A Faith
That Is Never Alone

a Response *to* Westminster Seminary California

Contributors:

John H. Armstrong
Don Garlington
Mark Horne
Peter Leithart
Rich Lusk
P. Andrew Sandlin
Norman Shepherd

P. Andrew Sandlin, Editor

KERYGMA
PRESS

La Grange, California

Primitive Truths for Postmodern Times

Copyright © 2007 by P. Andrew Sandlin

All rights reserved. No part of this publication may be reproduced or distributed in any form or by any means, or stored in a database or retrieval system — except for brief quotations in printed reviews — without the prior written permission of the publisher

Kerygma Press
P. O. Box 70
La Grange, California 95329
www.christianculture.com

Kerygma Press is the theological imprint of the Center for Cultural Leadership. CCL is a non-profit Christian educational foundation devoted to influencing Christians for effective cultural leadership — in church, the arts, education, business, technology, science, and other realms of contemporary culture

Printed in the United States of America

ISBN 978-0-6151-6915-6

To our esteemed colleague

Norman Shepherd

Persevering advocate for a faith that is never alone

Table of Contents

PREFACE	The Polemics of Articulated Rationality, *P. Andrew Sandlin*	vii
CHAPTER 1	Preaching the Faith That Is Never Alone, *by John H. Armstrong*	21
CHAPTER 2	Faith and Faithfulness *by Norman Shepherd*	53
CHAPTER 3	Reformed Covenant Theology and Its Discontents, *by Mark Horne*	73
CHAPTER 4	From Birmingham, With Love: A "Federal Vision" Postcard, *by Rich Lusk*	109
CHAPTER 5	Adam the Catholic? Faith and Life in the Adamic Covenant, *by Peter Leithart*	163
CHAPTER 6	The Gospel of Law and the Law of Gospel: An Assessment of the Antithetical Gospel-Law Paradigm, *by P. Andrew Sandlin*	193
CHAPTER 7	The Imputation of Active Obedience, *by Norman Shepherd*	249
CHAPTER 8	The New Perspective, Mediation and Justification, *by Don Garlington*	279
CHAPTER 9	Future Justification: Some Theological and Exegetical Proposals, *by Rich Lusk*	309
CHAPTER 10	Covenantal Nomism and the Exile, *by Don Garlington*	357
	Contributors	395

PREFACE

The Polemics of Articulated Rationality

P. Andrew Sandlin

Recently I had lunch with a friend, a theologically literate layman. He expressed savage disappointment at the internecine strife presently sundering the Reformed world (and not only there) on the topics addressed in this book. I could not honestly disagree with him. I then told him that theological controversy seems intrinsic to the DNA of the Reformed tradition. The very genesis of this tradition was a reactionary controversy with the Church of Rome, and disputes with its fraternal brothers, the Lutherans and the Arminians, followed in the wake. Throughout its history, the Reformed seem to have carried on a running battle not only with non-Reformed theologies and churches but also with deviations (or apparent deviations) within their own camp. The fact that the contemporary Reformed world would be rocked with controversy is therefore not surprising. The history of the Reformed world is a history of theological combativeness.

Articulated Rationality

What is it that renders the Reformed so susceptible to controversy, including intramural controversy? There are likely several accurate answers, but one stands out. I told my friend at lunch that of all sectors of Christendom, the Reformed is likely the most theologically oriented, where theology is defined as "articulated rationality" (see Thomas Sowell, *A Conflict of Visions*) — rational propositions (springing from primitive intuitions) that tend to generate a worldview. This apotheosis of "articulated rationality" is not a part of other leading traditions. For Rome, truth is encountered primarily in a collective context — the sacramental system of the church. For evangelicals, truth is founded on a personal relationship with Jesus Christ occasioned initially by conversion and regeneration and maintained by a warm experience with our Lord. For charismatics and Pentecostals, truth grows out of one's experience of the Holy Spirit. For Lutherans, truth is Jesus as the Word of God, which is conveyed in baptism, the Eucharist, and preaching. Conversely, no sector of the church has devoted such attention to confessions of faith (although the Lutherans come close) as the Reformed. Why? Affirming truth is, practically if not theoretically, a matter of fidelity to a system of propositions. Being "in the truth" is a matter of *believing the right things*. Because all self-consciously orthodox Christians grasp the necessity of correct theological beliefs, none would deny what the Reformed are affirming. However, they would likely question the emphasis on "articulated rationality" that stands at the heart of the Reformed belief system. The Reformed are especially susceptible to theological controversy because, for this tradition, deviation from precise doctrine is an unforgivable offense. Where accurate, precise theology is deemed paramount, deviation from accurate, precise theology is deemed abhorrent. The present controversy, like nearly all preceding it, is fueled by just such a commitment to theological precision, an essential component of "articulated rationality."

Justification, *Sola Fide* and Good Works

The current crisis of "articulated rationality" centers on the *doctrine* (as opposed to the practice) of justification and related themes. The Reformation dictum *sola fide* (faith alone) denotes the unique role that faith plays in appropriating justification (a legal declaration of innocence or righteousness on the ground of Jesus' death and resurrection). *Sola fide* contrasts with the medieval Roman (and Tridentine) notion of salvation by grace that nonetheless is appropriated by both faith *and* good works within the sacerdotal Church of Rome. In the Roman Catholic conception,

God infuses grace in baptism (usually infant baptism), and the believer cooperates with God's gracious provision in the church and its sacramental system in "being" justified progressively. For most Protestants, justification is an act, not a process. One is justified when he places faith in Jesus Christ, and his justification neither increases nor decreases.

But does the Protestant idea of justification negate the necessity of good works? The answer generally has been an emphatic No. Although good works do not cause justification, they are a necessary effect of union with Christ, another feature of salvation. But the Protestant relationship between faith and works has not always been answered so simply and confidently, and the differing answers (and shades of answers) have contributed to the polemics that plague the Reformed world today.

Lordship Salvation

It is difficult not to believe that the proximate source of much of the present fracas is the Lordship Salvation debate of the 70's and 80's. On one side were theologians who *opposed* what they labeled "Lordship Salvation." These included men like Charles Ryrie and Zane Hodges. Their view, in summary, is this. God saves one totally by grace through faith in Jesus. When we trust Jesus, we trust Him as Savior. Salvation is entirely by grace apart from man's works. When we trust Jesus, moreover, we trust Him *only* as Savior. We don't trust Him as Lord and Master. Chiefly this means that when one trusts Jesus, he doesn't make a commitment to be a disciple. Commitment to Jesus as Lord is desirable, but that decision likely comes later in the Christian life. In other words, salvation is to be separated from discipleship. Jesus wants disciples, but one can be a Christian without being a disciple. The leading point is that if we add commitment to salvation, we deny salvation by grace.

Then there is the opposing view. This is the side that *does* affirm "Lordship Salvation." Spearheaded by John McArthur and R. C. Sproul, the position is basically this. They agree with their opponents that God saves sinners totally by grace through faith in

Jesus. They agree that salvation is by grace through faith alone apart from works. But they do *not* agree that a woman can trust Jesus as her Savior without trusting Him as her Lord. For one thing, we cannot trust a divided Christ. (That's how the devotional pastor A. W. Tozer once put it.) Jesus is both Savior and Lord, and we cannot divide up His offices when we receive Him. That would be like saying, "I take this woman to be my wife, but I do not take her to be the mother of my children." No woman — at least no sensible woman — would tolerate that talk. Wifehood and motherhood in relation to a husband reside in one woman. To take a woman as a wife is to take her as the mother of one's children. We can't separate one from the other.

In addition, faith is a form of submission. In trusting Jesus Christ for salvation, we place our hope and destiny in Him. In trusting Him to save us, we are committing our lives to His care; and in committing our lives to His care, we are submitting to the lifelong process of discipleship. Therefore, in this way of thinking, there can be no salvation without submission to the Lordship of Jesus — "Lordship Salvation." The point was never that Christians would always obey ("sinless perfection"); rather, it was that one commits his *present* life to the Lord Jesus and not merely his eternal destiny.

The "Lordship Salvation" controversy uncovered a deep cleavage just under the surface of evangelical consensus, a cleavage that touched the very heart of evangelical conviction — salvation by grace through faith in Jesus Christ.

Law and Gospel

About the same time (1980), Daniel P. Fuller, professor at Fuller Theological Seminary, published a slender volume *Gospel and Law: Contrast or Continuum?* (Eerdmans) that invoked a firestorm of criticism from a large swath of the Reformed community. Fuller argued that a careful reading of the New Testament would not support traditional Reformed covenant theology. Fuller assaulted two cherished dogmas: (1) the prelapsarian (pre-Fall) covenant of works, the teaching that before the Fall man would have merited eternal life had he obeyed God at all times and that Jesus' law-keeping life merited eternal life for God's elect, and (2) the Law-Gospel distinction, the notion that all the commands of the Bible are divided into categories of (a) Law ("Do this and live"), a paradigm of legal obedience and reward, and (b) Gospel ("Trust Jesus for salvation"), a paradigm of passive trust in the promises of God.

Fuller contended, by contrast, that man never relates to God by means of legality and merit and that the traditional Law-Gospel distinction does not enjoy Biblical warrant under close scrutiny. To Fuller, the Biblical scheme of salvation is summarized in this way: Jesus died on the Cross in substitutionary atonement and rose from the grave in victory over the powers of darkness to take away our sins. We appropriate this redemptive work by entrusting our lives to Jesus, just as a patient trusts a doctor to cure his disease. The patient places his life in the hands of the doctor, on whom he relies to lead him to a disease-free life. Similarly, our trust in Jesus for salvation is a persevering trust, just as our obedience to the call of the Gospel is a persevering obedience. This trust is a form of obedience, just as the obedience is a form of trust. Faith is not passive but active, grasping the promises of God and following Him throughout our lives.

Fuller was by no means the first Protestant to articulate this unified Gospel-Law paradigm. Heinrich Bullinger, the Swiss Reformer and Zwingli's successor, held a position quite close to it. Moreover, the 20th century Swiss theologian Karl Barth, Fuller's seminary professor, reversed the traditional order of Law and *then* Gospel. For Barth, the Gospel, which comes first, is totally about God's grace in Christ, but it is a grace that requires loving obedience. The Biblical message is not "Do this and live, but since you can't, trust in Jesus who obeyed so you don't have to," but, rather, "Trust in Jesus alone with a persevering faith and follow Him all your days, since He alone saves you by His death and resurrection."

Like Barth, Fuller laid much of the blame at the feet of traditional Reformed covenant theology, which he identified as the precursor of dispensationalism in the former's discovery (invention) of two conflicting ways of salvation in the Bible — one by flawless law-keeping (prelapsarian) and another by Christ's flawless law-keeping (postlapsarian).

Fuller's manifold Reformed critics could never keep silent at this indignity to their tradition, and they charged him with polluting justification by faith alone.

The Shepherd Controversy

Closely related to the Lordship Salvation controversy as well as the Gospel-Law controversy was the nearly concurrent "Shepherd controversy" at Westminster Seminary in Philadelphia arising from the teachings of her long-time systematics professor (and successor to John Murray), Norman Shepherd. Shepherd argued that a close reading of the Westminster Confession — and the Bible — yielded a justification received by a living, penitent, obedient faith. Shepherd did not deny *sola fide* as such, and in fact he was quick to defend it against all notions of salvation by merit and human achievement. However, he contended not merely that the faith that justifies is never alone (most Reformed would agree with this assertion); he taught, in addition, that the faith that justifies is not only passive, resting on God's promises, but also active, following Jesus in submissive obedience. Shepherd's critics countered that his emphasis on an obedient faith was compromising *sola fide* and undermining salvation by grace. In recent years, Shepherd has (like Fuller) repudiated the idea that the "active" obedience of Jesus Christ (his law-keeping life) is imputed to the believer in justification; rather, according to Shepherd, justification (defined as the forgiveness of sins) is due solely to the death and resurrection of Jesus (his "passive obedience"). This move has only exacerbated the hostility of his critics.

The New Perspective on Paul

More theologically sophisticated than the Lordship Salvation debate and more wide-ranging than the "Shepherd controversy" has been the squabble over the so-called "New Perspective on Paul" (NPP). While obvious variations mark this revisionist viewpoint of Paul (which perhaps should be labeled the "New Perspective*s* on Paul"), sufficient commonality exists among its proponents to generalize. First championed by British scholars E. P. Sanders, James Dunn and N. T. Wright, the NPP argues that Protestants from Luther onward, in their running polemic with the Church of Rome, have tended to caricature the Judaism of Paul's time as espousing a legalistic soteriology — salvation by the Mosaic law or by meritorious good works. On the basis of a careful investigation of historical sources, the NPP has suggested that this typically Protestant understanding represents a serious misreading of the evidence. The Judaism of Paul's time (Second Temple Judaism) was not rife with legalism at all but rather depicted both individual and communal salvation as due to the gracious acts of Jehovah toward Israel. But if this is the case, what (who) is Paul's target in Romans and Galatians in his polemic against the misuse of the Mosaic law and of salvation by law-keeping? For the NPP, his target is not legalism, as though the Jews assumed that one could be saved by personal merit, but rather a conception of the Mosaic law *apart from* Jesus Christ. The Jews were wrong not because they were legalists, but because they refused to subordinate the Mosaic law to Jesus Christ as the Messiah.

This revision opens the way to a fresh understanding of the practice of the Mosaic law in NT-era Judaism. The NPP designates this understanding "covenantal nomism." If law-keeping and good works are not — and never have been — the instrument of gaining eternal life, what is their function? The NPP answer is that while one enters the covenant with God by grace, law and good works are the means of maintaining one's standing in the covenant. This non-meritorious obedience is not, however, incompatible with a mistaken view of Jesus Christ, and it is *this* fatal error that Paul targets.

Opponents of the NPP question both its interpretation of the soteriology of Second Temple Judaism as well as its "covenantal nomism," which seems allegedly to veer dangerously toward salvation by good works, NPP protests to the contrary notwithstanding.

The Federal Vision

Though the Federal Vision (FV) is a legitimate theological paradigm, it is driven more by pastoral concerns than theology proper. The FV has posited a covenantal conception of the Trinity and God's relation with humanity that emphasizes a more intimate unity between the visible church and the Trinity than has often been suggested by Protestants. A covenant is not merely a means of entering a relation with God but is the relationship itself. In ecclesial terms, this means that union with the church at baptism (and continuing union at the Lord's Table) constitutes union with Jesus Christ. The FV is intent to recover the "objectivity" of the covenant that had been lost in modern evangelicalism, in the latter's preoccupation with individual religious experience. We do not judge who is and is not a Christian by religious experience but by who stands in a visible covenant relationship to God by means of baptism and the Lord's Supper in the church. Though the FV claims precedent in the Reformed tradition, as, for example, in the Mercersburg Theology of John W. Nevin and Phillip Schaff, and all the way back to Calvin himself, its proponents are not averse to all innovation. For instance, nearly all advocate paedocommunion, the practice of bringing baptized children to the Lord's Table prior to a profession of faith. This practice is a consistent application of their idea of the objectivity of the covenant, since union with Christ rests not on man's experience but God's promises, and his promises to the parents of Christian children demand the latter's inclusion in both sacraments within the church.

Critics of the FV accuse it of positing an illegitimate "parallel soteriology" to the Reformed standards, that is, one that competes with decretal soteriology (which the FV does not, in fact, deny). In erasing or mitigating the distinction between the visible and invisible church, accuse the critics, the FV practically reduces salvific membership in the Body of Christ to membership in the local earthly church — in other words, objective membership in the covenant body (local church) does not, according to the critics, guarantee subjective membership in the Lamb's Book of Life. Finally, the critics charge that the FV sacramentology undercuts the definitive character of justification — in other words, that one must stay in the church's good graces in order to be justified at the Final Day.

Lordship Salvation, Law and Gospel, the Shepherd Controversy, the New Perspective on Paul, and the Federal Vision — diverse in content but united in affirming a faith that is never alone, have occasioned the prominent battle presently waged in Reformed churches, denominations, colleges, and seminaries. It is a battle whose divergent opinions are magnified by the emphasis devoted to "articulated rationality" in the Reformed tradition. "Ideas Have Consequences," Richard Weaver's influential post-World War II title championing political conservatism, accurately depicts the Reformed attitude toward their much-vaunted theology. "If we're wrong in our theology, even on matters not out of bounds of historic Christianity, our error will destroy churches and denominations and educational institutions — and lives and souls."

Perhaps the present painful warfare is the price that must be paid by any sector of the church for which "articulated rationality" is paramount.

The Scope of *A Faith That Is Never Alone*

The present work is a targeted response to *Covenant, Justification, and Pastoral Ministry: Essays by the Faculty of Westminster Seminary California*, edited by R. Scott Clark (P & R, 2007, hereafter *CJPM*). *A Faith That Is Never Alone* does not profess to be a comprehensive response to *CJPM*, but it does profess to address the leading lines of argument in the Westminster symposium, arguments representative of more widespread criticism of positions the contributors of the present volume embrace. We have chosen to interact with this work not because other works of similar conviction are unworthy but because *CJPM* so boldly articulates its position.

The contributors to this volume do not profess to represent a single school of thought. Some contributors, for example, are sympathetic to the NPP or FV and some are not. Instead, the contributors are united in their concern that the views expressed in

CJPM not become identified as *the* Reformed (or, more fatally, *the* Biblical) paradigm for the relation between faith and good works. Therefore, critics of the present work should avoid an easy guilt by association. Each contributor speaks for himself, and his arguments stand or fall on their own merit. In keeping with the wide conceptual latitude granted the contributors, we have, while operating with a basic style sheet, permitted stylistic variations with which the single contributor is most comfortable. *A Faith That Is Never Alone* stands as a unit in its response to *CJPM*, but it preserves the theological and stylistic distinctiveness of each contributor.

I offer special thanks to Walter and Megan Lindsay, friends and eagle-eyed proofreaders, who spared this editor much heartache. For all remaining editorial blemishes, however, I bear full responsibility.

For Further Reading

Barth, Karl. *Church Dogmatics*. Trans. Bromiley, G. W.; Thompson, G. T.; and Torrance, T. F. Edinburgh: T. & T. Clark, 1936-1977.

----. *Community, State and Church*. Gloucester, Massachusetts: Peter Smith, 1960, 1968.

Beisner, Calvin E., ed. *The Auburn Avenue Theology: Pros and Cons*. Fort Lauderdale, Florida: Knox Theological Seminary, 2004.

Bonhoeffer, Dietrich. *The Cost of Discipleship*. New York: MacMillan, 1937, 1959.

Braaten, Carl E. and Jenson, Robert W. Eds. *Union With Christ: The New Finnish Interpretation of Luther*. Grand Rapids: Eerdmans, 1998.

Bullinger, Heinrich. *A Brief Exposition of the One and Eternal Testament or Covenant of God*. In eds., McCoy, Charles S. and Baker, J. Wayne. *Fountainhead of Federalism*. Louisville, Kentucky: Westminster/John Knox Press, 1991.

Calvin, John. *Commentaries on the Epistle of Paul the Apostle to the Romans*. Grand Rapids: Baker, 1993.

Catechism of the Catholic Church. Washington, D. C.: United States Catholic Conference. [*Libreria Editrice Vaticana*], 1994, second edition.

Forde, Gerhard O. *The Law-Gospel Debate*. Minneapolis, Minnesota: Augsburg, 1969.

Fuller, Daniel P. *Gospel and Law: Contrast or Continuum?* Grand Rapids: Eerdmans, 1980.

Gaffin, Richard B. *By Faith, Not By Sight: Paul and the Order of Salvation*. Waynesboro, Georgia: Paternoster Press, 2006.

----. *Resurrection and Redemption: A Study in Paul's Soteriology.*. Phillipsburg, New Jersey: Presbyterian and Reformed, 1978, 1987.

Garlington, Don. *In Defense of the New Perspective on Paul: Essays and Reviews*. Eugene, Oregon: Wipf & Stock, 2005.

----. *Exegetical Essays*. Eugene, Oregon: Wipf & Stock, 2003, 3rd ed.

Husbands, Mark and Treier, Daniel J., eds. *Justification: What's at Stake in Current Debates?* Downers Grove, Illinois: InterVarsity, 2004

Johnson, Gary L. W. and Waters, Guy P. Eds., *By Faith Alone*. Nashville: Thomas Nelson, 2007.

Kline, Meredith G. *Kingdom Prologue*. Overland Park, Kansas: Two Age Press, 2000.

----. *The Structure of Biblical Authority*. Eugene, Oregon: Wipf and Stock, 1989 edition.

Kung, Hans. *Christianity: Essence, History and Future*. New York: Continuum, 1995.

Lillback, Peter. *The Binding of God*. Grand Rapids: Baker, 2001.

Luther, Martin. *Commentary on the Epistle to the Galatians.* Grand Rapids: Zondervan, 1962.

MacArthur, John. *Faith Works.* Waco, Texas: Word, 1993.

----. *The Gospel According to Jesus.* Grand Rapids: Zondervan, 1988.

McCormack, Bruce L., ed. *Justification in Perspective.* Grand Rapids: Baker, 2006.

McGrath, Alister. *Genesis of Doctrine: A Study in the Foundation of Doctrinal Criticism.* Grand Rapids: Eerdmans, 1990.

----. *Iustitia Dei: A History of the Doctrine of Justification — The Beginnings to the Reformation.* Cambridge: Cambridge University Press, 1986.

----. *Justification by Faith.* Grand Rapids: Zondervan, 1988.

----. *Luther's Theology of the Cross.* Oxford, England: Blackwell, 1985.

Oliphant, K. Scott., ed. *Justified in Christ: God's Plan for Us in Justification.* Geanies House, Fearn, Ross-shire, Great Britain: Christian Focus Publications, 2007.

Osterhaven, Eugene M. *The Spirit of the Reformed Tradition: The Reformed Church Must Always be Reforming.* Grand Rapids: Eerdmans, 1971.

Rayburn, Robert S. "The Contrast Between the Old and New Covenants in the New Testament," doctoral thesis, University of Aberdeen, 1978.

Robertson, O. Palmer. *The Christ of the Covenants.* Phillipsburg, New Jersey: Presbyterian and Reformed, 1980.

Ryrie, Charles C. *Balancing the Christian Life.* Chicago: Moody, 1969.

----. *Dispensationalism Today.* Chicago: Moody, 1965.

Sandlin, P. Andrew: *Backbone of the Bible: Covenant in Contemporary Perspective*. Nacogdoches, Texas: Covenant Media Press, 2004.

Shepherd, Norman. *The Call of Grace: How the Covenant Illuminates Salvation and Evangelism*. Phillipsburg, New Jersey: P&R Publishing, 2000.

Torrance, T. F. *Theology in Reconstruction*. Grand Rapids: Eerdmans, 1965.

Turretin, Francis. *Institutes of Elenctic Theology*. Phillipsburg, New Jersey: P & R Publishing, 1994.

Van der Waal, C. *The Covenantal Gospel*. Neerlandia, Alberta: Inheritance Publications, 1990.

Wilkins, Steve and Garner, Duane. *The Federal Vision*. Monroe, Louisiana: Athanasius Press, 2004.

Wright, N. T. *The Climax of the Covenant: Christ and the Law in Pauline Theology*. Minneapolis: Fortress, 1991, 1993.

----. *What Saint Paul Really Said*. Grand Rapids: Eerdmans, 1997.

CHAPTER 1

Preaching the Faith That is Never Alone

John H. Armstrong

The sixteenth century introduced massive changes in the life of the church and the way the ordinary Christian came to receive and understand the Christian faith. Changes were ecclesiastical, political, theological and even economic. But no change more directly transformed whole sections of Europe than the change that came about through the reformation of preaching. This change was, and always has been to varying degrees, part and parcel of evangelical Protestantism. One is hard pressed to think of a contribution that is more distinctly Protestant than that of the evangelical pulpit. Indeed, revivals and sundry Protestant movements that have focused upon the recovery of vital piety within the visible church have always been rooted in the pulpit.

The History of Reformation Preaching

Prior to 1517 Roman Catholic preaching was more often than not linked with rhetoric. Contrary to popular myths there were impressive and learned popular preachers prior to the Protestant Reformation. There were even itinerant preachers who moved whole crowds in a non-visual age. One author goes so far as to say, "Pre-Reformation sermons were filled with amusing, titillating, and interesting stories designed to make the biblical message meaningful."[1]

---

1. Larissa Juliet Taylor, in an entry titled: "Preaching and Sermons: France" in *The Oxford Encyclopedia of the Reformation*, ed. Hans J. Hillenbrand (New York: Oxford, 1996), III: 326-28.

France had its Mendicant preachers who even went from place-to-place speaking to significant crowds. Urban centers and towns had lots of preaching. And the primary source for this preaching was still the Bible. The sermons of Johann Geiler (1445-1510), for example, are described as "earthy, direct and full of humor." This dispels the foolish theory that all sermons were tedious and boring prior to the Reformation. The real story is quite a bit different than these Protestant myths.

These preachers measured their preaching by the church and their sermonic form was a rather artificial one that was often combined with "bawdy and humorous examples."[2] They employed what has been called a fourfold interpretative scheme. All passages were queried for: (1) A literal meaning; (2) An allegorical point; (3) a moral lesson, and; (4) An eschatological emphasis. When Luther became an enemy of the Catholic Church in 1518 the extant sermons of the time reveal that he was routinely countered in France, Spain and elsewhere by effective preachers who were quite aware of the controversies surrounding the time.

So, what actually changed about preaching during the Reformation? In short, the answer is this: Martin Luther captured the central emphasis of Scripture afresh—preaching is nothing unless it captures the central emphasis of Holy Scripture, namely the centrality of Jesus Christ and him crucified and raised from the dead! Simply put — *preaching is nothing if Christ is not preached!*

In *The Oxford Encyclopedia of the Reformation*, Ulrich Nembach writes that before the Reformation the purpose of the sermon was "to instruct in faith and morals."[3] Luther believed the purpose of the sermon was "instruction and exhortation." The difference here is not minor. A radical recovery of apostolic preaching was unleashed by this new emphasis. And this same emphasis can be seen in the sermonic work of theologians and reformers like Johannes Oecolampadius, Theodore Beza, Martin Bucer and

---

2. Taylor, "Preaching and Sermons: France," III: 326-28.
3. Ulrich Nembach, in an entry titled: "Preaching and Sermons: Germany" in *The Oxford Encyclopedia of the Reformation*, ed. Hans J. Hillenbrand (New York: Oxford, 1996), III: 223-26.

Heinrich Bullinger. And remember, it was bad preaching, *with terribly un-biblical content*, that so deeply disturbed Luther when he heard the famous Johann Tetzel, himself a member of the Order of Preachers. (Tetzel became the sixteenth century version of a market-driven preacher if there ever was one.)

But it was in places like France, in the 1560s and 70s, that Calvinist preachers began to do their greatest work of careful exposition with nothing short of amazing courage and power. They preached in secluded places, in private homes and generally at night so as to avoid their fierce opponents. Their preaching was marked by a plain exposition of the Bible, the giving out of simple exegesis in a plain spoken style, joined with the singing of Psalms at the beginning, middle and end of their sermons.

England followed this same pattern. Margaret Christian, in *The Oxford Encyclopedia of the Reformation*, writes: "The Reformation did not introduce preaching to England, but it gave preachers a new rationale and energy."[4] Hugh Latimer wrote to Edward VI in 1549, "And how shall they hear without a preacher? I will tell you it is the footsteps of the ladder of heaven, of our salvation. There must be preachers if we look to be saved."[5]

According to Medieval tradition preaching was *not* necessary to salvation. Sacraments, being central to grace and salvation, were the center of the church's work in worship. Sermons became, as noted above, "moral instruction." Sermons helped to explain the Bible readings on a particular holy day, or illustrated the Bible text with the pious legends of the saints. Far-fetched allegorical interpretations and extra-biblical embellishments were widely used to drive home the points of such a sermon.

Martin Luther's writings in the 1520s and beyond provided a whole new rationale, a well as a whole new context, for the recovery of preaching. These early Protestants highly valued personal faith and acceptance with God by free grace. This is why their ser-

---

4. Margaret Christian, in an entry titled: "Preaching and Sermons: England" in The Oxford Encyclopedia of the Reformation, ed. Hans J. Hillenbrand (New York: Oxford, 1996), III: 328-30.
5. Margaret Christian, "Preaching and Sermons: England," III: 328.

mons became powerful exhortations to true faith. The faith they called their hearers to was not a faith of notion, or a faith of passivity, but an active, trusting and recumbent faith.

The Reformed theologian/minister John R. deWitt believes that this reformation of the pulpit, this "distinctive view of preaching," is a mark of Reformed theology itself. He says it is synonymous with "a distinctive view of the ministry and of the life of the church in relation to it" as well. Indeed, all evangelicals are indebted to this "distinctive" mark whether they are Reformed or not. Dr. deWitt suggests that a high biblical view of the ministry will necessarily lead to a "a high view of the actual preaching of the gospel (1 Cor. 1:21; Rom. 10:13-15). It is by preaching that God confronts people and draws them to himself, conforming them to the pattern of his Son; indeed, it is by preaching that Jesus addresses himself to the hearts and consciences of men (Rom. 10:14)."[6]

The church experienced a reformation and revival in the early sixteenth century that changed civilization. Prior to Luther's time the institutions of piety were corrupt and theology had sunk into a dead scholasticism. The famous Anglican Frederic W. Farrar, in his Bampton Lectures of 1885, refers to this time as one that was built on a "foundationless superstructure, reared only on sand ... a sacerdotalism at once arrogant, intolerant, immoral and idle ... [which] divided the church into two classes, the ruling and the ruled." Farrar concluded that the necessary deliverance came through the study of Holy Scripture. And that study of Holy Scripture produced men with deep conviction and courage who became preachers of the gospel. They were the catalysts of a movement of the Spirit of God. This work was accomplished by means of both Word and Spirit.

It is my humble conviction and contention that biblical reformation always arises out of a proper emphasis given to the written Scripture and the vitality of the Holy Spirit's ministry in raising up people who "preach the Word" (cf. 2 Tim. 4:2). Severing the relationship between the Word and the Spirit, as is being done in

---

6. John R. deWitt, *What is the Reformed Faith?* (Edinburgh: Banner of Truth, 1981), 18.

a number of subtle and not-so-subtle ways in our time, brings serious dangers. These dangers hold back the blessing of God upon his people. There has never been a better time to rethink this subject than the present. And there has never been a more important time to preach the gospel effectively to people who are fast asleep under the influence of populist evangelicalism.

The Biblical Basis for the Reformation of Preaching

But was this recovery of preaching biblically sound? For some, to ask the question is to entertain doubts about the outcome. For me it is to ask the question the very Reformers themselves asked: "What do the Scriptures themselves teach us about preaching?"

The Apostle tells the ancient church in Ephesus: "Take the helmet of salvation, and the sword of the Spirit which is the word of God. And pray in the Spirit on all occasions, with all kinds of prayers and requests" (Eph. 6:17-18). When this text (starting with v. 14) is carefully read what is apparent is this—there are five pieces of armor enumerated by Paul here. Each of these five is to be used in a manner that can be called defensive. The church, for the church is who is in view here as the whole people of God (not so much the individual Christian), must defend itself against the "devil's schemes" (Eph. 6:11). But there is a sixth item of the soldier listed in this text and it alone is an offensive weapon. The apostle calls this "the sword of the Spirit which is the word of God." This sword is directly related to the helmet of salvation, which defends the church against assault from above. There can be no doubt that the sword of the Spirit here is the word of God; i.e., the apostolic word given to us in Holy Scripture. Regardless of one's own understanding of the doctrine of *sola Scriptura* all serious exegetes will conclude that the "word of God" here is a Pauline expression for the truth of the gospel that we find in the sacred Scriptures. And that truth is centered in the living Word, who is Christ Jesus. Even modern Roman Catholic biblical teachers agree with this conclusion.

What I am interested in demonstrating is how our Lord Jesus carried out this very truth in his own life. How did Jesus resist the evil one's schemes? The answer we have in Matthew 4:1ff. is plain—he used the Scriptures, in this instance the Old Testament, to resist the enemy. His authority was inherent in himself but he had no problem in relying upon this external authority, the sacred writings of God.

> We also have the prophetic message as something completely reliable, and you will do well to pay attention to it, as to a light shining in a dark place, until the day dawns and the morning star rises in your hearts. Above all, you must understand that no prophecy of Scripture came about by the prophet's own interpretation of things. For prophecy never had its origin in the human will, but prophets, though human, spoke from God as they were carried along by the Holy Spirit (TNIV, 2 Peter 1:19-21).

The point here seems to be clear. The Holy Scriptures had their *origin* in God. They came about through the ministry of the Holy Spirit. This fact about origin is also universally recognized. What is not so often recognized is that the same text makes it plain that these divine Scriptures *cannot be used effectively without the ministry of the Holy Spirit revealing Christ through them.* It is interesting that many came to conclude that the Reformation was nothing less than the dawning of a new day when the morning star arose in the hearts of God's people. In fact, the language of the "morning star" became closely associated with the men and the work of the reformers.

Paul refers, in 2 Corinthians 2:12, to his preaching the gospel of Christ in Troas where he "found the Lord had opened a door" for his personal ministry of the gospel. This "opening of the door" by the Spirit is what I mean when I refer to the ministry of the Word and the Spirit. Everything connected to the word of God, understood as the Holy Scriptures, is connected to Christ as the Word of God and particularly to the ministry of the Holy Spirit. Failure to grasp this vital connection has been the source of major problems throughout Christian history. I submit that it is no less true in our day and that the mistake is made by many Christians—Protestant, Catholic and Orthodox.

On one side we have various ideas about preaching that circulate throughout the church that suggest the idea of some kind of direct "inner light" that we receive mystically *without* the preaching of Holy Scripture. Illustrations abound in contemporary circles. In each case the Spirit is said to be all that we need. In this context the Scripture is dangerously devalued.

But the opposite mistake is often made by those who are troubled by the first. This error is to equate the Word with the Spirit so that the distinct ministry of the Holy Spirit is not welcomed or sought through prayer, as clearly taught in Ephesians 6 and elsewhere (Col. 4:2-6; 2 Thess. 2:13). In this emphasis, too often seen in churches associated with the Protestant Reformation, the Scriptures become equal to the Holy Spirit. This means that if you exegete the Scriptures correctly you can assume that you have the Holy Spirit and that's that.

Interestingly the Reformed confessions and catechisms will not support either of these extremes. The phrase "Word and Spirit" or "Spirit and Word" are both used regularly in the Reformed standards. (See, for example, Lord's Day 12, 21 and 48 in the *Heidelberg Catechism*, for one example.)

The Reformed side of the Reformation movement was particularly keen on preserving the freedom of God at this very point. God was not bound by his own means, even if He did choose to use the Scriptures as *the* means whereby the Spirit revealed Christ to the human soul. This caused Reformed preachers to avoid the idea that somehow the preacher could manipulate the Spirit in any sense of the term. No matter how good the exposition, or powerful the speaker in his oratorical skills, there was mystery. This mystery was bound up with God's freedom to use the preaching of Christ to *reveal* Christ to the human heart. So strong was this connection that John Calvin spoke of two ministers. The first was the human minister and the second was the Spirit. In his commentary on Micah Calvin suggests that when the Spirit reveals Christ through the Scripture today it is "the same now as when he formerly endued his servant Micah with a power so fair and extraordinary." (Read that again if you are a preacher!) I submit that this is an extremely high view of preaching and one that will also bear the weight of biblical scrutiny.

Elsewhere Calvin speaks of the Lord anointing his servants "in the heavenly power of the Spirit" and he even prays for those who preach that they may be "endued with . . . celestial power, that they may not attempt anything of themselves." In a sermon of Calvin's, based upon Jeremiah, he asks God to "to speak also to us inwardly by thy Spirit." Unless the Spirit is present, Calvin further argued in his commentary on John's Gospel, "to have the Word in our hands will avail little or nothing."

John R. de Witt argues, quite convincingly I believe, that what characterizes preaching in the New Testament is:

1. It is an exposition of the Word of God. We are dealing with the Scriptures when we preach rightly. We must wrestle with these words and grasp their meaning. Other branches of study will help us but "nothing must come between the preacher and his text."[7]

2. The application of the Word of God. Exposition and application must be linked together. As it was put in the "Introduction" to *The Form of Government* of the Presbyterian Church in the United States in 1788, "truth is in order to goodness; and the great touchstone of truth its tendency to promote holiness." This is correct. What it means is that truth must be driven home by the preacher. It has more than a cognitive function, it also has a moral dimension. In reacting against certain aspects of Roman Catholic preaching there has always been the tendency in Lutheran and Reformed circles to not stress this important biblical truth. Adds John R. deWitt: "To apply the truth in preaching is no easy matter; but we have not preached till we have done so."[8]

3. But even these two are not enough. Preaching is also proclamation. The word "preach" means exactly that. It is to proclaim and what is proclaimed, or better put, who is proclaimed, is the important point here. The message the preacher brings is not his

---

7. de Witt, 18.
8. de Witt, 19.

own, it is the message of his master, the message from God. Righty does de Witt observe: "What our generation needs is not a company of communicators, of clever speakers, of effective orators, of interesting teachers, but a company of proclaimers of the everlasting gospel in all its richness and comprehensiveness."[9]

4. The final quality de Witt cites in biblical and Reformed preaching is freedom. This, he argues, is the Apostle Peter's point when he writes: "If you speak, you should do so as one who speaks the very Word of God" (1 Peter 1:12). There is some restriction placed on contemporary preachers who handle the Word of God. Calvin understood this correctly when he wrote: "[The difference between the apostles and their successors is that] the former were sure and genuine scribes of the Holy Spirit, and their writings are therefore to be considered oracles of God; but the sole office of others is to teach what is provided and sealed in the Holy Scriptures."[10]

This prophetic function of the ministry of the Word must be maintained at all costs. The sixteenth century Reformers understood this as well as any Christians since the apostles thus they made this central to their struggle to reform the Christian Church. They understood the point Peter made when he said, "We must obey God rather than human beings" (Acts 5:29). I humbly submit that this view of preaching must not be allowed to perish even in the face of contemporary distortions of the very biblical principles that were used to so powerfully establish it in middle of the sixteenth century debates.

A Preaching That Exalts Christ

Thus the preaching that Martin Luther, and after him other Reformers, practiced gloried in the revelation of Jesus Christ as the end, or terminus, of true preaching. This preaching paid very careful attention to the text of the Bible. It was deeply rooted in the exegetical method. But it was also a rich theological exposition

---

9. de Witt, 20.
10. John Calvin, *The Institutes of the Christian Religion*, IV.8.9, cited in de Witt, 22.

that resulted in preaching that informed and challenged the hearts and lives of hearers. It understood the big themes of the Bible and how they led the reader, and the worshiper who heard such preaching, to see Christ as the sole object of true and living faith. It had a framework that was not sectarian but Christ crucified, Christ risen and Christ coming again.

When Luther was still, in his own words, "a mad papist" he wrote the now famous *95 Theses*. Several of these statements are worth repeating but most are forgettable. Luther himself acknowledged this some years after they were written. The more evangelical Luther saw the seeds of reformation in these statements but *not* the full flower. Of all the *95 Theses* perhaps the most important is No. 62: "The true treasure of the Church is the holy Gospel of the glory and grace of God." Indeed, this gospel *is* the true treasure of the Church. No one in present debates about the gospel disagrees. What we do disagree about is how certain language should be used and what this leads to both theologically and pastorally. This is why the book *Covenant, Justification and Pastoral Ministry* is important, but misleading at one and the same time. It is important because it addresses issues that profoundly matter to the well-being of the Church. No one disagrees. But it is misleading precisely because it misses the real heart of biblical Christianity by straining at some gnats and by using categories that are strained by a very tight, and considerably debated, confessional position that is not *precisely* biblical. (I will leave to others the debates over the actual statements in the Reformed Confessions but I for one do not think the authors of *Covenant, Justification and Pastoral Ministry* use these statements in the way that was intended by the Biblical writers. This is a vast subject and would itself result in another book.)

Covenant, Justification and Pastoral Ministry ostensibly addresses pastoral theology, at least according to the title. What it really does is lay out a case for correcting a number of perceived errors, mostly in other Reformed and evangelical theologies. At the same time it distorts important biblical and textual matters in the process. And it does this by appealing to a human theological tradition, namely the Reformed one, as the final word on pastoral ministry. Worse yet is appeals to this rich and varied human tradition, which I happen to love and affirm, in ways that numerous Reformed scholars do not share. It does this by assuming that the conclusions drawn by its authors are universally true for all the heirs of this great tradition. Put very simply—it argues from a tradition and for a tradition, and this from within a very narrow segment of that tradition, while it appears to stand, in the end, for the gospel itself. It does this by placing within its crosshairs the views of other serious evangelical writers and Reformed preachers. It is, at times, a well-written polemic but at other times it proves to be a weak argument argued poorly.

My particular task in this essay is to respond to Chapters 10 and 11, written by my highly esteemed friend, Dr. Hywel R. Jones. Jones argues: "Whenever the doctrines of justification and sanctification are to be considered, the instinctive reaction of Protestants ought to be to *draw a distinction* between them" (italics mine).[11] He further argues that the good news "lies at the very point where *these two doctrines are to be differentiated*" (italics mine).[12] This tells the reader a great deal and summarizes the major argument of the entire book. Jones, and his highly capable fellow faculty members, sincerely believes that we who are being critiqued in this volume are not making the proper distinction between justification and sanctification, thus we are in grave danger and are misleading the church. This, as he argues, has major implications for pastoral ministry, which is a major burden of his own life and teaching. As much as any statement in this book these quotes place the struggle precisely where these authors believe it truly lies.

Let's be clear about this — we who are critiqued do not question that there is a *distinction* between these two doctrines but we differ about the ways this distinction has been made and how the Scripture has been used by some to make this distinction. I believe that the way this distinction has been argued in this book does have

---

11. R. Scott Clark, ed. *Covenant, Justification and Pastoral Ministry* (Philipsburg, New Jersey: P & R Publishing Company, 2007), 285.
12. *Covenant, Justification and Pastoral Ministry*, 285.

pastoral ramifications. I also believe that these kinds of arguments have had a very negative impact upon the evangelical church. The clearest illustration of this point was made by Dietrich Bonhoeffer in his classic book, *The Cost of Discipleship*. The concept of "cheap grace" is neither new nor irrelevant for modern Christians in the West. If we, the authors of this volume, are essentially correct in how we *distinguish* doctrines and handle the Scriptures then I believe we are closer to solving the very real problem of "cheap grace" that profoundly plagues us to this day.

If I understand Professor Jones I do not fundamentally disagree with him in the basic point that he makes. Any suggestion that we add one thing—either by our human works or even by our own wise decision(s)—to our salvation is a deadly error. What he asserts, however, is that several modern writers, including me, are guilty of "blurring" the justification/sanctification distinction. This, he asserts, has massive implications for faithful preaching and good pastoral work. It is this argument that I wish to counter by my own argument.

Like the other authors in this volume of essays Jones believes "a quiet conflation is proceeding in which proper weight is not being given to *sola fide* when James 2 is being considered"[13] and this "conflation" is having a profound impact in the Church with regard to a right understanding of Romans and Galatians. He provides two examples of how this is actually taking place. One relates to Professor Norman Shepherd's book, *The Call of Grace*. The other example he uses refers to my essay, "The Obedience of Faith," which originally appeared in the book, *Trust and Obey: Obedience and the Christian* (ed. R. C. Sproul and Don Kistler; Morgan, Pennsylvania: Soli Deo Gloria, 1996).[14]

---

13. *Covenant, Justification and Pastoral Ministry*, 291.
14. It is curious, at least to me, that my essay in this volume was later removed. The editors must have found it acceptable originally or it would not have appeared in the book in the first place. I can deduce, so it seems, that one of the following explanations is true: (1) They read it and found nothing objectionable at the time; (2) They did not carefully read it in the first place, which I rather doubt; (3) Or, in view of the present debate, something caused them to read it again and under reconsideration they found offense in it. I was informed that the essay would be removed (by a second-hand source) and asked the

What Jones finds offensive in my own essay is my examination of Paul's "terse expression *the obedience of faith* (Rom. 1:5)"[15] His conclusion, after correcting what he believes to be my faulty scholarship, concludes: "Armstrong's 'richer' interpretation therefore contains the built-in potential of destroying justification by faith without works *unless some distinctions are clearly made* in relation to God's justifying declaration (italics are his)."[16]

What is particularly surprising, and it underscores the idiosyncratic nature of this book, is that Professor Jones questions some of the very same scholars who share much of his own perspective on the interpretation of Romans. He refers to Douglas Moo's work on Romans and James, to use one example. Moo makes a distinction between faith in James and Romans by suggesting that James is asking: "What *kind* of faith secures righteousness?" He gives to the verb *justify* in James the meaning of *declaring it to be so* thus James is referring to the last judgment where our faith will be openly shown to be real faith. By this means Moo believes we avoid a clash between James and the words of Paul in Romans and Galatians. But Jones says the Westminster Seminary authors ("our view" he calls it) see this view "as exegetically unnecessary and potentially dangerous. It also diminishes justification as the final verdict announced ahead of time!"[17] He proceeds to give two reasons for why this is true. Let me grant, for the moment, that his reasons for understanding the verb "justify" are correct, one wonders why he cannot allow a scholar who is in essential agreement with his arguments to have a differing voice in the discussion. The answer is not far removed. Jones answers: "It is highly significant that our confessional documents do

---

publisher if this was true. The answer I got was that it was true but no evidence of my mistakes was ever offered to me. I relate this story because I think it has bearing on how this debate proceeded once enemies were named and views were more carefully read. I did not see my essay as widely out-of-step with the rest of the volume, which I liked a great deal. I still love the title of the book: *Trust and Obey: Obedience and the Christian*. I thought that I showed, rather exegetically, how obedience relates to an active, living faith. Quite clearly this controversy drove the essay from the newer editions of the book.

15. *Covenant, Justification and Pastoral Ministry*, 292.
16. *Covenant, Justification and Pastoral Ministry*, 293.
17. *Covenant, Justification and Pastoral Ministry*, 295.

not use the word *justification* concerning the final judgment."[18] His conclusion, as a careful reading will soon see, is rooted in categories that were hammered out in the bitter debate with 16th century Roman Catholic polemics. His appeal is, in the end, to the confessional documents leaving this idea out. He, and with him his fellow writers, does not seem able to move beyond these categories toward any new attempts to understand Paul and James. Such a move would allow the battle to be surrendered and the gospel lost. I do not, in any sense, believe I am wrong in concluding this. I am quite convinced Jones, and these contributors, would applaud me for saying so. But this again underscores a major part of my problem with this book. It is rooted in a human interpretation of confessional language and limited to that language and situation in history. Only from within this framework does it then attempt to fit in the exegetical questions we need to face honestly. But I, being convinced of the continuing work of reformation and the power of the text of the Word of God to inform us in every age, think differently about the role of the confessions and how we should use them. (By the way, when Jones wrote this essay he was under the impression that I was still a Baptist, which is no longer the case. I am a minister in the Reformed Church in America and thus subscribe to the *Three Standards of Unity*.) I believe the very confessions that these teachers employ actually urge us to continue to shed the light of Scripture upon all our struggles with contemporary issues and doctrinal discussions. The danger of a faith rooted in historic confessions, *without doing fresh and charitable exegesis and biblical theology*, is a real danger for all of those who wrote for this present volume of essays. It is also a danger for those of us who respond to their volume. We are not denying a place for confessional subscription but we think that place must always self-consciously remain under the Bible's authority.

Jones then turns from his critique of Douglas Moo to another critique of me. He questions my using the word "vindication." He also questions my desire to dispense with the category of "merit" (in the sense that "merit" can in any correct sense be employed to

---

18. *Covenant, Justification and Pastoral Ministry*, 295.

describe how we are saved) and with the, so-called, covenant of works. These are all categories that are hugely important to the authors of *Covenant, Justification and Pastoral Ministry* even though they are neither central to the Bible nor to Reformed theology in the mainstream. Jones concludes, rather grimly, that my view "strikes a blow not only at the necessity of obedience but also at required righteousness as the condition of salvation."[19] How can this be? While I am arguing for the obedience of faith I am actually arguing against obedience and against the righteousness required for salvation. This is an amazing argument but one that will become clearer, I hope, in what follows.

Jones and the several other authors of this volume are clearly intelligent and good men. They surely know that the arguments they use in their essays are not new. My guess is that this is a reason why they feel that they must be right since they sincerely believe history is on their side. But they also should know that Reformed exegetes have openly raised these very same questions for several centuries now. The consensus they argue for simply does not exist, except in the circles of their own making.[20]

A Preaching That Seeks Faith in Those Who Hear

Hywel R. Jones is a magnificent preacher of the gospel. I have heard him declare the unsearchable riches of Christ as plainly as anyone I know. He is also a man who loves Christ deeply and preaches Him powerfully, in the fullness of the Spirit. This I do not question. What I question is his connection of certain doctrinal judgments and very sharp distinctions, rooted in a particular framework theologically, to a right preaching of the gospel.

Jones argues, in the conclusion to chapter 10: "Our aim in preaching and in living is therefore two-fold: sanctification must be (a) kept from where it does not belong and (b) given its proper

---

19. *Covenant, Justification and Pastoral Ministry*, 296.
20. See, for example, Charles S. McCoy and J. Wayne Baker, *Fountainhead of Federalism: Heinrich Bullinger and the Covenantal Tradition* (Louisville: Westminster/John Knox Press, 1991) and Bruce Gordon and Emidio Campi, *Architect of Reformation: An Introduction to Heinrich Bullinger, 1504-1575* (Grad Rapids: Baker, 2004).

place where it does belong."[21] He argues that *sola fide* safeguards the preaching of Christ alone. Again, I could not agree with him more. But the way he argues his point is where we follow different paths. He believes that my treatment of obedience and faith allows "the camel's nose of human merit [into] the tent" and thereby replaces "the Savior's voluntary and meritorious obedience in life and death as the only ground of a sinner's acceptance with God."[22] Jones is concerned that moralism might replace resting and trusting in Christ alone for salvation. He is right to insist that where there "are no good works there is no faith."[23] And he rightly concludes that "be good" and "do good" should never become "a summary of Christianity."[24]

The question a discerning reader should ask is whether or not he has made the case that this is what I, and other contributors to this present book, are *actually* saying. I have argued, for some years now, that the gospel calls us to *a living and vital faith in Christ alone*. I have further argued that we are justified by trusting in Christ alone. We are made right with God, thus declared not guilty in the present time and completely forgiven of all sin, through the instrumentality of this God-given faith. Our faith does not save, Christ alone saves! What I have also argued is that saving faith is, by its very nature, obediential. Here is the rub for me: *What is saving faith?* Inherent in real faith, properly defined, is a something that does more than *passively* trust in Christ to save me. Saving faith has in it an active principle that *trusts and obeys*, thus I see no real conflicts between James and Paul. I do not think we need to make various special appeals to *two kinds of faith*. Indeed, I believe that the right way to read these two great teachers of the gospel will make them harmonize in such a way that the non-technical reader can see the arguments I make very clearly.

Paul says the gospel is "the power of God that brings salvation to everyone who believes" (Romans 1:16). In this good news

---

21. *Covenant, Justification and Pastoral Ministry*, 304-5.
22. *Covenant, Justification and Pastoral Ministry*, 305.
23. *Covenant, Justification and Pastoral Ministry*, 305.
24. *Covenant, Justification and Pastoral Ministry*, 305.

both the power and the message are carefully linked. God's power is always cast in terms of two types. First, there is the power of God that creates, both physically and spiritually. God's power made the world. And it is this same power that ethically changes sinners when he transforms them through faith. This gospel, operative in those who believe, is "immeasurable" and thus God's grace works "according to the working of his great power" (Ephesians 1:19). Paul never says the gospel brings power. Nor does he say this power results in people hearing the gospel so that they are saved. He says his gospel, this message itself, "is [itself] power." The gospel includes historical facts—the life, death, burial and resurrection of Jesus—but when this message of good news is preached the late Leon Morris got it right when he concluded, "The power of God is at work."[25] Ponder this every time your hear the preaching of Christ!

Paul also says this gospel actually "saves." He says, quite specifically, that it "brings salvation." The Greek text uses the word *gar* here, thus Paul says this good news is proclaimed "for salvation." The power of God is not aimless but rather it is directed very specifically to saving people. Salvation is a comprehensive word in the New Testament that includes the various words used in debates about the gospel; e.g., justification, sanctification, glorification, redemption, propitiation, grace and forgiveness. The whole of this salvation is (1) of God; (2) by and through Christ; and, (3) not of human merit or works. And this salvation has three parts, or tenses: (1) Past (Titus 3:5; Ephesians 2:5), thus it has already been achieved; (2) Present (1 Thessalonians 5:23; 1 Corinthians 1:18; 2 Corinthians 2:15), thus it is a present, powerful and ongoing process; and, (3) Future (Romans 13:11; 1 Corinthians 5:5; 2 Timothy 4:18), it will be completed in our final vindication in the last day. This is why numerous commentators have said that in Romans 1:16 Paul has in view salvation in its largest meaning. *He is referring to the whole process of mercy from the death and resurrection of Jesus, through our believing in time [by and through the Spirit's work] which*

---

25. Leon Morris, *The Epistle to the Romans*, (Grand Rapids: Eerdmans, 1988), 67.

includes our deliverance from sin and death, right through to our final vindication before the judgment to come. The idea here is not one of making us better, or of moralism ("be good" and "do good") but rather of rescue. This salvation saves us from wrath to come, from hostility toward God, from alienation that comes as a result of sin, from being lost, from utter futility, from the yoke of slavery and from this corrupt present generation. God's power to save is never divorced from this message, a message that is to be proclaimed or preached to the churched and non-churched alike. This is why there are not two kinds of evangelism, one of word and one of power. The word itself is the power of God. The gospel is the power!

Further, this gospel demands faith. It comes to "everyone who believes" (Romans 1:16). This power is not *unconditionally* operative. Faith is required to receive it. And faith is not something that we naturally possess. When Roman Catholic theology speaks, as it has historically, of an implicit and an explicit faith I find no warrant for such distinction in the Scripture. Faith is not implicit assent to the teaching of the Church and then faith in Jesus to save. *It is one, whole, dynamic trusting of Jesus to save us, period.* And faith itself does not save us. We are saved by Christ alone, through faith, which is the channel, or "instrumental means" as Reformed Christians have rightly called it. This means we are not saved by faith, a frequently made and badly mistaken statement. We are saved by Christ through faith. And faith believes "into or upon" Christ to use the precise language of the New Testament (*eis* or, sometimes, *epi* in the Greek).

Thus the word of Hebrews 11:1, "Now faith is being sure of what we hope for and certain of what we do not see." Faith means we trust God, dynamically and actively, for our future based upon what he has done in the past. This is the whole point of Hebrews 11. We do not trust a set of propositions or our knowledge of facts. But to believe in the one God, and in his Christ, is *not* necessarily saving faith: "Even the demons believe that—and shudder" (James 2:19). Real faith believes God will be faithful and trustworthy and actively trusts him in the good news. Real faith is dynamic and transforming.

But the gospel reveals something else to those who believe. It is a revelation of God's righteousness "for in the gospel a righteousness of God is revealed" (Roman 1:17). Simply put, there must be revelation from God if a person is to be saved. Something must be given, or revealed, by the power of God. In fact, Paul says this righteousness of God is "being revealed" (Note: present tense). The gospel is not the answer to man's quest, or the end of his groping for light. This gospel is an announcement of glorious good news. And it is an unveiling. This means the power of God must be at work if one is to come into the light given in the gospel message. This is the obvious meaning of 1 Corinthians 2:4-5.

But what is meant by "the righteousness of God" in this text? Here is where I believe the present debate really resides.

1. Luther argued that this word refers exclusively to the believer's status before God. The *theou* (God) here is what we call a genitive of source. This means Paul has in view "the righteousness that is *from* God." This means righteousness refers to an alien gift that God gives to those who believe the good news. I agree with this conclusion but I believe Paul is saying more than this in Romans 6-8, as we shall soon see.

2. The expression can also be correctly understood, more broadly, in terms of God's saving power. The context of Romans, and even of this text, supports this broader reading I believe. In this case *theou* is a subjective genitive. The "righteousness of God" is understood as *more* than a righteous status. This means this righteousness, or justice, is *both* forensic and effective. It is this second conclusion, that the righteousness of God that justifies us, *is effective*, that is denied by those who write in *Covenant, Justification and Pastoral Ministry*. They deny this because they are deeply concerned to protect the gospel from the intrusion of human works. I respect this concern but believe it is misplaced because they are working within a paradigm that limits their perspective. This mono-perspectival reading of Paul ends up missing the arguments the apostle actually makes. It seems to me they do this because they are locked into a framework that reads Paul through Luther's lens and not Paul's. As much as I love Luther, and revere him as a great gospel preacher

who was used to unleash the power of God's grace anew for the Church, I do not think he is the last word on exegeting Scripture precisely. I also do not think he read Romans perfectly.

Let's be clear about this. Luther saw this righteousness as *only* forensic. I do not believe you must deny his reading to affirm the second. All the way back in 1969 the New Testament commentator Ernst Käsemann saw this term as apocalyptic, thus an expression that denoted God's power over all creation. This meant that the term "righteousness" in Romans was not to be defined in strictly individualistic terms, as it was in Luther. A host of scholars have followed suit in reading Romans in this way since.

A Faith That Truly Hears Christ Preached Is Never Alone

The Reformers genuinely struggled to demonstrate that faith alone was never alone. They expressed this concern in many different ways. Because they wanted to protect the forensic and alien dimensions of righteousness, against any idea that justification took place *inside* the believer as Rome taught, they were right to make this distinction. This is why Hywel R. Jones, and the other contributors to *Covenant, Justification and Pastoral Ministry*, is rightly concerned to distinguish between justification and sanctification and why I said earlier I agreed with the concern but not the approach. *Righteousness is a gift, from start to finish.* There is nothing inherent in the human person, even in the regenerated human person, that can make that person righteous before God unless it comes through grace alone.

The biblical arguments that "the righteousness of God" refers to one's standing before God are numerous. Here are a few compelling ones:

1. The frequent use of righteousness (*diakaisune*) in Romans with reference to one's status before God; cf. Romans 3:21-22; 4:3, 5, 6, 11, 13, 22: 9:30-31; 10:3, 4, 6, 10.

2. The language used leads us to conclude that faith or believing is being reckoned to us as status because of faith; cf. Romans 4:3, 5, 6, 9, 11.

3. Paul speaks "of the gift of righteousness" demonstrating that it is God's gift not our attainment in any sense; cf. Romans 5:17.

4. Righteousness is very likely used as a genitive in 1 Corinthians 1:30 where Paul says their righteousness is "from God."

5. Paul clearly contrasts the gift character of righteousness with that which comes from the law in Philippians 3:9.

6. The verbal forms of to justify (*diakaiou*) regularly favor a forensic sense.

So, we should conclude that believers are indeed vindicated, declared to be righteous, in the law court sense because of the righteousness of Christ alone. This language is clearly forensic. I believe it is right to argue for it passionately. The word "alien" is also helpful here since it underscores that this gift comes from outside of us. This righteousness is not intrinsic in any sense nor can we do anything that merits or earns it.

Having said this, and said it as clearly as I know how, I believe it is important to see that this term also carries with it the idea that God's righteousness is also His saving power as Romans 1 indicates.

1. The verb revealed (*apokaluptetai* in Romans 1:17) refers to the eschatological activity of God invading human history. For this reason it is correct to speak of this divine action as being revealed as well as speaking of it as a new status now disclosed. Romans 3:21 speaks similarly referring to a righteousness of God that is *being* manifested.

2. The connection between verses 17 and 18 in Romans 1 demonstrates that God's wrath is a divine activity and this is parallel to righteousness.

3. The gospel in verse 16 is described as *the saving power of God*, as noted earlier. The "for" (*gar*) of verse 17 demonstrates that verse 17 is *the result of what precedes in verse 16*, thus the saving power of God is clearly intertwined with the righteousness of God in this context.

4. Even more importantly, at least for a full-orbed biblical

theology, there is the Old Testament background itself. Consider Psalm 98:2-3 as one example and then cross-reference this Psalm with Psalm 71:1-2; 22:31; 31:1; 35:24, 28; 40:10; 69:27-29; 88:12 and 119:123. Also look at Isaiah 51:5-8 and then cross reference this passage with Isaiah 46:13; 42:6, 21 and 45:8, 13.

Peter Stuhlmacher, who again is not an advocate of everything that I am arguing here, concludes:

> In the Old Testament and early Judaism, God's righteousness thus means the activity of God through which he creates well-being and salvation in history (specifically that of Israel), in creation and in the situation of the earthly or eschatological judgment.[26]

Simply put, righteousness language is the characteristic way the Old Testament speaks of God's *total saving activity*. This is the way Paul also speaks in Romans 8.

> I consider that our present sufferings are not worth comparing with the glory that will be revealed in us. The creation waits in eager expectation for the children of God to be revealed. For the creation was subjected to frustration, not by its own choice, but by the will of the one who subjected it, in hope that the creation itself will be liberated from its bondage to decay and brought into the freedom and glory of the children of God.
>
> We know that the whole creation has been groaning as in the pains of childbirth right up to the present time. Not only so, but we ourselves, who have the firstfruits of the Spirit, groan inwardly as we wait eagerly for our adoption, the redemption of our bodies. For in this hope we were saved. But hope that is seen is no hope at all. Who hopes for what they already have? But if we hope for what we do not yet have, we wait for it patiently (TNIV, Romans 8:18-25).

---

26. Peter Stuhlmacher, *Paul's Letter to the Romans* (Louisville, Kentucky: Westminster/John Knox Press), 30.

God's righteousness is His salvific action whereby he creates well-being for those who experience this revelation. For this reason I conclude that we are warranted to biblically distinguish between justification and sanctification, as argued in *Covenant, Justification and Pastoral Ministry*, but we are also warranted to see more in the biblical witness than these good Reformed men have actually seen. Righteousness language does refer to forensic and declarative righteousness, wherein we stand fully justified in Christ alone. But the text warrants us to also see another nuance in this word. This use leads us to see that transformation necessarily takes place in association with this gift of righteousness. The conclusion I will make is, therefore, critical to developing a richer biblical and reforming theology.

Conclusion

Put simply, those whom God justifies, or vindicates, He also changes. This is necessarily the case because of the dynamic of God's righteousness. When we come into divine righteousness a revelation of God takes place that demonstrates the powerful activity of God in changing our status and our life as one. It may be helpful, at least for certain polemical reasons, and contra historic Roman Catholic theological errors, to separate or distinguish justification and sanctification sharply, as Jones argues. The problem with this is that we end up with a faith and a righteousness that have no direct link to obedience at all. This is, I will say again, precisely why Bonhoeffer reacted against "cheap grace" the way he did. It is no accident that strong law/gospel distinction routinely creates this type of problem in the church.

The goal of Paul, in Romans, is to "bring about the obedience of faith among all the Gentiles for the sake of his name" (NRSV, Romans 1:5). This same goal is restated at the conclusion of this epistle when Paul adds:

> Now to God, who is able to strengthen you according to my gospel and the proclamation of Jesus Christ, according to the revelation of the mystery that was kept secret for long ages, but is now disclosed, and through the prophetic

> writings is made known to all the Gentiles, according to the command of the eternal God, *to bring about the obedience of faith*—to the only wise God, through Jesus Christ, to whom be the glory forever. Amen! (NRSV, Romans 16:25-17, emphasis mine).

Regardless of the technical arguments that Hywel Jones makes against my exegesis of these two texts in Romans it seems clear, both on first and second reading, that Paul is saying *he wrote this letter to bring about transformation in his hearers.* That transformation he calls "the obedience of faith."

Let me express this as simply as possible: *True faith is not to be radically divorced from obedience or the result will be something less than the power the gospel brings to those who believe it.*

I have made a case, in the offending essay that Jones critiqued, for how to best understand the phrase "the obedience of faith." I will not make the same argument here but it seems to me exegetically unlikely that Paul intends to separate the righteousness of God as a first act, when the gospel is first believed, from a second and third act wherein we obey Christ by the same power that came to us through the first faith. We are back to the basic issue—what is the nature of true faith?

So clear is this point, to my own mind, that Romans 15 actually nails my case once and for all. Here Paul tells us what his mission was about among the Gentiles. It was not to simply announce righteousness as a forensic act alone, with something else optional or added on. It was to "win obedience." This obedience is rooted in the righteousness of God revealed in the good news that is in Christ alone.

> For I will not venture to speak of anything except what Christ has accomplished through me, *to win obedience from the Gentiles, by word and deed* (NRSV, Romans 15:18, emphasis mine).

And Romans 6 and 8 demonstrate that Paul believes the faith given by God's grace will transform everyday believers directly because they will, and must, trust and obey.

Is the point I make a tempest in a teapot? I argue it is not. And perhaps this is why good Christians have disagreed about the language I have used and the meaning(s) intended. Yes, the saving righteousness of God is a gift that declares God's present vindication but it is also eschatological—it is a breaking into this age of the age to come. It is an effective and powerful declaration—indeed the gospel is God's power! We are transformed by this righteousness and thus we are right to conclude that it is *both* gift and power.

One of the arguments consistently made in Covenant, Justification and Pastoral Ministry is that the imputation of Christ's active obedience to the believer is at the very center of the gospel. This means that Christ kept the law and transferred to us His full life of moral obedience, thus actually meriting our salvation through His works done in our place. This concept is framed by a larger theological argument but it is one that I find questionable, if not entirely without exegetical warrant. But if Christ does not give us His moral obedience then what does He give us? *I answer—He imputes to us the forgiveness of our sin and imparts to us His divine life; i.e., the gift of the Holy Spirit.* The Spirit enabled Christ to live as man in active obedience. The same Spirit is to be known in the power of the gospel and impacts my life as a believer so that I too am empowered to live unto God. This is the argument made in Romans 8:1-4, a passage very often misread by exegetes who are determined to see in this text what is not there. Paul says, "Therefore, there is now no condemnation for those who are in Christ Jesus" (Romans 8:1). We should ask, "Why?" The answer supplied by theological voices aplenty is that there is "no condemnation" because of imputed righteousness, i.e., the works of Christ keeping the law, put to our account. But is that what Paul actually says here? Hear the verses that follow:

> [There is no condemnation] because through Christ Jesus the law of the Spirit who gives you life has set you free from the law of sin and death. For what the law was powerless to do because it was weakened by the sinful nature, God did by sending his own Son in the likeness of sinful humanity to be

a sin offering. And so he condemned sin in human flesh, in order that the righteous requirements of the law might be fully met in us, who do not live according to the sinful nature but according to the Spirit (TNIV, Romans 8:2-4).

I must admit that I read this text for thirty years without really paying careful attention to what was actually being said. "The righteous requirements of the law . . . [are] fully met in us . . . according to the Spirit." The crux of my argument is simple. "No condemnation" is not rooted only in the death of Christ as a substitute for sinners but also in the work of the Spirit transforming sinners! This confuses the categories of many because of the way it suggests that justification depends somehow on sanctification. There are various ways that Protestant exegetes have tried to handle this seeming problem.[27]

One of the traditional approaches harmonizes the passage with traditional Protestant doctrine. Another interprets 8:2 as a reference to the death of Christ for sinners so that condemnation is averted through justification rather than through sanctification. This view sees sanctification in 8:2 but suggests that the "no condemnation" of Romans 8:1 refers not to a judicial verdict but to "penal servitude." The third approach accepts what is probably the most natural reading of the two clauses used here and then seeks to show how sanctification is *the consequence of justification*, not the grounds. This common approach is taken by many good modern Reformed commentators.[28]

A better argument, I believe, is found by realizing that all of these approaches are the result of theological doctrines that are read into this text and become "an unnecessary and unhelpful expedient."

> The apparent meaning of this text must be sustained: "no condemnation" (8:1) retains its usual forensic sense; the liberation of 8:2 refers to transformational, rather than alien,

---

27. Chuck Lowe, "There is No Condemnation" (Romans 8:1): But Why Not?" *The Journal of the Evangelical Theological Society*, 42:2, June 1999, 231-250.
28. Lowe, 232.

righteousness; and, gar ("because" [NIV] 8:2) grounds the former in the latter. According to 8:1-2, Christians escape condemnation because they have been transformed by the Spirit; this is, because they now live in such a way that condemnation is no longer warranted. All the same, this passage is amenable to historic Protestant theology.[29]

It is the last sentence in the above quotation that makes the authors of *Covenant, Justification and Pastoral Ministry* extremely nervous. They do not believe this reading is possible so they work diligently to make these kinds of texts fit within their framework. I, however, agree with this last sentence and thus I do not believe the basic categories of Protestant theology are radically altered by seeing the referent in Romans 8:1 as the transforming power of the Holy Spirit.

How so? The "condemnation in view is clearly the eschatological judgment of sin, which is escaped only through the alien righteousness of Christ."[30]

I ask: "What is the nature of the liberation that is in view in Romans 8:1-4?" Is it the guilt of sin cancelled through the atonement of Christ, or the power of sin, now made impotent through the transforming work of the Holy Spirit? I believe the correct answer is not that complex: "Theologically, the obvious answer is, 'Both!' Exegetically, however, only the latter is explicitly in view here."[31]

Every indicator in Romans 8:1-4 is that freedom from condemnation is to be linked with the work of the Holy Spirit in us. Space limitations do not permit an extensive exegesis of this text but Romans 8 quite plainly recalls the language and concept of participation that we discover in Romans 6:1-11. The words of Romans 8 take us back to the words that Paul uses there; words like baptism "into Christ Jesus (6:3a) and baptism "into his death" (6:3b). He also speaks of our being "buried with him" (Romans

---

29. Lowe, 232.
30. Lowe, 233.
31. Lowe, 242.

6:4, of our crucifixion "with him" (6:6), our death "with Christ" (6:8), our life "with him (6:9), and our life to God "in Christ Jesus" (6:11). What believers have in Romans 6 is *not* justification through faith alone (as is seen in the argument made in Romans 3:21-31) but rather transformation in the inner person. Thus the argument of Romans 8:1-2 connects with the arguments made in 6:1-23 where righteousness is transformational. (Note: In Romans 5:12-21 the righteous life *is* plainly grounded in the alien righteousness of justification!)

What I believe is self-evident is that the work of the Holy Spirit in Romans 7 is developed more fully in Romans 8:3-15. The Spirit's role is to transform believers so that they live for God and receive eternal life. He is "the Spirit of life." He changes the way people who believe the gospel actually live their lives. He does this by union with Christ (cf. again Romans 6). And it has been rightly indicated that there are obvious semantic parallels that abound in Romans 7:4-6.[32]

In Romans 8:3-4 Paul shows that the righteous requirements of the law are fulfilled in those who live in accordance with the Spirit. The Spirit builds upon the alien work of Christ to continue and complete a transforming work in and by the Holy Spirit. This does not fail to *distinguish* between justification and sanctification in the best sense but it does show *how they are biblically related*. I believe this emphasis is important in preaching precisely because we who preach the gospel much preach both the first and the second emphasis. While we must avoid all of the dangers that abound in injecting human works into the grace of God we must, on the other hand, distinctly avoid the dangers of the other side of the road as well. These dangers are far too common to be missed and far too troubling to be ignored by the faithful preacher.

---

32. Lowe, 240. The old way of life and the new are contrasted by the following:
   (A1) they died through Christ,
   (B1) so that they might bear fruit to God (v. 4);
   (A2) previously their lusts had held sway,
   (B2) so that they bore fruit to death (v. 5);
   (A3) now they have been released through death,
   (B3) so that they now serve in the newness of the Spirit (v. 6).

I can illustrate this whole matter by a conversation I had some years ago after preaching this Romans 8:1-4 text in a conference setting. After I spoke the other speakers wanted to converse with me about what I had said and why. We were enjoying a lunch conversation. Following lunch, in a more private time, one of the speakers, a well-known writer and theologian, engaged me in a gracious manner with one or two further questions. I then asked him: "What do you think is the central problem in the pew where people have heard our gospel message for decades and believe the gospel is singularly about dealing with our sin through trusting in the atoning work of Christ alone for our justification?" I thought he would answer, with me, that we needed to preach the necessity of a transforming righteousness that comes by our union with Christ and the work of the Spirit. He answered, however with the same answer I see in *Covenant, Justification and Pastoral Ministry*. In effect he said, "We need to explain justification more clearly through the alien righteousness of Christ. People do not understand this truth as they should and if they did they would live rightly." In effect, he was saying we must read and understand the law/gospel distinction better, see our righteousness as solely outside of us, look back to what Christ did in the first century on Golgotha, and return to *sola fide* as the cure to all our present confusion in the Church. He was saying we get to holiness and life transformation by a right reading of justification. Sanctification, in this way of thinking, is often reduced to simply understanding justification. Inferred in his answer was the very same message our Westminster Seminary friends communicate—a right view of salvation by the work of Christ keeping the law for us and transferring his obedience to us is the answer to the powerlessness of modern Christianity. I do not believe that is the correct answer at all. I have tried to show why. The Bible is my witness.

Remember Martin Luther's *95 Theses* cited earlier in this chapter. No. 62 said: "The true treasure of the Church is the holy Gospel of the glory and grace of God." Preachers must understand and preach the gospel in all its fullness. It is the gospel that impacts our lives and transforms us. And it does so in two ways:

1. At the moment the power of God grants us a revelation of God's righteousness in Christ we receive the gift of salvation. This gift brings forgiveness, reconciliation, peace and new standing. It also brings the Holy Spirit, the life giving power that puts us in the state of "no condemnation" (cf. Romans 8:1). We are not only seen by God as just (forensically) but we are brought into the actual state of being "in the right" (just) because God puts His Spirit within us.

2. As a result of this impartation we are released from condemnation (Romans 8:1) and given a positive bestowal. This righteousness should be understood as divine power, the power which unites us to Christ alone. This puts union with Christ at the very center of God's declaring and making us right before Him. This is why those who walk in the power of the Spirit fulfill the law of Christ as Paul reasons in Romans 6 and 8.

The late Leon Morris got this in proper perspective when he concluded:

> In the full sense only Christ has fulfilled the law's requirements, but when we are in him we in our measure begin to live the kind of life that God would have us live. Notice that Paul does not say "we fulfill the law's righteous requirement," but that "the righteous requirement of the law is fulfilled in us," surely pointing to the work of the Holy Spirit in the believer.[33]

To live in the righteousness of God is to live under the cross where both the saving and judging righteousness of God are manifested. This is why Paul can say, "For I decided to know nothing while I was with you except Jesus Christ and him crucified" (1 Corinthians 2:2). This means:

1. Christ crucified is the power of God to save.
2. Christ crucified is the power of God to bring us into a righteous standing before a holy God.
3. Christ crucified is the power to lead us into lives that are

---

33. *The Epistle to the Romans*, 304.

characterized by the obedience of a truly powerful saving faith.

But how can justification through faith, apart from any human works (or merit), which is clearly taught in Romans 1-5, be preserved if Romans 6 and 8 teach what I have claimed? In short, the answer lies in the text itself and thus it is not that difficult to understand as we have shown. In Romans 1-5 Paul treats works negatively while in 6-8 he treats them positively. In the second section he shows that human works are inevitable, necessary and connected to the righteousness of Romans 1-5. They are the corollary of justification. Righteousness is thus inevitable in the truly redeemed because they have been united with Christ in his crucifixion death, thus by definition they have also been united with him in his resurrection life. Let me borrow the words of Chuck Lowe, from the article I have cited several times in making my arguments above: "Moral transformation is thus a prerequisite for eschatological salvation."[34] I believe that this is precisely what Romans 8:3-4 is saying. Read this quote again and I believe it will be quite apparent to you that it is correct upon a careful second reading.[35]

Modern populist evangelicalism has virtually made an abso-

---

34. Lowe 246-7.

35. Simon Gathercole, "What Did Paul Really Mean? *Christianity Today*, August, 2007, 22-28. Gathercole's survey is the most recent attempt by an evangelical scholar to refute some of the arguments made in this chapter and this book. He gets some things helpfully correct but falls under the same law/gospel distinction of tradition categories when he read the Old Testament, insisting that "In the Old Testament, 'righteousness' is the status that an Israelite received when he or she fully observed the requirements of the law: 'And if we are careful to obey all this law before the Lord our God, as he has commanded us, that will be our righteousness' (Deut. 6:25)." He then speaks of this old covenant as tragic because no one lived up to the covenant and fully obeyed God. But a careful reading of the Psalms, as well as the rest of the Old Testament, shows clearly that this reading of the Bible is theologically rooted in a Lutheran paradigm more than a biblical one. Righteousness, which Gathercole calls a "status" gained by "living up to the ideal in Deuteronomy" is more dynamically used with the biblical text itself, as it is in Romans as well. See the quote cited in footnote 26 above he admits that God's righteousness means "the activity of God whereby he creates well-being and salvation in history . . . ." Gathercole, like so many who critique the New Perspective with mixed results, limits the concept of righteousness to the paradigm he is defending. He would be better to use the whole text of the Bible in its fullest sense and allow righteousness to be used more accurately.

lute distinction between faith and works, seeing works as negative in almost every instance related to salvation. Our works are important, to put it very simply, but quite optional. The only works that really matter are Christ's, which are transferred to our account. This is how we got a non-Lordship gospel message. Our Reformed friends reject that message just as we do. But they reject it by using a very different means. They appeal back to alien righteousness alone and, in effect, tell sinners there is no further work to be done. This cuts the nerve of real gospel preaching.

My argument is rooted in what we call the proper understanding of the indicative and the imperative. After stating the indicative of our salvation clearly in the early part of Romans Paul moves, in Romans 8:1-4, to the imperative. Paul is *not* saying that believers will ever produce "perfect works" or a righteousness that is morally perfected in this life by the work of the Spirit, but he is saying our obedience will be *substantial and observable*. This is what preachers of the gospel must tell their congregations today. We must rejoin these two truths so that our gospel message has the urgency known by the Reformers. By this means we will be faithful to both their message and method, even if not to their every single word. John Calvin did not fundamentally disagree, so it seems to me, when he wrote: "We, indeed, allow that good works are required for righteousness; we only take away from them the power of conferring righteousness."[36] Yes, and amen!

---

36. John Calvin, *Commentary on the Catholic Epistles* (Grand Rapids: Eerdmans, 1959), 317.

CHAPTER 2

Faith and Faithfulness

Norman Shepherd

In chapter 9 of *Covenant, Justification, and Pastoral Ministry*, W. Robert Godfrey offers a defense of "faith alone" under the title, "Faith Formed by Love or Faith Alone." He begins with a brief treatment of the Roman Catholic doctrine of "faith formed by love" (2 pages) followed by a longer treatment of John Calvin's doctrine of faith alone (7 pages), and concludes with the Biblical doctrine of faith alone (7 pages).

In this third section he raises what he calls a "crucial question" for some of the interpreters of Paul. The question arises from the rhetorical question Paul poses in Romans 6:1, "Shall we go on sinning so that grace may increase?" The crucial question for Godfrey is this: "Would anyone ever read the federal-vision writers or Norman Shepherd or the new perspective on Paul or Thomas Aquinas or the Council of Trent and come with the question to them: Should we sin that grace may abound?" He continues, "That question would never, could never, arise for anyone who has read these teachers." He appeals to Martyn Lloyd-Jones and other unnamed "defenders of the Reformation doctrine of justification" who say: "If no one ever comes to you after you preach the gospel and asks, 'So should we sin so that grace may abound?' you have probably never preached the gospel" (*CJPM*, 280).

Now I cannot speak for Thomas Aquinas or the Council of Trent, and I will not attempt to speak for the federal vision writers or the representatives of the new perspective on Paul. However, I would like to say a few words on behalf of Norman Shepherd. Why is it that when Shepherd finishes preaching the gospel no one asks, "Shall we go on sinning so that grace may increase?"

The answer is, of course, that when Shepherd preaches the gospel he calls on sinners to believe in Jesus with a living and active faith. He has learned from James 2 that true faith is a faith that works. James says explicitly that faith without works is dead (v. 26). It is no faith at all. James asks the question, if a man claims to have faith but has no deeds, can such faith save him in the final judgment (v. 14)? The answer is, "of course not!" It is dead faith and dead faith does not save in the final judgment, and it does not justify in the final judgment or at any other point. Even if we were to argue that James is talking about justification in a demonstrative rather than in a forensic, soteric sense, we still have the question whether a faith that cannot save can nevertheless justify, and the answer is a resounding "no."

Concerning this demonstrative sense of justify, we can also ask, why do works serve to demonstrate the genuineness of faith? What do works have to do with faith? The answer is that works demonstrate the genuineness of faith because of the indissoluble connection between faith and faithfulness to the commands of our Lord. You cannot really believe in Jesus without responding to his commands with obedience. As we read in 1 John 3:23, "And this is his command: to believe in the name of his Son, Jesus Christ, and to love one another as he commanded us." One command: to believe and to love. Faith alone, faith without works, is a theological abstraction that does not exist in the experience of converted sinners.

Shepherd finds that Paul preaches the same truth when he says that justifying faith is faith that expresses itself through love (Gal. 5:6). Paul says that the acts of the sinful nature are obvious and he gives a detailed list of them (Gal. 5:19-21). He concludes by saying, "those who live like this will not inherit the kingdom of God." When Shepherd preaches the gospel he includes this solemn warning as well as the similar warning in Galatians 6:8. This warning is coupled to the gospel promise, "the one who sows to please the Spirit, from the Spirit will reap eternal life." Shepherd also joins with Paul in this word of encouragement: "Let us not become weary in doing good, for at the proper time we will reap a harvest if we do not give up."

Not only does Shepherd think that justifying faith is living and active faith, he also thinks that it is a penitent and obedient faith. He believes that when we preach the gospel we ought to do what Jesus tells us to do in the Great Commission (Matt. 28:19-20). This is the mandate under which the church today carries out its evangelistic task. We ought to make disciples with a lot more than just "faith alone." We ought to make disciples by baptizing them in the name of the Father and of the Son and of the Holy Spirit, and by teaching them to obey everything that Jesus has commanded us.

This baptism in the triune name is a baptism of repentance for the forgiveness of sins as Peter made so clear on the Day of Pentecost when about three thousand people were baptized and added to the number of believers. Peter preached repentance for the forgiveness of sins, and forgiveness of sins belongs to the very essence of justification. So also in the form of the Great Commission as we have it in Luke 24:46-47, the gospel centers on the death and resurrection of Jesus and commands repentance for the forgiveness of sins to all nations beginning at Jerusalem.[1]

The prophets of the old covenant preached repentance, and the last of these, John the Baptist, preached a baptism of repentance for the forgiveness of sins with an appeal to the words of Isaiah the prophet (Luke 3:3-6). He told sinners to "produce fruit in keeping with repentance." Jesus began his ministry with the same call to repentance (Matt. 4:17) and taught his disciples to carry on with the same message. We see Peter doing this on the Day of Pentecost, and we see Paul doing this when he confronts the Gentiles in Athens. He speaks about the false conceptions of the divine being entertained by the Greeks and then says, "In the past God overlooked such ignorance, but now he commands all

---

1. The correct translation is "repentance *for* the forgiveness of your sins" as in the NASU, not "repentance *and* forgiveness of sins" as in the NIV, NRSV, and ESV. The same expression is used in Acts 2:38 and is translated correctly in all these versions: repentance *for* the forgiveness of sins.

people everywhere to repent. For he has set a day when he will judge the world with justice by the man he has appointed. He has given proof of this to all men by raising him from the dead" (Acts 17:30-31). In preaching the gospel Paul demands repentance in the name of the Lord in view of the judgment to come. Repentance is unto the remission of sins. Those who remain unrepentant do not know the forgiveness of sins now, and they will not be justified in the Day of Judgment.

Shepherd believes that justifying faith is not only a penitent faith, it is also an obedient faith. Repentance is not simply sorrow for sin. It is not a purely mental act. In Luke 3 we see the crowd responding to John's call to repentance by asking repeatedly, "What should we do?" and John tells them what they are to do with example after example of kingdom righteousness. Luke says, "And with many other words John exhorted the people and preached the good news to them" (Luke 3:18). The Westminster Confession of Faith is certainly correct when it says that by repentance "a sinner . . . so grieves for, and hates his sins, as to turn from them all unto God, purposing and endeavoring to walk with him in all the ways of his commandments" (chapter 15, section 2). Just as faith and repentance are indissolubly joined in the conversion of sinners, so also repentance and new obedience are indissolubly joined together in the life of the believer.

From the beginning of his public ministry as evidenced by the Sermon on the Mount, Jesus taught obedience to the word of God and to his own word because he was himself God. "Now remain in my love. If you obey my commands, you will remain in my love, just as I have obeyed my Father's commands and remain in his love" (John 15:9-10). In line with this Jesus taught his disciples to evangelize the world by teaching the nations to obey everything he commanded. And this is exactly what they did, not only orally but also in writing. We have the proof in our New Testament. The whole of each epistle is gospel, not only the promises made to faith but also the commands that are received by faith, faith that is living, active, penitent, and obedient. The good news is not that God forgives *impenitent* sinners, but that he forgives *penitent* sinners.

Because Shepherd teaches that saving and justifying faith is living, active, penitent, and obedient faith, Godfrey is quite certain that no one listening to him preach the gospel would ever raise the question, "Should we sin that grace may abound?" It is different, however, when Godfrey preaches the gospel. Presumably, when he is finished, crowds gather around the pulpit breathlessly inquiring, "Then why shouldn't we sin so that grace will abound?"

Why is there such a different response to the gospel Godfrey preaches?

The answer is that Godfrey preaches justification by faith *alone*, and he really means a faith that is alone. It is not a living and active faith that justifies as Shepherd says, but a faith that is all alone. He writes, "Paul really could not be clearer. Paul indeed taught that faith stands alone in receiving justification from the work of Christ ([Rom.] 3:24-26)" (*CJPM*, 282).

For Godfrey, justifying faith cannot be a penitent faith because once we join repentance to faith we no longer have faith alone. Even more so, we certainly cannot join faith and repentance to obedience. When faith is joined to repentance and obedience, as in Shepherd's formula, "a penitent and obedient faith," we then have justification by faith plus works; and that is the deadly combination that for Godfrey destroys the achievement of the Protestant Reformation.

When Godfrey preaches the gospel he does not tell sinners to repent of their sins, nor does he tell them to obey all that Jesus has commanded. In other words, he does not preach the gospel the way Jesus commands us to preach the gospel in the Great Commission. If we do what the Great Commission tells us to do then we mix what David Van Drunen calls a "cocktail" of faith and works (*CJPM*, 49). And it is a *toxic* cocktail because if we tell sinners to repent and obey our Lord, Godfrey and Van Drunen think we are teaching them to justify themselves by their own good works. They find this to be contrary to Paul's teaching that we are saved by faith alone and not by works of the law.

If all that is asked of us is simply faith to the express exclusion of repentance and obedience lest we concoct this toxic cocktail, then obviously someone is bound to suggest that we sin in order for grace to abound. That is how Godfrey explains the reason for the question in Romans 6:1.

Godfrey versus the Westminster Confession

Godfrey's chapter makes quite clear that he cannot really accept what the Westminster Confession says about the necessity of repentance for the forgiveness of sins. The Confession says, "Although repentance be not to be rested in, as any satisfaction for sin, or any cause of the pardon thereof, which is the act of God's free grace in Christ; yet it is of such necessity to all sinners, that none may expect pardon without it" (chapter 15, section 3). The Confession defines justification as including the pardon of sin, and therefore makes repentance necessary for justification. And as already noted it defines repentance so as to include not only a grief for and hatred of sin, but a turning away from sin with an endeavor to walk with the Lord in all the ways of his commandments. For Godfrey, the Confession really mixes a toxic cocktail of faith plus works as necessary for justification.

Godfrey's chapter makes quite clear that he cannot really accept what the Westminster Confession says about saving faith. In chapter 14, section 2, the Confession defines the principal acts of saving faith as "accepting, receiving, and resting upon Christ alone for justification, sanctification, and eternal life, by virtue of the covenant of grace." These are the "principal" acts, but they are not the only acts of this faith. They are "principal" in relation to all the other acts that are invariably associated with it including "yielding obedience to the commands, trembling at the threatenings, and embracing the promises of God for this life, and that which is to come." Thus according to the Westminster Confession justifying faith is an obedient faith. Godfrey cannot really accept this definition of saving and justifying faith because from his perspective it mixes a toxic cocktail of faith plus works for justification.

Godfrey's chapter makes quite clear that he cannot really accept what the Westminster Confession says about the nature of justifying faith in chapter 11, section 2. He strongly endorses the

Confession when it says that faith is the "alone instrument" of justification, but not when it goes on to say that this faith "is not alone in the person justified, but is ever accompanied with all other saving graces, and is no dead faith, but worketh by love." His point is, as noted above, that "faith stands alone in receiving justification from the work of Christ."

The Irish Articles (1615) that lie behind the language of the Westminster Confession sound a different note. "When we say that we are justified by faith only, we do not mean that the said justifying faith is alone in man without true repentance, hope, charity, and fear of God (for such a faith is dead, and can not justify)."[2] The Irish Articles tell us that a faith that stands alone is dead and cannot justify. They appeal to one of the two Bible texts cited in the Westminster Confession, James 2:24. The Westminster Confession also cites Galatians 5:6.

The Westminster Confession does not speak of justifying faith as an act that is over and done with in less than a moment of time. It does not define justifying faith as a mathematical point without dimensions. Justifying faith is an ongoing reality in the life of the believer. He believes and is justified with a penitent, obedient, and persevering faith. From Godfrey's perspective the Confession in Chapter 11, especially when it brings James 2:24 and Galatians 5:6 into connection with justification, mixes a toxic cocktail of faith plus works for justification and is really unacceptable.

Godfrey's chapter makes quite clear that he cannot really accept the way that John Calvin speaks of justifying faith as a faith that works. There are two passages in Calvin's *Institutes* that are especially relevant here and Godfrey includes both of them in longer citations of Calvin. The first is in 3:11:20, "Indeed we confess with Paul that no other faith justifies 'but faith working through love' [Gal. 5:6]. But it does not take its power to justify from that working of love. Indeed, it justifies in no other way but in that it leads us into fellowship in the righteousness of Christ."[3] The second is in 3:11:1, "The theme of

---

2. Philip Schaff, *The Creeds of Christendom*, 3 vols. (Grand Rapids, MI: Baker Book House, 1977 reprint), 3:533.
3. *Calvin: Institutes of the Christian Religion*, trans. F. L. Battles (Philadelphia: Westminster

justification was therefore more lightly touched upon because it was more to the point to understand first how little devoid of good works is the faith, through which alone we obtain free righteousness by the mercy of God."[4] (*CJPM*, 274-5).

In treating of these passages Godfrey is willing to say, "Calvin teaches that it is faith alone that *produces* love" (italics original). He says, "True faith is also the *fountain* of sanctification, love, and repentance" (italics added), and "the true faith that justifies is a faith that *leads* also to sanctification" (italics added). But Godfrey is careful not to say, as Calvin does, that faith working through love justifies, or that the faith itself through which we obtain free righteousness is not devoid of good works. Godfrey maintains to the contrary that faith stands alone in justification; and only after it has justified does it have works added to it. This may well be the view of Luther as Godfrey claims, and it certainly is the view of classic Lutheranism, but it is not the view of Calvin as Calvin states his view in the *Institutes*.

Actually Godfrey's view is similar to the Roman Catholic view that he rejects in the first part of his chapter. For Trent the faith that accepts what the Roman church teaches and leads to the sacrament of baptism, is faith alone. In baptism grace is infused and the sinner is justified by becoming a just person. In this justification by baptism, love is added to faith, and the initial faith alone becomes a faith formed by love. So also for Godfrey, initially faith stands alone and receives an imputed justifying righteousness. Then, after this faith has justified the sinner, it "leads to" sanctification, or "produces" sanctification. Thus love is added to faith alone, and faith alone becomes a faith formed by love.

The Reformed view as set out in the Westminster Confession is quite different. The Reformed view is that by the power of the Holy Spirit the sinner is effectually called into union with Jesus Christ (chapter 10), and in him simultaneously receives the gifts of justification (a forensic, soteric judgment), adoption, and sanctifi-

---

Press, 1960), 1:750.
4. *Institutes*, 1:725-6.

cation (personal transformation) (chapters 11, 12, 13). This union manifests itself in the exercises of faith, repentance, and good works (chapters 14, 15, 16).

Now Godfrey, of course, affirms the importance of sanctification for true religion, and that "Those who totally lack sanctification can make no claim of having true faith" (*CJPM*, 275). But he does not seem to appreciate the fact that if they do not have true faith now, they never did have true faith; and therefore they could not have been justified by a faith that stands alone. He does not seem to appreciate the fact that there is no true faith apart from faithfulness, even in the matter of justification by faith.

Habakkuk 2:4 says, "The righteous will live by his faith." The Hebrew word for "faith" can also be translated "faithfulness." This is the alternative translation offered in the margins of both the NIV and the ESV. Paul uses Habakkuk 2:4 in Romans 1:17 to prove that justification is by faith without the works of the law. Hebrews 10:36-38 uses Habakkuk 2:4 to prove that "You need to persevere so that when you have done the will of God, you will receive what he has promised." There is no way to escape the close association of faith and faithfulness when it comes to matters of eternal weal or woe. They are related in this way: justifying faith receives and rests upon Christ alone for justification, and it continues to rest upon Christ alone for justification throughout the believer's life. It issues in the faithfulness described as "doing the will of God," with the assurance that the believer will receive what is promised. The promise is the promise of eternal life.

A faith that stands alone is a theological abstraction that does not exist in the experience of the believer. No one less than Francis Turretin, an influential Reformed theologian of the scholastic period, describes this abstraction precisely with an illustration that speaks directly to the relation between faith and works. Turretin says,

> The question is not whether *solitary* faith (i.e., separated from the other virtues) justifies (which we grant could not easily be the case, since it is not even true and living faith), but whether it *alone* [*sola*] concurs to the act of justification

> (which we assert): as the eye alone sees, but not when torn out of the body. Thus the particle *alone* [*sola*] does not determine the subject, but the predicate (i.e., "faith only does not justify" [*sola fides non justificat*], but "faith justifies alone" [*fides justificat sola*]). The coexistence of love in him who is justified is not denied; but the coefficiency or cooperation in justification is denied.[5]

An eye, torn from its organic connection to the body, that can nevertheless see is a biological abstraction that cannot exist. So also faith that stands alone is a theological abstraction. Sinners are not justified by theological abstractions. As Turretin says, solitary faith, faith separated from other virtues, faith that stands alone (Godfrey's expression), does not and cannot justify because it is dead faith.

Calvin was therefore right to say that "no other faith justifies 'but faith working through love' [Gal 5:6]. But it does not take its power to justify from that working of love." This second sentence is most important and needs to be stressed. Turretin makes the same point in the passage cited above when he says that "[faith] *alone* concurs to the act of justification," and "The coexistence of love in him who is justified is not denied; but the coefficiency or cooperation in justification is denied." To say that faith working through love justifies does not mean for Paul, or Calvin, or Turretin, or Shepherd that works become the ground or instrument of justification. Godfrey, however, thinks that it does, because he cannot see works as functioning in any other way than as the ground or instrument of justification. For him, and contrary to Turretin, coexistence implies, even requires coefficiency. This is a basic mistake that Godfrey makes. That is why he cannot really agree with Calvin or Turretin, because from his perspective Calvin and Turretin are mixing a toxic cocktail of faith plus works for justification.

The view of the Apostle Paul and Calvin, that faith working

---

5. Francis Turretin, *Institutes of Elenctic Theology*, trans. G. M. Giger (Phillipsburg, NJ: P&R Publishing, 1992), 2:677. The quotation is from Topic 16, Question 8, Section 6.

through love justifies, has been the prevailing view in Reformed orthodoxy until just recently. Reformed writers have never been reluctant to speak of justifying faith as a living and active faith, even though this has been a continual irritant for our Lutheran brothers who are never sure that the Reformed can really make the proper distinction between law and gospel.

In his chapter on sanctification in *Our Reasonable Faith*, Herman Bavinck tells us that the sanctification Christ and the Holy Spirit have given to the church places a heavy obligation on believers. In the course of unfolding this point he makes this salient observation: "Just as in the justification the forgiveness of sins, completely prepared in Christ, can on our part only be received and enjoyed through a living and active faith, so God effects the sanctification in us only by means of us ourselves."[6] Here Bavinck says quite pointedly that justification is both received and enjoyed by a living and active faith. Since this justification is completely prepared for us in Christ, the fact that faith is living and active does not mean that works are added to faith as a ground for justification.

Godfrey rightly calls Bavinck "one of the great Dutch Reformed scholars and theologians of the late nineteenth and early twentieth centuries" (*CJPM*, 268), and Bavinck says that believers are justified by a living and active faith.[7] This is a formula Godfrey cannot accept because this is what Shepherd says, and for him it creates a toxic cocktail of faith plus works for justification.

J. Gresham Machen gives expression to the Reformed view in the way that he treats the difference between Paul and James. Paul says that we are not justified by works, and James says that we are.

---

6. Herman Bavinck, *Our Reasonable Faith*, trans. Henry Zylstra (Grand Rapids, MI: Eerdmans Publishing Co., 1956), 479. *Our Reasonable Faith* is Bavinck's one volume condensation of his four volume *Reformed Dogmatics*, and was first published in Dutch under the title, *Magnalia Dei*. The quoted passage reads in the original: "Zooals in de rechtvaardigmaking de vergeving der zonden, die volkomen in Christus gereed ligt, onzerzijds alleen ontvangen en genoten kan worden door een levend en werkzaam geloof, zoo brengt God de heiligmaking in ons slechts door ons te stand." H. Bavinck, *Magnalia Dei* (Kampen: J.H. Kok, 1909), 544.
7. The dogmatic formulation Bavinck uses here is exactly the formulation for which Shepherd was roundly chastised in the lengthy footnote 89 of the official 2006 Orthodox Presbyterian Report on Justification.

Machen is too fine a New Testament scholar to resort to the exegetically untenable demonstrative sense for "justify" in James 2 in order to reconcile James and Paul. This is how Machen resolves the issue:

> The solution of the whole problem is provided by Paul himself in a single phrase. In Gal. 5:6, he says, "For in Christ Jesus neither circumcision availeth anything, nor uncircumcision; but faith working through love." "Faith working through love" is the key to an understanding both of Paul and of James. The faith about which Paul has been speaking is not the idle faith which James condemns, but a faith that works. It works itself out through love. And what love is Paul explains in the whole last division of Galatians. It is no mere emotion, but the actual fulfilling of the whole moral law.[8]

Here Machen says that the faith of which Paul speaks in Romans 3:28 when he says that a man is justified by faith apart from observing the law, is a faith that works. A faith that does not work is not a justifying faith. It is a demonic faith, a dead faith. Godfrey cannot really accept the solution to the Paul-James question that Machen offers because it mixes faith with works and serves up more of the toxic cocktail that he and David Van Drunen so strenuously condemn.

When Godfrey preaches the gospel people crowd around to ask, "Shall we go on sinning so that grace may increase?" They ask this because Godfrey preaches justification by faith alone. He asks his listeners only for faith, faith without repentance and faith without obedience. As we have seen, Reformed writers such as Calvin, Turretin, Bavinck, and Machen did not think Paul was asking for that kind of faith, though Lutheran theologians would concur with Godfrey's interpretation of Paul.

From Calvin to Paul

Godfrey is on target when he writes, "It is good to know what Calvin said; it is much more important to know what Paul said"

---

8. John H. Skilton, ed., *Machen's Notes On Galatians* (Philadelphia: Presbyterian and Reformed Pub. Co., 1972), 220-1.

(*CJPM*, 269), and so we turn now to Paul. What kind of faith did Paul have in mind in Romans 3:28 when he said that we are justified by faith without the works of the law? Was it a faith that stands alone, or a penitent and obedient faith?

To begin, Romans 3:28 does not use the word "alone," when it speaks of justification by faith. Luther inserted this word into the translation of his German Bible because he thought it necessary to tweak the inspired word of God so that it would clearly say what he thought it ought to say. Godfrey begins his chapter by pointing out and defending this Lutheran gloss. Godfrey can also find widespread support for the Lutheran gloss among Reformed writers who rightly want to guard the Biblical doctrine of justification from being grounded in the merit of good works. This was certainly Calvin's point in defending the gloss. However, as we shall see in a moment, the defense rests upon a misunderstanding of "works of the law," and the gloss is now used to deny what Reformed orthodoxy has always affirmed, namely, that justifying faith is a living and active, penitent and obedient faith.

In Romans 1:5 Paul declares it to be his ministry "to call people from among all the Gentiles to the obedience that comes from faith." Godfrey takes note of this NIV translation and sees in it a reference to the obedience that comes after faith standing all alone has done its justifying work. However, in this case he does not want to tweak the translation, and prefers the more literal ESV, "the obedience of faith." He understands the obedience as obedience that consists in faith (*CJPM*, 279). This interpretation has the advantage of rightly defining faith as itself an act of obedience, and therefore as a work. However, from Godfrey's perspective this literal translation really begins to flirt with the toxic cocktail. But now, is that all that Paul is asking of the Gentiles? Is the purpose of his ministry among the Gentiles to cultivate faith without repentance, and faith without obedience to the commands of Christ?

Paul certainly carries out his mission to the Gentiles in terms of the Great Commission's command to "make disciples of all nations." He will do that by preaching a baptism of repentance for the remission of sins and by teaching the Gentiles to obey everything that Christ has commanded. Jesus does not mention faith explicitly in the Great Commission, though it is certainly there by implication; however, this faith cannot be a faith that stands all alone.

As he proceeds in Romans, Paul not only exposes the sins of both Jew and Gentile, but also specifically the sin of refusal to repent in spite of the patience of the Lord. The problem Paul addresses here is not that no one will be able to merit their salvation by their good works because they have no works that are any good. The basic problem is that because of this sin God is dishonored and his name is blasphemed (Rom. 2:23-24). The problem is the offense against God and the insult to the divine majesty that sin represents. Paul is concerned for the honor of God and therefore calls the Gentiles as well as the Jews to repentance, to the obedience of faith, to the obedience that comes through faith in Jesus and is invariably associated with faith in Jesus. Faith bears fruit in faithfulness that is honoring to God.

In chapter 2 Paul reminds God's people, the Jews, of the demand for repentance and the fact that because of their unrepentant hearts they are storing up wrath against themselves for the Day of Judgment. When we get to chapter 3 it is not as though Paul forgets all about this demand for repentance and asks simply for faith without repentance or faith without obedience. He says in Romans 2:13 that in the Day of Judgment "it is those who obey the law who will be declared righteous." This is not justification by the merit of good works, but justification by faith, faith that is genuine, faith that works, faith that expresses itself through love. We are not justified by dead faith (faith without works) and we are not justified by dead works (works without faith). We are justified by living and active faith. This is the kind of faith Paul calls for in chapter 6 when he tells us not to let sin reign in our mortal bodies, and not to offer the parts of our bodies to sin. He commends his readers because they have now by the grace of God "wholeheartedly obeyed the form of teaching to which you were entrusted" (6:17). This is the obedience of faith.[9]

---

9. See also Heb. 5:9, "He became the source of eternal salvation for all who obey him."

Paul speaks about the obedience of faith once again at the end of the letter in chapter 15 when he speaks of what Christ has accomplished through him "in leading the Gentiles to obey God by what I have said and done" (v. 18). This follows his statement in v. 16 that it was his privilege to offer up the Gentiles to God as "an offering acceptable to God, sanctified by the Holy Spirit." The obedience of faith in Romans 1:5 is not simply obedience that consists in faith, but obedience that flows from faith and is the result of the *sanctifying* work of the Holy Spirit. This is the faith in Romans 3:28 that justifies "without the works of the law."[10]

Now we have to ask, what are these "works of the law?" They are not simply any and all good works, as Godfrey and many others think, nor are they simply the ceremonial aspects of the law without the moral aspects. These interpretations completely overlook the historical circumstances in which Paul is writing and the historical issues with which he is dealing. The loss of this Biblical-historical perspective distorts a proper understanding of Romans 2 and 3.

By "works of the law" Paul is referring to the old covenant, the Mosaic covenant delivered to Israel on Mount Sinai, summarizing the promises and obligations under which Israel lived from the time of the Exodus to the advent of Christ and the establishment of the new covenant. Paul's argument in Romans 3 is that if salvation ultimately comes by the works of the law, the provisions of the Mosaic covenant, then the Gentiles are excluded from the possibility of salvation. They are not excluded because they could not *keep* the law, but because they did not *have* the law.[11] This is the

---

10. In support of his view that the obedience of faith is obedience that consists in faith, Godfrey appeals to John 6:29, "The work of God is this: to believe in the one he has sent" (*CJPM*, 279). He thinks that Jesus deliberately excluded the obedience that invariably accompanies true faith, as though Jesus was asking for faith without repentance. He overlooks John's own testimony in his First Epistle, 3:23, "And this is his command: to believe in the name of his Son, Jesus Christ, and to love one another as he commanded us." John speaks of a single command with two aspects.
11. Romans 2:15 does not say that the Gentiles have the law. V. 14 says explicitly that they do not have the law. Psalm 147:19-20 says that God revealed his laws to Israel. "He has done this for no other nation; they do not know his laws." The Gentiles are a law to themselves; but they show by their actions "the *requirements* of the law written on their

point Paul makes in Romans 3:29.

Further, Paul shows that those Jews who made their boast in this Mosaic law and thought they were right with God because they were doing works of the law, were not really keeping this law. This is the point Paul makes in Romans 2. How could works of the law justify them when they were deliberately leading immoral and impenitent lives? We have examples of this phenomenon in Matthew 23. There the Lord condemns religious teachers and leaders who were tithing mint, dill, and cummin, but at the same time were neglecting the more important matters of justice, mercy, and *faithfulness*. In Romans 3 Paul is not now teaching, contrary to Jesus, that faith without repentance, faith without justice and mercy, and *faith without faithfulness* is the real key to justification after all![12]

Answering the Question

Godfrey is mistaken when he thinks that the question in Romans 6:1, "Shall we go on sinning so that grace may increase?" arises from the fact that Paul is teaching justification by faith that stands alone apart from repentance and obedience. Rather, the question arises because for Paul justification is the forgiveness of sins. Paul's emphasis in Romans 3, 4, and 5 is on the fact that justification is grounded in the death and resurrection of Jesus. His sacrifice of atonement is the righteousness from God (3:21), the one act of righteousness (5:18), that secures the forgiveness of sins. Therefore we are justified through faith in the blood of Christ (3:25; 5:9). Jesus "was delivered over to death for our sins and was raised to life for our justification" (4:25).[13] Because justification is the free forgiveness of sin grounded in the mediatorial accomplishment of Christ, Paul asks the rhetorical question, "Shall we go

---

hearts." See John Murray, *The Epistle to the Romans*, 2 vols. (London: Marshall, Morgan, and Scott, Ltd., 1960), 1:74-5. This reference is to Murray's comments on Rom. 2:15.

12. For a fuller discussion of the meaning of "works of the law," see my "Justification By Faith in Pauline Theology," in *Backbone of the Bible*, ed. P. Andrew Sandlin (Nacogdoches, TX: Covenant Media Press, 2004), 94-100.

13. For a fuller explanation of justification as the forgiveness of sins, see "Justification By Faith in Pauline Theology," in *Backbone of the Bible*, 87-9.

on sinning so that grace may increase?" The thought behind the question is that the more we sin, the more Jesus can forgive us and thereby magnify his grace.

Now how does Godfrey answer this question? He does not tell us, and understandably so. From his perspective there really is no good answer. If our sins are forgiven by the imputation of Christ's passive obedience so that there is nothing to keep us out of heaven, and if the meritorious ground for entrance into heaven is granted by the imputation of Christ's active obedience, and if all these benefits are ours through a faith that stands all alone, then why not sin so that grace may abound? Godfrey can say, of course, that if the believer has true faith this faith will *produce* good works. But this does not answer the question. The question is not, "*Will* we go on sinning so that grace may increase," but "*Should* we go on sinning that grace may increase?" What difference would it make whether faith produces works or not? But if it does make a difference then Godfrey is beginning to sound like Shepherd who keeps saying that justification is by a penitent and obedient faith.[14]

Shall we sin that grace may abound? In Germany during the time of the Protestant Reformation, Philip of Hesse contracted a second and bigamous marriage with a seventeen-year-old maid. When word of this got out, and in order to do some damage control, Martin Luther advised Philip to tell "a good, strong lie."[15] Luther's advice on this occasion is a thoroughly consistent application of a doctrine of justification by faith that stands alone; but it is not an acceptable answer to the question, shall we sin that grace may abound? No one wants to answer, "yes." But if we say "no," then

---

14. Q&A 87 of the Heidelberg Catechism asks, "Can those be saved who do not turn to God from their ungrateful and impenitent ways?" The answer given in the Catechism is, "By no means. Scripture tells us that no unchaste person, no idolater, adulterer, thief, no covetous person, no drunkard, slanderer, robber, or the like is going to inherit the kingdom of God." Of what practical benefit to the sinner is his justification by faith that stands all alone if, after being justified in this way, he is then told that he must now repent in order to be saved? Saved from what? Saved from divine condemnation. But that is exactly what justification is supposed to secure!

15. Kenneth Scott LaTourette, *A History of Christianity* (New York: Harper & Brothers, 1953), 728.

from Godfrey's perspective we are beginning to introduce a measure of legalism. Apparently there are just some things that we ought not to do if we expect to be justified in the judgment of God.

Shepherd answers the question of Romans 6:1 the same way Paul does in the rest of the chapter. Paul does not point the believer to his own personal faith and rest content with the thought that solitary faith will somehow eventually produce fruit. He immediately points to Jesus Christ and tells us that the same Jesus who died and rose again to secure the forgiveness of sin, also by this same death and resurrection has secured our death to sin and our life of righteousness (our sanctification). Paul says that in Jesus we have died to sin and therefore we cannot live in sin any longer. In Jesus we were raised from deadness in sin to live a new life in righteousness and holiness. On the basis of what Jesus has done for us Paul does not hesitate to command us to offer ourselves to God and to offer the parts of our bodies as instruments of righteousness. He is not afraid that somehow he will be mixing a toxic cocktail of faith plus works for justification.

It is significant that Godfrey, along with Martyn Lloyd-Jones, thinks of the question in Romans 6:1 as coming at the end of the sermon, after the gospel has been preached. Godfrey quotes Lloyd-Jones approvingly when he says, "If no one ever comes to you after you preach the gospel and asks, 'So should we sin so that grace may abound?' you have probably never preached the gospel."[16] For these men the gospel is justification by faith alone, and when that truth has been expounded the gospel has been preached. Again, this is a typically Lutheran way of looking at soteriology. For Paul and for the Reformed faith it is different. The whole gospel is not simply the *forgiveness* of sin but also the *destruction* of sin, both justification and sanctification, as the twin benefits that come to us in union with Christ.

When Paul comes to the end of chapter 5 in Romans he has not finished preaching the gospel as Godfrey and Lloyd-Jones

---

16. *CJPM*, 280. Godfrey does not place the words in quotation marks as a direct quote, nor does he give a bibliographical reference.

think. The question in 6:1 is a rhetorical device to make the transition to the rest of the gospel, the glorious truth that Jesus sets us free not only from the guilt of sin (justification) but also from the power of sin (sanctification). As the first question and answer of the Heidelberg Catechism teaches us, our only comfort both in life and in death is our union with Jesus Christ as Lord and Savior. He has not only fully paid the penalty for our sin by his death on the cross, but has also set us free from the tyranny of the devil. As Paul says in Romans 6:7, if we have died and are risen with Christ we are "freed from sin." Literally he says we are "justified" from sin, both from its guilt and from its power.

Paul does not finish his sermon until the end of letter. When he has finished preaching the whole gospel no one asks him whether he may sin so that grace will abound. If Godfrey and these unnamed "defenders of the Reformation doctrine of justification" are constantly being bombarded with this question when they have finished preaching the gospel, as Godfrey implies, then the crucial question for them is, Are they preaching the whole gospel? Are they commanding sinners to repent? Are they warning sinners that without repentance they will perish eternally? Are they teaching sinners not only to receive the gracious promises of Jesus in faith, but also to submit to him in love and gratitude for all that he has done for them? Are they obedient to the Great Commission? Do they think of the Great Commission as pure gospel, or as a toxic cocktail of faith plus works for justification?

From Shepherd's perspective Godfrey makes two basic mistakes. First, he thinks that the faithfulness that is invariably associated with faith and is the manifestation of faith is inherently meritorious and therefore antithetical to justifying faith that relies wholly on the righteousness of Jesus Christ for justification. The second mistake flows from this misconception. Godfrey is unable to cope with the many texts of Scripture that in one way or another make eternal weal or woe contingent on what we do in this life. They are found in virtually every book in the New Testament. That is why he simply ignores them in this chapter on faith alone. From his perspective such texts can only represent a toxic cocktail of faith plus the merit of works for justification.

Jesus says, "Not everyone who says to me, 'Lord, Lord,' will enter the kingdom of heaven, but only he who does the will of my Father who is in heaven" (Matt. 7:21). James writes, "What good is it, my brothers, if a man claims to have faith but has no deeds? Can such faith save him? .... You see that a person is justified by what he does and not by faith alone" (Jas. 2:14, 24). These texts do not teach that justification is grounded in the merit of human works. Justification is grounded wholly and exclusively in what Jesus has done for us; and this gift is ours by a living and active faith, a faith that responds to the gospel overtures of grace with repentance and obedience to our Lord who loved us and gave himself for us.

We must not set faith and faithfulness over against each other as antithetical and mutually exclusive principles of gospel and law when it comes to the justification of a sinner before almighty God. The same Lord who promises, "Believe in the Lord Jesus Christ, and you will be saved — you and your household" (Acts 16:31), also encourages us with these promises, "Be faithful, even to the point of death, and I will give you the crown of life" (Rev. 2:10). "Blessed is the man who perseveres under trial, because when he has stood the test, he will receive the crown of life that God has promised to those who love him" (James 1:12). This is the pure gospel that ought to inform our pastoral ministry.

CHAPTER 3

Reformed Covenant Theology and Its Discontents

Mark Horne

... mainstream Reformed theology has dealt with the obvious conditionality in Scripture, including Paul. This tradition has never said that there are no conditions in the covenant—or even in justification. Rather, it argued that the condition of justification is faith and that the conditions of salvation as a whole process are many: lifelong repentance and faith, sanctification, and glorification. This theology . . . emphasized that these conditions are fulfilled by the gifts that come to us through union with Christ. Thus, God promises to give faith and perseverance, justification and sanctification, throughout the course of our life, all the while distinguishing justification from the process of inner renewal. Furthermore, even the law that accused us now appears to us as a delight.

Michael Horton, *CJPM*, 217

Dr. Horton has given us an excellent statement about "mainstream Reformed theology." However, his essay ("Which Covenant Theology?", *Covenant, Justification and Pastoral Ministry*, pp. 197-227) as a whole does not provide a historically accurate picture of mainstream Reformed theology. Based on this picture, he also states that the so-called "Federal Vision," and even what N. T. Wright is proposing, are not faithful to historic Reformed theology's approach to "the obvious conditionality in

Scripture." In response, this is an essay about the *whole* of *mainstream* covenant theology.

My claim is simply this: Zacharias Ursinus (an early source, principal author of the Heidelberg Catechism) is not a heretic. Francis Turretin (a much later source) does not deny the Gospel. The Westminster Standards (a confessional standard in my own Reformed denomination in which I am a minister) do not articulate a false soteriology. Reformed people are free to quibble about whether they would want to state things in the same way, but Ursinus, Turretin, and the Westminster divines as they have come to us in their ratified documents cannot be cast off as departures from the Reformed Faith.

My response to Dr. Horton's essay will correct historical inaccuracies. Thus, it will deal with very little with Scripture. It will also deal very little with the accuracy of Dr. Horton's portrayal of his targets. To pick apart every inaccuracy in Dr. Horton's paper versions of Rich Lusk, Steve Schlissel and others would be a long and unfocused series of comments. My response will fill holes in Dr. Horton's portrayal, and the material I quote will make clear to those familiar with the Federal Vision that it is not at odds with how mainstream Reformed Covenant Theology deals with the conditionality of Scripture.

Getting the Tradition Right

The Westminster Shorter and Larger Catechisms set out *three necessary requirements* that must be met for salvation at the Day of Judgment.

The Westminster Shorter Catechism:

> **Q84:** *What doth every sin deserve?*
> **A84:** Every sin deserveth God's wrath and curse, both in this life, and that which is to come.
>
> **Q85:** *What doth God require of us, that we may escape his wrath and curse due to us for sin?*
> **A85:** To escape the wrath and curse of God due to

us for sin, God requireth of us faith in Jesus Christ, repentance unto life, with the diligent use of all the outward means whereby Christ communicateth to us the benefits of redemption.

Q86: *What is faith in Jesus Christ?*
A86: Faith in Jesus Christ is a saving grace, whereby we receive and rest upon him alone for salvation, as he is offered to us in the gospel.

Q87: *What is repentance unto life?*
A87: Repentance unto life is a saving grace, whereby a sinner, out of a true sense of his sin, and apprehension of the mercy of God in Christ, doth, with grief and hatred of his sin, turn from it unto God, with full purpose of, and endeavour after, new obedience.

Q88: *What are the outward means whereby Christ communicateth to us the benefits of redemption?*
A88: The outward and ordinary means whereby Christ communicateth to us the benefits of redemption, are his ordinances, especially the Word, sacraments, and prayer; all which are made effectual to the elect for salvation.

The Westminster Larger Catechism:

Q152: *What doth every sin deserve at the hands of God?*
A152: Every sin, even the least, being against the sovereignty, goodness, and holiness of God, and against his righteous law, deserveth his wrath and curse, both in this life, and that which is to come; and cannot be expiated but by the blood of Christ.

Q153: What doth God require of us, that we may escape his wrath and curse due to us by reason of the transgression of the law?

A153: That we may escape the wrath and curse of God due to us by reason of the transgression of the law, he requireth of us repentance toward God, and faith toward our Lord Jesus Christ, and the diligent use of the outward means whereby Christ communicates to us the benefits of his mediation.

Q154: What are the outward means whereby Christ communicates to us the benefits of his mediation?
A154: The outward and ordinary means whereby Christ communicates to his church the benefits of his mediation, are all his ordinances; especially the word, sacraments, and prayer; all which are made effectual to the elect for their salvation.

Perhaps it might be helpful to display some confirming testimony here. Consider then the Congregationalist theologian, John Owen. In his "lesser catechism" we find the following series of questions and answers:

Q. *What is the Church of Christ?*
A. The universal company of God's elect, called to the adoption of children.

Q. *How come we to be members of this church?*
A. By a lively faith.

Q. *What is a lively faith?*
A. An assured resting of the soul upon God's promises of mercy in Jesus Christ, for pardon of sins here and glory hereafter.

Q. *How come we to have this faith?*
A. By the effectual working of the Spirit of God in our hearts, freely calling us from the state of nature to the state of grace.

Q. *Are we accounted righteous for our faith?*
A. No, but only for the righteousness of Christ, freely imputed unto us, and laid hold of by faith.

Q. *Is there no more required of us but faith only?*
A. Yes; repentance also, and holiness.

Q. *What is repentance?*
A. A forsaking of all sin, with godly sorrow for what we have committed.

Q. *What is that holiness which is required of us?*
A. Universal obedience to the will of God revealed unto us.[1]

So we have here two witnesses to the mainstream Covenant theology, the Westminster Divines and John Owen. In both these two, faith is only one of several other requirements. I doubt anything is different for John Owen (though it might be possible to parse it differently), but the Westminster Catechisms are clear that "requirements" means conditions. If the requirement is not met then the person will fail to "escape" God's "wrath and curse due to us by reason of the transgression of the law."

These catechism questions and answers, I submit, are representative of mainstream Reformed Covenant Theology.

Zacharias Ursinus

Zacharias Ursinus, the principal author of the Heidelberg Catechism, lectured on this catechism in his *Commentary on the Heidelberg Catechism*. Though the catechism says very little about the covenant, Ursinus includes a section on the covenant when discussing Christ's work as mediator. He explains a covenant thus: "This agreement, or reconciliation, is called a *Covenant*, because God promises to us certain blessings and demands from us in return our obedience" (p. 97). Ursinus is *not* referring solely to God's covenant with Adam, nor to the work of Christ in being obedient to the Father. Rather, he is saying that all covenants have this structure with their members. Indeed, in explaining the difference between Law and Gospel in the prolegomena at the beginning of

---

1. Available in PDF format at http://public.csusm.edu/public/guests/rsclark/owen.pdf.

his commentary, he states, "The law promises life upon the condition of perfect obedience; the gospel, on the condition of faith in Christ and the commencement of new obedience" (p. 3).

Faith and commencement of new obedience are the conditions that *members* of the covenant of grace, not their *mediator*, must meet. They are for Christians, not for Christ as covenant head. Jesus did indeed lead a sinless life, and his obedient death for our sins and resurrection for our justification, are indeed the only ground by which a covenant member can have righteous standing before God. But when mainstream Reformed Covenant theology refers to the "conditions of the covenant," it is not referring to those unique and essential works done by Jesus. The term is used for those who are saved by grace alone—a grace that is precisely the only reason why anyone fulfills the conditions of faith and the commencement of new obedience and thus benefits from Christ' mediatorial office.

It should be also noted that, by contrasting Law and Gospel, Ursinus is not referring to a contrast between Moses and Christ. In his section on the covenant, he insists that the Mosaic Covenant and that of the Christian Church are substantially the same. Since there is "one way of reconciliation, one faith, and one way of salvation for all who are and have been saved from the beginning," the covenants are "one in substance" (p. 98). Further, Ursinus explicitly addresses the issue of obligations:

> There is but one covenant, because *the principal conditions*, which are called the substance of the covenant, *are the same before and since the incarnation of Christ*; for *in each testament God promises to those that repent and believe*, the remission of sin; whilst men bind themselves, on the other hand, to exercise faith in God, and to repent of their sins (p. 99; emphasis added).

And he goes on to assert that the Old and New Covenants agree, "in the condition in respect to ourselves," and explains, "in each covenant, God requires from men faith *and obedience*" (ibid; emphasis added). "The new covenant, therefore, agrees with the old in that which relates to the principal conditions, both on the part of God and on the part of man." The benefits of these two covenants, incidentally, are "the remission of sins and eternal life" (ibid).

Naturally, one might expect these sorts of affirmations to lead to the question *"whether good works are necessary to salvation,"* which is precisely what Ursinus asks on pages 484 and 485. He writes, "There have been some who have maintained simply and positively, that good works are necessary to salvation, whilst others, again, have held that they are pernicious and injurious to salvation." Ursinus held that "both forms of speech are ambiguous and inappropriate."

However, the claim that good works "are pernicious and injurious to salvation" is "especially" "ambiguous and inappropriate." Indeed that claim is "to be rejected" altogether, while the claim that "good works are necessary to salvation" is merely to be "explained."

Ursinus explains the way in which "good works are necessary to salvation" with two negations and three affirmations. They are necessary "[1] not as a cause to an effect, [2] or as if they merited a reward, but [1] as a part of salvation itself, [2] or as an antecedent to a consequent, [3] or as a means without which we cannot obtain the end."

Ursinus goes further and says, "In the same way we may also say, that good works are necessary to righteousness or justification, with which regeneration is inseparably connected." Still, regarding such statements about justification and regeneration, Ursinus "would prefer not to use these forms of speech." He gives three reasons: "1. Because they are ambiguous. 2. Because they breed contentions, and give our enemies room for caviling. 3. Because these expressions are not used in the Scriptures with which our forms of speech should conform as nearly as possible."

> We may more safely and correctly say, *That good works are necessary in them that are justified and that are to be saved.* To say that good works are necessary in them that are to be justified, is to speak ambiguously, because it may be so understood as if they were required before justification, and so become

> a cause of our justification. Augustine has correctly said: "*Good works do not precede them that are to be justified, but follow them that are justified.*"

In concluding this section, Ursinus consistently relies on a distinction between necessity and merit:

> We may, therefore, easily return an answer to the following objection: That is necessary to salvation without which no one can be saved. But no one who is destitute of good works can be saved, as it is said in the 87th Question. Therefore, good works are necessary to salvation. We reply to the major proposition, by making the following distinction: That without which no one can be saved is necessary to salvation, viz: as a part of salvation, or as a certain antecedent necessary to salvation, in which sense we admit the conclusion; but not as a cause, or as a merit of salvation. We, therefore grant the conclusion of the major proposition if understood in the sense in which we have just explained it. For good works are necessary to salvation, or, to speak more properly, in them that are to be saved (for it is better thus to speak for the sake of avoiding ambiguity,) as a part of salvation itself; or, as *an antecedent of salvation*, but not as a cause of merit of salvation (p. 485, emphasis added).

In trying to settle on Ursinus' definitive view and practice, it is important to realize that, on the previous page, he gives three classes of reasons why "good works are to be performed by us" (p. 483). These reasons are listed in reference to God, ourselves, and our neighbors. In explaining why we must perform good works for ourselves, he states they should be done so that "we may escape temporal *and eternal* punishment" (p. 484; emphasis added). He goes on to state this positively: that we should do good works "that we may obtain from God those temporal and spiritual rewards, which, according to the divine promise, accompany good works both in this and in a future life." He then makes the "Biblicist" point that, "if God did not desire that the hope of reward, and the fear of punishment should be moving causes of good works, he would not use them as arguments in the promises and threatenings which he addresses unto us in his word." Plainly, Ursinus does believe that the saints must embrace both God's promises of blessing and his warnings of punishment, even eternal punishment, in order to pursue resurrection glory.

What Ursinus taught about sin is also relevant here. Earlier in his *Commentary on the Heidelberg Catechism*, he wrote that sometimes the regenerate

> fall into errors which oppose the very foundation of their faith, or who sin against conscience, on account of which they lose the consciousness of their acceptance with God, and the gifts of the Holy Spirit, who, were they to continue therein to the end of their lives, would be condemned and rejected of God; but they do not perish, for the reason that they are led to see the error of their ways, and thus brought to repentance (p. 49).

We see then the need for the "promises and threatenings which" God "addresses unto us in his word." By them a person who would otherwise "be condemned and rejected of God" will "escape temporal and eternal punishment."

Finally, we should note that the contrast between Law (in Adam's covenant) and Gospel (when Jesus made a new covenant beginning after the fall of Adam) does not involve merit. Ursinus regards Christ's work as exclusively meritorious, while humanity's works, including Adam's, were not.

> even if our works were perfectly good, yet they could not merit eternal life, inasmuch as they are due from us. A reward is due to evil works according to the order of justice; but not unto good works, because we are bound to do them as the creatures of God; but no one can bind God, on the other hand, by any works or means to confer any benefit upon him. Evil works, again, in their very design oppose and injure God, whilst good works add nothing to his felicity (p. 335).

In fact, one of the very reasons why it was "required of the Mediator" that he be truly God as well as truly man was precisely so that "he might be a perfect Savior in merit and efficacy," and cover our demerit—which would not be possible if Jesus had merely been a sinless creature (p. 87). The contrast between Adam and us as far as conditions go, then, is not that his were meritorious and ours weren't, but that his required perfect sinless obedience, and God requires of us faith in Jesus Christ and to commence new (and sin-stained) obedience. The only human being to ever "merit" anything was Jesus, and that was precisely because he was not only a human being, but also truly God. "Nor is the obedience of Christ meritorious in this respect, as though it added anything to God, but it is called meritorious on account of the dignity of his person, because he who suffered was the Son of God" (p. 328).

Francis Turretin

In explaining "*The Nature of the Covenant of Grace*" in volume 2 of his *Institutes of Elenctic Theology* (14.2), Francis Turretin insists the covenant is "mutual" (14.2.26; p. 183), and involves "a mutual exchange of benefits and duties so that if God is our husband, we should be his chaste and faithful spouse" (Ibid). This mutuality is described in Jeremiah 31.33: "I will be their God, and they shall be my people." Thus, "as all God's blessings towards us are comprehended in this one promise alone, so all man's duties are prescribed in this single condition (which indicates together and at once both what they ought to be and what they are bound to do)." Turretin next explains that single condition by saying, in part:

> To be the people of God is not only to be subjected to his dominion and to depend upon and be governed by him (for thus all men universally are his people), but to cleave to him in worship and obedience, so as to be nothing, to have nothing, to be capable of and do nothing which is not of God, i.e., which may not be referred to his glory (14.2.27; p. 183).

Turretin goes on to describe this condition as being wholehearted devotion. Especially relevant to our investigation is his claim:

> In vain do we hope that God will be our God, *unless* in turn we are his people and bear witness to the love of the Father, *unless* we give the obedience of children to him. In vain do we hope that he will bestow the promised blessings, *unless* we perform the duties required of us (14.2.38; p. 184; emphasis added).

Next, Turretin addresses whether the Covenant of Grace is either conditional or unconditional. He answers that it depends on one's perspective:

> It may be taken either broadly and improperly (for all that man is bound to afford in the covenant of grace) or strictly and properly (for that which has some causality in reference to life and on which not only antecedently, but also causally, eternal life in its own manner depends). If in the latter sense, faith is the sole condition of the covenant because under this condition alone pardon of sins and salvation as well as eternal life are promised (Jn. 3:16; Rom. 10:9). There is no other which could perform that office because there is no other which is receptive of Christ and capable of applying his righteousness. But in the former, there is nothing to hinder repentance and the obedience of the new life from being called a *condition because they are reckoned among the duties of the covenant* (Jn. 13:17; 2 Cor. 5:17; Rom. 8:13) [p. 189; emphasis added].

While Turretin's position is nuanced according to various possible perspectives, he plainly affirms that conditions are laid down in the Bible for the covenant. He lists three reasons why it "cannot be denied that the covenant is conditional." Among his reasons he includes that, "It is proposed with an express condition (John 3.16, 36; Romans 10.9; Acts 8.37; Mark 16.16 and frequently elsewhere)" (12.3.3; p. 185). He also argues that, if the covenant were not conditional, "there would be no place for the threatenings in the gospel (which could not be denounced except against those who had neglected the prescribed condition)—for the neglect of faith and obedience cannot be culpable, if not required" (Ibid). He also points out that if "the promises of the covenant are understood concerning the end, no one can deny that they are conditional because they are always made under the condition of faith and repentance" (12.3.4; p. 185).

We will see below that Turretin also addresses the question "Are good works necessary to salvation?" In affirming that they are necessary, again, Turretin refers to the nature of the covenant of grace, saying, "And as to the covenant, everyone knows that it consists of two parts: on the one hand the promise on the part of God; on the other the stipulation of obedience on the part of man" (17.3.7) He goes on to clearly state that the stipulations are conditions for enjoying the promises: "Although God by his special grace wishes these duties of man to be his blessings (which he carries out in them), still the believer does not cease to be bound to observe it, *if he wishes to be a partaker of the blessings of the covenant*" (ibid.; emphasis added).

Of course, like all Calvinists (including Rich Lusk, Steve Schlissel and other of Horton's targets), Turretin knows that, in an important sense, God's salvation is unconditional. Thus, while it is possible to speak of the covenant of grace being given under condition of faith *alone* rather than faith and repentance, it is equally possible to speak of the covenant as being strictly *unconditional*. Again, it depends on one's perspective—how the covenant is "viewed." He writes:

> If the covenant be viewed in relation to the first sanction in Christ, it has no previous condition, but rests upon the grace of God and the merit of Christ alone. But if it is considered in relation to its acceptance and application to the believer, it has faith as a condition (uniting man to Christ and so bringing him into the fellowship of the covenant). If, however, in relation to its consummation with faith (obedience and the desire of holiness), it has the relation of condition and means because without them no one shall see God (12.3.5; p. 185).

Turretin takes his conditionality so seriously that he realizes he is open to the charge of confusing the Covenant of Works with the Covenant of Grace. He replies to this objection, writing, "Although the covenant of grace be conditional, the promises of the law and the gospel are not therefore to be confounded" (12.3.6; p. 186). Denying the conditionality of the covenant of grace because it allegedly confuses law and Gospel is explicitly addressed by this father in the faith, and is rejected.

This brings us to Turretin's view of law and gospel. He defines "merit" in a way that rules out the possibility that a creature could merit anything from the Creator:

> To be true merit, then, these five conditions are demanded: (1) that the "work be undue"—for no one merits by paying what he owes (Luke 17.10), he only satisfies; (2) that it be ours—for no one can be said to merit from another; (3) that it be absolutely perfect and free from all taint—for where sin is there merit cannot be; (4) that it be equal and proportioned to the reward and pay; otherwise it would be a gift, not merit. (5) that the reward be due to such a work from justice—whence an "undue work" is commonly defined to be one that "makes a reward due in the order of justice." (17.5.4; p. 712).

This would lead one to expect that Turretin would deny that sinless "legal obedience" could ever be meritorious in God's sight. Turretin explicitly meets this expectation. Even if sinless, "there is no merit properly so called of man before God" (Ibid). "Thus, Adam himself, if he had persevered, would not have merited life in strict justice" (Ibid). One time in his Institutes he describes the obedience of a sinless being as meritorious, but immediately makes it clear that he does not refer to true merit: "the legal condition has the relation of a meritorious cause (*at least congruously and improperly*)" (12.3.6; p. 186; emphasis added).

Furthermore, Turretin insisted that Adam's righteousness was a "grace" from God. (5.11.16). Joel Garver summarizes (http://www.lasalle.edu/~garver/covwor.htm):

> Regarding the gratuitous promise of life held forth in the prelapsarian covenant of nature, Turretin argues that God promises not only bodily immortality, but also a transformed

heavenly life. Had Adam persevered in obedience, the immortality of his body would only have been "through the dignity of original righteousness and the power of God's special grace" (5.12.9). Moreover, Adam's elevation to heavenly life would not have been a matter of mere justice, but also "the goodness of God" who is "plenteous in mercy" and by whom Adam would "be gifted" with heavenly life (8.6.6, 8).

For Turretin, not only was grace involved in Adam's creation, in God's promise, and in its reward, but Adam was also given "sufficient grace" by which to remain obedient to that first covenant, a grace that Turretin describes as "habitual and internal" (9.7.14-17).

We cannot move on from Turretin on this issue without discussing his teaching on what has come to be called, "final justification." He writes what he calls "justification *a posteriori*." While defending *sola fide* in his Eighth Question, "Does Faith alone justify? We affirm against the Romanists" (Sixteenth Topic, p. 675ff.), Turretin says that, for the issue to be "more easily understood," one must understand that "a twofold trial can be entered into by God with man" (16.8.3, p. 676). The first trial is "by law" in which a person "is viewed as guilty of violating the law by sin and thus comes under the accusation and condemnation of the law" (ibid). The other trial is "by the gospel" in which a person "is accused by Satan of having violated the gospel covenant and so is supposed to be an unbeliever and impenitent or a hypocrite, who has not testified by works the faith he has professed with his mouth" (ibid). This situation requires "a twofold justification" which entails not the "Romish sense" but something different.

> The first is that by which man is absolved from the guilt of sin on account of the righteousness of Christ imputed to us and apprehended by faith; the other is that by which he is freed from the charge of unbelief and hypocrisy and declared to be a true believer and child of God; one who has fulfilled the gospel covenant (if not perfectly as to degree, still sincerely as to parts) and answered to the divine call

by the exercise of faith and piety. The first is justification properly so called; the other is only a declaration of it. That is justification of cause a priori; this is justification of sign or of effect a posteriori, declaratively. In that, faith alone can have a place because it alone apprehends the righteousness of Christ, by whose merit we are freed from the condemnation of the law; in this, works also are requited as the effects and signs of faith, by which its truth and sincerity are declared against the accusation of unbelief and hypocrisy. For as faith justifies a person, so works justify faith (ibid).

Thus, when a person is said to be justified by faith alone, the statement "does not concern justification a posteriori and declaratively in the fatherly and gospel trial—whether faith alone without works concurs to it." In the case of such a justification, not only do "works come in here" but "works only [not faith] are properly regarded" as the "effects and indubitable proofs" of faith (16. 8. 4, p. 676).

As Turretin's nephew and the last orthodox pastor of Geneva, Benedict Pictet serves as a second witness to what his uncle believed. In his writings he reiterated this Reformed Orthodox position. Indeed, he was influential, like his uncle, in American Presbyterianism. Frederick Reyroux translated his Christian Theology and the Presbyterian Board of Publication in Philadelphia published it before January of 1846. At that time, the issue of the *Princeton Review* announced the publication and declared,

> In this small but compact volume, we have a comprehensive epitome of Theology; from the pen of one of the most distinguished theologians of Geneva. The great excellence of Pictet is simplicity and perspicuity. He is, even in his large work, much less scholastic, than his predecessors, and less disposed perhaps to press his statements beyond the limits of certain knowledge. We are glad to see so sound and readable a book placed within the reach of all classes of readers (vol 18, issue 1, "Short Notices," p. 180).[2]

---

2. The translator gives similar reasons for providing an English version of Pictet's work: Those who are in any measure conversant with the theological works of the age of the Reformation, and of that immediately succeeding it, cannot fail to bear testimony to

Benedict Pictet's consistent position is revealed in his chapter "of good works" (pp. 331-334). He writes:

> As to the necessity of good works, it is clearly established from the express commands of God, from the necessity of our worshipping and serving God, from the nature of the covenant of grace, in which God promises every kind of blessing, but at the same time requires obedience, from the favors received at this hands, which are so many motives to good works, *from the future glory which is promised, and to which good works stand related, as the means to the end, as the road to the goal, as seed-time to the harvest, as first fruits to the whole gathering, and as the contest to the victory*... (p. 332; emphasis added).

On justification, Pictet follows Turretin's *a priori a posteriori* scheme by using two chapters on justification, the first on "the justification of a sinner," and the second on "the justification of a righteous man." He writes in the latter chapter,

> We have spoken of the justification of man as a sinner; we must now speak of his justification as a righteous man, i.e. that by which he proves that he is justified and that he possesses a true justifying faith. Now *this justification is by works, even in the sight of God*, as well as of men; and of this James speaks when he declares that "by works a man is justified and not by faith only" (Jam 2:24). To illustrate this, we must remark that there is a twofold accusation against man. First, he is accused before God's tribunal of the guilt of sin, and this accusation is met and done away by the justification of which we have already treated. Secondly, the man who has been justified may be accused of hypocrisy, false profession and unregeneracy; now he clears himself from this accu-

---

their value; as presenting the most accurate and luminous views of divine truth, and as constituting a sort of standard of reference and appeal in the present age. Among these works, those of the divines who flourished in the Reformed churches abroad, occupy a distinguished place, and supply a fund of valuable information on every branch of Christian Theology, properly so called... The volume which is now presented to the public, claims attention as a body of Christian divinity, more concise and perspicuous, and therefore more acceptable to general readers, than similar productions of the same age and school.

sation and justifies his faith by his works-this is the second justification; it differs from the first; for in the first a sinner is acquitted from guilt, in the second a godly man is distinguished from an ungodly. In the first God imputes the righteousness of Christ; in the second he pronounces judgment from the gift of holiness bestowed upon us; both these justifications the believer obtains, and therefore it is true that "by works he is justified and not by faith only."

Pictet wrote regarding God's covenant with Adam that it involved both promise and warning. The warning involves a rather straightforward exposition of the text of Genesis. Proving that a promise was also involved, however, requires some extrapolation, because the future reward is not stated in the text. Pictet reasons from God's character saying that "although God owes nothing to his creature, yet as the whole scripture sets him forth to us as slow to anger and abundant in mercy." Therefore, "it is not at all probable, that God denounced upon man the threat of eternal punishment, and at the same time gave him no promise" (p. 141).

Pictet also deals with the possibility of meritorious works later in his book. In dealing with the good works of a believer, and proving "the necessity of good works" (see below), he goes on to point out that such necessary good works are not meritorious before God. In doing so he gives four reasons (pp 332, 333). At least two of these would apply to all creatures regardless of sin or innocence. First "a meritorious work must be one that is *not due*, for no one can have any merit in paying what he owes; but good works are *due*; 'When ye shall have done all those things which are commanded you, say, We are unprofitable servants: we have done that which it was *out duty to do*' (Luke 17.10)." Second, there must be a "proportion" between "the good work and the promised reward; but there is no proportion between the two in the present case; not even when the good work is martyrdom, the most excellent of all. For (all) 'the sufferings of this present time are not worthy to be compared with the glory which shall be revealed,' (Romans 8.18)."

But Pictet not only speaks of good works in general, but specifically addresses the issue of how good works would have related to Adam's vindication and glorification if he had continued in faith and obedience rather than falling into unbelief and disobedience. He writes that "if the first man had persevered in innocence, he would have been justified by the fulfillment of the natural law which God had engraven on his heart, and of the other commandments which God might have enjoined on him; in short, by perfectly loving God and his neighbor" (p. 312). Thus, if Adam had persevered he would have been declared righteous and "acquired a right to eternal glory, not indeed as if he had properly merited it, for the creature can merit nothing from the Creator, but according to the free promise and Covenant of God" (Ibid.).

As can be seen by the fact that Pictet was translated, American theologians did not reject Turretin's faithful summary of the Reformed heritage; far less did they condemn it as a subversion of the Gospel. A. A. Hodge, for example, wrote in his *Outlines of Theology*, published in 1860, that the covenant of works "was also essentially a gracious covenant, because although every creature is, as such, bound to serve the Creator to the full extent of his powers, the Creator cannot be bound as a mere matter of justice to grace the creature fellowship with himself." He reiterated the point in his posthumously published *Evangelical Theology: A Course of Popular Lectures*, "God offered to man in this gracious Covenant of Works the opportunity of accepting his grace and receiving his covenant gift of a confirmed holy character."

I will cut short my discussion of the evidence here. Readers are directed to Joel Garver's much more detailed and better-organized essay (http://www.lasalle.edu/~garver/covwor.htm) for more evidence, though it too could be much longer.

An Area of Disagreement between Ursinus and Turretin

One notable disagreement between these two men who have been set out, was their respective views of the imputation of the active obedience of Christ (i.e. that Christ's obedient works throughout his life are imputed to us, while the imputation of the passive obedience of Christ refers to Christ's suffering and death on the cross). Turretin affirmed the doctrine and demanded that all ministers in his church do so also. Earlier, however, Ursinus had understood Christ's obedience in a different way. He expounded on what was entailed or meant by this doctrine of the imputed righteousness of Christ in several places in his lectures on the Catechism. We have them now, in an English translation as his *Commentary on the Heidelberg Catechism*.

We can see Ursinus' view by looking at his question

> **Q60:** How are thou righteous before God?
> **A:** Only by a true faith in Jesus Christ; so that, though my conscience accuse me, that I have grossly transgressed all the commandments of God, and kept none of them, and am still inclined to all evil; notwithstanding, God, without any merit of mine, but only of mere grace, grants and imputes to me, the perfect satisfaction, righteousness and holiness of Christ; even so, as if I never had had, nor committed any sin: yea, as if I had fully accomplished all that obedience which Christ has accomplished for me; inasmuch as I embrace such benefit with a believing heart.

In their "testimony," Westminster the faculty uses this answer to defend the imputation of the active obedience of Christ along with the imputation of his passive obedience. For Ursinus, however, such double imputation is redundant. He writes of the "legal righteousness" that is imputed in this answer of the catechism, that it "is performed either by obedience to the law or by punishment. The law requires one or the other" (p. 325). He then elaborates:

> The righteousness with which we are here justified before God, is not our conformity with the law, nor our good works, nor our faith; but it is the satisfaction which Christ rendered to the law in our stead; or the punishment which he endured in our behalf; and therefore the entire humiliation of Christ, from the moment of his conception to his glorification, including his assumption of humanity, his subjection to the law, his poverty, reproach, weakness, sufferings, death, &c., all of which he did willingly; yea, whatever he did and suffered to which he was not bound, as being righteous, and the Son of

> God, is all included in the satisfaction which he made for us, and in the righteousness which God graciously imputes to us, and all believers. This satisfaction is equivalent to the fulfilling of the law, or to the endurance of eternal punishment for sin, to one or the other of which the law binds all.

Beginning with Paul on knowing nothing but Christ and him crucified (1 Corinthians 2.2), Ursinus appeals to a string of texts: Colossians 2:10, Romans 5.19; Isaiah 53:5, 6; Luke 22:20; Romans 3:24, 25; 4:7; 5:9, 10; 2 Corinthians 8:9; Galatians 3:13; Ephesians 1.7; and 1 John 1.7. One might be tempted to read, "subjection to the law," as "active obedience," but it only refers to passive obedience in Ursinus' mind. This is readily explained in his comments on the Creed's "He suffered" as found in question 37 of the Heidelberg catechism. Christ's sufferings included "the temptations of the devil; 'He was in all points tempted like as we are, yet without sin.' (Heb. 4:15)" (p. 213). Ursinus' makes an initial comment on Christ's sufferings that show how far active obedience was from his mind:

> The passion or suffering of Christ is placed immediately after his conception and nativity; 1. Because *our entire salvation consists in his passion and death*. 2. Because his whole life was one continued scene of suffering and privation (emphasis added).

Going back to question 60, Ursinus continues to explain himself by saying that Christ fulfilled the law so that he would be qualified as a mediator to have the "shedding of his blood" be the righteousness which is imputed to us.

> Christ fulfilled the law by the holiness of his human nature, and by his obedience, even unto the death of the cross. The holiness of his human nature was necessary to his obedience; for it became our mediator to be holy and righteous in himself, that he might be able to perform obedience, and make satisfaction for us. "For such an High Priest became us, who is holy," &c. (Heb. 7: 26.) This obedience now is our righteousness, and it is upon the ground of this that God is pleased with us. The blood of Christ is the satisfaction on

account of Which God receives us into his favor, and which he imputes unto us, as it is said, *the blood of Jesus Christ his Son cleanseth us from all sin*, both of commission and omission. The shedding of his blood is the complement of his satisfaction, and is for this reason called our righteousness.

Ursinus continues in this way, never varying from his explanation. Even when he says that "a sinner can be regarded as righteous only on the ground of the imputation of Christ's merits," he explains his meaning thus: "Nor is the obedience of Christ meritorious in this respect, as though it added anything to God, but it is called meritorious on account of the dignity of his person, *because he who suffered* was the Son of God" (p. 328).

He explains "the satisfaction which Christ rendered to the law in our stead" as "the punishment which he endured in our behalf." For Ursinus, the righteousness sinners receive in Christ by faith is the righteousness of Christ's "passive obedience." He does call it "obedience" to be sure, but nowhere do we find this obedience to be anything other than his willing suffering. When Ursinus calls Christ's obedience meritorious, he immediately defines that obedience as suffering: "it is called meritorious on account of the dignity of his person, because he who suffered was the Son of God" (p. 328). Ursinus's mention of "subjection to the law" could be used to refer to "active obedience," but that is obviously not what Ursinus meant.

Finally, Ursinus does deal with Christ's active obedience in relationship to his passive obedience in commenting on question and answer 16 of the catechism. He writes,

> It behooved him to be a perfectly righteous man, one that was wholly free from the least stain of original and actual sin, that he might deservedly be our Savior, and that his sacrifice might avail, not for himself, but for us: for if he himself had been a sinner, he would have had to satisfy for his own sins...
>
> If the Mediator himself had been a sinner he could not have escaped the wrath of God, much less could he have procured for others the favor of God, and exemption from

punishment: neither could the passion, and death of him, who did not suffer as an innocent man, be a ransom for the sin of others (p. 86).

Ursinus then quotes 2 Corinthians 5.21 as one of his prooftexts that only a righteous man could have suffered to obtain "exemption from punishment."

In the next paragraph (bottom p. 86 to top of 87), Ursinus writes that "The man Christ was perfectly righteous, or has fulfilled the law in four respects," which he then enumerates. The third fulfillment in the law is its fulfillment in us by his Spirit. The fourth fulfillment is his correct teaching of the law that frees it from errors that were being taught. Regarding the first two fulfillments, he writes:

> 1. By his own righteousness. Christ alone performed perfect obedience, such as the law requires. 2. By enduring punishment sufficient for our sins. There was a necessity that this double fulfillment of the law should be in Christ: for unless his righteousness had been full, and perfect, he could not have satisfied for the sins of others; and unless he had endured such punishment as has been described, he could not thereby have delivered us from everlasting punishment. The former is called the fulfilling of the law by obedience, by which he himself was conformable thereto; the latter is the fulfilling of the law by punishment, when he suffered for us, that we might not remain subject to eternal condemnation.

Thus, the "double fulfillment" involves a qualifying obedience that allows Christ to suffer for our sins and in so suffering provide the righteousness that can be imputed to us.

In Ursinus view one either needs to be perfectly obedient or one needs to have suffered eternal punishment. Jesus Christ perfectly obeyed the Law in order to qualify as a representative sufferer. He suffered an eternal punishment so that we could be counted as perfectly obedient since the curse of the Law would have nothing more to do with us.

Turretin disagreed with Ursinus for a variety of reasons that he thought good and sufficient. Since his position is not under dispute, there is no need to argue for it as there is in the case of Ursinus and the Heidelberg Catechism. In defending the imputation of the active obedience of Christ, Turretin specifically deals with the objection that this would render the obedience of Christians to be superfluous for salvation. He answers that we must yield "the same obedience to God" in order "to enter upon the possession" of what Christ has acquired for us:

> Although Christ fulfilled the law for us as to obedience, it cannot be inferred that we are no longer bound to render obedience to God. It certainly follows that we are not bound to obey for the same end and from the same cause (to wit, that we may live by it, from our federal subjection). But this does not hinder our being bound by a natural obligation to yield the same obedience to God, not that we may live but because we live; not that we may acquire a right to life, but that we may enter upon the possession of the acquired right. Just as (though Christ died for us) we do not cease to be still liable to death—not for punishment, but for salvation (14.13.27, p. 452).

So if someone claimed the imputation of the active obedience of Christ meant that the obedience of the Christian was not necessary as a means of entering into eternal life, Turretin would regard that as an argument *against* his doctrine. In order to fully prove the imputation of the active obedience of Christ, Turretin felt it was necessary to show that obedience was still so necessary.

Finally, regarding the Westminster Confession and Catechisms, it is well known (and is only beginning to be denied in recent and highly politicized situations) that it was written to accommodate both Ursinus and Turretin.

The Westminster Confession and Catechisms

A quick look at the Westminster Standards reveals the same basic perspective as Ursinus and Turretin. We have already seen what is in the Catechisms about what God required for eternal life, repentance, faith, and the diligent use of all ordinances. This correlates rather precisely with Turretin's statements that "In vain do we hope that he will bestow the promised blessings, unless we perform the duties required of us" (14.2.38; p. 184), and that the covenant, "is proposed with an express condition (John 3.16, 36; Romans 10.9; Acts 8.37; Mark 16.16 and frequently elsewhere)" (12.3.3; p. 185).

But the basic agreement goes far deeper. Like Ursinus and Turretin, the Westminster Confession declares that faith is a requirement of believers (one provided, as everyone in this dispute agrees, only by God's grace to those elect to eternal life):

> Man, by his fall, having made himself incapable of life by that covenant, the Lord was pleased to make a second, commonly called the covenant of grace; wherein he freely offereth unto sinners life and salvation by Jesus Christ; *requiring of them faith in him, that they may be saved*, and promising to give unto all those that are ordained unto eternal life his Holy Spirit, to make them willing, and able to believe (Ch. 7, "Of the Covenant," paragraph 3; emphasis added).

And thus the Larger Catechism's formulation:

> **Q. 32.** How is the grace of God manifested in the second covenant?
> **A.** The grace of God is manifested in the second covenant, in that he freely provideth and offereth to sinners a mediator, and life and salvation by him; and *requiring faith as the condition to interest them in him*, promiseth and giveth his Holy Spirit to all his elect, to work in them that faith, with all other saving graces; *and to enable them unto all holy obedience*, as the evidence of the truth of their faith and thankfulness to God, *and as the way which he hath appointed them to salvation* (emphasis added).

Here we have not only the priority given to faith as the condition of the covenant, but also a point about holy obedience being "the way" to salvation by God's appointment.

This is backed up by what the Westminster Confession says about good works (chapter 16), that they are not only "evidences" of faith and "fruit" but—quoting from Romans 6:22—also means to "the end, eternal life." I wonder if Pictet had this statement in mind when he wrote in his Christian Theology, that there are "many motives to good works, from the future glory which is promised, and to which good works stand related, as the means to the end, as the road to the goal, as seed-time to the harvest, as first fruits to the whole gathering, and as the contest to the victory… (p. 332).

The Confession maintains the same ground in its teaching on repentance. According the Westminster Divines, "repentance to life" is an "evangelical" (WCF 15.1) and "saving" (WLC #87) "grace."

> By it, a sinner, out of the sight and sense not only of the danger, but also of the filthiness and odiousness of his sins, as contrary to the holy nature, and righteous law of God; and upon the apprehension of his mercy in Christ to such as are penitent, so grieves for, and hates his sins, as to turn from them all unto God, purposing and endeavoring to walk with him in all the ways of his commandments (WCF 15.2).

Notice here that repentance is not some one-time act of contrition (though it may involve such a thing at times) but also includes "endeavoring to walk with him in all the ways of his commandments." The Shorter Catechism concurs saying that repentance means, among other things, that a person in regard to sin will "turn from it unto God, with full purpose of, and endeavor after, new obedience" (#87).

The Westminster Standards also teach that no one will receive pardon from God if he refuses to repent. Lest this requirement be misunderstood, the Divines were careful in their formulation: "Although repentance be not to be rested in, as any satisfaction for sin, or any cause of the pardon thereof, which is the act of God's free grace in Christ; yet it is of such necessity to all sinners, that none may expect pardon without it" (WCF 15.3). Repentance (including new obedience) is necessary for pardon.

The fact that repentance, and thus new obedience, is required for pardon is amplified by question 153 of the Larger Catechism and question 85 of the Shorter Catechism, mentioned at the beginning of this essay. In those questions, we have a list of three requirements, the last of which covers the faithful attendance at worship (it is unpacked as including, but not limited to, the Word—especially the preaching—the sacraments, and prayer). It seems the answer in these catechisms is distinguishing repentance from the new obedience that the Confession includes in it. This is no real contradiction. To say that a repentance that includes new obedience is necessary for pardon is not much different from claiming that repentance and new obedience are required to escape God's wrath. And we would expect nothing less from a Reformed document in the heritage of such men as Ursinus who said, ""The law promises life upon the condition of perfect obedience; the gospel, on the condition of faith in Christ and the commencement of new obedience" (*Commentary on the Heidelberg Catechism*, p. 3).

The Westminster Divines saw faith as a turning to God that entailed a turning away from idols. Thus, they defined faith as inclusive of obedience and repentance as inclusive of faith. To see this, let us consider, first, how they defined faith:

> By this faith, a Christian believeth to be true whatsoever is revealed in the Word, for the authority of God himself speaking therein; and acteth differently upon that which each particular passage thereof containeth; yielding obedience to the commands, trembling at the threatenings, and embracing the promises of God for this life, and that which is to come. But the principal acts of saving faith are accepting, receiving, and resting upon Christ alone for justification, sanctification, and eternal life, by virtue of the covenant of grace (WCF 14.2).

Recently some have tried to insist that only the last sentence is actually the definition of saving faith. The first sentence is a list of other things that are done "by" faith. There are several problems with this idea. First, it is a commonplace that "have faith" and "believe" are virtual synonyms of one another. Both refer to trust. But if we separate these two sentences and only allow the latter to define saving faith, then we are in the anomalous position of saying that believing God in His Word ("believeth to be true whatsoever is revealed in the Word, for the authority of God himself speaking therein") does not count as faith. Even more strange would be to insist that trusting God savingly is something distinct and different from "embracing the promises of God for this life, and that which is to come."

Secondly, if the statement "by this faith…" is taken to exclude an actual definition of faith, then we would have to insist that the chapter on repentance never bothers to tell us what repentance is: "By it [i.e. this repentance], a sinner…. so grieves for, and hates his sins, as to turn from them all unto God…" According to the proffered novel hermeneutic of the chapter on faith, repentance must not be defined as turning from sin to God, but as something else, previous to that turning, which causes or enables one to do it.

Thirdly, if we recognize this, then it will make perfect sense why "yielding obedience to the commands" is part of the definition of faith. The promise of pardon is, according to the Westminster Assembly following Scripture, conditional. Repentance is "of such necessity" for pardon because God "requireth" it. How could one embrace such a promise and not repent? It is a self-contradiction to even think of such a thing. It would be like saying that Abram could believe God's promise that he would be given a wonderful land somewhere else and yet, at the same time, remain in Ur and refuse to leave. Leaving Ur was not simply the result or consequence of faith. Leaving Ur was an act of faith! To make sure we understand all this, the Divines also include in the definition of faith, "trembling at the threatenings." How can one say that one believes God and not take His warnings seriously? A person who doesn't take God's warnings seriously is refusing to believe or trust God as a reliable guide and protector.

Finally, the second sentence does not say "But faith actually is…," but rather "But the principal acts of saving faith are accepting, receiving, and resting upon Christ alone for justification, sanctification, and eternal life, by virtue of the covenant of grace." The contrast is not between some things that one does "by" faith and what faith actually is. Rather, the contrast is between general acts of faith and "principal acts" of faith, which are *both* part of the definition of faith itself. Since our faith is weak and we remain sinners in this life, none of us will trust God so much as to perfectly obey him. If the divines had left us with only the first sentence in their definition, then one would become unsure as to whether one truly received the imputed righteousness of Jesus in his life of obedience and his suffering the penalty that our sins deserved. One needs to know that, in the midst of weak faith, one can continue to rely on God through Christ for all things necessary to salvation.

So repentance is required of those who would be pardoned by God precisely because one is justified and saved only by faith. New obedience is not an attempt to be good enough to win God's favor, nor a checklist of conditions by which one maintains God's favor. Rather, it is simply faith in God through Christ as he has offered himself in the Covenant of Grace. It is the embodiment of trust in God.

What such a life of faith will look like will vary according to many considerations. Any attempt to make some apparent level of sanctification the condition for salvation is hostile to the Gospel and not the teaching of the Westminster Standards. Indeed, claiming that such a level is merely the "fruit" of faith is no less legalistic and dangerous. Matthew 18 gives us the process by which a professing believer may be considered an unbeliever, and that same chapter strongly warns against judging people or cutting them off from hope simply because of repeated sinning. The question is not how much someone obeys God but if they trust God. That trust, operating within a revealed structure of promise and warning, will be visible to oneself, to others, and to God.

Finally, like both Ursinus and Turretin, merit is asserted of Christ, but not Adam or his works before the Fall. In fact, in explaining why our works cannot merit eternal life, the Confession lists several things that Ursinus and Turretin mention that apply not only to sinners, but to creatures generally (ch. 16, paragraph 5). The first covenant ends at the Fall and the covenant of Grace begins from the fall in two administrations, that of the Law, and that of the Gospel (Ch. 7).

Some Observations Regarding Michael Horton and Rich Lusk

Michael Horton decided in his essay to attack a variety of targets, both Evangelical and Liberal, and roll them all together. Unraveling the resulting tangle would take more time and space than I have. In general, I will observe that Horton chooses the confusing over the clear whenever he can. The first subheading is indicative of this, "Is Obedience a Condition of Justification?" Could this not be said just as easily of Francis Turretin when he writes "When Christ enjoins upon the young man the duty of following him (Mt. 19:23), he does not give a counsel, but a command to all in common because no one can have a hope of salvation unless he follows Christ (2 Pet. 2:21), although from a particular cause it is peculiarly adapted to him"? (11.4.11; p. 32) Is this not exactly what the Westminster Confession states when it says that none may expect pardon without repentance? In fact, if faith itself is not an act of obedience, then the Westminster Confession is in error for saying that it is an "evangelical obedience" (ch. 11, paragraph 1).

Michael Horton has every right to ask whether it might not be wiser to use a different form of words (in line with Ursinus, though James 2 should forever prohibit any Christian from banning the phrase in all contexts). He has every right to ask in what way obedience is a condition for justification (i.e. faith as an instrument). But instead he writes as if the answer of the Protestant Reformation is an unambiguous "no" and never mentions "the justification of a righteous man" as a opposed to that "of a sinner" (Benedict Pictet) or "justification a posteriori" as opposed to "a priori" or a host of other matters. In fact, the entire tradition of the Reformed Faith regarding Judgment According to Works at the Last Day, the final justification that believers will receive when they are "openly acknowledged and acquitted" at the Resurrection (SC #38; LC #90)—is treated as a purely Tridentine Roman Catholic doctrine. The mention of conditionality in Scripture quoted above looks like it belongs to a completely different essay.

It is impossible to say anything good about his critique of Lusk or anyone else on the basis of such a fictional standard of "orthodoxy." The entire world of the Reformation that Horton portrays is a clear exercise in imagination, not an actual exposition of the Reformation heritage. (Readers should note that because I am focusing only on Lusk does not mean I concede any of Horton's accusations; it simply reflects the limitation of time and this book's space.)

In addition, not much of this is new. Horton wrote this in *Modern Reformation* ("Déjà vu All Over Again," July/August 2004, pages 23-30). Lusk wrote a response entitled "Blurring the Federal Vision." Anyone who is genuinely interested in what Lusk believes is more than welcome to print it out and read it. It can be found at http://www.auburnavenue.org/articles/Blurring_the_Federal_Vision.htm. On matters such as the exegesis of Philippians 2.8ff (in which Lusk follows Moises Silva and Frank Thielman) see his reply to the OPC Justification report, part 3 (http://www.trinity-pres.net/essays/opc-justification-reply-3.pdf).

I do think it is important to say something here about union with Christ.

Imputation and Union with Christ

Here is the offending passage from Lusk's contribution to the Knox Colloquium with some missing context:

> This justification requires no transfer or imputation of anything. It does not force us to reify "righteousness" into something that can be shuffled around in heavenly accounting books. Rather, because I am in the Righteous One and the Vindicated One, I am righteous and vindicated. My in-Christ-ness makes imputation redundant. I do not need the moral content of his life of righteousness transferred to me; what I need is a share in the forensic verdict passed over him at the resurrection. Union with Christ is therefore the key. Note well, this does not downplay the significance of the active obedience. Without it, Jesus' body would still be in the tomb. But to be precise, I am not justified by a legal transfer of his "obedience points" to my account. I am justified because the status he has as The Sinless One, and now as The Crucified and Vindicated One, has been bestowed upon me as well.

Allow me to illustrate. Suppose a woman is in deep, deep debt and has no means at her disposal to pay it off. Along comes an ultra wealthy prince charming. Out of grace and love, he decides to marry her. He covers her debt. But then he has a choice to make about how he will care for his bride. After canceling out her debt, will he fill up her account with his money? That is to say, will he transfer or impute his own funds into an account that bears her name? Or will he simply make his own account a joint account so it belongs to both of them?

In the former scenario, there is an imputation, a transfer. In the second scenario, the same final result is attained, but there is no imputation, strictly speaking. Rather, there is a real union, a marriage.

I would suggest the first picture (the imputation picture) is not necessarily wrong, though it could leave adherents exposed to the infamous "legal fiction" charge since the man could transfer money into the woman's account without ever marrying her or even caring for her. It could become, as Wright has said, "a cold piece of business."

The second picture (the union with Christ picture) seems more consistent with Paul's language, and for that matter, with many of Calvin's statements. It does not necessarily employ the "mechanism" of imputation to accomplish justification, but gets the same result. Just as one can get to four by adding three plus one or two plus two, or just as one can get home by traveling Route A or by Route B, so there may be more than one way to conceive of the doctrine of justification in a manner that preserves its fully gracious and forensic character.

For Calvin, the central motif of Pauline theology is not "imputation," but union with Christ....

Now, the only problem with Lusk here, as far as I can tell, is that he thinks his second analogy is not as much an "imputation" as the first one. But plainly, in responding to Morton Smith, Lusk is not saying that Paul was redundant to speak of *logizomai* (reckon, regard, impute) in Romans 3. Rather he is talking about imputation as it has recently started to be used as inherently a transfer term and a separate event from God's reckoning us as in Christ as having everything that He has by virtue of his death and resurrection.

Responding to Richard Gaffin's (in my view completely implausible) reaction to the statement, Lusk wrote, "I freely admit that the sentence from my colloquium essay, 'My in-Christ-ness makes imputation redundant,' is open to misunderstanding. Indeed, I gladly withdraw that statement, and let the rest of the argument stand on its own." ("A Reply to the 'OPC Justification Report on Union and Imputation,'" p 20, http://www.trinity-pres.net/essays/opc-justification-reply-1.pdf). He points out also,

> Again, in retrospect, I am happy to withdraw the offending sentence about the "redundancy" of imputation. My argument does not depend on that particular way of stating the matter, and perhaps overstates it. I wish now I had been even more explicit that it was specifically imputation-as-extrinsic-transfer (a.k.a. "alien righteousness") that I was critiquing. As with most of the debate surrounding the so-called "Federal Vision," subsequent clarifications in things I have written on this point do not seem to have gotten through to the critics.
>
> The really chief thing, as I see it, is that we conceive of imputation as the way God reckons, or regards, us, in Christ. That is to say, imputation is an aspect of, or angle on, union with Christ. It is the declarative, or forensic, dimension of union with Christ. God imputes faith as righteousness, meaning that he regards believers as judicially one with Christ. If we must speak of a transfer, let us talk of God's transferal of our persons from Adam's covenant headship to Christ's (Rom. 5:12ff; cf. Col. 1:12-14).

So what on earth is wrong with this? The record shows contra Horton, that Lusk is not giving us a false choice between union with Christ and imputation, but speaking to a situation where, despite our heritage, imputation has virtually overwhelmed any mention of union with Christ other than as an afterthought.

Imputation and Union with Christ According to Horton

But Horton has his own version of the Reformed Faith on this point, saying that Protestantism made "imputed righteousness the legal ground of union" (CJPM, p. 204) and cites a forthcoming book, *Justification and Participation* to back his point. This is completely backward.

While it is true that union with Christ would provide salvation for no one without Christ's atoning death and vindicating resurrection, the clear teaching of the Westminster Standards is that union is the basis for our righteous standing in God's sight. The *ordo salutis* of the Westminster Standards is

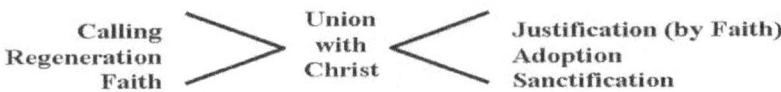

In chapter 11 of the Confession of Faith, entitled "of Justification" we find that we do not merely receive Christ's righteousness but Christ and his righteousness.

- Paragraph 1: Christ's obedience and satisfaction are imputed to those who are "receiving and resting on him and his righteousness."

- Paragraph 2: "Faith, thus receiving and resting on Christ and his righteousness, is the alone instrument of justification."

- Paragraph 4: "God did, from all eternity, decree to justify all the elect, and Christ did, in the fullness of time, die for their sins, and rise again for their justification: nevertheless, they are not justified, until the Holy Spirit doth, in due time, actually apply Christ unto them."

Here, one is justified when and because the Spirit unites one to Christ. Turning from the Confession, let us look at the Westminster Larger Catechism:

> **Q69:** What is the communion in grace which the members of the invisible church have with Christ?
> **A:** The communion in grace which the members of the invisible church have with Christ, is their partaking of the virtue of his mediation, in their justification, adoption, sanctification, and whatever else, in this life, **manifests their union with him** [emphasis added].

Union with Christ is what provides the believer with Christ's legal standing, His righteousness imputed to the Christian, as well as his adoption and sanctification. Questions 72 and 73 reiterate the same point:

> **Q72:** What is justifying faith?
> **A:** Justifying faith is a saving grace... whereby he ... receiveth and resteth upon Christ and his righteousness...
>
> **Q73:** How doth faith justify a sinner in the sight of God?
> **A:** Faith justifies a sinner in the sight of God ... only as it is an instrument by which he receiveth and applies Christ and his righteousness.

The Shorter Catechism presents the same pattern. Thus:

> **Q29:** How are we made partakers of the redemption purchased by Christ?
> **A:** We are made partakers of the redemption purchased by Christ, by the effectual application of it to us by his Holy Spirit.
>
> **Q30:** How doth the Spirit apply to us the redemption purchased by Christ?
> **A:** The Spirit applieth to us the redemption purchased by Christ, by working faith in us, and *thereby uniting us to Christ in our effectual calling* [Emphasis added].
>
> **Q31:** What is effectual calling?

A: Effectual calling is the work of God's Spirit, whereby ... he doth persuade and *enable us to embrace Jesus Christ,* freely offered to us in the gospel.

Notice in Answer 31, in a catechism for children, there is no need to add "and His righteousness" to embracing Jesus Christ in effectual calling. If one embraces Jesus Christ one cannot fail to have his righteousness.

The Westminster Standards are clear and consistent: The only people who receive/have imputed to them Christ's righteousness are those who receive/are united to Christ only by faith. The reason why the effectually called are justified is precisely because they are united to Christ by faith in that calling.

The only way one could deny this truth would be to reject paragraph 4 of chapter 11, "Of Justification," and assert that, in fact, somehow sinners are justified prior to the time that "the Holy Spirit doth, in due time, actually apply Christ unto them." But then, how can "justification *by faith*" be professed? It is amazing to me that this revolutionary statement, which is actually at the heart of his critique of Lusk, though never really acknowledged as such, is slipped in with no argumentation but a request for trust in a future vindication.

Conclusion

Has this essay vindicated Rich Lusk or others? In the sense that it is impossible to prove a universal negative, the current quality of discourse in Reformed circles dictates that I answer *no*. It is always possible that there is some dangerous heresy lurking somewhere in someone's past or future writings waiting to be discovered. Perhaps, Michael Horton will devote his ingenuity to proving Lusk is unorthodox by the standards of the actual Reformed heritage instead of the distorted version he used in his essay. But until an acknowledgment of mainstream Reformed theology is forthcoming, along with a truly compelling case, accusations against Lusk and others reveal more about the accuser than the accused.

CHAPTER 4

From Birmingham, With Love: "Federal Vision"[1] Postcards

Rich Lusk

The book *Covenant, Justification, and Pastoral Ministry (CJPM)* is yet another frontal assault in the latest Reformed Civil War. According to the editor, Scott Clark, there is "open disagreement within Reformed and Presbyterian churches over the most basic elements of the doctrine of justification" (*CJPM*, 3). According to David VanDrunen, the Reformed doctrine of justification is "under attack" – "even in the name of Reformed theology itself" (*CJPM*, 48).[2] It is my hunch that the issues at stake in the current fracas are not worth the amount of time and en-

---

1. I despise the use of theological labels to segregate the church into various parties and factions. In this case, I have only used the "Federal Vision" label because it crops up so frequently in the book to which this present volume of essays is responding. The "Federal Vision" is essentially a *conversation* among Reformed catholic Christians, who see a retrieval and maturation of Reformed biblical theology and ecclesial practice as the need of the hour. The "Federal Vision" is not a monolith or a fixed target, though I do not doubt that a "Federal Vision" theology (of sorts) could be identified. Readers should note that the "Federal Vision" is not uniform, and the views expressed here are my own, not necessarily those of another person who has been assigned the "Federal Vision" label.
2. My assigned task in this essay is to respond primarily to the first two chapters of the *CJPM* volume, edited by R. Scott Clark. My reply will be more indirect than direct; I am aiming more at description and defense than full scale critique. Space will not permit taking up each major assertion made by authors Clark and David VanDrunen, since these chapters are introductory summations. Instead of individual counter-arguments, I will (mostly) engage in painting counter-portraits ("postcards") of different aspects of the doctrine of justification. Of course, the two composite pictures, when placed side by side, are not contrary at every point, but I will generally pass over areas of overlap to focus on areas of disagreement.

ergy they have already consumed. That is not to say the issues that have caused the impasse are unimportant. But the high-stakes rhetoric is very one-sided, full of distortion, and reflects the ghettoizing of the Reformed church into an ingrown sect. The critics of the so-called "Federal Vision" really believe the gospel and the Reformed faith are being openly denied by the "Federal Vision."[3] On the "Federal Vision" side, the issues are seen as an intra-mural Reformed discussion which should be conducted in a brotherly manner since those things we hold in common outweigh our differences. That imbalance is very significant. The issue is not only the doctrines over which we disagree, but also the way in which those disagreements are communicated.

This contribution cannot even begin to canvas all the theological territory in dispute. While the sections of this meandering essay would not actually fit on a series of postcards, as the title suggests, it is my aim to break the massive discussion of justification down into several bite-sized, digestible pieces. The progression of "postcard" pictures I present will unpack the way I view key issues raised in the *CJPM* book: the righteousness of God, the nature of justification and justifying faith, imputation, and union with Christ. In another essay in this book, I will take up the topic of future justification. My aim is to give a brief overview of the doctrine of justification as it's understood on this side of the controversy, in such a way that the doors to further dialogue and discussion are

---

3. It is almost impossible to give a comprehensive overview of the issues involved in the current Reformed discussion. The issues are wide ranging, and yet the differences among various positions are often very subtle and nuanced. Certainly justification is at the heart of the discussion as the *CJPM* volume shows. Ecclesiology, sacramental theology, and covenantal conditionality (e.g., the possibility of apostasy) are also central. Less attention has been given to other, equally important matters, such as hermeneutics (especially the role of narrative and typology in interpretation), eschatology, the finer points of Trinitarian doctrine and theology proper, the relationship of biblical to systematic theology, the relationship of Reformed denominations to the church catholic, and the legitimacy of a Christian social order (Christendom). At the same time, these differences should not obscure major swaths of agreement on issues such as divine monergism in salvation, the ultimate authority of the Scriptures, the primacy of faith, etc. All parties to the present debate are cut from the same Reformed cloth, even if they are flowing down different currents in the Reformed stream.

left open. I am not trying to break any new ground here; rather, I want to gather up, summarize, and clarify what has already been said, so that we can press forward. My essay is not intended to be the last word, but hopefully a helpful word on the way to better understanding of each other and of Scripture.

I will limit myself primarily to biblical considerations (and primarily to Paul's epistles, at that), though I think it could be easily demonstrated that the doctrine of justification articulated here is within the boundaries of historic Reformed confessional orthodoxy (and I will gesture in that direction at points). It is important that we consider the teaching of the Reformed confessions and catechisms, the writings of great Reformers like John Calvin, and the works of contemporary scholars like Norman Shepherd, Richard Muller, and N. T. Wright. But the bottom line question for all Protestant Christians must be, *"What does Scripture teach?"* and so that will be the focus. Obviously, this paper is entering into an ongoing discussion; the uninitiated may want to consult the various works cited in the footnotes to get up to speed.[4] *Kyrie eleison* as we proceed.

The Righteousness of God

Our first postcard is a sketch of God's righteousness. Paul launches the argument of Romans from the base of "the righteousness of God" (Rom. 1:16-17).[5] But Paul did not invent this theological foundation. The OT already offered a very thick de-

---

4. My own key contributions, related to this present essay include "Rome Won't Have Me," "Blurring the Federal Vision," "A Response to Bryan Chappell," "A Response to the 2006 OPC Justification Report (Parts 1-3), "The PCA and the NPP," "Christ Church Ministerial Conference: The Life of Justification (Lecture Notes)," "Miscellanies on the 'New Perspective' and Pauline Biblical Theology," "Bombing the Theologians Playground: An Extended Review of N. T. Wright's *NIB* Romans Commentary," and "Theologians in Pajamas" (forthcoming). All of these are (or will be) available at http://www.trinity-pres.net/pastor.php.

5. The bibliography on "God's righteousness" has grown too massive to survey here. A succinct, helpful summary may be found in Michael Bird, *The Saving Righteousness of God*, (Waynesboro, GA: Paternoster, 2007), ch. 2. In *CJPM*, VanDrunen explores the meaning of God's righteousness mainly in connection with his summarizing the views of "New Perspective on Paul" scholars (41ff).

scription of God's righteousness, from which the apostle draws. Consider some texts:

> Oh, continue Your lovingkindness to those who know You, And Your righteousness to the upright in heart (Ps. 36:10)
>
> The LORD has made known His salvation; His righteousness He has revealed in the sight of the nations (Ps. 98:2)
>
> But the mercy of the LORD is from everlasting to everlasting On those who fear Him, And His righteousness to children's children (Ps. 103:17)
>
> I bring My righteousness near, it shall not be far off; My salvation shall not linger (Isa. 46:13)
>
> But My salvation will be forever, And My righteousness will not be abolished... But My righteousness will be forever, And My salvation from generation to generation (Isa. 51:6, 8)

Obviously, these passages are stripped of their full context here. But the key point should still be evident. In these texts, God's righteousness is clearly a *divine attribute* revealed in *divine action*. God's righteousness is his integrity, which manifests itself in history as fidelity to his covenant promises, which in turn manifests itself in the salvation of his people and the destruction of their enemies. God's righteousness is his character, reflected in his actions, vindicating true Israel and condemning the wicked. God's righteousness is his power, exercised on behalf of his people, to rescue them from sin through his Son.

God's righteousness is not just something to fear; it is also the ground of our hope of redemption. Note that repeatedly in these texts above "righteousness" is put in poetic parallel with "lovingkindness" (or "covenant love") and "salvation." God shows his righteousness when he keeps his covenant of love with his people, achieving their salvation. Yes, righteousness condemns, as we might expect. But it also saves. God's righteousness has two sides to it: When God acts in righteousness (covenant loyalty) to rescue his people, he also acts to destroy their enemies as well (e.g., the exodus).

There can be no doubt this is the understanding of divine righteousness Paul employs in Romans 1. This is the righteousness manifested in the gospel. The OT provides the framework within which Paul develops his argument that the righteousness of God has *now* (eschatologically) been revealed. The righteousness of God includes dark shades of wrath (1:18ff), but also the bright light of grace (3:21ff). Early in Romans 3, Paul uses God's "righteousness" and "faithfulness" interchangeably (3:3, 5). Later in chapter 3, Paul shows how God has overcome human unrighteousness (described in 3:9-20) and demonstrated his own righteousness in setting forth Christ as a propitiatory sacrifice (3:21ff), which Paul explains by alluding to the mercy seat on the ark of the covenant (*hilasterion* in 3:25). What happened symbolically in secret in the Holy of Holies on the Day of Atonement has now happened in reality in public on Good Friday. The cross proves and enacts the righteousness of God, for through the cross God upholds both his character and his covenant promises.[6] Israel's unfaithfulness has not caused God's word to fail; God has maintained his integrity even though Israel has failed to uphold her end of the covenant.

Why does Paul locate the righteousness of God in the faithful death of Jesus Christ (3:21-25)? On the one hand, the cross shows that God, as the Holy One, must pour wrath out upon sin. That wrath takes the shape of an execution (Gen. 2:17; 3:19), as Jesus endures the curse for the sake of his people. On the other hand, the cross shows God keeps his gracious promises, fulfilling the covenant

---

6. Romans 3:21ff explicates 1:16-17. Some have suggested that 1:17 should be translated "righteousness *from* God" but that does not make a huge difference. The reading "righteousness *of* God" emphasizes righteousness as God's *character*; the very Godness of God is found in his integrity and faithfulness. The reading "righteousness *from* God" emphasizes that God has *acted* in righteousness to keep his covenant promises in Jesus Christ and give salvation (righteousness) to his people. The phrase "from faith to faith" probably means the gospel moves from divine faithfulness to human faithfulness; that is, from God's powerful, saving action in Christ, to the human response of the obedience of faith. Alternatively, it could refer to the fact that the Christian life proceeds from the initial act of faith to persevering faithfulness (cf. Rom. 1:5; Gal. 3:2-3: Col. 1:22-25; Heb. 12:1-4).

pledge he made to redeem his people and form the global family of Abraham (Gen. 12:1-3; cf. Rom. 4:13) through Jesus and the Spirit (cf. Gal. 3:1-14). Hence, Paul describes God as just and the justifier of those who share in the faith of Jesus (Rom. 3:26). Romans 1:16-17, filled in by the rest of the letter, shows us that God's righteousness is defined as his powerful and saving self-revelation in the death and resurrection of Jesus Christ.[7] In Christ, God has proven that he is trustworthy and has made good on the covenant promises. God's righteousness is his covenant faithfulness embodied and enacted in the person and work of Christ, the Son of God, the Son of Man, overcoming human unrighteousness/unfaithfulness.[8]

---

7. In other words, the "righteousness of God" in Romans is more or less synonymous with the gospel narrative, announced at the very beginning of the letter in 1:1-6 as "the gospel of God." The gospel is "good news" precisely because it contains and reveals the righteousness of God. Jesus fits into the righteousness of God as the one in whom the divine promises have been fulfilled (1:2), as well as the one in whom the royal vocation of Israel as has been fulfilled (1:3; note Jesus' identity as the "seed of David").

8. We need to be careful to do justice to the simplicity of God here, lest we set God against himself. God is not schizophrenic, with his holiness and love internally warring against each other. All of God is involved in all that God does. All of his attributes are equally ultimate. It is a distortion of the divine being to speak of justice as being more basic than love. There is a tension to be found within the Bible's storyline, to be sure, but it is not a tension within the life of God. Rather, it is a tension between God and sin. That tension is resolved into perfect harmony at the cross, where the Triune God, in absolute holiness and love, achieves our salvation and defeats sin.

Further (while I am on this topic), we should be careful how we understand propitiation in Romans 3:25. We must dispense with the notion that the loving Son came (merely) to appease the wrath of an angry Father, or to persuade the Father to love us, or to acquire merits that would leverage the Father's favor towards us. After all, the Father's love for us sent the Son in the first place (John 3:16); even if we choose to speak of the Son's obedience "meriting" the Father's mercy to us (as John Calvin did), we still have to ask what merited the sending of the Son in the first place. The gospel, like creation itself, has its origins in the unmerited, unbounded love of God. The only alternative is to fall into an infinite regress. Yes, the Father's wrath against sin must be propitiated, but the Father himself provides the sacrifice that accomplishes this propitiation. He is not propitiated so that he can love sinners; rather, he loves sinners, and therefore sets forth his Son as propitiation for them.

Also, note that the Son is wrathful against sin every bit as much as the Father, such that his wrath must be propitiated as well. In that sense, the cross is the Son's self-propitiation. Our whole redemption is the project of the Triune God, from beginning to end. Each person of the Godhead has a unique work in the economy of redemption, yet those distinct roles interpenetrate one another as the persons act in perfect concert with one another.

The Victory of Righteousness

Paul's picture of divine righteousness in Romans is a picture of divine triumph. But that is not immediately apparent. Paul's stance in Romans is largely (if not essentially) apologetic. Paul argues his case that the gospel reveals the righteousness of God precisely because historical events (specifically, the story of Israel) have called that righteousness into question. Why haven't the promises been fulfilled as expected? What are we to make of the fact that the covenant people, Israel, have rejected their Messiah and been cut off? Is this God really trustworthy if his own people do not seem to be sharing in his blessings? The heart and climax of Romans demonstrate that God is indeed true to his word, even in the case of Israel (Rom. 9-11; 15-16).[9] He can be trusted. History is unfolding according to plan, even if appearances sometimes veil God's work, such that victories are cleverly disguised as defeats. Israel's covenant breaking leaves her with no grounds for hope, yet still God remains faithful and gracious. God has demonstrated his righteousness once and for all in the death of his Son, fulfilling the law and the prophets and bringing in the new covenant. The whole of history will ultimately serve God's glory and the whole cosmos (minus reprobate angels and humans) will share in the bounties of his goodness. All questions about God's covenant loyalty to his creation and his people are answered at Calvary. God's righteousness means that forgiveness, redemption, and renewal can only come through death. But on the other side of death lies resurrection.

To say God is righteous is to say God is *committed* – committed to restoring creation to peace and bringing his project for the world to its mature glory. God's righteousness is his unswerving purpose to glorify himself through keeping covenant with his people, and behind that, with his creation. The gospel – the good

---

9. Note that the programmatic quotation in Romans 1:17 comes from Habakkuk, which is also an apologetic work of theodicy. Paul, like Habakkuk, has to wrestle with the issue of God's faithfulness in relation to Israel's unfaithfulness. How will the righteous God keep covenant with an unrighteous people? What happens when covenant promises collide with human rebellion? For more on this line of thought in Romans, see Richard Hays, *Echoes of Scripture* (New Haven: Yale, 1989), ch. 2.

news about what God has done in Jesus' death and resurrection – is the announcement of God's cosmic and restorative righteousness. The creation's cries will be answered at last (Rom. 8:18ff).

So God's righteousness is the hub of the wheel; the blessings we receive in Christ radiate out from God's righteousness like so many spokes. The rest of the NT fills out this understanding of divine righteousness. Consider a couple of examples:

> Finally, there is laid up for me the crown of righteousness, which the Lord, the righteous Judge, will give to me on that Day, and not to me only but also to all who have loved His appearing (2 Tim. 4:8)

> If we confess our sins, He is faithful and just to forgive us our sins and to cleanse us from all unrighteousness (1 John 1:9)

In these texts, the righteousness of God is clearly his covenant faithfulness. As in the OT, it includes the legal, but also the relational, aspects of the covenant. His righteousness (or justice) is a comfort because it assures us of our present forgiveness and final vindication; it is the ground of our hope. This is the same view of God's righteousness found in Romans. God's righteousness is his total gift of salvation to believers and his fitting punishment of those who reject him. God is true to himself and to his people. The righteousness of God is ultimately Christ himself; he is the gift that brings justification and life. God is righteous – meaning he has won the victory over sin and death, just as he promised he would.

What Is Justification?

In many ways, our respective pictures of justification are similar. Everyone on both sides of the controversy agrees that justification is a forensic, lawcourt category. To be justified is the opposite of being condemned. Justification is a judicial declaration. "To justify" is to *declare righteous* in a legal context, not to *make righteous* by way of moral transformation. To be justified is to be declared in the right with God. No one desires to sideline or minimize the

Bible's robust judicial theology.[10]

Justification is found *in Christ* (Rom. 8:1; 1 Cor. 1:30). As the Son of God and Son of Man, he lived a perfect life, died on the cross for our sins as the spotless Lamb of God, and rose again in victory and vindication. By faith, we are united to him; by faith everything that is his becomes ours. Union with Christ is the matrix of our justification (and every other salvific blessing). As we trust him, we are united to him; in union with him, we participate in the vindicating verdict the Father passed over him and share in his righteous status.[11]

Paul gives a wonderful summary of how God justifies us in Romans 4:25. He firmly anchors justification in the death and resurrection of Christ. Our sin was the basis of his death; his resurrection is the basis of our acquittal. Jesus died that we might be forgiven. His death is our death, as he bears the curse we deserve. By his blood, our transgressions are washed away. Further, his resurrection was *his* justification, and therefore *our* justification as well, since we share in the verdict the Father declares over him. Had Jesus remained dead, he would have remained under the condemnation and power of sin. An unjustified Christ cannot justify anyone else. So Paul rightly says that Christ was raised *with a view to* our justification. This prospective, causal reading of Romans 4:25b is ably defended by Michael Bird.[12] Bird points out that standing behind this Pauline text is Isaiah's pre-announcement of the gospel in 53:11, where the Suffering Servant

---

10. This is the case even with regard to those like Peter Leithart who wish to point out the full breadth of the forensic category in the Scriptures. Leithart has demonstrated that justification includes a definitive deliverance from sin's power, as well as release from sin's condemnation (cf. Rom. 6:7). But this enriched, enlarged notion of justification is still fully forensic. See Leithart, "Judge Me, O God," in *The Federal Vision*, edited by Duane Garner and Steve Wilkins (Monroe, LA; Athanasius Press, 2004), 203-235, and my own essay, "Justification: Ecclesial, Cosmic, and Divine," available at http://www.hornes.org/theologia/content/rich_lusk/justification_ecclesial_cosmic_and_divine.htm.

11. Obviously, then, justification is *by faith*. Faith's unique function is unitive; we believe "into" Christ, as the NT often puts it. Faith justifies precisely because it embraces and receives Christ. The seminal work on our union with the risen Christ, especially as it relates to our justification, is Richard Gaffin, *Resurrection and Redemption* (Philipsburg, NJ: Presbyterian and Reformed, 1978). Gaffin would certainly not endorse everything in this essay, but many of his insights cohere well with my argument.

12. Bird, *The Saving Righteousness of God*, 50ff, 76f.

"justifies many" because he has "borne their iniquities" (a reference to the cross) and has now seen "the light" and is "satisfied" (a reference to the resurrection). I will not produce Bird's full argumentation here, but his summary is very apt:

> [U]nion with Christ is union with the justified Messiah and the now Righteous One. Jesus by fact of his resurrection is the locus of righteousness and redemption (cf. 1 Cor. 1:30; 2 Cor. 5:21; Eph. 1:17) and believers are justified only because they have been united with the justified Messiah. Whereas believers formerly shared the verdict of condemnation pronounced on Adam, now they partake of the verdict of justification pronounced of Christ...It is union with Christ in his death *and resurrection* that constitutes the material cause of justification.

Bird then quotes John Calvin's *Institutes of the Christian Religion* (3.11.8):

> For though God alone is the fountain of righteousness, and the only way in which *we are righteous is by participation in him*, yet as by our unhappy revolt we are alienated from his righteousness, it is necessary to descend to this lower remedy, *that Christ may justify us by the power of his death and resurrection*..[13]

The resurrection is a fitting paradigm for justification. Resurrection, taken in its many facets, is the core of our salvation. The resurrection is both a judicial and transformative event; and as such, it reveals the inseparability of these different aspects of our salvation. Moreover, Scripture attests that Jesus was not active in his resurrection. The typical way of describing the resurrection in the NT (aside from perhaps John 10:17-18) is to say the Father and/or Spirit enlivened Jesus from the grave (Acts 2:24; Rom. 8:11; etc.). Jesus did not "rise" from the dead so much as he "was raised." In the same way, our justification is not our own work; rather, we are recipients of the acquitting, enlivening verdict of God, even as Jesus was. Romans

---

13. Bird, *The Saving Righteousness of God*, 56 (emphasis his).

4:25 captures this dynamic: via our union with the risen Christ, we share in both his new judicial status and his new life. As we share in his resurrection, we are delivered from sin in all its consequences and ramifications, including death itself ultimately.

Paul further unfolds the meaning of justification in Romans 5:12-21, in which Adam and Christ represent not only two families, but two ages. This passage looks at humanity from the vantage point of covenant headship. Every person is found either in union with the first Adam (sharing in his disobedience, condemnation, and death) or the last Adam (sharing in obedience, justification, and life). Christ secured justification for his people by his one act of obedience (on the tree of the cross), answering to the one act of disobedience committed by the first Adam (which also took place at a tree). In the key verses, 5:18-19, it is "one man's righteous act" (note: not his entire life of obedience, but his singular act of obedience unto death as the unique *culmination* of that lifelong obedience) that has brought justification. This is contrasted with the "one man's offense" that brought sin and death.[14]

By the time we get to the end of Romans 8, Paul has shown the pastoral comfort that justification gives us. No charge can be brought against us. It is God who justifies – and he did not spare his own Son, but rather freely gave him up for our sakes. Surely he will give us everything else we could possibly need (8:32-33). All legal/judicial threats against us are answered by the death, resurrection, and intercession of Christ (8:34).[15]

This is not to deny a future dimension of justification still to come. But that future aspect of justification is still a legal verdict (not a process of moral renewal), and in a very real sense is based upon our initial justification, as described here.

---

14. Again, Bird's exegetical discussion in *The Saving Righteousness of God* hits on all the right nuances. Bird says that the obedience in view is not Christ's whole life, but specifically his obedience unto death (78). That is the best way to preserve the parallel with the first Adam. Further, he chastises John Piper for reading imputation into the text, when participation makes better sense (79).

15. It is worth noting that Paul's beautiful summary of Christ's glorious justifying work at the end of Romans 8 does not say a word about his "active obedience." More on that below.

Justifying Faith: Living or Dead?

How should we picture justifying faith? In *CJPM*, Clark asserts that the "Federal Vision" group believes that faith derives its justifying power from its moral qualities. He writes: "To conclude that in justification faith justifies because it obeys...has the most serious implications for the historic (and confessional) doctrine of justification" (4). VanDrunen echoes Clark's objection, focusing the problem on Norman Shepherd: "In his book, Shepherd repeatedly stresses that justifying faith is an active, living, obedient faith. Given the context of debates over justification, such language is inherently ambiguous" (49).

But Clark's view is a misreading of those he opposes and, contra VanDrunen, there is nothing ambiguous about Shepherd's "living faith" formula. This is actually quite simple: We are either justified by a *living faith* or a *dead faith*. Clark and VanDrunen apparently want to argue that a dead faith justifies. Doing my best impersonation of the apostle James, I want to ask (rhetorically, of course), *"Can such a faith save?"* When our theological formulations directly contradict the apostles, we need to back up and try again.[16] As James says, a dead faith does not profit (2:14). As Paul says, the only faith that avails for justification is a faith that works through love (Gal. 5:5-6). Believers receive and rest upon Jesus for justification in the same act of faith that also clings to him for moral transformation. Faith is faith; faith cannot be divided into two types, "justifying faith" and "sanctifying faith." Saving faith is an integrated whole, and can no more be divided than Christ himself.

---

16. The *CJPM* men are also contradicting Protestant doctrinal standards. Consider WLC 73 says, "other grace do *always* accompany" justifying faith, and WCF 11.2, which says faith is "not alone in the person justified, but is *ever* accompanied with all other saving graces" (emphasis added). The Lutheran teaching in the Formula of Concord (Solid Declaration, 3.41) quotes Luther to the same effect: "it is faith alone that lays hold of blessing, apart from works, and yet *it is never, ever alone*" (emphasis added). Faith does not come alive *after* justification; the faith that lays hold of Christ for justification is *already* a living, loving, virtuous faith. Any other kind of faith is dead, and such faith cannot bring a share in the life of Christ. It has always been standard Protestant teaching to apply the "alone" in the formula "justification is by faith alone" to "justification" and not "faith," precisely because faith is never alone.

These claims by Clark and VanDrunen are part of a larger presupposition the *CJPM* authors share. They believe the gospel must *sound* antinomian if it to be kept pure of legalism. Indeed, sounding antinomian is a test of orthodoxy. In chapter 9, Robert Godfrey, following Martyn Lloyd-Jones, says "If no one ever comes to you after you preach the gospel and asks 'So should we sin so that grace may abound?' you have probably never preached the gospel" (280).[17]

Aside from the fact that all of the "Federal Vision" men have been accused of preaching antinomianism at one time or another (and thus pass this test), the Godfrey/Lloyd-Jones point is really an exercise in missing the point. The objection of Romans 6:1 ("Shall we continue in sin that grace may abound?") is not raised *after* the gospel has been preached; it is raised *in the middle* of preaching the gospel. In other words, the antinomian objection is not a sign that you have preached the gospel; rather, it is a sign that you have *not yet finished* preaching the gospel. Paul's presentation of the gospel does not end in Romans 5:21; Romans 6 is pure gospel as well. Thus, the gospel is not preached in full if union with Christ in his death to sin and rising to new life are ignored (Rom. 6:2ff). The gospel is not preached in full unless a call for obedience to all of Christ's commands is issued (Matt. 28:20). The gospel is not preached unless the promised gift of the Spirit, given to enable us to put to death the misdeeds of the body (Rom. 8:13), is included in the offer. The gospel is not preached unless there has been a summons to repent (Acts 17:30).

The pure grace of the gospel is not threatened by a call to obedience. Indeed, the gospel, properly preached, understood,

---

17. See also *CJPM*, 208-9. I've always wondered what this test does for those who *don't* object to the antinomian presentation of the gospel, but instead simply draw the conclusion that the gospel *is* in fact an antinomian message, and go their merry way. In case the *CJPM* authors haven't noticed, not every totally depraved person is looking for rules to keep in order to earn God's favor; many (especially in a postmodern context) are looking for ways to escape any kind of rules whatsoever, while still being able to feel good about themselves. Antinomianism is (and always has been) every bit the danger that raw legalism is. For every sinner who tries to earn his way to God, there is another sinner turning grace into license. Some sinners are even skilled at doing both! This is why we need to focus *not* on sounding as antinomian as possible, but presenting a full-orbed gospel that includes both forgiveness and renewal as gracious gifts of God in Christ.

and embraced, demands *and promises* obedience. In the Scriptures, heralds of the gospel essentially interchange faith and repentance as appropriate responses to the message (cf. Acts 2:38 and 16:34). In other places, Scripture speaks of "the obedience of faith" and calls hearers to "obey the gospel" (Rom. 1:5; 2 Thess. 1:8). In still other texts, faith and obedience (cf. Rom. 10:16) as well unbelief and disobedience (Heb. 3:18-19) are interchangeable. The basic gospel confession is, "Jesus is Lord" (Rom. 9; 1 Cor. 12:3) – which is to say, "He has given himself for me, and I now owe him my allegiance." In the gospel, we find that God's righteous requirements are not legalistic impositions, but gracious gifts he promises to work in us (cf. Rom. 8:1-4).

The only kind of faith that justifies is a faith that lives – that is to say, a faith that loves, obeys, repents, calls, and seeks. Thus, faith can be *seen* (cf. Mark 2:5) and *demonstrated* (Jas. 2:18); it is embodied and embedded in outward action. True, at the moment of initial justification, faith has not yet done good works. But *the kind of faith* that lays hold of Christ for justification is a faith that will issue forth in obedience, not because something will be added to that faith a nanosecond after its conception (as if faith had to be "formed" by additional virtues, ala Roman Catholic teaching), but because that faith already carries within itself the seeds of every virtue.[18] The faith God works in us, in order that we might be justified by faith, simultaneously begins the process of transformation by faith. Faith never exists on its own, even at its inception. The kind of faith God gives his elect is a living, working, penitent, persevering faith. It is a faith that is inseparable from repentance and obedience. When faith grasps Christ, it grasps the whole Christ, so that he simultaneously becomes Savior and Lord. Indeed, given that faith is a gift of God, its presence in us is proof that the Spirit has already begun his work of transforming us.

Works, then, are the public manifestation of faith. When Paul describes the life of faith, in union with Christ, he immediately turns

---

18. How could good works be regarded as the "fruit" (cf. WCF 16.2) of faith unless faith contains the *seeds* of those works from the outset?

to how we re-pattern the use of our bodies (Rom. 6:12-13). Faith redirects and reorients the way we use the body. We put to death the body's misdeeds and begin to embody future resurrection life even in this present mortal existence (Rom. 8:1-17). While faith is certainly a matter of the heart, and renews the mind (Rom. 12:1-2), it has an inescapable communal, even political/cultural, dimension as well. The person acting in faith offers his body as an instrument of righteousness (Rom. 6:13); he becomes a holistic slave of God, even as he was previously a slave to sin (Rom. 6:19). Faith gives us a new posture, a new way of "leaning" into all of life.

The faith/obedience nexus is a critical aspect of biblical theology. The key thing to note here is that the gospel is bigger than merely the offer/promise of forgiveness; it is also the offer/promise of a changed life. God accepts us as we are, but he doesn't let us stay that way. The necessity of obedience is not bad news tacked onto an otherwise antinomian gospel message. People need (and should want) transformation and freedom from sin's enslavement, every bit as much as they want pardon and release from the burden of sin's guilt. A gospel that did not ultimately aim at and guarantee the complete destruction of sin in our lives and the complete renovation of our humanity would actually be mediocre news at best, not the good news of Jesus Christ. Every demand God makes is also a promised gift in the economy of grace. It is good news to hear that God not only desires to clear us from sin's penalty, but also re-humanize us so that we can begin to enjoy the kind of life we were designed to live.

Contra Clark's assumptions, none of that is to say that faith justifies *because* it obeys. Faith justifies because it lays hold of Christ, the Just One. Rather, the point here is that justifying faith has certain qualities. The same faith that receives the gift of justification receives the gift of transformation. It's a package deal.

The Meaning of Imputation

The eye of the storm in the present controversy is Paul's doctrine of imputation. Here the picture is a little cloudier. There is no question Paul uses imputation (*logizomai*) language to explicate his gospel. But the questions are: What does this language mean? How does it work? How does imputation relate to justification and the rest of our salvation in Christ?[19]

The exegetical issue is somewhat complicated by the fact that the term "imputation" took on a life of its own in Reformed systematic theology. The Reformed polemic against Rome was structured in terms of a debate between those who believed in justification by imputed righteousness vs. those who believed in justification by infused righteousness. In Reformed systematic theology, the notion of "imputation" took on a great deal more theological freight than it carries in the Pauline epistles. Over time, it became the defining mark of Protestant theology, or, as Bird puts it, a "boundary marker" for the Reformed faith. For some, imputation has become synonymous with the gospel itself.[20]

But the role of imputation in Paul and the role of imputation in Reformed theology are not necessarily identical. Failure to notice the slippage between biblical and systematic terminologies is a major culprit in the present controversy. Terms have to be understood in light of their context. While theologians are certainly free to use terms in stipulated, shorthand ways, we also need to keep in view the distinctive biblical sense(s) a given term may have as well. This is not an attack on doing systematic theology (which is inescapable), but an endorsement of doing biblical exegesis (a burden we have all too often escaped).

Popularly understood, imputation describes a *transfer* of righteousness. The model looks something like this: Through his active (lifelong obedience) and passive obedience (suffering on the cross),

---

19. In *The Saving Righteousness of God*, Bird perceptively points out that many theologians who have replaced the scholastic *ordo salutis* model of salvation with a union-with-Christ model (e.g., Sinclair Ferguson, Anthony Hoekema, Gaffin, etc.) have not accounted for the relationship of imputation to union. For example, Bird shows that Gaffin rightly perceives "the overarching significance of union with Christ" in Paul's soteriology, yet Gaffin "fails to explicate the relationship between an imputed righteousness and participative righteousness" (47; cf. 2, 60, etc.). It is precisely this relationship between union and imputation that we must explore.

20. Bird rightly notes that Reformed theology's overemphasis on imputation has led our theologians to all too often overlook the soteric significance of the resurrection and the forensic dimension of union with Christ (85f).

Jesus accumulated merits in his account. Those merits are imputed to our accounts when we trust him. Because the merits of Christ have been transferred to us, God declares us justified. When the Scripture says, "faith is counted for righteousness," it really means that by faith, God transfers Christ's righteousness to us in order to declare us just. Justification is a consequence of this imputation; God's act of justification is based on his (logically prior) act of imputation.[21]

Obviously, such a model is true insofar as it preserves the free, forensic, gracious, and christological character of our justification. It is also attractive in making a sharp, tidy contrast with the Roman Catholic doctrine of justification on the basis of personal moral transformation or infused righteousness.[22] But this is not *exactly* what Paul means when he speaks of imputation.[23]

---

21. For example, consider R. C. Sproul's summary in *Getting the Gospel Right: The Tie That Binds Evangelicals Together* (Grand Rapids: Baker, 1999), 64:

> The Reformers insisted that the sole ground of our justification is the righteousness of Christ wrought for us in his life of perfect obedience. This is done by imputation. This means that God transfers to our account the righteousness of Christ wrought in his own person and that this righteousness is "counted" or "reckoned" to us by imputation.

In Sproul's explanation, the "active obedience" of Jesus comes to the foreground, while the cross and especially the resurrection recede to the background. This is just the opposite of the NT emphasis. Further, imputation is treated as a discrete action of God which in turn leads to justification. Imputation is explicitly defined as a transfer.

But is this order of things really reflected in the biblical descriptions of justification? Does Paul view imputation as an isolated, transitive event that produces the verdict of justification? Does he ever suggest that God justifies us by counting righteousness to us by imputation, which then provides the ground for the verdict? Against Sproul, I will argue that justification is the imputative, forensic *aspect* of union with Christ. Apparently, this option is not on Sproul's theological map.

Another example of "imputation" being used taken as "transfer" language is the recent paper "The PCA Federal Vision Study Committee Report," found at http://www.byfaithonline.com/partner/Article_Display_Page/0,,PTID323422%7CCHID664014%7CCIID2326076,00.html. This document assumes that "imputation" must mean "transfer," but without offering any argumentation from the Westminster Standards or the Scriptures, and without any interaction with alternative views. See pages 2224-2225.

For a complete overview of my own view of imputation see my essay "A Response to the 2006 OPC Justification Report," Part 1.

22. Although, ironically, it shares a "treasury of merit" concept with Rome!

23. Note that does not mean that Paul's doctrine is Roman either, as though imputation

In Paul, imputation language describes how God *counts* or *regards* the believer *in view of his union with Christ.* Imputation docs not describe a *transfer* of righteousness from Christ's account to ours; rather it is how God *reckons* us, or *considers* us, in union with Christ.[24] The key text is Romans 4, since this is the place imputation language is most heavily concentrated. We cannot do a complete exegesis or linguistic analysis, but a few notes on the passage should establish the point.

Paul's concern in Romans 4 is twofold: *Who* are the children of Abraham – the true people of God? And *how* are they justified – by faith or by works of Torah?[25] Paul argues that Abraham's faith-ancestry, not merely his flesh-ancestry, is the decisive issue. Abraham was put right by faith, not works, lest he have something to boast in; the same must be true of his children (Rom. 4:1-3). But what is

---

(as transfer) and infusion are the only options. There is a third way, an alternative to both imputation (as transfer) and infusion, namely, incorporation. Of course, incorporation includes both imputative (declarative) and transformational aspects. This will be developed below.

24. I will not provide a full-scale analysis of the problems (exegetical, theological, philosophical, linguistic) with the "transfer" view. My aim is simply to point out that the standard prooftexts for the "transfer" doctrine of imputation say something slightly different and that the "transfer" model ends up distorting Paul's meaning. "Imputation" (*logizomai*) language is never used in Paul's writings to describe the transfer of something from one party to another.

Some Reformed theologians have tried to maintain a focus on union with Christ, while simultaneously holding on the concept of transferred righteousness. But this adds an unnecessary and artificial step to the application of salvation. It much more Pauline to integrate imputation into union rather than to treat it is an independent aspect of salvation. God's act of imputing us as righteous in Christ is essentially identical to his act of declaring us justified in Christ.

25. Both of these questions flow out of the immediately preceding context, Romans 3:21-31. In those verses, Paul has twined together justification as it relates to sin (3:22-26) and ethnicity (3:27-30). In chapter 4, Paul is working with both threads, continually weaving them into a single coherent argument in favor of justification by faith. Paul has just shown how God forgives sin through the cross (3:25). He also said "there is one God" (3:30) — which monotheism entails a single (Abrahamic) family. Thus, as the argument unfolds in Romans 4, Abraham emerges as a typological "father figure" (4:1), representing the ungodly who trust in God (4:2-8), as well as both Jewish believers and Gentile believers (4:9-12). In other words, the multiple facets of Abraham's life narrative (e.g., the timing of his circumcision in relation to his faith) allow him to be the paradigm for how God justifies sinners by faith alone *and* how justification in Christ draws together disparate people groups into a single new family.

entailed in becoming righteous like Abraham?

The apostle uses the language of imputation throughout Romans 4, notably in 4:3, 4, 5, 6, 8, 9, 10, 11, 22, 23, 24. In *none* of these instances does imputation mean that the righteousness of Christ is *transferred* to believers.[26] Instead, we will find that imputation is used in a way roughly synonymous with justification itself. To say "faith is accounted for righteousness" is to say God reckons, or counts, the believer to be righteous *in Christ*. This is just another way of saying God justifies us (that is, declares us just) by faith. Faith does not *consist in* righteousness as such (as though it were meritorious), but faith is reckoned as righteousness by God because of faith's object (the God who raised Christ; cf. 4:22-25).

In Romans 4:4-5, we find that God did not declare Abraham righteous in Genesis 15:6 because Abraham had been obedient. To be sure, Abraham had been obeying God for quite some time by that point. He walked with the Lord by faith when he moved out of his homeland some years previous (cf. Gen. 12; Heb. 11:8). But those works of Abraham (e.g., rescuing Lot in Genesis 14) did not put God in his debt; even at this mid-point in Abraham's growth as a believer, he is declared righteous by grace through faith. Abraham did not view himself as an employee, serving God for wages; rather,

---

26 In 4:3, 5, faith is imputed for righteousness, which is to say God regarded Abraham's faith as the token of his covenant membership and accordingly reckoned him as righteous. To take "imputation" in the sense of a "transfer" makes no sense here. How can a person's own faith be "transferred" to him? In fact, if we look at imputation language elsewhere in Paul, we find the same thing (though English translations often obscure this). For example, in Romans 2:26, 3:28 and 6:11, imputation language clearly means "consider" or "reckon." It has no overtones of transfer. Thus, Romans 4 does not indicate God transfers righteousness to us any more than 2:26 means circumcision is transferred from one person to another, or 6:11 means we transfer death to sin from Christ to ourselves. In Romans 4, imputation concerns how God regards us in Christ; in 6:11, it concerns how we regard ourselves in Christ.

Outside of Romans, we find the same kind of usage. In Philippians 4:17, Paul uses imputation language in a financial rather than forensic context, but still no transfer is involved. The Philippians' sacrificial deeds will be "imputed" (or "counted," or "marked") to *their own* account. There is obviously no transaction. 2 Timothy 4:16 uses imputation in a similar way: Paul hopes that the misdeed of those who forsook him will not be imputed ("charged" or "counted") against them. Obviously, there is no transfer involved; Paul is hoping for the non-imputation of sin ala Romans 4:8.

he viewed himself as someone still in need of God's grace, and so he continued clinging to the promise of a coming seed. God considered this faithful response to be the true fulfillment of the covenant, and as a result declared Abraham to be a right-standing covenant member. Abraham's life story shows that in a very deep sense, faith is the *sole condition* of the covenant *from beginning to end*..[27]

Romans 4:6-8 explain the nature of imputed righteousness. To have righteousness imputed means that sins are forgiven – or, to put the same reality another way, it means that God does not count (impute) a man's sin against him. When God refuses to reckon sin (4:8, quoting Ps. 32:2), it means he "covers" our sin (4:7, quoting Ps. 32:1). It means he has cast our sins away (Isa. 38:17), removed them (Ps. 103:12), blotted them out (Isa. 43:25, 44:22), and forgotten them (Isa. 43:25). The non-imputation of sin means God is not pressing charges against us; instead, he is accounting us as in the right. So we have this equation: "righteousness imputed" = "sins forgiven/covered" = "sins not imputed." Note that it is *impossible* for imputation language to describe a transfer in verse 8 since a person's *own* sin is in view. (How could a person's own sin be transferred to him?) But that means that it will take some pretty strong argumentation to prove imputation terminology should be read as transfer language elsewhere in the passage.

Verses 9-10 ask if the blessing of imputed righteousness (defined as forgiveness in the immediate context) is only for Jews (the circumcised). Verse 11 answers the question. Paul says God counts

---

27. The fact that the declaration of Genesis 15:6 does not come at the beginning of Abraham's life of faith has baffled commentators, and I admit to being somewhat baffled myself. Nevertheless, at the very least, the quotation seems very apt for Paul's purposes in Romans 4 (as well as Galatians 3, where he also employs it). If the declaration came at the very beginning of Abraham's encounter with God, there might have been room for later Jews to conclude that Abraham started in faith, but had to finish in his own strength (cf. Rom. 4:19-25; Gal. 3:1-9). But the fact that Genesis 15:6 is placed in the narrative a long time after Abraham initially came to faith (and presumably received some sort of initial justification/acceptance) indicates that faith is *always* the means of justification. God continued to accept Abraham because Abraham continued to trust in the promise of a coming seed, even though the odds grew longer and longer against the promise ever coming true. In my companion article in this volume I demonstrate how this *sola fide* theology is still consistent with a final judgment/justification according to works.

the uncircumcised as righteous by faith as well as the circumcised (cf. Rom. 2:25-29). In other words, the uncircumcised can have the same status as the circumcised *by faith* – as the 2-stage life experience (pre-circumcision/post-circumcision) of Abraham demonstrates (4:10-12). Abraham was justified as a Gentile, before he was circumcised – a point with obvious typological implications for Gentile believers in the new covenant, since it proves them to be children of the patriarch, along with believing Jews. This reinforces the thought of 3:28: If justification was by works of Torah, it would only be available to the circumcised. But the case of Abraham refutes that notion. It is impossible to circumscribe the bounds of Abraham's family with circumcision or the Torah.

Romans 4:12-18 further reinforces the same point. Abraham is to be heir of *the world*, not just one nation among many; thus, the salvation promised in the Abrahamic covenant must be for Gentiles as well. In 3:29-30, Paul used monotheism to establish the point that there must be one covenant family composed of Jew and Gentile. Now Paul says there must be one "father of us" – which, again, suggests one covenant family (4:16). Those who are "of circumcision," or "of the law," are saved by faith. But those without circumcision or the law are saved in the same way. If the promise was only to the circumcised, it would appear to be a matter of ethnicity/race, rather than faith and grace. But Paul will have none of that. Abraham is destined to be the father of *many* faithful nations, all rolled into one covenant community.

Paul finally wraps up this phase of his argument in 4:19-25, a text we have already touched on above. Abraham's faith was justifying because it was resurrection faith (4:19-21). Christian believers follow in Abraham's footsteps, as their faith is directed towards the God who raised Christ (here, hinted at as the new Isaac) from the dead (4:22-25), bringing life out of death, justification out of condemnation, birth out of barrenness, and family out of enmity. Abraham's faith gives glory to God (4:20) – answering to the very problem with fallen humanity Paul identified in 1:21ff and 3:23. Through Christ, God has created a new humanity that escapes the wrath revealed from heaven and brings him glory.

Sharing Resurrection Status

Now we can sketch a fuller picture of justification. For Paul, this is how justification works: God (through the Torah) curses Christ and condemns him as a sin offering on Good Friday (Rom. 8:1-3); he then reverses that sentence, and justifies him as the Righteous One on Easter Sunday (1 Tim. 3:16). Thus, the condemnation of sin on the cross and the resurrection of Christ from the grave form the ground of our justification. Standing in the background of Paul is Isaiah 53 (among other texts), where the execution/vindication pattern is already woven into the heart of biblical Christology. When we are united to Christ, our sin is taken care of by his cross and we share in his resurrection verdict. This justification is (obviously) fully forensic and christological.

To sum up:

1. Christ *is* our righteousness; we are righteous *in him* (Rom. 4:22-25; cf. Rom. 5:12-21; 8:1; 1 Cor. 1:30).

2. Faith is imputed as righteousness = justification by faith (Rom. 4:3ff). To "impute" in this context is to "declare" or "reckon." It is not a transfer.

3. God imputes faith as righteousness because it is by faith that we are united to Christ, the Righteous One. Faith's key function in justification is unitive, though this cannot be severed from faith's other functions.

"Justification by faith" is theological shorthand for saying we are united to Christ by faith, and in Christ there is no condemnation. For the sake of exegetical purity, I do not think we should speak of Christ's righteousness (or merit) being imputed (transferred) to believers. That's not how Paul puts it; that's not how he uses imputation as a category. Rather, we should say things like,

"God imputes/declares/regards as righteous those who, by faith, are united to the crucified and risen Christ," *or*

"God imputes faith as righteousness because faith unites us to Christ, the Righteous One," *or*

"God does not impute sin against those who are united to Christ by faith, but rather imputes them as righteous."

This is the "grammar of the gospel," so to speak, as I see it. These are better summaries of the heart of Paul's theology than those that focus on the ostensible transfer of Christ's active obedience or merit to our accounts. Again, there is *no text* in Scripture where imputation language is used to describe a transfer of Christ's righteousness from his account to ours. Instead Scripture says he *is* our righteousness; thus, we are righteous *in him*. Imputation simply means God counts us as we are in Christ. If I already have Christ by way of union, what can be added to me by way of transfer?[28] Imputation is not transitive but declarative.

It is clear, then, that union with Christ is the key that unlocks the doctrine of justification. The centrality of union with Christ in the Protestant tradition (Calvin, Westminster) is well documented elsewhere, and I shall not repeat that work here. One Luther quote is enough to sum up the matter: "The moment I consider Christ and myself as two, I am gone."[29] Indeed.

---

28. This is why I suggested the transfer formulation is actually redundant in my essay "A Response to 'The Biblical Plan of Salvation,'" in The Auburn Avenue Theology: Pros and Cons, edited by E. Calvin Beisner (Ft. Lauderdale, FL: Knox Theological Seminary, 2004), 142. Because that language has been misunderstood and the cause of controversy, I have subsequently clarified and retracted it in Part 1 of my "A Response to the 2006 OPC Justification Report." My intention was to echo the view of Leon Morris, *The Apostolic Preaching of the Cross* (Grand Rapids, MI: Eerdmans, 1965), 282:

In plain view of statement like these [in Romans 4] it seems impossible to hold that Paul found no place for the imputation of righteousness to believers. On the other hand he never says in so many words that the righteousness *of Christ* was imputed to believers, and it may fairly be doubted whether he had this in mind in his treatment of justification, although it may be held to be a corollary from his doctrine of identification of the believer with Christ.

While I admit my own lack of clarity in that essay, critics were too quick to judge my work by their own sloganized formulations to understand my argument. This paper intends to help correct those problems.

For more, see Joel Garver's fine assessment of my "redundancy" remark, posted at http://sacradoctrina.blogspot.com/2007/06/pca-report-on-nppfv-some-concerns-4.html.

29. Quoted in Ralph Wood, *Contending for the Faith* (Waco, TX: Baylor University Press, 2003), 171. For more on union with Christ, see Anthony A. Hoekema, *Saved by Grace* (Grand Rapids, Mi: Eerdmans, 1989), and Mark Horne, "Justification by Union with

Why does it matter that we conceive of imputation in terms of union? Union with Christ makes imputed righteousness *a matter of fact*, rather than *legal fiction*. It makes justification a judgment according to truth, rather than a bare legal fiat with no grounding in reality. We actually are what God declares us to be in Christ; we do have not some "deeper identity" outside of union with Christ, or impervious to God's declaration over us. We are who God says we are in Christ; to say otherwise about ourselves is to quarrel with God in unbelief. God's act of justification does not merely *recognize* who we are; it *determines* who are. Our righteous status is not a matter of God doing mental tricks or shuffling righteousness around heavenly ledgers; it is a matter of our concrete, personal relationship with Christ himself. More on this below.

The Imputation of Christ's Active Obedience and Inclusive Substitution

In the picture drawn in the *CJPM* volume the imputation of Christ's active obedience is necessary to a truly Reformed doctrine of justification (cf. ch. 8). Why doesn't my picture include this element in the same way? What is *required* in an orthodox formulation of justification? Is the imputation of Christ's active obedience a systematically fundamental doctrine in the Reformed system? Questions about theological constructs, like whether or not Christ's "active obedience" (or Torah-keeping) is imputed, are interesting, but not *essential* to an articulation of the gospel.[30] Indeed, if such is essential to the gospel, where did Jesus (in the gospels) or the apostles (in their sermons in the book of Acts) *ever* preach the gospel?

Christ," available at http://www.hornes.org/theologia/content/mark_horne/justification_by_union_according_to_calvin_and_westminster.htm.

30. The main impetus behind the doctrine of the imputation of Christ's active obedience is the meritorious covenant of works, which is itself a highly dubious theological construction. When the *CJPM* authors point to Reformed antecedents for the meritorious covenant of works (e.g., 208, 335), they do not accomplish their aim because these historical precedents are too ambiguous to establish the *key features* of their doctrine over against the "Federal Vision" side. On the problems with the meritorious covenant of works, see the classic study by Cornelius van der Waal, *The Covenantal Gospel* (Neerlandia: Alberta: Inheritance Publications, 1990).

Their message is much simpler and sleeker, focusing on how God forgives us and renews us in and through the death and resurrection of Christ, as we respond with faith and repentance.[31]

The importance of the doctrine of the imputation of Christ's active obedience has been overblown in contemporary debate. Paul

---

31. In light of Romans 4:25, I have asked the question in several places: Why would it be better, soteriologically speaking, to have Christ's active obedience imputed to us than to have a share in the forensic verdict passed over him at his resurrection? So far, none of the critics of the "Federal Vision" have provided anything like an adequate answer. If anything, we could even make a case that getting the resurrection verdict implicitly includes getting the pre-cross obedience that led up to it. But it should be noted that Paul never locates our justification in Christ's Torah-keeping as such, and in fact, openly denies that the Torah was given for the purpose of justification.

For an exegetical critique of the imputation of the active obedience formulation, see Daniel Kirk's work, "Nothing but the Blood: The Cruciform Matrix of Justification," available at http://www.act3online.com/act3reviewArticlesDetail.asp?id=288. Kirk makes a very solid case for viewing our justification as grounded in the death and resurrection of Christ, rather than his obedience to the Torah. Kirk shows that those who insist on the imputation of Christ's active obedience run the risk of making Christ's blood *insufficient* for salvation, which is surely at odds with Scripture.

One of the strongest arguments against the imputation of the active obedience is found in the sacrificial system of the OT. This system, of course, was given to serve as a blueprint of Christ's work. A worshipper would bring a spotless animal to the tabernacle or temple. The cleanness of the animal obviously represented Christ's perfect obedience. The worshipper would lay hands on the animal, *incorporating* himself into the sacrifice, and setting the animal apart to the "office" of representative substitute. But the reverse action was never performed; never did the animal lay its hooves on the worshipper, never was anything *transferred* from the animal to the worshipper. After the worshipper is united to the animal, the animal must die for the sin of the one he represents. Thus, the animal is killed and its blood presented for propitiation – pointing forward to the cross. Afterwards, the animal carries the worshipper into the Spirit-fire of the altar, and ascends before the Lord's throne as a sweet smelling aroma. This entire pattern corresponds to cross-resurrection-ascension-glorification. Thus, the sacrifices provided a comprehensive preview of the whole work of Christ. The matrix for the entire model is union, not transfer, as the worshipper participates in the movement of the animal through death into God's glorifying presence. The worshipper is "in" the animal and therefore shares in its death to sin and subsequent nearness to God (resurrection). But nothing in the Levitical rites corresponds to the *imputation* of Christ's *active obedience*. For a fuller account of how the sacrifices worked, see Peter Leithart, *A House For My Name* (Moscow, ID: Canon Press, 2000), 87-95.

The same point can be made regarding the sacraments of the new covenant, baptism and the Lord's Supper. Neither sacrament symbolizes or enacts a *transfer* of merits or active obedience; instead, they focus on *union and communion* with the risen and glorified Christ.

never says Christ's Torah-keeping is imputed to us; rather when he unfolds the substance of imputed righteousness, he *always* turns to Christ's death and resurrection (cf. Rom. 4:22-25; 8:32-34; 14:9). If the doctrine of imputed active obedience is so important, surely Paul would have mentioned it more explicitly, or given it greater prominence. The emphasis of the *CJPM* authors does not match that of the apostle.

To be clear, I am *not* questioning the active obedience of Christ to the Torah as such. He had to be sinless in order to qualify as the sin bearer on the cross. Nor am I denying our union with Christ in every phase of his life-long obedience. Nor am I denying that Jesus is the True Adam and True Israel, fulfilling God's original plan for humanity. To be sure, he does fulfill the Adamic covenant (as well as every other covenant). What I *am* suggesting is that the NT locates our justification not in his active obedience as such, but in his death and resurrection, or in his "blood" and (resurrection) "life," as Paul puts in Romans 5:9-10.

Many critics of the "Federal Vision" are wrong at just this point, and have caused the church a great deal of unrest by insisting on arcane, over-wrought, debatable formulations as tests of orthodoxy. This is a recent and unfortunate development within the Reformed world. For example, in *CJPM*, Scott Clark says one side in the present controversy teaches "the imputation of Jesus' passive obedience only" and he perceives this to be an attack on the gospel (5). Clark insists vociferously on the imputation of Christ's active obedience, in addition to his passive obedience; anything less is a departure from Reformational orthodoxy and compromises grace. But when he critiques the passive-obedience only view, he never examines what those men put in the place of the active obedience (namely, the resurrection; cf. *CJPM*, 241-243, where Clark briefly summarizes my view but does not engage the core arguments).

Thankfully, a rising generation of scholars is questioning the usefulness of holding to the imputation of Christ's active obedience, at least at the level of exegesis, if not systematics. Of course, in doing so, they are not only developing a sound biblical theology, but following the lead of a wide range of early Reformed theologians as well (an historical point that Clark recognizes but refuses to reckon with). The doctrine of imputed active obedience has not always had the prominence that it holds today; for several generations of Protestants, it was a secondary doctrine, over which there could be legitimate differences. Simon Gathercole is representative of today's trend back to the classic Reformed view:

> The Reformed tradition's most common way of explicating the christological character of justification...has recently aroused considerable controversy. This is the doctrine of the imputation of *Christ's* righteousness (as opposed to imputed righteousness understood in some other way)...[I]t should be said that there is a great deal of diversity of opinion on the matter. This is, of course, not sufficient in itself to let discretion take the better part of valor. But in this case, the diversity seems to arise out of the complexity of the New Testament evidence, not because one side is particularly hidebound to tradition and the other wallowing in the desire for novelty or for a doctrine that is more amenable to culture...[B]ecause of the complexity of this issue, I would propose that the requirement that it is specifically Christ's righteousness that is imputed to believers should not feature in evangelical statements of faith. To make such a finely balanced point an article of faith seems a dangerous strategy. Nonetheless, it is very clear that justification is still christological through and through. Both the cross and the present action of Christ are the vital grounds of justification.[32]

---

32. Simon Gathercole, "The Doctrine of Justification in Paul and Beyond: Some Proposals," in *Justification in Perspective*, edited by Bruce L. McCormack (Grand Rapids: Baker Academic, 2006), 222f. Gathercole specifically has in view the position of Robert Gundry. Though my view is significantly different than Gundry's, it falls well within the parameters of Reformed orthodoxy as Gathercole lays them out.

Gathercole's view should be compared to that of Mark Seifrid, in *Christ Our Righteousness: Paul's Theology of Justification* (Downers Grove, IL: Inter-Varsity Press, 2000), 174-5. Seifrid expresses some uneasiness about the "imputed active obedience" formula: "It is worth observing that Paul never speaks of Christ's righteousness as imputed to believers, as became standard in Protestantism." He goes on to argue that this formulation is redundant, as it "multiplies entities within 'justification.'" There is no need to add the imputation of Christ's active righteousness to the forgiveness of sins. See 174ff and 120-121n for more of Seifrid's insightful analysis.

Thus, Gathercole carefully refrains from making the "imputed active obedience" formulation a test of orthodoxy since it is exegetically dubious.

As I see things, the imputation/transfer of the active obedience of Christ, as usually expressed today, never really finds a home in Paul's description of salvation. For example, in Romans

---

D. A. Carson at least acknowledges that the imputation of Christ's active obedience is a "second order doctrine," at most teased out of Paul's letters rather than explicitly stated. While he argues vigorously for the imputation of Christ's active obedience, this is still a significant admission. See Carson's article "The Vindication of Imputation: On Fields of Discourse and Semantic Fields" in *Justification: What's at Stake in the Current Debates?*, edited by Mark Husbands and Daniel J. Treiers (Downers Grove, IL: InterVarsity Press, 2004).

A number of earlier Reformed theologians, including the venerable John Owen, did not consider the imputation of Christ's active obedience to be *essential* to the Reformed doctrine of justification. Owen believed in the imputation of Christ's active obedience, but was wise enough to know that other orthodox Reformed theologians did not use that formulation. In his work *The Doctrine of Justification* in *The Works of John Owen: Volume 5*, (Edinburgh: Banner of Truth, 1965), 62-63, Owen says, "But as to the way and manner of the declaration of this doctrine among Protestants themselves, there ever was some *variety* and difference in expressions." This variety "among persons who agree in the substance of the doctrine" included "the righteousness of Christ that is said to be imputed to us. For some would have this to be only his suffering of death…" In other words, Owen did not regard the debate over the imputation of Christ's active obedience to be a debate over the "substance" of the doctrine of justification!

William Cunningham, in *The Reformers and the Theology of the Reformation* (Edinburgh: Banner of Truth, 1989 reprint), 404, questioned whether or not John Calvin would have accepted an active obedience/passive obedience construct at all:

As to the distinction between the passive and the active righteousness of Christ… this does not appear to be formally brought out in the writings of John Calvin. It is to be traced to which the doctrine of justification was afterwards subjected; and though the distinction is quite in accordance with the analogy of faith, and may be of use in aiding the formation of distinct and definitive conceptions,—it is not of any great practical importance and need not be much pressed or insisted on, if men heartily and intelligently ascribe their forgiveness and acceptance wholly to what Christ has done and suffered in their room and stead. There is no ground in anything Calvin has written for asserting, that he would have denied or rejected this distinction, if it had been presented to him. But it was perhaps more in accordance with the cautious and reverential spirit in which he usually conducted his investigations into divine things, to abstain from any minute and definite statements regarding it.

A solid historical case can be made that the Westminster divines did not require imputation to be understood in the sense of a transfer, rather than a declarative reckoning. Nor did they require belief in the imputation of Christ's active obedience. It is fair to conclude that in the 1640s, believing that the passive obedience of Christ is sufficient to justify would have been adequate to sit on the Westminster Assembly and subscribe to the Westminster Standards. To claim anything else is historical revisionism.

8:29-30, Paul gets as close as anywhere to a dogmatic *ordo salutis* ("order of salvation"). Paul moves from *calling* (the work of the Spirit, bringing us to faith, and thereby uniting us to Christ) to *justification* (being declared righteous in Christ) to *glorification* (mature life in the Spirit of Christ). There is no separate step of "imputation" in the sequence. Paul does not say, "Whom he called, to them he transferred Christ's righteousness, and on that basis declared them justified."[33]

Why make an issue of these things? God's justification of his people is not a matter of doing a calculation in his head. It is not a bookkeeping event, in which righteousness is treated like electronic currency and shuffled around in heavenly bank accounts. Rather, justification is an aspect of our concrete union with the Savior. It is intensely and thoroughly personal. It is not an abstract transaction, but a personal participation. It's not a business deal but a marriage. (Remember, marriages are covenanted relationships, but they have a legal dimension included within the relationship.)

Personal union is at the core of biblical theology. Going back to the OT, Messiah's job description includes doing *for* his people and *as* his people what they cannot achieve for themselves. That's just how messiahship works. As N. T. Wright has pointed out in various places, "messiahship" (or "Christology") is, in the very nature of the case, an incorporative concept.[34] Take an example from the OT. How did the Israelites share in David's victory over Goliath (1 Sam. 17)? That victory was not transferred to each individual Israelite. Rather, David stood in the place of the people as their anointed (Messianic) representative (1 Sam. 16). His victory was counted as their victory because he was their covenant head. David, prefiguring Jesus, is no mere individual; he was a *corporate*

---

33. It seems to me that treating imputation as a transfer of Christ's righteousness/merits, and therefore as a discrete step in the *ordo*, causes insuperable problems. Does this transfer come *before* union with Christ? If so, we have the oddity of being righteous outside of Christ, contra Romans 8:1 and 1 Corinthians 1:30. Does it come *after* union with Christ? In that case, we have to ask what the transfer adds since if we already have Christ, we have righteousness and every other blessing.

34. This is why the whole people (*totus Christus*) can be named "Christ" in texts such as 1 Corinthians 12:12 and Galatians 3:16.

person, bearing Israel on his shoulders. The nation was lodged in David's very person, by means of covenant union, so that when he cast the sling, Israel cast the sling. The nation defeated Goliath in him and as him, as he stood as their representative champion.

So it is with Jesus. As Messiah/Christ, he bears his people in himself. We share in his legal status because we are in him. He does not transfer righteousness or merits to our accounts; rather, he incorporates us into himself, making his account a joint account. All that he possesses is freely shared with us. If the head is justified, how could the body be condemned? If the husband is one flesh with the bride, how can she fail to share in all that he possesses? He has "married" us to himself precisely so he can own our liability and so we can share in his status. The old saying goes: As the Savior, so the saved. Or: As the Christ, so the church. He is the Righteous One (cf. Isa. 53:11; Acts 3:14, 7:52, 22:14; 1 John 2:1); as we are identified with him, we are righteous as well.

Reformed theologians have sometimes subtly slipped off of this point. For example, it is not uncommon to hear talk of being clothed with Christ's righteousness as a way of explaining imputation (cf. Zech. 3:1-5). But the reality is that we are clothed with *Christ himself* (cf. Gal. 3:27)! The Lord does not transfer righteousness to us, as if the Giver and his gift could be pried apart; rather, he *is* our righteousness (Jer. 33:16). In 1 Corinthians 1:30, Paul does not say Christ's righteousness is our righteousness; he says *Christ* is our righteousness. Righteousness inheres in him as a property of his person as the crucified-and-risen God-man; we access and possess that righteousness not by means of a transfer (as if Christ could separated from his righteousness) but by means of personal union (as a man and woman come into possession of one another's goods upon getting married). 2 Corinthians 5:21 does not say anything about a transfer of righteousness from Christ to us; rather it describes the status that is ours *in Christ*. The only imputation in this text is the non-imputation of sins which, as we have seen in our discussion of Romans, is equivalent to the forgiveness of sins. Becoming God's righteousness happens via union, as we share in the death and resurrection of Christ.[35] In Philippians 3:9, Paul expresses his desire to have a righteousness (right standing/status) not from the law, but from God. But in the surrounding context, it is very evident that this gift of divine righteousness is found only through union with Christ, as we *share* in his sufferings and resurrection by faith. The passage no more teaches the imputation of God's righteousness to us than it teaches the imputation of the law's righteousness.[36]

The view being articulated here – that there are no benefits apart from or outside of union with the Benefactor – has been called "inclusive substitution." The point is that Christ and his people are so conjoined and incorporated into one another that when he died on the cross, he not only died *for* us, but *as* us. He bears our sin and liability because we have been grafted into him. Note Paul's language in 2 Corinthians 5:14: "If One died for all, then *all* died." Christ's people died with and in him on the cross. In other words, Christ was not some third party standing between us and God. He *is* his people. He is one flesh with them (Eph. 5:31-32). His death is their death; his life is their life. He represents humanity as the Last Adam, the Truly Human One.[37]

---

35. See Bird, *The Saving Righteousness of God*, 82ff.
36. See Bird, *The Saving Righteousness of God*, 81.
37. "Inclusive substitution" is the surest defense against the charge that the Protestant view of justification is a legal fiction. So far from giving way to Rome, my formulations actually fortify our anti-Roman defenses! See Miroslav Volf, *Free of Charge: Giving and Forgiving in a Culture Stripped of Grace* (Grand Rapids, MI: Zondervan, 2005). Volf, ch. 4, contrasts "inclusive" and "exclusive" substitution in terms that end up sounding a lot like classic (e.g., John Williamson Nevin vs. Charles Hodge) and current debates. Volf argues that Christ did not so much die *for* us, setting us free from having to die, as he died *as* us, so that what happened to him has actually happened to us. Christ's doing and dying and rising counts as ours because of the deep personal bond that exists between himself and his people. As Volf says (149), Christ's life is not "an alien life, imposed on us from the outside." It is not "like a Mickey Mouse figure that waves at kids at the entrance of Disneyland – a mere costume..." Rather, "united with Christ, we live in God and God lives in us." Volf (150f; cf. 200), following Luther, argues at length that imputation is a judicial effect of union:

> To describe the imputation of Christ's righteousness, Luther used a metaphor from the world of personal relations. Following the apostle Paul, he likened the soul's union with Christ to marriage. Christ is the bridegroom, and the soul is the "poor, wicked, harlot" who becomes his bride. Since they are one flesh, he takes from her

Even so, at the same time, Christ is God.. After all, "*God was in Christ* reconciling the world to himself" (2 Cor. 5:19). So we were in Christ when he died – but God was in Christ as well. The incarnate Son was acting as both True Man and True God when he gave himself unto death. Again, he was not a third party representing God, but God himself in human form. Thus: All that he did, we did. All that he did, God did. Christ stands on our side, a sinless substitute for sinful humanity. But he also stands on God's side, as the wronged-yet-forgiving God who deals with his own wrath on the cross.[38] He is the embodiment of God's faithfulness and human faithfulness at one and the same time, satisfying both sides of the covenant relationship.

A Modified Version of the Imputation of Christ's Active Obedience?

Before moving ahead, it might be helpful to clarify one aspect of the picture just drawn. As some have analyzed my view of union and imputation, they have concluded that I am not *really* rejecting the imputation of Christ's active obedience (as my writings have claimed), but merely *modifying* (and perhaps expanding) what it means. After all, I *do* affirm that we are united to Christ in

---

all her failings and incapacities and gives her all his uprightness and power. He "suffered, died, descended into hell that he might overcome" all her sins. "Her sins cannot now destroy her, since they are laid upon Christ and swallowed up by him. And she has that righteousness in Christ, her husband, of which she may boast of as her own and confidently display alongside her sins in the face of death and hell.". . . Because we are one, Christ's life is our life. Because we are one, Christ's qualities are our qualities. Because we are one, we have died in Christ's death, and our sins are no longer ours but are "swallowed up" by Christ.

The marriage illustration is useful in this discussion because it situates the legal within a covenant relationship, instead of leaving it abstract.

38. Again, the best contemporary statement of this view of Christ's work is found in Volf, *Free of Charge*, ch. 4. Volf argues that moral liability as such cannot be transferred. God can only separate sinners from their sin – he can only condemn the deed while forgiving the doer – by becoming one with humanity in Christ's very person, and dying humanity's death. *Only death separates the sin from the sinner*. At the same time, Christ is one with God – such that God has placed human sin onto himself so that he can bear away its curse. The divine judge judges against himself. Christ is not a third party, inserted between God and man; he is the obedient man and the wronged God in one divine-human person.

the fullness of his work, so that his "story" is now our "story," and I do believe Christ was actively obedient to his Father for the whole of his life.

All that is well and good. I am happy to admit that I hold to a "modified" version of the popular doctrine. But I would throw in four important caveats to qualify what that might mean and to show where I would still criticize what has become the standard model of "the imputation of Christ's active obedience."

First, to say that we are united to Christ in his pre-cross obedience is not the same as saying that that pre-cross obedience is justifying. After all, his pre-cross life could not deliver us from our death sentence/condemnation, which is what justification is all about. In addition, I would rather say that Christ's *righteousness* (in the sense of his judicial right-standing before the Father as the Risen One) is *shared* with us, rather than saying his *active obedience* (his thirty-three years of law-keeping) is *imputed* to us. I can understand how a verdict can be shared via union, as God makes the same declaration over us that he made over his Son. It is not as clear to me that his life of obedience can be imputed, given the way Paul uses imputation language (see the above discussion). If Christ's righteousness is understood as his resurrection verdict, rather than his life of obedience prior to the resurrection, we actually get more of what Christ possesses, rather than less.

What role, then, does the pre-cross active obedience play? As stated above, Paul always seems to ground our justification specifically in the death and resurrection of Christ. His law-keeping is important, but remains in the background. It might be best to say that Christ's obedience is the ground of his own justification/resurrection, and his justification/resurrection (that is, his righteous status) then becomes ours. So, we move backwards from our justification on the basis his resurrection, to the basis of his resurrection, which is his obedience. The active obedience explains why death could not hold him, why he had to be vindicated against death, why the verdict of justification was sure. Thus, we get his active obedience indirectly, as we share in the judicial verdict that obedience brought about in the resurrection. This is not how the "imputation of Christ's active obedience" doctrine usually works in contemporary Reformed theology, but it is another way of getting to the same result. But note that the place of the active obedience in our justification is never on the surface of the biblical texts; we have to dig down deep to find its role. It is not the centerpiece in Pauline theology the way it has become such in some versions of Reformed theology.

Second, the view of the imputation of Christ's active obedience I have been critical of presupposes and is correlative to a meritorious covenant of works. The imputed active obedience doctrine, as it is presently espoused in Reformed circles, was created to satisfy the requirements of a particular view of the Adamic covenant, in which Adam was called to earn eschatological life through his works. But that view is highly suspect. There is no doctrine of merit to be found in Genesis 1-2. Everything in the text indicates that Adam was graced with gift upon gift, all unearned. His glorious starting position was a free blessing; the mature, eschatological life he was implicitly promised upon condition of perfect, faithful obedience would have been a gift as well. He was a favored son awaiting an inheritance, not an employee seeking an earned wage. But if the first Adam was not required to earn merit through works, then the active obedience of the last Adam need not be regarded as meritorious either.[39]

The idea is sometimes set forth that the cross removes the curse, and thus brings us back to "neutral ground" (e.g. Ian Duguid in *CJPM*, 83). The active obedience, then, earns the blessings God had promised in his covenants to covenant keepers. But this is a tragic devaluation of the cross and simply does not square with anything in the Scriptures. There is no such thing as "neutral ground" before God. Adam was created not in a state of neutrality

---

39 For a more complete analysis of the Adamic covenant, see Peter Leithart's contribution to this volume, "Adam the Catholic," as well as my essay "A Response to 'The Biblical Plan of Salvation'" in Beisner, *The Auburn Avenue Theology*. If "merit" simply refers to Christ overcoming the demerit of the Adamic situation, or the infinite worth of his finished work, then it is not problematic (except for the confusion the term itself brings). But when a doctrine of merit is rooted in the Adamic covenant itself, it becomes a distortion of the filial nature of the Bible's covenant theology.

but righteousness and blessing. So the model of Duguid is flawed from the outset. Moreover, the biblical witness never says that the cross simply returns us to a neutral position before God. Instead, it ascribes our whole redemption to his blood (Rom. 3:24-25; 5:9). In addition, there are no biblical texts that describe Jesus' pre-cross obedience in terms of "earning." In fact, *there are no specific redemptive benefits attributed to his pre-cross obedience.* Scripture does not ever present the pre-cross work of Christ as a discrete step in his achievement of redemption. If the "imputation of Christ's active obedience" is paired with a "meritorious covenant of works" we may end up with a logically tight theological system, but it will not rest on a solid exegetical base.

There are other problems we could identify here. If we have the forgiveness of sins in his cross and justification in his resurrection, what more could we want? How can forgiveness be equated with mere neutrality? Doesn't forgiveness presuppose and include reconciliation and acceptance? What can the active obedience add that would not already be included in the death (removing the curse) and resurrection (bringing legal vindication and new life)? What further blessings are there to earn or merit?

Third, whereas as the active obedience formula found in *CJPM* emphasizes how Jesus *kept* the law, the version of active obedience advocated in my writings emphasizes how Jesus *fulfilled* the law. Yes, Jesus lived the truly obedient human life that Israel, as a new Adamite nation, should have rendered. But this wasn't a matter of obeying a set of discrete commands in order earn justification. Rather, it was matter of *typologically fulfilling Israel's whole history in order to bring in the eschatological era.* Certainly that included keeping the commands of the Torah, by which old covenant life was maintained (Lev. 18:5). But it also included much more – ultimately bringing in a new covenant. The gospels were written in such a way as to focus on Jesus not merely as keeping the righteous demands of the law, but especially to show Jesus bearing and fulfilling Israel's national identity and vocation. Jesus succeeds precisely where Adam and Israel failed, in essence rewriting their unfaithful histories with his own life of faithfulness. But that faithfulness is more than his sinlessness; it is his recapitulating and completing the covenant story that began to be told in the Hebrew Scriptures. The problem with the active obedience formula in *CJPM* is that it is too thin; it does not give wide enough scope to the fullness of Christ's work.[40]

Fourth, the "imputation of Christ's active obedience" formula, as usually espoused today, works with a flawed understanding of "imputation." This has already been demonstrated above, and there is no need to rehash the arguments. In short, the model of "imputation" I am critiquing (as found in *CJPM* and elsewhere) assumes that the purpose of Jesus' obedience was to acquire merit which would then be transferred over to his people. But this is off point, as far as the biblical writers are concerned. Jesus did not obey in order to acquire merits. He obeyed in order that he might be the sinless sacrifice for sin, thereby bringing Adamic humanity to full glory and maturity through his resurrection. We get the benefits of his work not by means of a bookkeeping event (transferring merits from his account to ours), but by virtue of our personal union with him. When the Spirit unites us to the Son by faith, the Father's righteous verdict over him is pronounced over us as well. To be true to Scripture's use of imputation language, we should speak of being united to Christ in his obedient life, so that his resurrection status is imputed as ours, rather than having his active obedience (or merits) imputed to us as a distinct part of his work.

---

40. See my "Christ Church Ministerial Conference: The Life of Justification (Lecture Notes)" for more details. At points, *CJPM* approximates what I am arguing for here, in terms of a typological understanding of Christ's active obedience, even though it is not where they usually put the accent. See, e.g., Ian Duguid's overview of the exile/exodus pattern and Matthew's gospel on pages 82-85. See also VanDrunen and Clark's discussion of Philippians 2:9 and New Adam Christology on pages 183-184. The irony, of course, is that these authors are leaning heavily on the insights of N. T. Wright in those sections. For an exemplary overview of how Jesus' life fulfills Israel's history from within the narrative of Matthew's gospel, see Peter Leithart's essay "Jesus as Israel: The Typological Structure of Matthew's Gospel," available at http://www.leithart.com/pdf/jesus-as-israel-the-typological-structure-of-matthew-s-gospel.pdf. Leithart proves Matthew's gospel is written to show that Jesus "does Israel right" from beginning to end. Obviously if we are united to Christ, that whole history is regarded as ours.

Union, Imputation, and Legal Fiction

How, then, should we picture union with Christ in relation to imputation and justification? How do we fit imputation into union? We already touched on this, but it might be helpful to paint a more detailed picture at this point. My own journey into these issues began when I was a newbie Bible study teacher years ago. I was teaching a group of kids a lesson on justification and used a familiar illustration that went something like this:

> Imagine that you have to take a test on quantum physics. You are clueless, completely unable to answer any of the questions correctly. You write in answers, but all of them are wrong. You are bound to fail. But then Someone comes and offers to take the test for you. He erases all your wrong answers and writes in perfectly correct answers. He then hands in the test with your name on it.

After giving the illustration, I asked the kids, "What would you call that?" I was expecting an answer that pointed to the graciousness of the arrangement. I was expecting them to note that erasing the wrong answers corresponded to Christ's blood; writing in the right answers corresponded to Christ's life of perfect obedience. Instead, a rather precocious junior high boy blurted out "Cheating!" I knew right then that I was going to have to rework the way I presented the doctrine. My homely illustration (which I had heard used multiple times by preachers over the years in various forms) was open to the "legal fiction" charge. In that moment, I suddenly understood more fully why scholars like Richard Gaffin and Anthony Hoekema put such emphasis on union with Christ. I understood what Gaffin meant when he called union with Christ the "central motif" in Paul's view of salvation applied and denied that imputation could have a "discrete structure of its own."[41] I

---

41. Gaffin, *Resurrection and Redemption*, 132. Gaffin's book masterfully demonstrates the exegetical and theological problems with conceiving of imputation as an extrinsic transfer of righteousness. Gaffin's work rightly locates our justification in the resurrection of Christ, which becomes ours via union. He says, "the act of being raised with Christ in its constitutive transforming character is at the same time judicially declarative; that is, the

understood in a fresh way what one of the Puritans meant when he said union with Christ is "the sole fountain of blessedness."

The only way to properly ground imputation (and other attendant doctrines, like the "great exchange," and penal substitution) is with a rich, thick doctrine of union with Christ. There has to be some relational framework which makes it "legal" for Christ to act in our stead, and for us to share in what is his.[42] Focusing on union with Christ as the sum and substance of salvation does not mean the various aspects of salvation are blurred or confused, any more than the light and heat of the sun are indistinct. Within the *one gift* of salvation in Christ, there are *manifold particular gifts*. We can still speak of justification, regeneration, adoption, sanctification, etc. as distinct blessings, like so many colors refracted through a prism from one beam of light. But all of those blessings are ours by virtue of union with the Savior. That is to say, the gift of Christ is the Gift of gifts because he contains all other gifts in his glorified person.

The book of Philemon gives a helpful illustration of the relationship between union and imputation, even though it is not about justification per se. Philemon 18 is the closest we come to imputation-as-transfer in Pauline corpus, but it also shows that imputation of *any* sort only works within a framework of relational union. Paul tells Philemon to charge to him whatever Onesimus owes. Note that this is a different term than the one found in Romans 4. Paul uses *logizomai* in Romans 4; *ellelgo* is used in Philemon. Terminological differences are important, but the overall shape of things in Philemon still meshes well with what we have seen in

---

act of being joined to Christ is conceived imputatively. In this sense the enlivening action of resurrection (incorporation) is itself a forensically constitutive declaration."

42. For a contrary view, see Scott Clark's comments in *CJPM*, 258-9 and his blog post at http://www.oceansideurc.org/the-heidelblog/2007/2/13/what-is-your-only-comfort-5.html. Clark admits that he has changed how he views the relationship of union to imputation over the years. But he has ended up with a view that essentially caves in to the legal fiction charge. Because he has severed forensic imputation from organic union, all he can say is that God gives us Christ's righteousness by a bare divine fiat. Thanks to Jonathan Barlow for pressing the issue with Clark and exposing the implications of his approach.

Romans. The underlying rationale for Paul assuming Onesiumus' debts is their relational bond, described in terms of regenerative/adoptive sonship (Phlm. 10) and brotherhood (Phlm. 16). Paul considers Onesimus one with himself (Phlm. 17; cf. Phlm. 10, 12). Paul making Onesimus' debt his own presupposes their brotherly union with one another "in the Lord" (Phlm. 16). They are in partnership, which indicates a common life and shared goods (Phlm. 17). Paul is imitating Christ in bearing the burden of his brother in Christ and paying his debts (cf. Gal. 6:2). But note: here, as elsewhere, union provides the matrix for imputation. Or, to put it another way, imputation (Paul being charged with Onesimus' debts) is the financial aspect of their union with one another (their brotherly partnership), just as imputed righteousness is the forensic aspect of the believer's union with Christ. Paul shares in Onesimus' debts and Onesimus shares in Paul's resources via their incorporation into one another in Christ. The analogies with our salvation are easy to detect. Obviously, Paul is playing Jesus to Onesimus and acting in Onesimus' stead as his representative substitute. Paul wants Philemon to receive Onesimus as if he were Paul, in the same way that the Father receives the believer as if he were Jesus.

The overarching point of our rather extended discussion, then, is that Paul *always* situates imputation in the framework of union. Imputation is not a transfer but a reckoning in view of a covenanted relationship. Thus, Paul *never* uses imputation language to describe the extrinsic transfer of merit or righteousness from Christ to the believer. That's just not the way the language works. Instead, imputation describes God's declaration or reckoning of us as righteous *in Christ*. Imputation does not point primarily to a bookkeeping metaphor but to God's judicial reckoning of our new relationship with him through Christ. Union with Christ is the broad, all-encompassing framework in which the application of redemption is worked out, including its imputative element. Those who speak in terms of imputation as a transfer of righteousness are not compromising the gospel in any serious way (obviously), but they are blurring the Pauline picture in a significant way. Justification is not something that happens outside of or in abstraction from union with Christ, but is found within the gift of Christ himself

When we situate justification (and the related doctrine of imputation) within the framework of union with Christ, we are able to keep justification firmly connected to the church, sacraments, and moral transformation. Union with Christ has a declarative (imputative), judicial aspect, along with other aspects. Union with Christ integrates the forensic and the transformative, the individual and the corporate, the experiential and the ecclesial/sacramental.[43] Union with Christ holds together those blessings that tend to drift apart in alternative approaches to applied soteriology.

My continual impression with critics of the view I have been depicting, such as those in the *CJPM* volume, is that they take "salvation" to be basically synonymous with "forensic justification." "Sanctification" is then tacked on, as extrinsic proof that justification has taken place. Justification and sanctification derive from independent principles (e.g., distinct legal and mystical unions with Christ) and do not really form a united, organic whole. Union with Christ as outlined here is the answer to this kind of disjointed, amalgamated soteriology.[44]

---

43. Contrary to the theological intuitions of some, I would argue that union with Christ is experiential *precisely because* it is ecclesial and sacramental. It is in the life of the church (including participation in the sacraments) that we come to experience the grace of Christ in a personalized way. This essay does not address the relation of the sacraments to justification, but see Peter Leithart's web entries, "Justification by Faith," http://www.leithart.com/archives/003081.php, and "Justification and Sacramental Theology," http://www.leithart.com/archives/000818.php for the connection between a robust view of baptismal efficacy, union with Christ, and *sola fide*. See also my essay, "Do I Believe in Baptismal Regeneration?" available at http://www.trinity-pres.net/liturgy.php. This is a topic "Federal Vision" writings have treated rather extensively, so I will not broach it any further here.

44. Clark ends up talking about two different kinds of union with Christ (legal and vital) in *CJPM*, 262. But is there some higher kind of union that holds these two sorts of union together? How do legal and vital unions relate? For Clark, these are unanswered (and perhaps unanswerable) questions.

In that same context, Clark takes me to task for implying that "we retain that union partly by cooperating with grace," thus turning "gospel" into "law." But this is a flawed argument. I certainly acknowledge the indicative (we *are* united to Christ) as the basis of the imperative (we *must remain* united to Christ). While remaining united to Christ is a matter of persevering faith (cf. Jn. 15), it is not something we do in our own strength, but

Justification, Legalism, and Corporate Identities

Both the "Federal Vision" and the "New Perspective on Paul" have been tarred and feathered with the charge that they make justification more social than salvific. But in a union with Christ model, there is no dichotomy. Salvation is for the one and the many; union with Christ is an intrinsically communal concept, but it applies soteriologically to individuals as well. Individuals are saved, but not individually; salvation is always a corollary of incorporation into *totus Christus*. As Bird puts it, "Paul's notion of God's saving righteousness includes *both* a declaration that those who profess faith in Christ have been graciously granted a right-standing in a right relationship with God, and also that they are thereby constituted as full equal members of God's covenant people."[45] In other words, Paul's in-Christ theology answers to both works-righteousness and race-righteousness, both merit theology and Jewish nationalism, both individual pride and corporate pride. Justification in Christ is a basis for both assurance of forgiveness and table fellowship with other believers. Justification not only issues us into a new relationship with God; it also constitutes a new, cosmopolitan community. There is no need to dichotomize individual salvation and corporate identity.[46]

Paul argues Israel's pursuit of justification in Torah is flawed not only because it abuses the Torah and thus misses the true *telos* of the Torah, not only because it promotes prideful self-reliance, but also because it excludes Gentiles (Rom. 9:30-10:21; cf. Gal. 2:11-21). But these really resolve into a single problem. Indeed, from an ultimate point of view (as I have argued elsewhere),[47] nationalism is just

---

as the Spirit enables (as I have always made clear). Clark's critique amounts to a cheap shot.
45. Bird, *The Saving Righteousness of God*, 113. See also 4-5, 33-35.
46. It is hard for me to see what is gained by continuing to screen out the Jew/Gentile issue from the doctrine of justification. My guess is that the larger issue here derives from a rejection of the flow of redemptive history, which goes hand in hand with the transmutation of the "law" in Paul from the Mosaic Torah to a timeless system of moral principles. The scandal of particularity rears its head all over the NT.
47. See my essay "The PCA and the NPP" as well as my "N. T. Wright and Reformed Theology: Friends or Foes," *Reformation and Revival Journal*, Vol. 11, No. 2, 47-48n6. Self-

another form of legalism. Though nationalism/racism is typically a corporate idol and Pelagianism/self-salvation is typically an individual idol, both are simply primal manifestations of human pride and unbelief. The answer to both is union with Christ and justification by faith. In Christ, our attempts to earn God's favor are shown to be bankrupt. Our hope must be pinned to the death and resurrection of Israel's Messiah and not our own efforts or abilities. At the same time, our desire to belong to a "new humanity" is redirected to the church catholic, which offers an equal share in redemption to every tribe, nation, people, and tongue. Union with Christ binds together the social and soteriological as two sides of the same coin; in Christ we are reconciled to God and to one another as part of a single, integrated work of salvation.

Nowhere is this seen more clearly than in Galatians. In this epistle, Paul uses the doctrine of justification to resolve Jew/Gentile tensions over Torah observance in the new age inaugurated by Christ. The Jewish "agitators" were using the badges of Torah to construct a false identity. Paul deconstructs that identity by showing that Torah does not do what they think it does, and moreover, the Torah-covenant has been eschatologically superseded by Christ and the Spirit, a point they should grasp if they are attuned to the flow of the biblical metanarrative. For example, the Torah's built-in obsolescence, compared to the Abrahamic covenant, is demonstrated in 3:15-4:31). God is one, and thus must have one family in the end. But the Torah cannot mediate the one family, so it cannot be a part of the final, eschatological form of the covenant. Like a gallon of milk, it is good for a while, but after its expiration date, turns sour. The Torah focused the curse on Israel, but once Jesus (as the True Israel) exhausted that curse on the cross, the Torah covenant had fulfilled its historical purpose and it is no longer in force.[48]

---

salvation and sectarian exclusivism feed off of one another, in the same way that justification by faith through grace brings together reconciliation with God and fellowship with his people. Those with the deepest understanding of justification should also have the strongest commitment to Christian community and ecumenicity.

48. Obviously the old covenant revelation remains authoritative Scripture for us, and

It is important to note how justification *functions* in Paul's letter to Galatians. It is not just an answer to the question, "How do I get saved?" Paul is doing a lot more than refuting Pelagianism in the epistle. The whole redemptive-historical backdrop to the letter would be unnecessary if that was the entire agenda. Instead, Paul uses the doctrine of justification by faith apart from works of the law/Torah to demarcate the bounds of table fellowship and to specify the identity of Abraham's covenant family. In other words, the doctrine of justification answers questions about fellowship and church life. It provides structure and shape for the covenant community. It is a sociological doctrine (though not in a way that weakens its soteriological force).

What does Paul mean by "works of the law" in Galatians? No one involved in the "Federal Vision" that I am aware of argues that the phrase "works of the law" refers to the law exclusively in its "boundary marker" function.[49] Rather, it describes life under the Mosaic covenant as a whole (especially as that form of life took shape in the second temple period). Thus, "works of the law" refers to the whole way of life God gave to Israel, indeed, to the whole of the Torah's legislation, not merely the symbolic/ceremonial "boundary marker" elements. The phrase "works of the law" describes Jewish life and culture; the phrase sums up the Jewish mode of life as it existed under the old covenant order.

That being said, when Jews intermixed with pagans in the wider world (especially in the post-exile situation), those covenant "boundary markers" became especially important ways of maintaining and manifesting Jewish identity – "acid tests" of loyalty to

---

thus we find Paul appealing to it to establish various doctrinal and ethical points. But the Mosaic covenant is not our covenant; it can only be useful to us as it is interpreted and applied in light of Christ's death and resurrection.

49. When Michael Horton claims otherwise (without any proof), he shows he is quite ignorant of the positions he is supposedly critiquing (*CJPM*, 211). Horton's entire thesis in *CJPM* chapter 7 rests on a totally misguided attempt to collapse the "Federal Vision," the "New Perspective on Paul," the "covenant nomism" of second temple Judaism, and medieval Catholicism into one another. Horton's overly ambitious project fails at virtually every turn, as I demonstrated in "Blurring the Federal Vision." There are wide differences in these various movements and perspectives; Horton's article is only able to advance his agenda by distorting, ignoring, and glossing over these distinctions.

the covenant, as Don Garlington has put it. Thus, it is not surprising to see circumcision, dietary regulations, and calendrical observances rise to the surface in the discussion in Galatians. But we should keep in mind Paul is always dealing with the Torah as unit, an integrated whole, a covenantal system. His target is those who are insisting that one must become a Jew in order to be a Christian (cf. Acts 15:1), so he has to take up the place of old covenant law in the new creation situation. Because that law created social/sacral boundaries between people, he has to show why those are no longer in force.

Is this a "New Perspective" reading of Galatians? In some ways, yes. But Paul's polemic against seeking justification in "works of the law" is actually a place where the "old" and "new" readings of Paul can converge quite nicely. If distinctively Jewish "works of the law," prescribed by Torah, could not serve to justify humanity before God, then it makes no sense to say Gentiles must come under Torah and do its works to be justified. If works of the law were ineffectual to justify Jews, they are unnecessary for Gentiles. If the "works of the law" program doesn't justify those who have the law "by nature," it won't work for those who don't have the law "by nature" (cf. Gal. 2:15) either. *No flesh* can be justified by "works of the law." This is true whether considered from the standpoint of human sin (which is impotent to please God in itself) or from the standpoint of why God gave Torah in the first place (which was never to provide a way of self-justification, but to set aside Israel as the bearer of his redemptive program for a time).

Here is the key point: This polemic against specifically Jewish "works of the law" (the view of the "New Perspective") feeds quite easily into a polemic against *any* form of moralistic, Pelagian works (the view of the "Old Perspective"). If no Jewish works can justify, then neither can any Gentile works (however understood). If not even the God-ordained Torah can serve as an instrument of justification, then no Gentile code of ethics (natural law, Kant's categorical imperative, Fletcher's situational ethics, Aristotle's golden mean, or whatever) can. If Moses cannot justify, neither can Plato or Mill or Sartre. In other words, the "New Perspective" reading, focused on Paul's polemic against Torah, can actually serve *to re-*

inforce and strengthen the chief application of the "Old Perspective" reading! The "New Perspective" interpretation, in all its redemptive-historical specificity, aimed at apostate Judaizers, actually undergirds the more generalized reading offered by traditional Protestants, aimed at human hubris in whatever form it appears. So Paul's soteriology (justification by faith) and sociology (Jew and Gentile believers formed into one new humanity) mutually reinforce one another; we cannot advocate one without also advocating the other. And by reading the text in its first century context, we actually lose none of the applications we want to make to the church and world in our own day; indeed, the applications are only enriched and enlivened.

The same points ultimately hold true in Romans. We cannot build the exegetical case here, but it seems fitting that the closing chapters (15-16) should be viewed as the summit of the letter. In his final words, Paul calls Jews and Gentiles to blend together (with their lips and their lives) into one song of praise to the Lord (15:1-13). Paul's goal is that a unified Christian community in Rome would embody and fulfill the prophetic hope, described in the chain of quotations in 15:9-12. The greeting list Paul gives in chapter 16, then, is not just a sign of apostolic friendliness; it is an embodiment of the gospel message Paul has been declaring in the letter, as he turns "justification by faith" into "fellowship by faith." For Paul, justification apart from works of the law inevitably gives rise to a new family and new way of life. This is a main thread of his gospel, one he has woven into the heart of the letter again and again.[50]

Conclusion: Forging Ahead in the Reformed Tradition

Our series of "postcards" is now complete.[51] We can stand

---

50. For a helpful study of the connection between Paul's doctrine of justification and his eschatological ethics, see Oliver O'Donovan, *Resurrection and Moral Order: An Outline for Evangelical Ethics* (Grand Rapids, MI: Eerdmans, 1994).
51. Obviously, I have left out some key issues. In particular, readers may wonder how the "Federal Vision" view of apostasy fits into the pictures of justification drawn here. Is it possible for someone to be justified initially but fail to reach final justification? Though I do believe apostasy is a reality, that's not quite the way I would put it. Whatever "justification" a covenant member can receive by virtue of church membership or temporary

back and compare the composite pictures of the "Federal Vision," and contributors to *CJPM*. The uniqueness of the "Federal Vision," over against the authors of *CJPM*, is that it tries to account for *all* that the Bible teaches about justification, instead of filtering out portions of Scripture that do not fit with a preconceived dogmatic structure. The "Federal Vision" ends up with a considerably thicker, richer doctrine of justification. At the same, the "Federal Vision" is probably less concerned with making particular mechanics of justification a test of orthodoxy (e.g., the imputation of Christ's active obedience), and more concerned with relating justification (and other applied aspects of our union with Christ) to the overall flow of covenant history.

But this is not just a conflict over who has the better, fuller understanding of justification. It is really a conflict between "catholic" and "sectarian" versions of the Reformed faith. The *CJPM* authors would be content to remain ensconced in a Reformed ghetto, maintaining denominational and institutional status quo. They only venture out of their Reformed bunker to fire a few shots at Christians from other traditions now and then. The "Federal Vision," on the other hand, would like to learn from and share with other traditions within Christendom, trusting that God will continue to bring his church to greater confessional maturity and unity in the time to come.[52] Those involved in the "Federal Vision"

---

faith (e.g., Matt. 18:21-35; 2 Pet. 2:1) must be distinguished from the justification that a persevering, elect individual receives. If nothing else, the "justification" received by the one who will apostatize is not an anticipation of the verdict he will receive at the last day, as it is in the case of the one who will persevere. God knows this because he decreed it, and that undoubtedly colors his attitude (in some way) towards the one who will apostatize, even before that apostasy takes place. Without going into more detail, I would point to the language of the Belgic Confession, Article 22 which sums up the matter nicely by calling faith "the instrument that *keeps us* in communion with him [Christ] and with all his benefits" (emphasis added). Whatever conclusions we may draw about apostasy and the temporary benefits that covenant breakers possess before they fall away, it must be insisted that faith is the means by which the elect are *kept* in union with Christ, and therefore the means by which they *remain* in a state of justification. If faith dies, union with Christ is lost, as well as the corresponding benefits.

52. Predictably, Clark accepts the notion of doctrinal development/maturation up until the writing of his favorite Reformed confession (333f). Then everything freezes. So, for example, law/gospel confusion in the church fathers does not make them unorthodox,

are not looking for heretics hiding behind every bush. Ecumenical interaction certainly poses certain risks, but it is a calling we are commanded to undertake, as we pursue oneness with all of God's people (John 17:2-26; Eph. 4:1-16). In other words, the problem is that the "Federal Vision" appears to be messing with supposedly fixed boundary markers. It tampers with Reformed identity, by its openness to the Bible, other traditions, and the ongoing work of the Holy Spirit in the church.[53] In the spirit of *semper reformanda*, those on the "Federal Vision" side are not so much "reformed" as "reforming." The "Federal Vision" refuses to treat cherished theological positions as finished products; there is always more to learn, new questions to ask, new insights to discover.

However, at the same time, the "Federal Vision" is a radically conservative movement, going back behind Enlightenment rationalism and American revivalism, in an effort to recover the original, full orbed vision the Reformers. The "Federal Vision" has largely been fueled by a rediscovery of the high ecclesiology of Calvin and Bucer. The "Federal Vision" has largely been driven by a renewed movement back to the original sources of the Protestant Reformation. "Federal Vision" writings very often play

---

but when the same "error" crops up in the "Federal Vision," it's considered an "attack" on the gospel because it occurs sometime after 1517. The arbitrariness of Clark's understanding of historical theology should be obvious. Clark also illegitimately narrows the breadth of the historic Reformed tradition, but we cannot explore that here.

53. It is telling that Clark spends a good portion of his introductory chapter wrestling with the issue of Reformed identity, taking pains to distance the Reformed faith as much as possible from every other identifiable tradition in Christendom, including evangelicalism (6ff). Clark attempts to give a sociological explanation for the rise of the "Federal Vision." However accurate he may be with regard to the blending of confessional Reformed churches into broad evangelicalism (and much of what he says is undoubtedly correct), I think he has misconstrued the origins, agenda, and placement of the "Federal Vision."

Even more telling is Clark's blog post claiming that (his version of) Reformed theology is a perfected system (http://www.oceansideurc.org/the-heidelblog/2007/2/2/wilson-is-right-2.html). He says of the "Federal Vision" men, "They are like kids taking apart a Hamilton 992B (a fine railroad watch). They don't know what they're doing. The pieces are all over the floor. Who gave them the authority to play with the watch in the first place? It was running perfectly." So much for *semper reformanda*! The "Federal Vision" conversation is obviously going to be a challenge to anyone who thinks Reformed theology is already "running perfectly."

out in dialogue with classic Reformational works. It is something of a Reformed *ressourcement* movement.

So there is a "treasures old, treasures new" dynamic at work in the "Federal Vision." It is forging ahead, even as it seeks to retrieve the past. It seeks to learn something new and fresh, even as it seeks to relearn the old and proven. The critics, however, do not seem to like *either* aspect of the "Federal Vision." But thus far, they have done little more than demonstrate that the "Federal Vision" makes them uncomfortable; they have not offered compelling answers to the kinds of questions (cutting-edge biblical-theological and confessional/historical) that the "Federal Vision" has been asking. There are several reasons why those involved in the "Federal Vision" conversation are unlikely to be moved by the essays in *CJPM*.

The *CJPM* book as a whole is pervaded by a certain sloppiness. I have already brought attention to some of that sloppiness above, but a few more examples might be helpful. There is most certainly a terminological sloppiness. The *CJPM* authors repeatedly fail to define key terms, the definitions of which are *everything* in the current debate. For example, the index shows that the term "merit" appears on over 25 pages. But not *once* do they offer something like a working definition of "merit" that is exegetically defensible! This is remarkable, given how important they make merit out to be. If merit is so important to orthodoxy, surely it isn't that hard to define or prove from the text of Scripture. A lot of Latin gets thrown around, but at the end of the various discussions, *none* of the really crucial objections to merit theology have been answered. Surely the *CJPM* authors are aware of the fact that the meaning and (especially) the exegetical foundation of merit theology is hotly contested in the current (and historic) discussions. It is not something that can be taken for granted.[54]

---

[54] My own discussion of merit is found in "Rome Won't Have Me." I wrote there that, "In interacting with other Reformed theologians over the issue of merit in the aftermath of the colloquium, I have found a wide variety of views on merit, some of which I could easily live with (I don't just want to fight over words, after all)." See also Part 3 of my "A Response to the 2006 OPC Justification Report." In that essay, I raise a number of

The same is true with regard to the term "imputation." From the beginning of the "Federal Vision" controversy, the main issue here has been the meaning of this term. Is it a matter of how God reckons and regards us in Christ? Or is it an extrinsic transfer of righteousness from Christ's account to ours? But the *CJPM* book, while harping on the imputed righteousness of Christ as the *sine qua non* of orthodoxy, never engages in the work of defining and debating what "imputation" actually means. The result is that *CJPM* ends up failing to grapple with the concerns that are at stake in the "Federal Vision" conversation. The core issues are dodged and the driving questions remain unanswered.

The authors of *CJPM* are also quite sloppy in matters of historical theology. With remarkable audacity, Clark essentially calls everyone who does not share in his particular version of Reformed theology a "revisionist" (3; cf. 24, where he speaks as though the *CJPM* book represents the only perspective within authentic Calvinism). But Clark and colleagues have revised the Reformed faith themselves in all kinds of idiosyncratic ways.[55] Oft course,

---

questions about the theological coherence of merit. I also deal extensively with Philippians 2:9, a key prooftext. My discussion should be compared with *CJPM*, 183-4 and 202. Ultimately, the issue is not the word "merit," but how the category is defined, how it functions, and whether or not there is a better way to express what needs to be said.

55 For example, Clark has dismissed the teaching of the early Reformers and classic confessions on the issue of creation/Genesis 1. He has rejected the theocratic social order that all the magisterial Reformers presupposed, as reflected in the original confessions. And in many areas where there was diversity in the early Reformation period (e.g., the imputation of Christ's active obedience, which was disputed at least up through the Westminster Assembly in the 1640s) and in more recent eras (e.g., the structure of covenant theology in the John Murray/Meredith Kline debates), Clark has insisted that one particular strand within Reformed theology become an absolute, non-negotiable boundary marker for orthodoxy. Essentially, the authors of *CJPM* gerrymander the boundaries of the Reformed faith around their own feet. But Reformed orthodoxy has always been a field, with plenty of room to play and discuss, not a pinpoint, in which there is no room carved out for legitimate diversity or growth in exegetical maturity. Clark's claims to a monolithic Reformed tradition become even more suspect when one remembers that many of the Reformed confessions were compromise documents to begin with, drawn up with a built-in latitude on a number of doctrines. They were never meant to be the last word, and are undoubtedly historically and culturally conditioned. They are wonderful testimonies of our faith, but they do not settle every issue before the church today. For a succinct overview of Reformed confessionalism, see John Leith, *The Assembly at Westminster* (Richmond, VA: John Knox Press, 1973).

they are able to pull off the plausibility of their claims by setting themselves up as a magisterium that will interpret the Reformers and their confessions for the rest of us.

In reality, Clark repeatedly presses traditional Reformed theology into a mold that suits him. For example, as a way of buttressing his law/gospel hermeneutic, Clark and VanDrunen, following Godfrey, make the claim that the Reformed and Lutheran confessions share a common doctrine of justification (5n3, 56). But how plausible is that claim? If nothing else, it is very clear that the authors of *CJPM* do not give baptism the same role in justification that the Lutherans do. Indeed, on this point, the "Federal Vision" is much closer to Lutheranism![56]

The *CJPM* authors are sloppy dealing with the work of those they critique. By lumping the "Federal Vision" in with a variety of clearly aberrant movements, they create an aura of "guilt by association." In several instances, they simply sidestep the challenges that the "Federal Vision" poses to their particular version of Reformed theology. For example, Michael Horton's essay in chapter 7 is substantially a republication of his article "Déjà Vu All Over Again?" from the July/August 2004, issue of *Modern Reformation* (pages 23-30). I already responded to that piece a few years ago in my article "Blurring the Federal Vision."[57] But Horton's contribution to the *CJPM* does not even acknowledge the existence of my response, much less interact with its arguments and clarifications. That kind of irresponsible, half-baked scholarship pervades the whole book.

---

56. For example, Lutheran Johann Gerhard wrote, "the word and sacraments are instrumental causes [of justification] on the part of God, faith is the instrumental cause on God's part." Quoted in Lane, *Justification By Faith in Protestant-Catholic Dialogue: An Evangelical Assessment*, (New York: T and T Clark, 2002), 70n. This is standard Lutheran theology, but probably isn't compatible with the views set forth in *CJPM*. It would be very hard to imagine Lutherans writing a 465 page treatise on justification that only mentioned baptism on 3 pages! See also David Scaer, *Baptism* (St. Louis: The Luther Academy, 1999). Scaer writes, "The [Lutheran] Small Catechism lists the benefits of Baptism as effecting the forgiveness of sins, delivering from death and the devil, and granting eternal salvation...Basic to the Lutheran understanding of Baptism's effects is its bestowal of the forgiveness of sins, which assumes the presence of all of God's other benefits" (41).

57. Reading *CJPM* chapter 7 was definitely a "déjà vu" experience for me – but not a pleasant one!

The *CJPM* men have tried to make their critical task too easy by creating straw men and distorting the positions of those they oppose. If they really want to refute the supposed challenge of the "Federal Vision," they need to understand what it is and deal with it at its best. Most, if not all, of their significant objections have already been answered many times over. Their book is essentially a huge waste of time for those who would actually like to see the discussion over these issues move forward.

Another example: Clark suggests that some in the Reformed church are teaching that faith justifies *because* it is obeys (5). But *no one* in the current context has offered that formulation (even if Richard Baxter did). If anything, the "Federal Vision" has said that faith justifies because it unites us to Christ (as this essay, once again, demonstrates). Clark's critique has confused the qualities of justification's instrument with the causal ground of justification. On the same page, Clark describes the "Federal Vision" as a "monocovenantal" theology. But, again, no one on the "Federal Vision" side is advocating anything like that.[58] So Clark's claim creates a horribly false impression.

Anyone who thinks the "Federal Vision" promotes works-righteousness is in the grip of a schismatic agenda and is not seeking the peace and purity of the church. That does not automatically make the "Federal Vision" right in every detail – all of our theologies remain deeply flawed if measured by the divine standard of inspired Scripture. But if we are always *simul iustus et peccator* in this life, that applies to theology as much as any to any other human endeavor. The logic of the gospel requires us to cut one another slack when it comes to nuanced, detailed theological discussions. Many of the points at issue in today's debate have been up

---

58. "The "Federal Vision" certainly acknowledges key differences between the Adamic covenantal administration and Christ's covenantal administration. A detailed assessment of the bizarre "monocovenantal" charge is in "Rome Won't Have Me." See also one of the formative theological works in the rise of "Federal Vision" theology, James B. Jordan's *Through New Eyes* (Brentwood, TN: Wolgemuth and Hyatt, 1988), which is certainly not "monocovenantal." Ironically, since the authors of *CJPM* subject both Adam and Christ to the *same* covenant of works, they are actually much closer to a monocovenantal schema than the "Federal Vision"!

for grabs for centuries within the Reformed church. Why should anyone want to suddenly cut off debate, unless they are protecting vested interests in some form or fashion? In reality, there should not be a "Federal Vision" *controversy* at all; rather, there should be an ongoing "Federal Vision" *conversation*. And that conversation should not be aimed at proving one "party" or "subculture" in the Reformed church as standing in the right all the way down the line. Rather, it should be aimed at lovingly edifying the brethren in our mutual pursuit of understanding and applying Scripture more faithfully in the life of the church and the world.

In the end the *CJPM* volume ends up revealing more about the weaknesses of present day Reformed culture than it does the problems with the "Federal Vision." A. T. B. McGowan has captured the ongoing dynamic in this particular controversy, and points the way forward:

> In some circles today, when anyone seeks to explore a new idea or restate an old one in new words, there is an immediate rush to judgment. Often this approach amounts to theological bullying and oppression, leading to a situation where scholars do not feel free to go where they believe God through his Word is leading them, for fear that they will be declared heretics before they have even had time to explore the matter properly. In some situations, people run to the church courts and demand an ecclesiastical "trial," where the more sensible approach would be to take a good long time to think and pray and study God's Word. Sometimes the pressure is more subtle, with younger scholars being advised to avoid certain issues or certain positions "for the sake of their career." This is a deeply regrettable and unfortunate situation. Evangelical scholars must have the courage of their convictions and be prepared to challenge (where necessary) the Creeds, Confessions and practices of the churches.[59]

---

59. A. T. B. McGowan, editor, *Always Reforming: Explorations in Systematic Theology* (Downers Grove, IL: InterVarsity Press, 2006), 16.

My hope for the Reformed wing of the church is that we would learn to do our theologizing and conversing with one another in way more befitting of the glorious gospel of grace we are all seeking to uphold. *Kyrie eleison* as we proceed.

CHAPTER 5

Adam the Catholic? Faith and Life in Eden

Peter J. Leithart

Early in the twentieth century, Catholic theology was rocked by a debate over the notion of "pure nature."[1] Theologian and future Cardinal Henri de Lubac and others challenged a reading of Thomas Aquinas that had reigned supreme since the counter-Reformation, and in so doing they challenged the entire structure of Catholic theology and laid the groundwork for the remarkable shifts in Catholic theology and practice that received conciliar approval at Vatican II.

Though the full development of this notion of "pure nature" did not occur until the sixteenth and seventeenth centuries,[2] medieval theologians had already toyed with it.[3] In this context, "pure" is not the opposite of "impure." The theologians who developed this idea were not claiming that Adam was created innocent, though they believed that. Rather, "pure nature" means "nature and nothing but nature," "undiluted nature." Examining human beings from the perspective of "pure nature" provided a way of speculating on their capacities – reason, will, moral capacities – while bracketing man's communion with God. "Pure

---

1. The next several pages are adapted from my *Deliverdict: A Contribution to the Theology of Justification* (Moscow, Idaho: Canon Press, forthcoming).
2. For this later development, see Henri de Lubac, *Augustinianism and Modern Theology* (Milestones in Catholic Theology; New York: Crossroad, 2000), esp. ch. 6.
3. Gabriel Biel for example. See Heiko Oberman, *The Harvest of Medieval Theology* (Grand Rapids: Baker, 2000), pp. 47-50, 139-141.

nature" spoke of human nature untouched by grace, a human nature that has received no revelation, human nature undiluted by the special presence and gifts of God. For the earliest medieval theologians who employed this concept, the state of pure nature was conceived as purely hypothetical, since theologians taught that in reality Adam the natural man was also endowed by his Creator with some sort of supernatural gifts that would enable him to reach his ultimate destination. For some theologians, however, this hypothetical condition opened the possibility of defining human nature in purely natural terms, without any reference to grace.

The question of "pure nature" comes into play especially in connection with the questions of desire and the ends (or purposes) of humanity. On Aristotelian assumptions, every nature aspires and desires to reach the perfection of its nature. For Aristotelians, the question, What does man aim for and desire as his highest perfection? is answered by examining the unique capacities of his nature. A nature cannot, by Aristotelian definition, transcend itself; a nature *is* a principle of action and life that is limited by the capacities of nature. So, if man is considered as purely natural, he has only a natural end and desires only a natural, this-worldly fulfillment. As a pure nature, he aspires only to employ his reason and will within the natural world and for natural ends. As pure nature, he may be interested in scanning the heavens, but has no desire for the Love that moves the sun and all the other stars. He may use his reason to manipulate numbers, but he will not purpose to know the God who is One and Three. He may *in fact* aspire to commune with his Creator, but on this paradigm this desire for God must be *added* to his nature. It is not an intrinsic impulse of his "natural" being, but "extrinsic" to that being. It is a "supernatural" gift, a gift "over and above" his natural being. A theologian operating on a strict natural/supernatural dichotomy would therefore conclude that man has a double desire and a double end, more or less unrelated to each other. He can reach his natural end of building skyscrapers and exploring space without union with God, and, by the same token, he can bypass his natural desires and aims in his progress toward the beatific vision of God.

This dualistic conception of human nature is not the view of the church Fathers or the best of the medieval scholastics, whose "focus was on one, sole order: the concrete order of grace in which humans were made for God and human nature could be intelligible only by reason of its finality, divination."[4] On this earlier view, there is no such thing as "pure nature," since man is created with a desire to seek his fulfillment in communion with God. Thomas Aquinas retained this earlier conception. His notion of a "natural desire" for God was an Aristotelian version of Augustine's "unquiet heart" seeking rest in God. Thus, despite his use of Aristotelian terms and categories, Thomas maintained two propositions in tension: On the one hand, he claimed, human beings have a natural desire to enjoy the vision of God, and, on the other hand, this natural desire is only fulfilled by an act of pure grace on God's part. The fact that man has a natural desire for God does not in any way obligate God to fulfill it. Nor is the "supernatural" fulfillment of man's natural desire a divergence from his original nature. Man's "supernatural" fulfillment "fits" his character as created. Supernatural grace is not a crown on a canary; it crowns a creature created to be a king, though this creature is made a king only by the favor of the High King.

Later scholasticism failed to maintain this tension, and the notion of a natural desire for God was qualified out of existence. For later scholastics, to speak of "pure nature" was to speak of a nature without any intrinsic desire or trajectory toward God. Thomas is not wholly free from blame for this development, largely because his attempt to combine the patristic/biblical emphasis on man as image of God with an Aristotelian view of nature was not entirely successful:

> The tension, bordering on contradiction between the patristic notion of human being as image of God and the Aristotelian classification of it as a "nature" is a recurrent motif in [de Lubac's book] *Surnaturel*. Human being as im-

---

4. Stephen J. Duffy, *The Dynamics of Grace: Perspectives in Theological Anthropology* (New Theology Studies #3; Collegeville, MN: Liturgical Press, 1993), p. 296.

age of God is meant to grow into the likeness of God in vision of the divine glory. This patristic position was rooted in "the essential differences between the beings of nature, whose diverse ends are proportioned to their diverse natures, and the spirit, which is open to the infinite." Whereas the Fathers distinguished human spirit and nature, with Aristotle one could speak of human being as one did of everything else, viz., as being a nature, a principle of operation with a defined and limited set of powers. Thus the "nature" to which Thomas refers ... even though spiritual, does not differ essentially from other natures. It was "philosophical" nature as conceived by the Ancients, who did not speak of a Creator God. No longer was it the image of God as understood by the Fathers, whose climate was "mystery" and who were less taken by Plato than by Scripture.... For the Fathers there is no *nous* [mind] without an anticipatory sharing, gratuitous and precarious as it is, in the one *pneuma* [spirit]. For Aristotle, nature, as a center of properties and source of strictly delimited activity, is locked up, sealed off in its own order. In Thomas, the Aristotelean and patristic conceptions of nature uncomfortably lie side by side and uneasily intermingle in unresolved tension.[5]

As a result, the "Aristotelean transposition of the patristic heritage" in Thomas "paved the way for later misrepresentations of his thought by those paleo-Thomists who betrayed the nourishing soil of the tradition with their over-rationalized theology." Thomas rightly asserted that man is created, as a "natural" being, for communion with God. But he erred in accepting too much of the Aristotelian conception of nature. As a result, "Thomas transformed Augustinianism and ended by allowing an autonomous philosophy to take up residence in the Christian house of intellect. ... In time his position came to be read as menacing orthodoxy and provoking the extrinsicism that sealed off the supernatural from nature and welcomed in all the demons of dualism that have come to haunt the Catholic household."[6]

---

5. *Ibid.*, p. 298. Duffy is summarizing the work of Henri de Lubac, and the quotations in the paragraph are from de Lubac's *Surnaturel* (1946).
6. *Ibid.*, p. 299.

Thomas's unstable, but still unified, vision of natural and supernatural broke apart in the sixteenth century. In his commentary on Thomas, Cardinal Cajetan argued that the notion of a natural desire for God was a "theological" rather than a "philosophical" opinion, and argued that "Thomas saw the desire simply as a response to God's revelation calling humans to a supernatural finality." Following this suggestion, later sixteenth and seventeenth century theologians developed an ever more explicit theory of "pure nature" according to which "humans could possibly be created with a goal proportioned to their natural powers and not called to beatific vision." By the nineteenth century, this vision "had solidified and become a wedge driven between the natural and the supernatural" and by the twentieth century had become so entrenched than any questioning of it was viewed as a threat to the gratuity of grace.[7]

For counter-Reformation Thomists, the logic went like this: If man has no inherent natural capacity, and not even any natural inclination or desire for reaching the final end for which he is created, then that end must be a sheer gift from God, a surprisingly unexpected gift. Even the *desire* for this supernatural end is an "extra" gift of God, given in addition to man's nature. On the other hand, if man has natural inclination toward God, then he might have some *capacity* in himself to reach communion with God. And, if God created man with a natural desire for and inclination toward God, it seems that God would be unjust if He refused to fulfill that desire and realize that inclination. If man is created with a natural desire for God, then human fulfillment is not gracious; God is virtually obligated to bring man to his final end. Thus, to retain the surprising gracefulness of grace, these theologians posited a notion of "pure nature" without any human capacity for, inclination toward, or desire for God. For grace truly to be grace, it must come from *outside* the human situation as created. If it is always already there, then it cannot be truly grace.

But in their desire to protect the gratuity of grace, these theo-

---

7. *Ibid.*, pp. 296-297.

logians forged a profound dualism at the foundation of Christian theology. They were forced to conclude that the realm of the supernatural is "external" or "extrinsic" to what man is by virtue of creation. Grace appears not so much to elevate or perfect nature as simply to replace nature with a different (super)nature. As a result,

> grace seems irrelevant to human existence in this world precisely to the extent that it is supernatural, and the question arises of why human beings in their strictly human nature should not be indifferent to it. Moreover, if the very sharp distinction between what is natural and supernatural slides into a separation between these two orders, other separations naturally follow: between religious life and temporal "natural" life; between the Church and the world; between salvation history and the rest of world history.[8]

On this paradigm, supernatural grace does not bring the natural inclinations and interests and capacities of human life to fulfillment; rather, it cancels them in favor of other inclinations, goals, and capacities. Naturally, human beings aim for dominion over the natural world; supernaturally, they aim for communion with God. And these two aims have virtually nothing to do with each other.

In this scheme, grace is truly gracious, but this gratuitous grace is the crown on the canary.

The cosmological, anthropological, political and cultural consequences of positing "pure nature" and the natural/supernatural dualism are vast:

> the "supernatural" was a miraculous gift appended to nature.... The supernatural was accessible only by revelation; the natural could be known by unaided reason. Indeed some held that just as one might place a variety of caps on a bottle, all of which leave the bottle unchanged, so too no matter what destiny was assigned to human nature, "natural

---

8. *Ibid.*, pp. 72-73.

realities would perdure just as they are now." The natural and supernatural orders are only extrinsically and juridically linked by divine decree. This dualism led to splitting the study of human being in two; philosophical anthropology goes on its own way in disregard of theology. No longer is desire for God central to anthropology. Theology's stress on what human nature can do relying on its own resources opened a door to secularized construals of existence and the supernatural became increasingly foreign. Pure natural, a hypothetical possibility, was becoming a historical reality . . . . Nature and supernature were paired off and the latter was seen as an adornment of the former, a rather superfluous add-on to a system already integral and complete in itself. "Christianity took on an artificial character and the bread of doctrine was presented as a stone." The theologians, not the philosophers, were the villains in the piece. They were the ones who cordoned off and isolated the supernatural. On the intellectual labors of reason it must not cast even its shadow, not a hint of its presence of possibility. Any rational reflection allowing the slightest opening of the human spirit to the absolute mystery had to be illusory. No wonder religion and culture were estranged.[9]

John Milbank offers a similar assessment: "Cajetan, unlike Thomas, explicitly says that human nature *in actuality* is fully definable in merely natural terms. This means that there can be an entirely natural and adequate ethics, politics, and philosophy and so forth. Man might even offend the moral law and yet not be directly guilty of sin."[10]

By a tragic historical irony, the advocates of the natural/supernatural scheme often saw themselves as defenders of the faith, "opposing naturalism and exalting the transcendence of the supernatural," while in fact they had become "the unwitting ally of naturalism and secularism" because they pushed "the supernatural to splendid isolation. Christianity thus became marginal to culture's

---

9. *Ibid.*, p. 297.
10. *The Suspended Middle: Henri de Lubac and the Debate Concerning the Supernatural* (Grand Rapids: Eerdmans, 2005), p. 17.

life."[11] Put differently, the natural/supernatural scheme implies that the natural realm is a closed system with its own goals and standards. Pious as the motivations behind it may be, the natural/supernatural paradigm plays into the hands of secularists.[12]

Though the categories and issues in debate are quite different, this Roman Catholic debate comes to mind in connection with contemporary Reformed debates concerning the covenant of works. For some Reformed theologians, Adam must have been created in a state free of grace; otherwise, grace cannot be grace. Only "extrinsic" grace, on this view, is truly grace. It must enter a situation that is not graced if it is to be free grace; it must enter a situation where man has already been damaged, or else it is not grace. For Michael Horton, God's creation of Adam was an expression of "divine *goodness*" but he refuses to call it an act of "divine *grace*."[13] He criticizes O. Palmer Robertson for suggesting that "grace is fundamental to any divine-human relationship."[14] Grace cannot "retain its force as divine clemency toward those who deserve condemnation" if we claim that the Adamic covenant was founded in grace.[15] Law is "natural" and human beings are "simply 'wired' for it." Grace, Horton implies, is not natural, but comes onto the stage only after Adam's sin.[16] In this scenario, it is not surprising that Horton claims that "Adam is created in a state of integrity with the ability to render God complete obedience," thus earning his "right" to receive the tree of life.[17] Adam has all he needs in his own natural capacities; he did not, apparently, have to rely on God's assistance to obey. His obedience was not the obe-

---

11. *Ibid.*, p. 300.
12. Roger Haight, *The Experience and Language of Grace* (New York: Paulist, 1979), pp. 74-75: "the validity of this supernaturalist language of grace . . . is dependent on the naturalism it presupposes. Once a closed system of natures with immanent and proportioned goals gives way to one in which nature and human existence are seen as radically open, to an indefinite future and even an infinite goal, the concept of the supernatural may be discarded even as the notion of utter gratuity must be retained."
13. *God of Promise: Introducing Covenant Theology* (Grand Rapids: Baker, 2006), p. 100.
14. *Ibid.*, p. 96.
15. *Ibid.*, p. 93.
16. Ibid., pp. 92-93.
17. *Ibid.*, p. 89.

dience of faith, but the obedience of nature. Though Horton is hardly a Thomist, the similarities between his account of Adam's natural condition and that of post-Reformation Thomists are significant. And, I would suggest, the anthropological, cultural and political consequences of Horton's construct are as vast as the consequences of the Catholic natural/supernatural distinction, and of a similar hue. It is no wonder that the debate over the covenant of works has been so heated and protracted. The Adamic covenant is at the foundation of Reformed covenant theology, and differences over this issue resonate throughout one's theological system.

If Horton's non-gracious, meritorious version of the Adamic covenant can be sustained, then a great deal follows both theologically and culturally. If his version of the covenant can be sustained, then there really is a dualism of nature and grace, nature and supernature; and there really is a secular realm that rightly remains impervious to the gospel. It is my contention, however, that this version of the Adamic covenant cannot be exegetically sustained. To demonstrate that, I will examine Bryan Estelle's essay, "The Covenant of Works in Moses and Paul," which presents a position close to that of Horton's. About half of Estelle's article is devoted to a discussion of Romans 5, but to keep my essay within reasonable limits, I have concentrated attention on the first half of the article, which discusses the Adamic covenant.

Preliminaries

Follow the footnotes. That is a good hint for evaluating any scholarly work, but it is particularly apt for Estelle's essay.

The first and most obvious thing to notice is that there are quite a lot of them. The purpose of several is difficult to discern. Reading through Estelle's essay, I began a list of what I considered unnecessary or bloated footnotes. By the end of the essay, I had listed more than half a dozen. Footnote 17 (p. 95) is a lengthy reflection on Marcion (a 2nd century Gnostic who rejected the Old Testament and taught that the apostolic texts were too Jewish and thus obscured the radical newness of Jesus' message) and modern Marcionites like Harnack (1851-1830, who taught that NT texts are not canonical and that doctrine was too Greek and obscured the practical nature of the faith), which claims that the problem of Old and New can be seen as "*the* problem Christian theology." I happen to agree with that point, but I am puzzled as to why it ended up in *this* paper. Perhaps Estelle is responding to a charge that he and his colleagues at Westminster California are ignoring or belittling the Old Testament, but footnote 17 is an odd place to present his rebuttal. Footnote 91 refers to a number of works in sociolinguistics. No doubt these works are intriguing, but their relevance to the current debate is unclear.

This criticism may seem unfair and beside the point, but the footnotes play an important role in establishing the rhetorical tone of Estelle's essay. He has 185 footnotes in a paper of 37 pages, an average (for the statisticians out there) of five footnotes per page. Many of these are quite lengthy and detailed. Quite apart from the content of the paper and its footnotes, this apparatus of erudition sends a message: "This paper is thoroughly researched, grounded in the best scholarship, and perhaps irrefutable." More strongly, it tells the reader, especially the reader without the patience or inclination to follow up the footnotes, "Who can – who dare – argue with so many footnotes?"

The footnotes are worth following for another reason. Among the unique features of Estelle's paper, he says, is that "it incorporates modern research in biblical studies in order to supplement the traditional presentation of the doctrine" (p. 91). Hence, his exposition of Genesis 2 draws on work by Gordon Wenham, T. Stordalen, Jon Levenson, Randall Garr, and other contemporary scholars. Once he gets to the crunch moment, however, when he has to defend the specific contents of his covenant of works doctrine, the footnotes lurch in a different direction. Footnotes 64 and 65 happily summarize the interpretation of Genesis 2 at Qumran and in 2 Enoch, but in footnotes 66-69 contemporary Old Testament scholarship suddenly disappears as Estelle begins citing Berkhof, Witsius, Machen, Dabney and Turretin in support of the central claim that "Faith and works function quite differently *before* the fall than *after* it" (p. 109). Citing systematicians is fair game, of course, and perfectly consistent with Estelle's early notice that he is going to combine biblical and systematic argumentation. But the sudden shift is striking. One is left wondering if Wenham, Stordalen, and the other biblical scholars Estelle cites would follow Estelle in finding this distinction between faith and works. One suspects not, else he would have cited them.

This shift in the footnotes is anticipated a few pages earlier when Estelle makes a jolting transition from biblical categories and exegetical material into systematic theological categories. Having carefully established, from the text of Genesis, that the garden was a sanctuary, that Genesis 1-2 is infused with a "royal ideology," and that Eden was a "cosmic mountain," he claims that the two trees of the garden, though mysterious, are "in their quintessential double signification ... the seminal teachings of law and gospel (Turretin, *Institutes* 1.582)" (p. 105). Again, I have no difficulty with using systematic categories or citing Reformed scholastics, but the shift was jarring enough to leave me with a mild case of whiplash (for which I do not intend to sue either Estelle or his publisher). And, importantly, Estelle makes no effort to explain or defend the transition. His claim that the trees of life and knowledge correspond to law and gospel is neither an argument nor buttressed by argument. It is assertion, buttressed by a parenthetical citation of Turretin.

Estelle defends many of the features of one version of the covenant of works, but it is not always clear against whom he is developing his defense. At some points, he appears to rebut disciples of John Murray and other Reformed theologians who are reluctant to describe the Adamic order as a "covenant."[18] He devotes a significant amount of space to defending points on which many parties in the current controversies are agreed. Here is a non-exhaustive list of points of agreement, at least between Estelle and myself:

---

18. For more along these lines, see the excellent essay by John Bolt, "Why the Covenant of Works is a Necessary Doctrine: Revisiting the Objections to a Venerable Reformed Doctrine," in Gary L. W. Johnson and Guy P. Waters, *By Faith Alone: Answering the Challenges to the Doctrine of Justification* (Wheaton: Crossway, 2007), pp. 171-189.

1. Adam was in covenant with God.
2. God commanded Adam not to eat from the tree of knowledge.
3. Adam was a representative of the whole human race, so that his sin introduced sin and death into the world and brought all his seed under the reign of sin and death.
4. Adam was supposed to obey on pain of death.
5. Biblical Theology is structured by the parallels of the First and Last Adams.
6. Adam's probation was temporary.
7. Adam was created with a built-in eschatological trajectory.
8. The prohibition against Adam eating the tree of knowledge was a test of his allegiance.
9. God is king and judge.
10. The New Perspective writers, and E. P. Sanders in particular, raise "a whole host of issues with which New Testament scholars and scholars in related fields must now grapple and perhaps even nuance or adjust previously held opinions" (p. 126, fn. 146).

Check, check, check, check, and on up to ten. Few dispute any of this. The most controversial point is probably #10, but Estelle's colleagues at Westminster California – that is, other contributors to *CJPM* – are the ones who would most vigorously dispute it.

Not only does Estelle defend these points on which there is widespread agreement, but he devotes a great deal of space and deploys massive technical artillery to establishing these points of consensus. More power to him, for he offers solid support for many things that he and I happily agree about. But consider again the rhetoric of the paper, which, in charity, I judge to be unconscious. Estelle goes to great lengths to show that Adam was required to obey God, on pain of death. A reader innocent of contemporary disputes (blessed man, that reader) is bound to be left with the impression that some Reformed theologians declare that Adam could disobey His Creator anytime he pleased, and without consequence. Why else would Estelle be so careful to establish that point? He takes up a lot of space showing that God is King. Given the polemical nature of the whole volume, Estelle must be debating with *someone*, and that someone must be very, very wicked and dangerous if he or she or they deny that God is King.[19]

By contrast, Estelle devotes little or no space to defending claims that are vigorously under debate. I have already noted the assertion about "law and gospel" in the garden. In addition, he offers a detailed linguistic analysis of the Edenic prohibition in Genesis 2:16-17, and concludes that the syntax indicates the command was a "provisional instruction, headed with a positive allowance which is followed by one specific prohibition" (p. 112, quoting Stordalen). This linguistic claim

> comports well with a traditional reading of the covenant of works. If Adam, as the federal head of the human race, had passed his temporary probation, he would have justly merited God's approval and moved on to a higher state, contrary to Daniel Fuller, who wants to redefine merit. In other words, something potentially greater – namely, the state of permanent, confirmed righteousness – was waiting for him if he passed this probation (pp. 112-113).

This is Estelle's first reference to "merit" in the article, and he leaves it both undefined and undefended. Yet, this is the precise point at issue in many sectors of the Reformed world. Many agree that Adam's probation was temporary, and that he was responsible to obey, and that he would have entered into a "higher state" if he had passed the probation. The question is whether "merit" is a felicitous way to describe the basis for this advance. Yet, Estelle does not address this question in any detail.

---

19. The rhetoric of the recently released statement from the Mid-America Reformed Seminary (MARS) has a similar effect. The statement makes passing reference to the "New Perspective on Paul" and the "Federal Vision," but then launches into a defense of many points on which there is wide agreement among Reformed theologians. The implication is that someone, somewhere must be teaching very horrible things, or the faculty would not have spent so much time refuting them. The statement is available at http://www.midamerica.edu/pubs/errors.pdf.

In a footnote, Estelle quotes Daniel Fuller's *Law and Gospel* (1980), and says, in rebuttal to Fuller, that "as will be shown below, God does use a works principle (cf. Rom. 5:18), and it matters greatly that there was something meritorious about the Last Adam's work" (pp. 112-113, fn. 88). When we turn to his exposition of Romans 5:18, however, we find again that he offers very little defense or explanation of "merit."

> In 5:18, the apostle affirms that the one man Jesus Christ has secured, through his obedience, the promises of God talked about in 5:1-11. In 5:19, the apostle elaborates further. After describing Adam's transgression as "disobedience" (*parakoe*) resulting in "many made sinners," the apostle characterizes Christ's act as "obedience" (*upakoe*) resulting in "many made righteous." . . . Christ, by reversing the consequences brought about by Adam's disobedience, has triumphed over sin by his obedience (p. 124).

But of course Fuller, and everyone else who believes the Bible, agrees with Paul that Jesus reversed the first Adam's sin by His obedience. But this is not what Fuller, or anyone else, means by a "works principle." Yet, in the entire article this is the only defense Estelle offers of his meritorious reading of the covenant of works.

At a few points, Estelle enters directly into dialogue with writers associated with the Federal Vision, but when he does it is not clear that he has understood what he has read. He dismisses James Jordan's essay "Merit versus Maturity"[20] with the comment that "Jordan seems to have ignored Gerhard von Rad's comments" in his Genesis commentary (p. 93, fn. 11). Perhaps. Or, perhaps Jordan disagrees with Gerhard von Rad. Or perhaps he does not think Gerhard von Rad worth disagreeing with. Whatever the reasons, this kind of criticism is pointless. It would be as if I complained that Estelle had not paid careful attention to Suarez.

More substantively, he responds to Jordan's argument in footnote 65. After referring to 2 Enoch's understanding of Adam's

---

20. "Merit Versus Maturity: What Did Jesus Do For Us?" in Steve Wilkins and Duane Garner, eds., *The Federal Vision* (Monroe, LA: Athanasius Press, 2004), pp. 151-200.

state, he concludes that

> ... early readers of the Genesis account interpreted the testing dimension of the tree of knowledge of good and evil as not demonstrating a new acquisition of knowledge; rather, it was a matter of putting into practice what Adam knew. Although it could prove profitable, we are not venturing into a detailed discussion here of the issue of Adam's potential maturation with respect to attaining knowledge of good and evil (p. 107, fn. 65).

While Jordan does say that Adam would have grown in knowledge of his own inadequacy and his need for God, Jordan's notion of "maturation" is not merely about knowledge. Adam's maturation would have involved glorification, the acquisition of a new office and status, through crisis moments like the deep-sleep operation that led to Adam's first advance in glory – namely, Eve.

Estelle quotes me once, in support of the charge that there is "antipathy for abstract theological frameworks and systematic theology in both the new perspective on Paul and the so-called federal-vision adherents and others" (p. 94; cf. fn. 15). Had Estelle asked, I could have supplied him with plenty of support from my writing to illustrate "antipathy for abstract theological frameworks." I stand guilty: I am opposed to certain modes of systematic theology, and certain uses of it, particularly ones that are overly abstract. But the quotation he uses says the opposite. Far from *attacking* systematic theology, I am pushing for more thoroughly and rigorously *systematic* theology, one that thinks through the Trinitarian and Calvinistic categories of our Confessions more systematically.

Adam in the Garden

Estelle's actual argument for the Covenant of Works begins well, even very well. He carefully examines a number of features of Adam's original situation in the garden, insisting quite accurately that the garden was a sanctuary where Adam served as priest; that God is King over man, his co-ruler; that Eden is connected to the cosmic mountain of Ezekiel's vision (pp. 100-105). Apart from a strange, but stray, reference to "God's physical presence" (p. 101), there is nothing to disagree with here.

Disagreements begin to arise when he turns to discussing the trees of the garden. The two trees of the garden represent, he says, "in their quintessential double signification . . . the seminal teachings of law and gospel." Since he fails to expand this point, it is not immediately clear what this means, or how he arrives at this conclusion. The following paragraphs apparently are designed to make his case. Estelle makes several points. First, he claims that the tree of knowledge was not forbidden because of anything inherent in the tree, but solely because "God assigns a particular meaning to that tree in order to sharpen the test" (p. 106). He cites Dabney to the effect that the tree was a tree of knowledge "not because it was a particular species of tree, but because it had been selected as the tree whereby to test the implicit obedience of Adam" (p. 106, fn. 61). This is unexceptionable, though it leaves unsaid most of what needs to be said.

Second, he claims that by designating the tree as the focal point of his test of Adam, the tree is the place where God confronts Adam with his "absolute Lordship." At this tree, "good and evil would become the opposites between which a choice must be made and a right judgment would become evident." In short, the tree focuses the question of whether "Adam, the federal (representative) head of the human race [would] listen to the apocryphal word . . . of the unholy intruder, that is, the snake, thus betraying his allegiance to another, or would he maintain fealty to his Lord and king and yield his will, his love, and his veneration to only his Creator" (p. 106). Though I find this awkwardly stated, it appears that Estelle is saying that the tree is a tree of knowledge of good and evil because it is the place where Adam's obedience or disobedience will be manifested. At this tree, Adam's choice between good and evil will become evident. Again, this is unexceptionable as far as it goes.

In a related footnote (p. 106, fn. 62), Estelle notes that the phrase "to know good and evil" is used elsewhere in the Old Testament to refer to the "wise discerning choice" made by a king passing judgment (2 Samuel 14:17; 1 Kings 3:9). This does not, unfortunately, affect his analysis of the tree of knowledge. If we take these passages into consideration, we get a far more specific idea of what the tree represents. It is indeed a tree that tests obedience, but the specific privilege it holds out is the privilege of passing judgment. It is a royal tree that communicates the knowledge of good and evil that Adam needs to be elevated to his throne as Yahweh's earthly co-ruler. Meredith Kline quite rightly describes the tree as the "judgment tree."[21] Somewhat more on this below.

Third, after briefly drawing support for his interpretation from Qumran documents, Estelle discusses the other tree, the tree of life. God was already in fellowship with Adam, but He planned to deepen that fellowship, and aimed to bring man from the "relative perfection" of his original condition to a state of eschatological perfection. This is what the tree of life represented, Estelle argues:

> The tree of life pointed beyond the immediate life that Adam and Eve presently had to a consummated period: eternal life. What did it signify? It signified life consummated through eschatological blessing. It did not merely signify endless existence, for that could be a curse as well as a blessing. Indeed, had man passed the probation, he would have received the approbation of God and no longer been under the probation of God. Mankind would have been established in righteousness and holiness (pp. 108-109).

For support for the idea that the tree of life represents eschatological life and fellowship, Estelle points to Revelation 21, where "only the eschatological community may partake" (p. 109).

Estelle here gives a fair brief summary of the traditional doctrine of the covenant of works, but in a number of particulars this traditional doctrine is at odds with the text. For starters, Estelle and much of the Reformed tradition to the contrary, Adam was

---

21. *Kingdom Prologue* (3 vols.; self-published, 1986), vol. 1, pp. 80-83. Jordan recognizes the judicial connotations of the tree of knowledge as well ("Merit Versus Maturity," pp. 165-169), but in my judgment he develops the point more convincingly than Kline.

not prohibited from eating the tree of life. In Genesis 2:16-17, God moves from saying "You may eat freely from every tree of the garden" immediately to "but as for the tree of knowledge of good and evil, you shall not eat from it." It is hard to imagine how this could be clearer: *Every* tree is "freely" given to Adam. There is *only one* restriction – the tree of knowledge. Consequently: The tree of life is available to Adam. Imagine:

> *God:* Eat from every tree in the garden.
> *Adam: Every* tree?
> *God:* There's one exception: You may not eat from the tree of knowledge of good and evil.
> *Adam:* That's the only exception?
> *God:* That's the only exception.
> *Adam:* So what about this tree of life?
> *God:* The only prohibition is on the tree of knowledge.
> *Adam (heading to pick fruit from the tree of life):* Great!

If Adam were a certain kind of Reformed theologian, this dialogue would end with:

> *Adam (looking skeptical):* I think I'll be safe and not eat from the tree of life either.

That would not be playing safe. That would be unbelief, and ingratitude. God offers life, and Adam refuses it. Estelle assumes, without much argument, that the tree of life represents eschatological life. The passage of Revelation does indeed say that the eschatological community eats from the tree of life, but that is because the eschatological community is restored to the garden. But the garden is where Adam started. For Adam, the tree of life is not a *telos* but a beginning. It is the Alpha tree, not the Omega.

Estelle is correct that Adam was created with a built-in eschatological trajectory: If there is a natural body, there is a spiritual (1 Corinthians 15:45). But the tree of knowledge, not the tree of life, is the eschatological tree. Adam did not have access to this tree, but would, at some point, have been permitted to eat it, thus assuming fully the role of co-ruler with God, sharing in God's discernment and judgment concerning good and evil. Estelle, and much of the Reformed tradition, have it backward: Life is there for the plucking in Eden. Rule, and judgment, comes later. The probation gives time for Adam to grow to the point where he will be able to share in God's rule. Adam violates the prohibition by seizing this royal privilege before the time.

Near the conclusion of this section, Estelle states the really crucial, and contested, point of his entire argument: "Faith and works function quite differently *before* the fall than *after* it" (p. 109). I commend the clarity with which this puts the real issue in debate. I cannot commend the argument that leads up to this conclusion. Even if Estelle is correct that the tree of life represents eschatological life, it is not obvious that his conclusion follows. Consider: God spoke to Adam; Adam was to obey. But that obedience would arise out of Adam's trust in the God who commanded him, and obedience would be the fruit of that trust. Obedience always assumes trust of the one who commands. If Adam became convinced (as Eve apparently did) that God prohibited access to the tree out of jealousy for His divine rights, then Adam's distrust would (and did) lead to disobedience. Even in the garden, works emerged from trust in the God who speaks and in the speaking of that God.

But Estelle is *not* correct about the tree of life, and that wholly vitiates his argument. Life was available to Adam. All Adam had to do was to accept Yahweh's offer – "eating you shall eat," an offer Estelle rightly characterizes in his translation as an offer "freely" given. Life was not something Adam had to earn. He had to pass no test. The only "qualification" for eating from the tree of life was hunger, and trust in the God who all but handed Adam the fruit.

Estelle cites Turretin to support his claim about the difference between prelapsarian (before the Fall) and postlapsarian (after the Fall) faith-and-works. Turretin makes things much worse:

> Nor can it be objected here that faith was required also in the first covenant and works are not excluded in the second. ... They stand in a far different relation. For in the first covenant [i.e., the covenant of works], faith was required

> as a work and part of the inherent righteousness to which life was promised. But in the second [i.e., the covenant of grace], it is demanded – not as a work on account of which life is given, but as a mere instrument of apprehending the righteousness of Christ (on account of which alone salvation is granted to us). In the one, faith was a theological virtue from the strength of nature, terminating on God, the Creator; in the other, faith is an evangelical condition after the manner of supernatural grace, terminating on God, the Redeemer. *As to works*, they were required in the first as an antecedent condition by way of a cause for acquiring life; but in the second, they are only the subsequent condition as the fruit and effect of the life already acquired. *In the first, they ought to precede the act of justification; in the second, they follow it* (p. 109, fn. 69, emphasis Estelle's).

This is a mess. First, faith changes its character – from a work to a "mere instrument" – once Adam leaves the garden and lives outside. How does *that* happen? How can faith change its character in this way because of sin? And where is the exegetical support for such a notion? Certainly not in Genesis. Second, faith in the garden is a "virtue from the strength of nature," which means apparently that it arises from Adam's own constitution, and is not a gift of God's grace. Only after the fall does faith become an "evangelical condition" that depends on "supernatural grace." But wasn't Adam dependent on God for everything, literally *everything*? Was he not a creature? Does his nature possess *anything* or produce *anything* that is not already a gift received? Of course not. Even if Adam's faith was a work, it would be as much a gift for Adam as it is for us. Finally, and most dramatically, whatever can it mean for faith to "terminate" at one time on God as Creator and on another time on God as Redeemer? Are we talking about different gods? It will not do to say that Adam needed no salvation because he was sinless, and therefore knew God only as Creator. God put him into deep sleep, a state of near-death, and brought him back to meet his glory, his bride. Was that not a rescue? Soon after, Adam faced a dragon at the gate, and he needed to act in faith to protect his bride. Confronted with Satanic danger, Adam was indeed in need of rescue. His only hope for remaining in his integrity, in fact, was a hope that God would save him, because Adam was surely not prepared to deal with the serpent on his own. Adam was to confront Satan with the same hope that the sinless Jesus had – that His Father would raise Him after His conquest of Satan and His obedience to death.[22]

Step back a few paces, and the strangeness of Estelle's scenario becomes more evident. With much of the Reformed tradition, he is saying that, had Adam not sinned, mankind would have reached its eschatological fulfillment by its own works and not by God's work. The fulfillment of the man's destiny would have been the result of human effort, and Adam would have received life as wages earned by his good works. Theoretically, though not actually, humanity could have made its way in the world without divine intervention. Natural man, without grace, could have built the kingdom of God on earth. Thus Reformed theology opens up, theoretically only to be sure, the possibility of a highly successful but utterly secular human project. Thus Reformed theology, for all its zeal to attack naturalism and secularism, helps to underwrite them.[23]

Adam the Catholic?

Over the next few pages, Estelle offers a close examination of Genesis 2:15-17. Much of this discussion is very good, and I agree with much of it: God as the superior gave a command to His inferior, Adam (p. 109); a promise was implied in the command, though I differ with Estelle about the nature of the promise; failure to obey resulted in death; since "God spoke as the king," Adam

---

22. Turretin's argument implies that God could not have been known in all His character apart from sin. Had Adam remained unfallen, God would have ever after been known only as Creator, not as Redeemer. This cannot be the case. It cannot be that God's revelation of His character to man depends on man's fall, for that makes the fall not contingently or decretally necessary, but an absolute necessity.
23. Conversely, this line of argument implies that God would have intervened personally in history, perhaps through incarnation, even if Adam had not sinned. The achievement of human destiny would never have been left in human hands. Jordan presents a somewhat different argument for incarnation in a sinless world in "Merit Versus Maturity," pp. 184-189.

would suffer punishment for disobedience. The manner Estelle chooses to make these points is rather puzzling. He appeals to speech-act theory to establish that the command of Genesis 5:16-17 is "an excercitive" and he explains that the phrasing of the command departs from the standard phrasing of commands in the Pentateuch to suggest that the prohibition was "a provisional instruction, headed with a positive allowance which is followed by one specific prohibition" (p. 112, quoting Stordalen). Though the linguistic data are intriguing in themselves, they do not have a lot of cash value here, and they only confuse Estelle's arguments. It is not always clear exactly what he is trying to establish: Is he trying to show that God issues the command as Adam's king? No one disputes that. Is he trying to establish that Adam was responsible to obey? Who questions that? Is he trying to prove that the prohibition of the tree of knowledge was temporary? I agree.

Where his linguistic argument does have some import for the specific issues in debate, it works against Estelle. The statement from Stordalen quoted above indicates that there is "*one* specific prohibition" in Genesis 2:16-17 – namely, the prohibition of access to the tree of knowledge. But Estelle implies that the prohibition extends to the tree of life. Estelle uses a good deal of his heavy equipment to establish that the command of Genesis 2 is a *royal* command, a point that Estelle appears to think is disputed. He summarizes with "The language is command, legal, and judicial: the language is simultaneously relational because the king, that is, the Lord delivers it" (p. 114). He adds that "Understanding these discourse-pragmatic functions of the language, therefore, may help readers and writers avoid fruitless discussions regarding the relational and legal aspects of the language used here in Genesis" (p. 115). In the accompanying footnote (fn. 99), he cites John Barach, who says "Covenant membership is not just a bare legal relationship." Estelle seems to think he is disagreeing with Barach, but he is not. Estelle says, "God's command is legal; but there is a relational dimension to the command. Adam's covenant relation to God is legal and personal." Barach says, "God's relation in the covenant is not *just* legal," which implies that the relationship is *also* personal. Both say legal; both say relational. Let's call the whole thing off.

Yet, there is a dispute, and it is not merely a matter of "balance" between relational and legal elements. It arises from different conceptions of the relationship within which the command is issued. Estelle notes that the expression for "command" used in Genesis 2 "typically denotes 'a provisional instruction from a ruler (or father) concerning subordinates'" (p. 111, quoting Stordalen). If the syntactical form could be a command issued by a father, and not by a king, one wonders how Estelle knows from the syntax that the command is royal and not paternal. Put that particular question to the side. The differences between Estelle and Barach have to do with this royal/paternal question. The question is not whether God is both King and Father. Estelle, Barach, and I are in cozy agreement: God is both Adam's King and Father. The question is what Adam is: Is he merely *subject*, or is he – already, as created, without "earning" anything – a *son*? Is the command issued by a loving Father to a peasant who might, if he obeys, earn a right to the throne? Is he a subject who might earn the Father's adoption? Or is the command issued by a loving King to His beloved Crown Prince? Though Estelle surely believes that God was Adam's Father and that Adam was God's son, his inclination is to see Adam as subject and not son. Genesis leans in the first direction.[24]

---

24. Meredith Kline writes, "Man's identity as a child of the Creator is suggested by the special intimacy of the mode of God's creating him. Setting the Bible's description of the origin of man apart from its account of the origin of the subhuman creatures of land and sea and sky are the special consultation involves in the former (Gen. 1:26) and the immediacy of God's personal touch and breath in bringing forth Adam and Eve (Gen. 2:7, 21f.). Though with careful restraint, biblical revelation thus intimates that this creating of man is a kind of divine authoring analogous to human procreation. What is simply suggested of father-son imagery in the record of creational origins becomes virtually explicit in the record of the birth of Seth in Genesis 5:1-3. In this passage a statement of Adam's creation in the likeness of God is directly juxtaposed to a statement that Adam begat a son in his own likeness and image. Clearly we are being advised that there is a similarity between those two processes, both of which result in products like their authors. Adam's fathering of a son provides a proper analogy to God's creating of man and the relations of Seth to Adam is analogous to man's relationship to his Maker." Kline further cites Luke 3:38 to confirm that Adam was created as "son of God" (*Kingdom*

The real issue at stake here comes up very briefly in the midst of Estelle's argument, so briefly that it might be missed. Having drawn from syntactical and linguistic considerations that the command is a "provisional instruction," Estelle concludes:

> This explanation comports well with a traditional reading of the covenant of works. If Adam, as the federal head of the human race, had passed his temporary probation, he would have justly merited God's approval and moved on to a higher state, contrary to Daniel Fuller, who wants to redefine merit. In other words, something potentially greater – namely, the state of permanent, confirmed righteousness – was waiting for him if he passed this probation (pp. 112-113).

This is, as mentioned above, the first reference to "merit" in the essay. Estelle does not define the term, which has been used in a multitude of ways in both medieval and Protestant theology. Equally importantly, he is ambiguous about what Adam was supposed to merit. On the one hand, Adam might have "justly merited God's approval," which appears to mean that Adam would have been accepted by God if he had obeyed. That would imply that Adam was not approved before his obedience; after he obeyed, he would have earned approval. On this interpretation, God apparently regarded Adam with a kind of neutral indifference until he proved himself. This fits with Estelle's earlier claim (in the quotation of Turretin) that Adam would have been justified by works if he had passed the probation. On the other hand, Estelle appears to be saying that Adam's obedience would have justly merited an advance in his status – not approval as such, but a "higher state" of "permanent, confirmed righteousness." These are two different things. If Estelle is suggesting that Adam was already accepted and beloved as a son, but needed to obey in order to reach some higher condition, then he is not so far from those he opposes.[25] If, on the other

---

Prologue, volume 1, p. 35).
25. Though even if this is his view, I differ with him. I agree with Jordan ("Merit Versus Maturity") that Adam would never have advanced to a "high position" simply by obeying. That higher station, represented by the tree of knowledge, would have been given to Adam as a sheer gift, and would have likely have involved something like the deep-

hand, he is suggesting that Adam needed to obey in order to earn, by a "works principle," the favor of God, then he is indeed differing with his opponents. He is saying that Adam was created a Catholic, but became a Protestant after he fell. Protestantism is reduced to a postlapsarian form of Christianity.[26] Worse, he is suggesting that God Himself began creation as a Catholic merit-based project, but turned things in a Protestant direction because of the fall.[27]

Given the ambiguity of Estelle's claims, it is helpful to turn to other recent defenses of the covenant of works for clarification. As I mentioned above, Estelle's Westminster colleague, Michael Horton, gives a great deal of attention to the covenant of works in his recent introduction to covenant theology.[28] Defending the proposition that the Adamic arrangements are rightly described as "covenantal," Horton says,

> ... every covenant in Scripture is constituted by a series of formulae, most notably, oaths taken by both parties with stipulations and sanctions (blessings and curses). These elements appear to be present, albeit implicitly, in the creation narrative. Adam is created in a state of integrity with the ability to render God complete obedience, thus qualifying as a suitable human partner. Further, God commands such complete obedience, and he promises, upon that condition, the *right* (not the *gift*) to eat from the Tree of Life. While creation itself is a gift, the entrance into God's Sabbath rest was held out as the promise for loyal obedience in the period of testing (p. 89, his emphasis).

---

sleep and waking sequence by which Adam advanced from lonely singlehood to glorious marriage.
26. I recognize that there are multitudinous complications in both "Protestant" and "Catholic" theology, and that my use of the terms is close to caricature. If anything, Estelle, and particularly Horton (see below) are closer to the caricature of Catholicism than actual Catholics. Catholics, after all, believe that supernatural grace was necessary for Adam to achieve his ultimate destiny of communion with God; for Horton at least, Adam needed no grace at all, but could rely wholly on his own natural resources.
27. I realize that Estelle, as a Calvinist, would say that this Catholic-Protestant sequence was eternally planned. I am not saying that Estelle implies that God changes. But the sequence that Estelle believes God decreed (if I read him rightly) is a sequence that begins Catholic and progresses Protestantly.
28. *God of Promise*.

Lest anyone think that Adam's obedience was itself a gift of God, Horton insists in several places that Adam's ability to obey comes from himself: "Created for obedience, he was entirely capable of maintaining himself in a state of integrity" (p. 84); "Adam . . . was in a state of rectitude, perfectly capable of acceding to the divine mandate" (p. 91). For Horton, in short, Adam had to earn his right to the tree of life, and had to earn that by obeying from his own resources, resources given to him by virtue of his creation. For Horton as for Estelle, the tree of life represents eschatological life, entry into Sabbath. For both, Adam was not created with free access to life. For both, faith and works function differently before and after the fall. For both, humanity begins its life as a Catholic and *falls* into Protestantism.

Adam the Protestant

Estelle and Horton to the contrary, I submit that Protestantism, not Catholicism, is the natural state of man. How could it be otherwise? By definition, a creature is wholly dependent on his Creator for everything. We call the human recognition of that dependence "faith." In the nature of the case, the natural stance of a *creature* has to be one of faith, albeit a faith that is never alone. What would a Protestant Adam look like? I can only sketch a few lines here, but, for both my editor and me, a sketch is better than a blank page.

First, the Adamic covenant is, as the Westminster Shorter Catechism puts it, a covenant of *life*. It was a covenant of life if there ever was one. Adam just had to reach out, pluck the fruit, and he could eat life. He did not have to achieve anything to gain access: He *had* access. The so-called covenant of works can rightly be described as preeminently a covenant of "access."

Second, as I have mentioned in passing throughout this article, Adam did have an eschatological trajectory. He was the "natural" man, but was destined to become the "spiritual" man. This is symbolized in the garden by the presence of two trees. The tree of life was the Alpha tree, the tree given to Adam from the first moment of his creation. He had life, and was created in a state of blessing and fellowship with God. God issued a command, and by keeping that command in the obedience that arose from his faith in Yahweh, he would have retained access to the tree of life.

The other tree, the tree of knowledge, symbolized and conferred royal authority, the right and ability to judge between good and evil, and to share in Yahweh's kingly rule over creation. At some point, through some process, God would have permitted Adam to eat from the tree of knowledge, and Adam would have then taken a throne fully as a co-ruler with his Father, the King. This was the glorification held out to Adam, and Adam sinned by seizing this glorification for which he was not prepared, a glorification that Yahweh had not yet conferred on Him as gift.

Third, what is the difference between Adam's prefall and his postfall situation? If we stick with the text of Genesis, we find nothing at all about a reversal in the relation of faith and works, or a transubstantiation of the nature of faith. The text does not mention faith or works. What it does mention is that Adam was driven from the garden, and particularly from the tree of life (Genesis 3:22-24). Under the terms of the original covenant, Adam was in the garden; because of his sin, Adam was outside the garden. The original covenant was a covenant of access; the postlapsarian covenant is premised on Adam's *exclusion*. The difference between the covenants has *nothing* to do with how one has fellowship with God, or receives rewards from God, or with the shape that the life of godliness takes. In the garden and out, what God requires of Adam is the "obedience of faith." The difference is locational and structural (or "cultural"): Adam is in the garden and then he is out; at first he can just pick the fruit, but then he is excluded from the fruit and has to offer sacrifice to get close and even then he does not get as close as he used to.

Fourth, the Old Testament unfolds a series of covenantal arrangements that are all premised on humanity's exclusion from Eden. No one can enter the cloud on the mountain except Moses. As Estelle notes, the garden was the original sanctuary, and throughout the Old Testament no one can enter the Most Holy Place in the tabernacle or temple (except the high priest, who enters briefly one day a year).

Fifth, this is the situation into which Jesus, the Last Adam, enters. He does not come "under the Adamic covenant" but "under the law." He does not operate under the terms and conditions of the covenant of access but under the terms of the covenant of exclusion. He begins outside the heavenly sanctuary and then goes in. He faces Satan in the wilderness, not in the land or the garden. This fits perfectly with Romans 5: Jesus' obedience comes "after many transgressions" (v. 16), while Adam's disobedience is a single transgression. Jesus regains access to life by rendering His Father the obedience of faith under the terms of the covenant of exclusion, and as a result all who are transferred from Adam into Him also regain access. By His obedience, He has ended the covenant of exclusion, torn the veil, taken us back into the garden, where life is there for the picking. God still demands the obedience of faith of us – as He did from Adam, as He did for all believers throughout the Old Covenant – but He demands it now in different conditions and with us in a different location.

Finally, Jesus has not only restored us to the garden, but has taken the throne at the right hand of the Father, the throne reserved for glorified humanity. By continuing steadfast in obedience, and by undergoing death and resurrection, He has received access to the tree of knowledge, and through Him we also are exalted on thrones as kings and priests, and share in God's judgments and rule over the nations. Jesus does not merely restore us to life, but advances us beyond Adam, to glory.

Conclusion

Whether in its Catholic or Reformed guises, the entire natural/supernatural scheme rests on unbiblical assumptions about creation. To describe nature as a closed system is to deny creation *ex nihilo*. The doctrine of creation means, if it means anything, that the creation is completely dependent upon the Creator, which in turn means that the creation exists only by virtue of Someone outside the creation. Created existence is, by definition, *open* existence, "decentered" existence. Nor can human beings created through the Word of an eternal, free God exist for even a moment without being confronted with the revelation of the Creator. God's call to communion is always already there, though man may close his eyes and ears to it. Human capacities of every sort – whether "natural" or "supernatural" or "ultranatural" – are always and only gifts of God. By treating human nature as detached from God and autonomous, even if only hypothetically or theoretically, the natural/supernatural scheme implies that human beings exist by something other than God's gifts, that we have something "in us" that is not given and sustained entirely by God. These gifts, further, were given with creation in a way that is suitable to our end both in this world and in a new creation. Biblically, man is not a "nature" in the Aristotelian sense. Made in the image of God, we do not reach our fulfillment by virtue of a principle within us; on the contrary, we reach our fulfillment by virtue of being conformed more and more to what we are not and never will be; we reach our end through an infinitely extended process of approximation to the God who is other than us.

For both Protestants and Catholics, the solution to the dilemmas created by the natural/supernatural scheme is not to strive for more precision in relating the natural and supernatural, but to reject the whole paradigm. The natural is always already infused with the gifts and graces of God, always already the arena of revelation; man always already, in every action, is aiming for communion with God or alienating himself from that communion. There is no way to draw the line between the two. Insofar as some formulations of the Adamic covenant try to pry grace from nature, they aid and abet secular enemies of faith.

CHAPTER 6

The Gospel of Law and the Law of Gospel: An Assessment of the Antithetical Gospel-Law Paradigm

P. Andrew Sandlin

It is our duty to adhere firmly by faith to the one God, inasmuch as he is the one and only author of all good things, and to walk in innocence of life for his pleasure. For anyone who has neglected these things and has sought false gods, who has lived shamefully or impiously, and who has worshiped God more with ceremonies or external things than with true holiness of life, will be excluded, disinherited, and rejected from the covenant.

Heinrich Bullinger, A Brief Exposition of the One and Eternal Testament or Covenant of God (1534)[1]

[T]he law presented at Sinai was one of faith, with essentially the same content needed for salvation as the message people received in the New Testament times.

Daniel P. Fuller, The Unity of the Bible (1992)[2]

---

1. Heinrich Bullinger, *A Brief Exposition of the One and Eternal Testament or Covenant of God*, in eds., Charles S. McCoy and J. Wayne Baker, *Fountainhead of Federalism* (Louisville, Kentucky: Westminster/John Knox Press, 1991), 105, 110-111.
2. Daniel P. Fuller, *The Unity of the Bible* (Grand Rapids: Zondervan, 1992), 350.

The Role of Presuppositions and Paradigms

In his chapter addressing Gospel and Law (*CJPM*, 331-363.), Professor S. Scott Clark observes that all Biblical interpretation presupposes some theological grid, a "system of doctrine" and "history of interpretation" (*CJPM*, 331). Beginning with Martin Luther, he furnishes an impressive catalog of a number of Protestants' views on the relation between Gospel and Law, which he takes as the "system of doctrine" and "history of interpretation" for Reformed theology and the Reformed Faith (*CJPM*, 352). He then complains about a "naïve biblicistic approach to the proclamation of the word [of Scripture]" (352). The minister may not preach the word "indiscriminately"; he must preach in conformity to "our [Reformed] confessions and theologians," which divide the Bible into two separate words or "moods," Gospel and Law.

Accordingly, the objective of Clark's chapter is not so much to offer a Biblical defense of his definition of Gospel and Law as a hermeneutical category (or more accurately, hermeneutical categories) as it is to document that this category dominates the Reformed interpretive tradition. The paramount question, which Clark's chapter mostly skirts, is whether in fact this category is correct and, even if it is, why it and it alone should serve as the hermeneutical category of the Reformed tradition.[3]

In his introductory chapter of *CJPM*, Clark asserts his preference for "read[ing] the Scriptures [through the eyes of] the visible institutional church as expressed, publicly and authoritatively, in the Reformed and Presbyterian Standards" (*CJPM*, 12). In other words, the confessional standards of the Reformed and Presbyterian sector of the Faith serve as an overarching grid for Biblical interpretation. (In this approach he mirrors confessional Lutherans, who "do not regard [their own confessions] as a sec-

---

3. One wishes Clark had interacted with the sort of observations we find from A. T. B. McGowan in the Introduction to his edited work *Always Reforming* (Downers Grove, Illinois: InterVarsity, 2006): "The sixteenth-century Reformation and the theology that developed from it was a movement rather than a completed event" (14). This six-page Introduction is worth serious pondering for its brief, balanced treatment of the meaning and application of *semper reformanda* (always reforming).

ond norm standing alongside of Scripture," but rather the pure teaching of Scripture itself.[4]) Perhaps this is why Clark does not feel compelled to offer significant Biblical evidence for his viewpoint — he assumes that his readers recognize in the Reformed and Presbyterian tradition the correct interpretation of the Bible, to which no appeal now need be made.

Yet if the dictum *sola Scriptura*[5] constitutes an actual functioning principle[6] as, for example, the Westminster Confession of Faith demands ("The supreme judge by which all controversies of religion are to be determined, and all decrees of councils, opinions of ancient writers, doctrines of men, and private spirits, are to be examined, and in whose sentence we are to rest, can be no other but the Holy Spirit speaking in the Scripture," Ch. 1, No. 10), it will not suffice for Clark simply to appeal to Reformed tradition or even the Confession itself. To be sure, every exegete brings to the text certain presuppositions, including theological presuppositions.[7] In this sense, every interpretation is relative.[8] Each of us interprets the Biblical text — and the world — within a pre-conceptual grid.[9] An objective of faithful Biblical interpretation, however, is, by the enlightening ministry of the Holy Spirit, to identify that grid and other presuppositions that may cause us to misread the text.[10] The

---

4. Ralph A. Bohlmann, *Principles of Biblical Interpretation in the Lutheran Confessions* (St. Louis: Concordia, 1968), 15.
5. See Philip Schaff's balanced, *The Principle of Protestantism* (Philadelphia and Boston: United Church Press, 1964), 80-124. For a recent equally balanced view of *sola Scriptura*, see also Kevin J. Vanhoozer, *The Drama of Doctrine* (Louisville, Kentucky: Westminster/John Knox Press, 2005), 233.
6. Here we must agree with Oscar Cullmann: "[W]hen I approach the text as an exegete, I may not consider it to be certain that my Church's faith in Christ is in its essence really that of the writers of the New Testament," *Salvation in History* (New York and Evanston: Harper & Row, 1967), 68.
7. Among the current evangelicals, the Emergent Movement seems to lend greater weight to theological subjectivity and historical situatedness than the confessionally Reformed. See Will Samson, "The End of Reinvention: Mission Beyond Market Adoption Cycles," in eds., Doug Pagitt and Tony Jones, *An Emergent Manifesto of Hope* (Grand Rapids: Baker, 2007), 153-161.
8. Webb B. Garrison, "The Necessity and Relativity of Biblical Interpretation," *Interpretation*, Vol. 7, No. 4 [October 1953], 426-438.
9. Gerhard Ebeling, *The Problem of Historicity* (Philadelphia: Fortress Press, 1967), .
10. John Warwick Montgomery, "The Theologian's Craft: A Discussion of Theory For-

text must at all times be permitted to call into question alien presuppositions, long cherished though they may be.[11] It will not suffice to rely at all points on a deductive theological scheme.[12]

At some point, therefore, Clark or those who advocate his position must present from the Scriptures persuasive counter-evidence to the position they are explicitly opposing – the position that (1) the divine commands of the prelapsarian era and Mosaic law and other forms of obligatory revelation imposed on humanity reflect at root God's grace and mercy toward man, and (2) the Gospel of Jesus Christ, grounded exclusively in His atoning death and bodily resurrection by its very nature imposes on man certain obligations, such that through a resting, submissive faith man actively appropriates justification, an obedient faith without which he cannot expect to be saved in the end.[13]

Clark is thoroughly committed to what Daniel P. Fuller pejoratively calls "theological interpretation."[14] Of course, all Biblical interpretation is theological in the sense that it relates to God, but Fuller has in mind something more specific. When we refuse to let Biblical texts stand on their own and, instead, deduce a certain broad, overarching scheme of the Bible's message by appealing

---

mation and Theory Testing in Theology," *The Suicide of Christian Theology* (Minneapolis, Minnesota: Bethany Fellowship, 1971), 267-313.
11. Ned B. Stonehouse, "The Infallibility of Scripture and Evangelical Progress," in ed., Ronald Youngblood, *Evangelicals and Inerrancy* (Nashville: Nelson, 1984), 24.
12. Michael Horton complains about the "remarkably poor scholarship [among "covenantal nomists"] in treating the Reformers and their successors" (*CJPM*, 199). Yet Horton offers little or no exegesis in defense of his criticism; he acknowledges the inevitability of bias in all exegetical work (*CJPM*, 199) but does not explain why readers should accept his bias rather than that of his opponents. Exegesis does not eliminate all bias, but it can minimize the harm those biases may pose to understanding the Bible.
13. For example, see Karl Barth, "Gospel and Law," *Community, State and Church* (Gloucester, Massachusetts: Peter Smith, 1960, 1968), 71-100; John M. Frame, "Law and Gospel," http://www.frame-poythress.org//frame_articles/2002Law.htm; Daniel P. Fuller, *Gospel and Law*; P. Andrew Sandlin, "Covenant in Redemptive History: Trust and Obey," in ed., Sandlin, *Backbone of the Bible* (Nacogdoches, Texas: Covenant Media Press, 2004), 63-84, and "The Grace of Law and the Obligation of Gospel," *Reformation and Revival Journal*, Vol. 14, No. 1 [2005]; and C. van der Waal, *The Covenantal Gospel* (Neerlandia, Alberta, Canada: Inheritance Publications, 1990), 57-64
14. Fuller, *Gospel and Law*, 62. For answers to his Reformed critics, see his "The Gospel and Law: A Syllabus," Fuller Theological Seminary, 1988.

to a few "clear" or "important" verses in terms of which the rest of the Bible must be read, we tend to circumvent the concrete message(s) of the Biblical texts in favor of a single, harmonious message to which our deductions have previously committed us. The conclusion is already apparent in the premise.

While Clark (surprisingly) does not quite say so explicitly, he seems to be anxious that depicting Law as gracious and Gospel as obligatory (1) pollutes the free grace of God in salvation (Gospel) and (2) undercuts the deadening effect of Law to drive hopeless, depraved men to Jesus Christ to trust in Him (*CJPM*, 358-363). Yet the majority of those who disagree with Clark's antithetical Gospel-Law paradigm in no way deny that salvation is God's unmerited gift in Jesus Christ appropriated entirely by man's faith. To my knowledge, for example, Professor Clark and this writer agree that the ground of justification (one's right standing before God) is the Cross of Jesus Christ[15] and the reality of His empty tomb (Rom. 4:25).[16] We agree that the exclusive means of that justification is faith (Rom. 4:4-5; Gal. 3:6-14; Eph. 2:8-9).[17] *We agree* that human merit, achievement, good works, church membership, and sacraments cannot contribute one iota to a one's acceptance as a forgiven sinner before God (Rom. 4:6; Tit. 3:5).[18] But it is not evident (certainly not self-evident) that Clark's overarching Law-Gospel paradigm is the proper way to perceive and preserve that gracious salvation. Indeed, as will be argued below, Clark at points tends to compromise salvation by grace through faith alone in adopting his antithetical Gospel-Law paradigm.[19]

While space limitations forbid an extensive assessment and full inductive investigation, the remainder of this chapter is in-

---

15. Leon Morris, *Glory in the Cross* (Grand Rapids: Baker, 1966).
16. Richard Gaffin, *Resurrection and Redemption* (Phillipsburg, New Jersey: Presbyterian and Reformed, 1978, 1987).
17. We disagree, however, on the definition of faith. See below.
18. Bruce L.. McCormack is quite right, contra Calvin, that sacramentology has been given excessive emphasis in Christian theology. See his "What's at Stake in Current Debates over Justification?", in eds., Mark Husbands and Daniel J. Treier, *Justification* (Downers Grove, Illinois: InterVarsity, 2004), 111.
19. On the Biblical Gospel, see Leon Morris, *The Apostolic Preaching of the Cross* (Grand Rapids: Eerdmans, 1955, 1960).

tended to show not merely that "gospel" and "law" as they are expressed in the Bible do not conform to Clark's categorization, but also that his antithetical Gospel-Law paradigm does not do justice to significant data of the Bible. Attention to and interaction with selected Biblical texts suggests that a chief message of God to man in the Bible — from creation to consummation — is that eternal life is God's gracious offer to all who by simple faith cast themselves on the glorious promises of God in the redemptive work of His Son Jesus Christ, a faith that by its nature entails repentance of sin and surrender of one's life to Christ's Lordship.

History

Clark has offered historical and theological justification for a widely attested Protestant view of the relationship between Gospel and Law. The Reformer Martin Luther, Clark contends, influencing many subsequent Protestants, broke sharply with the Western tradition in positing a sharp antithesis between Gospel and Law. Beginning in the patristic church (*CJPM*, 333ff.), these two theological categories were melded, and by the early 16th century they had become so intertwined as to severely undercut the Biblical picture of salvation, which demands their division. For Clark, while Gospel and Law are equally valid messages from God, and while each has its place in Biblical preaching and in the Christian life, they are different — radically different — messages that must be kept carefully distinct in Bible study, in theology, and in preaching (*CJPM*, 349-350). "Unless a sharp distinction is maintained between the purpose and function of the Law and the Gospel," writes Luther, "the Christian doctrine cannot be kept free from error."[20] With this stark, momentous pronouncement, Professor Clark agrees.

The Dilemma of Definition

Unfortunately, confusion with the terminology "Gospel and Law"[21] immediately confronts the listener or reader. The prime

---

20. Martin Luther, *Commentary on the Epistle to the Galatians* (Grand Rapids: Zondervan, 1962), 131-132.
21. I capitalize Gospel and Law in this dissertation when they refer to theological catego-

culprit is the term "Law," which is a salient example of a word in theological usage whose denotation is different from that of its Biblical usage.[22] When we hear the English word law, we tend to think of legality, argumentation, coercion, surveillance, policing, enforcement, dispassion, objectivity, abstraction, sterility, and justice — summarized in the expression "the cold, dead letter [of the law]." These connotations have often carried over into theological usage. "Law" is that which God inflexibly demands of his rational creatures on pain of penalty and in promise of reward. It is thought by some (including Clark) that in the Garden of Eden, God gave man a command ("Law") that, if he obeyed, would merit him eternal life; if man disobeyed, he would invite on himself God's eternal judgment. This plan of salvation (discussed below) is, like much the legislation given to Moses at Sinai, a prime example of Law in theological usage: obey and live; disobey and die (Rom. 10:5; cf. Lev. 18:5).

Nonetheless, "Law" in the Bible does not carry this precise denotation. In the English Old Testament (OT), "law" is almost always the Hebrew *tôrâ*, though *tôrâ* is translated by other expressions as well. In the Septuagint (the non-inspired Greek Old Testament) and the Greek of the New Testament (NT), *tôrâ* is translated *nomos*, which in English does equate to law. But "law" does not accurately convey *tôrâ* ("Torah" in English).[23] The Torah is the divine teaching, instruction, even direction. It does not carry the simple denotation of "law." It covers the entire OT range of godly instruction and direction for life, which includes the sacrificial system in terms of which Israel was (temporarily) redeemed. When, for example, we read in Deuteronomy 17:11, "According to the sentence of the law [*tôrâ*] in which they [the priests] instruct

---

ries; I do not capitalize them when they refer to Biblical categories. These categorical distinctions are sometimes difficult to maintain; therefore, the distinction in the text is at some points overlapping or arbitrary.
22. Vern S. Poythress, *Symphonic Theology* (P & R Publishing: Phillipsburg, New Jersey, 1987, 2001), 74.
23. Walter C. Kaiser, Jr., "The Law as God's Gracious Guidance for the Promotion of Holiness," in ed., Wayne G. Strickland, *The Law, the Gospel, and the Modern Christian* (Grand Rapids: Zondervan, 1993), 192-193.

you ... you shall do," "law" is not the most helpful translation, when it is understood in the narrow, modern sense.[24]

But Clark is not arguing chiefly on the basis of etymology or terminology. He understands that the Bible uses the term "law" in varied senses. By Law, Clark denotes a particular, distinctive kind of divine message, chiefly in opposition to another message, Gospel (*CJPM*, 339, 341, 349-350). This message of Law is one of requirement or obligation: do not kill, do not commit adultery, do not eat swine flesh, do not serve other gods, love your brother and sister, turn the other cheek, repent of your sins, observe the Sabbath, and so on. Anytime we read the language of requirement or obligation of God to man — something man must actively do to please God — we encounter "Law." Law demands without accommodation or adjustment.

Gospel, however, is a radically different kind of divine message (*CJPM*, 357, 362). Unlike Law, Gospel is a message of offering without demand or obligation. While Law is requirement, Gospel is promise. In Gospel, God grants to man freely and does not make demands or issue requirements or conditions (apart from faith, or resting in what God has done in Christ's actions). On the basis of Jesus Christ's substitutionary life and death, God grants the elect eternal life apart from obligations and requirements. This is Gospel, not Law. "[T]he stuff of gospel is not the stuff of law," writes Clark (*CJPM*, 349).

By Law ("a hermeneutical and homiletical category") Clark relies on the Westminster Confession of Faith in referring to "the demand for 'perfect, personal, and perpetual obedience'" (CJPM, 332). In sharp contrast, on the same page he defines the hermeneutical category of Gospel as God's message that "speaks of the gracious, sovereign redemption of Christ's people." "The law," he summarizes, "is a demanding taskmaster"; "the gospel," conversely, "does not demand but grants freely" (*CJPM*, 339). These confluent but different messages are not divided into the Biblical testaments, as though the OT is Law and the NT is Gospel (*CJPM*,

---

24. Kaiser, "The Law as God's Gracious Guidance for the Promotion of Holiness," 193.

349). Rather, we encounter Law and Gospel in both canonical testaments. Wherever (in either testament) we see demands (to which blessing and curse are often attached), we confront Law; whenever in the Bible we encounter God's sovereign, salvific grace accomplished in Jesus offered to man without human obligation (and anticipated in the OT), we confront Gospel. This theological construct may be termed the antithetical Gospel-Law paradigm.

To furnish precedent for this paradigm, Clark turns to certain prominent theologians in the history of the Reformed Faith, beginning with Calvin, and then addresses lesser lights (*CJPM*, 340-348). He labors to demonstrate beyond reasonable doubt that these figures, to a greater or lesser degree, follow Luther's antithetical Gospel-Law paradigm — Law demands without mercy; Gospel grants without obligation.

But not all Reformed figures. For instance, Clark does not mention early Swiss Reformer Heinrich Bullinger (Zwingli's successor), who in his short but incisive book on the covenant from 1534[25] defends a bilateral covenantalism, which posits salvation totally by grace through faith alone in Jesus Christ that nonetheless imposes as conditions of justification man's obeying God. Gospel and Law are not antithetical but are united in a single divine message to man; Bullinger, therefore, did not accept Luther's Gospel-Law distinction.[26] Perhaps this covenantal construction of Gospel and Law is one example of what Peter Lillback has in mind when he writes: "Luther was convinced that the Swiss were teaching the same as the pope concerning justification."[27] They were not teaching the same as the pope taught, but they were not teaching what Luther taught, either, especially as justification (defined below) is related to Gospel and Law.

While, therefore, the dominant strand in the Reformed tradition perpetuated Luther's antithetical Gospel-Law paradigm, secondary strands in that tradition did not.[28]

---

25. Heinrich Bullinger, *A Brief Exposition of the One and Eternal Testament or Covenant of God*, 105, 110-111.
26. McCoy and Baker, *Fountainhead of Federalism*, 24.
27. Peter Lillback, *The Binding of God* (Grand Rapids: Baker Book House, 2001), 113.
28. McCoy and Baker, *Fountainhead of Federalism*, 30-34. On the conditions man must

Salvation by Law-Keeping: Christ's and Ours

Foundational to the antithetical Gospel-Law paradigm in both its Lutheran and Reformed versions is a surprising role that Law is asked to occupy in relation to eternal life. In fact, the non-specialist reader may be perplexed to encounter Clark's assertion, "The good news of the gospel is understood only in the light of the relentless demand of the law for perfect obedience" (*CJPM*, 338). Has not Clark already argued, in apparent contradistinction, that Law is that which demands without adjustment, while Gospel is that which grants without obligation? Did he not write that "[f] or the unregenerate, law and gospel are antithetical" (*CJPM*, 349)? Did he not state, further, that "[o]ne learns of grace, not in law, but in the gospel" (*CJPM*, 355)? How then could "[t]he good news of the gospel [be] understood only in the light of the relentless demand of the law for perfect obedience," unless, after all, the Law, with all of its obligations and demands, and threatening and curses, plays some role in conferring eternal life on man? Clark seems to suggest that man may — and must — be saved by keeping the Law. But how is this suggestion possible if Law demands while, contrarily, Gospel confers? This apparent incongruity is at the root of the purported Gospel-Law antithesis.

In this antithetical Gospel-Law paradigm, God confronts man with the revelation that Jesus has not merely died on the Cross to discharge our sin-debt and has risen from the grave for our justification; Jesus has, in addition, kept the Law on our behalf during His life, a Law that one is actually bound to keep if he is to be rewarded with eternal life (*CJPM*, 350-363; cf. 229-265). The message at root is one of salvation by Law-keeping[29] — Jesus substituted for us, keeping the Law in our place during His life, and

---

meet for salvation, as understood in Reformed theology, see John Murray, "Covenant Theology," *Collected Writings of John Murray* (Edinburgh: Banner of Truth, 1984), 4:229-234.

29. "Heaven must be earned.... [T]he principle of works forms the foundation of the gospel of grace," Meredith G. Kline, *Kingdom Prologue* (Overland Park, Kansas: Two Age Press, 2000), 107-108. Kline is an avid proponent of the "Covenant of Works" in its most pronounced form.

He substituted for us in His death and by this death kept the Law for us, suffering the penalty of that Law that we incurred by our sin. One might wish immediately to inquire why, if Jesus has suffered the penalty for our Law-breaking in His death, He must also be obliged to substitute for us in His Law-keeping life. After all, if He has paid our sin debt by substituting for us on the Cross, are we not free from God's judgment?

By no means, according to the antithetical Gospel-Law paradigm. Eternal life for man after the Fall is a gift of God on the ground of Christ's redemptive ministry, but it is a gift that must be earned and merited — earned and merited by Jesus Christ on behalf of God's elect. Before the Fall (in the "prelapsarian" era, to use theological language), God set before man the conditions of eternal life. In other words, it is not enough for man to avoid sin; he must also treasure up sufficient merit. This arrangement of salvation by deeds is called, not surprisingly, the Covenant of Works. The Westminster Confession of Faith elucidates it this way:

> The first covenant made with man was a covenant of works, wherein life was promised to Adam; and in him to his posterity, upon condition of perfect and personal obedience. (Ch. 7, No. 2)

Subsequently in the Confession, we read:

> God gave to Adam a law, as a covenant of works, by which He bound him and all his posterity, to personal, entire, exact, and perpetual obedience, promised life upon the fulfilling, and threatened death upon the breach of it, and endued him with power and ability to keep it. (Ch. 19, No. 1)

Crucial to this scheme of salvation is the distinction within Christ's redemptive work of two phases of obedience. Christ's law-keeping death is known as His passive obedience; His law-keeping life is known as His active obedience.[30] Chapter 19 the Confession states that, after the Fall, this law ("active obedience") continued to

---

30 T. F. Torrance, *Theology in Reconstruction* (Grand Rapids: Eerdmans, 1965), 154-155.

be the definition of righteousness that man is bound to obey. This is just what the Mosaic law actually constitutes — a republication of the ethical stipulations of the prelapsarian Covenant of Works, though within a different covenant framework that takes sin into account. Chapter 7 of the Confession had already made clear that this Covenant of Works as an arrangement for man's obtaining eternal life had been replaced by the Covenant of Grace, an arrangement in which man is no longer saved by his own merit and good works, but by faith in Jesus Christ, whose good works merit that eternal life for sinful man. In chapter 8, number 5, the Confession states that Jesus kept this law perfectly and that in keeping it, as well as in dying on the Cross, He satisfied God's justice (i.e., in substituting for God's elect). To simplify, the Covenant of Grace is a covenant of grace for us but a Covenant of Works for Jesus.

Jesus was a Law-keeper so that we do not need to be Law-keepers as a condition of our salvation. Since the passivity of the sinner is a vital distinctive of accepting the Gospel (*CJPM*, 362-363), we can say that in this scheme, Jesus' active obedience fulfilled the Law so that man's passive reception of that active obedience will appropriate the Gospel to eternal life.[31] Man passively trusts the One Who actively keeps the Law on his behalf. In appropriating eternal life for the elect, Jesus is active and man is passive.

In any case, despite obvious differences between Lutheranism and much post-Reformation Calvinism,[32] both hold that eternal life is at root something man merits by keeping divine commandments. It will be readily seen that in this scheme of salvation, salvation is fundamentally by Law, if Law is defined (per Clark) as fulfilling ethical stipulations and obligations God has established for man.

---

31. See also David VanDrunen, "To Obey Is Better Than Sacrifice: A Defense of the Active Obedience of Christ in the Light of Recent Criticism," in eds., Gary L. W. Johnson and Guy P. Waters, *By Faith Alone* (Nashville: Thomas Nelson, 2007), 127-146.
32. Norman Shepherd provides evidence that the Covenant of Works and its foundational tenet of the imputation of Christ's "active" obedience were not a part of the original Reformation soteriology. See his "Justification by Works in Reformed Theology," in ed., P. Andrew Sandlin, *Backbone of the Bible* (Nacogdoches, Texas: Covenant Media, 2004), 104-111.

Therefore, when Clark writes, "Paul reckons that Christ canceled that record [of sin debt] because he actively obeyed the law for us (*CJPM*, 254)," he situates Christ's meritorious, Law-keeping life as the heart of His atoning work for man. "[T]he cross is the highest expression of Christ's righteousness for us" (*CJPM*, 254) in that it definitively finalizes His substitutionary, Law-keeping life.

Given his commitment to the Covenant of Works, it is understandable why Professor Clark would posit such a radical antithesis between Gospel and Law, as he defines these terms. If at its core salvation is what Jesus by His Law-keeping merited for elect sinners, any suggestion that Law-keeping is entangled with Gospel-believing implies an abhorrent mixture of salvation by man's merit or works or achievement. After all, Jesus fulfilled the Covenant of Works, and for man to mix Gospel and Law would imply that man, too, must fulfill that Covenant on his own. Man then treads on the impeccable, redemptive work of Jesus, arrogating to Himself the Law-keeping, meritorious righteousness that belongs exclusively to Jesus. In this case, the conflation of Law and Gospel profanes the monergistic (one-sided), redemptive work of Jesus.

However, if Professor Clark's antithetical Gospel-Law paradigm is not what the Bible actually teaches, it might be possible to relate Law and Gospel more positively to each other without in any way subverting salvation by grace through faith alone in Jesus Christ, which Clark champions (though only with reference to the postlapsarian era). It may be possible, in fact, to hold that Law is an aspect of Gospel and that Gospel is an aspect of Law (as Clark defines them), while validly supporting the highest form of monergistic soteriology and the finality of the work of Christ, a work that is appropriated by faith alone. If Clark's theological approach to Law and Gospel is found to be mistaken, his criticism that alternative viewpoints subvert Biblical preaching is likely also mistaken (CJPM, 352), and we are free to suggest that Gospel and Law may be related in a way different from Clark's antithesis that nonetheless preserves an entirely gracious soteriology.

This chapter argues, in fact, that Clark's paradigm is mistaken and that Gospel and Law are not antithetical to each other.

The Gospel as a Message of the Cross and Resurrection Includes Gracious Obligations ("Law")

Gospel in both Testaments. Contrary to the antithetical Gospel-Law paradigm, the Bible does not teach that the Gospel is merely a message that grants freely, to an exclusively passive faith and apart from demands and conditions of sinners. It is a Gospel of grace through and through (Jn. 1:13; Eph. 2:8-9; cf. Gal. 3:1-14), but it is not a Gospel without demands and requirements.

Gospel and Obligation ("Law"). Salvation, while gracious from beginning to end, is not without obligation or condition. The idea that man's obligation in salvation counts as good works or merit or achievement in which man could boast makes a mockery of the Scriptures, for the Bible emphatically teaches that man stands under obligation to meet certain conditions if he is to be saved by grace and if he is to be justified in the Final Day. That is, in the Gospel, God's grace is not incompatible with human obligations. Three obligations stand out clearly as conditions for man's salvation — faith, repentance, and submission to the Lordship of Jesus.

God demands that sinners exercise faith in His Son Jesus Christ. In Biblical usage, faith is sure confidence and trust, casting oneself on the credibility of the person and/or message of another.[33] It is a requirement of the Gospel: again and again, God demands that sinners exercise simple faith in Him and His Son if they are to be saved.

God's salvific call to Abraham is a prime example in the OT, and the NT confirms that this obligatory faith is the instrument by which Abraham was justified (Rom. 4; Gal. 3:1-18). Paul, in fact, invokes Abraham's experience as the example to NT saints, who must be justified by faith and not by works (Rom. 4:1-5). Paul is refuting the notion that justification (God's legal declaration of innocence on sinful man)[34] can be attained by adherence to the law of the

---

33. W. A. Whitehouse, "Faith," in ed., Alan Richardson, *A Theological Word Book of the Bible* (New York: MacMillan, 1956), 75-76. This entry is a brief but insightful treatment of the topic.
34. John Murray, *Redemption Accomplished and Applied* (Grand Rapids: Eerdmans, 1955), 115-116, 129-131.

Mosaic covenant and therefore only the province of the Jews, who were its exclusive recipients (see vv. 11-12);[35] for he observes that Abraham's justification preceded the mark of circumcision, which identified Abraham as the first Jew and which became a sign of covenant inclusion (vv. 9f.). God justified Abraham by faith and not by circumcision (a chief external mark of law-keeping) so that He could justify both Jews and Gentiles (Rom. 3:29-30; 4:16-18). Had Abraham appropriated justification by circumcision or other good works, he could have boasted as a Jew (v. 2), but faith is an obligation in which man cannot boast. Note carefully that Paul is not refuting the idea that circumcision is a condition of justification in that there could never be obligations for justification whatsoever. Rather, he is arguing that circumcision is a specious condition of justification while faith is a valid condition. Faith itself, like works, is a law, but it is not a law in which man may boast (Rom. 3:27-28).

This faith is not optional. Historically the most quoted verse in the Bible (Jn. 3:16) implies that those who do not believe in Jesus will perish (stated flatly v. 18). St. Mark trumpets that whoever does not believe in Jesus will be condemned (16:16). Paul warns that it was Israel's unbelief (in Jesus) that incited God to turn from that covenant nation and bring salvation wholesale to the Gentiles (Rom. 11:10). Faith in Jesus is an obligation for salvation.

This is why faith is not only intimately linked to obedience in the NT but also is itself a form of obedience. At least three times in Romans (1:5; 10:3, 16:26) in setting forth facets of his own Gospel ministry, and once in 2 Thessalonians (1:8), warning of judgment at Christ's Second Advent, Paul so closely aligns obedience with acceptance of the Gospel that it is impossible to dismiss the element of active human obligation. The reference here is to expressions variously translated (1:5; similarly in 16:26) "obedience to the faith" or "obedience that comes from faith" (NIV). Whether the grammatical construction suggests "obedience which

---

35. William Hendriksen, *Romans* (Grand Rapids: Baker, 1980, 1981), 149-155. For a fine introduction to the Biblical materials, see Alister E. McGrath, *Justification by Faith* (Grand Rapids: Zondervan, 1988), ch. 2.

consists in faith" (this is, obedience is of the essence of faith),[36] or "obedience which flows from faith" (that is, faith is the source of obedience), or simply, "obedience to faith" (that is, faith induces obedience),[37] it is clear that, for Paul, belief in the Gospel includes and imposes obligation.

In Romans 10:3 Paul laments that Israel as a whole has not submitted or subjected itself to "the righteousness of God." The context is clear that this righteousness (however it is precisely defined) is an aspect of the Gospel (9:30; 10:1, 8, 10, 13-15). In lamenting that Israel has not submitted herself to God's righteousness, he is firmly implying that the belief at the cornerstone of the acceptance of the Gospel includes ethical obligation — submission. When we believe the Gospel, we *bind* (submit) ourselves to Jesus as Savior and Lord.

More striking, perhaps, is Paul's statement in 2 Thessalonians 1:8 that Jesus will one day appear in great glory "[i]n flaming fire taking vengeance on those who do not know God, and on those who do not obey the gospel of our Lord Jesus Christ." We know from Paul's message to the Athenians that in the present age God commands all individuals everywhere to repent (Ac. 17:30), and, by implication, to believe the Gospel. Is response to this command to repent and believe the Gospel what Paul had in mind when he referred to the impending judgment on those who do not obey the Gospel? We have every reason to believe that it is. It is the Gospel of Jesus Christ that individuals must believe (that is, obey) if they are to avoid God's wrath.

It has been suggested that this obedience (in Romans 10:16, for example) is simply a synonym for belief itself and does not connote any ethical stipulation as such. It is merely (in the words of Clark) the "passive trust in the finished work of Christ."*38* Trust in

---

36. C. E. B. Cranfield, *Romans 1-8* (London, T & T Clark: Eerdmans, 1975), 66-67. I agree with Cranfield that for Paul, faith itself is an act of obedience.

37. Charles Hodge, Romans (Edinburgh: Banner of Truth, 1972), 21. See also John H. Armstrong, "The Obedience of Faith," *Reformation and Revival Journal*, Vol. 12, No. 4 [Fall 2003], 13-21.

38. R. Scott Clark, "When the Good News Becomes Bad," *Evangelium*, Vol. 2. Is. 2 [March/April, 2004], 7.

the finished work of Christ is, to be sure, the object of the sinner's (and Christian's continuing) faith, but it is anything but passive. We contend that had it been suggested to the writer of Hebrews 11 that faith in Jesus Christ is merely "passive," he would have responded without comprehension. The faith of the faith*ful* OT saints that he is upholding as examples for wavering NT saints is by its nature a living, active, working faith. In Romans 10:16 Paul does equate obedience with belief, but it is a belief that is the antithesis of the unbelieving disobedience of an apostate Israel (v. 21). The Gospel command to believe is in fact a call to active obedience — trust in the finished work of Christ and submission to His Lordship (on which, more below). Faith is an obligation that God lays down for the reception of the Gospel.

The Gospel demands, in addition to faith, repentance, whose Biblical definition is a turning from sin to God, an act that elicits God's forgiveness. Repentance is not simply external conformity, for while it "is emphatically a matter of conduct …. it is also a matter of the heart."[39] Sinners abandon their rebellion against God and His law and turn to Him in humility, with the determination henceforth to obey Him. Alan Richardson observes:

> The fundamental idea in the biblical conception of repentance is that of turning or returning to one's due obedience, as of rebels returning to serve their lawful king, or of a faithless wife coming back to her husband. It represents a fundamental reorientation of the whole personality.[40]

This demand for a holistic repentance as a dimension of the Gospel begins in the OT. For instance, in Deuteronomy 30, at the conclusion of Jehovah's covenant ratification with Israel, He conditions His forgiveness on her repentance (v. 2). Significantly, He suspends regeneration, installing a new heart, on that act of repentance (v. 6). We are left to speculate about the precise rela-

---

39. W. Morgan, "Repent, Repentance," in ed., James Hastings, *A Dictionary of the Bible* (New York: Charles Scribner's Sons, 1909), 4:225.
40. Alan Richardson, *An Introduction to the Theology of the New Testament* (London: SCM Press, 1958), 31.

tion between repentance and regeneration;[41] but, whatever may be the answer to that question, it is clear that Israel could not expect to enter (or re-enter) into a living, organic relation with God until she had repented.

Paul in Romans 4:6-8 enlists David as an OT illustration of justification by faith in Christ, and not by good works, notably those of Jewish exclusivity (v. 10). David, like Abraham (vv. 1-3), was justified by faith. The Gospel is not a message of human performance but of God's grace, received by faith (4:23-5:2). In adducing David as an example of this wholly gracious justification conferred in the Gospel, Paul cites the beginning of Psalm 32. In verse 5 of this psalm, interestingly, we learn that the man to whom the Lord does not impute iniquity (*i.e.*, whom He justifies) is the man who acknowledges and confesses his sins and who determines to be led of the Lord (vv. 6-9). In other words, the one justified is the one who repents.

Isaiah 55:3-7, moreover, furnishes a clear, succinct example of the Old Testament's inclusion of repentance as a component of the Gospel:

> " ... Incline your ear, and come to Me.
> Hear, and your soul shall live;
> And I will make an everlasting covenant with you —
> The sure mercies of David.
> Indeed I have given him as a witness to the people,
> A leader and commander for the people.
> Surely you shall call a nation you do not know,
> And nations who do not know you shall run to you,
> Because of the LORD your God,
> And the Holy One of Israel;
> For He has glorified you."
> Seek the LORD while He may be found,
> Call upon Him while He is near.
> Let the wicked forsake his way,

---

41. Thomas C. Oden, *Life in the Spirit* (Peabody, Massachusetts: Prince Press, 1992, 1998), 156-177.

And the unrighteous man his thoughts;
Let him return to the LORD,
And He will have mercy on him;
And to our God,
For He will abundantly pardon.

God ratifies His covenant of mercy with and abundantly pardons the "unrighteous man" who abandons His sin, and we are fully warranted in inferring that He will *not* shower His covenant mercies on or pardon those who do not repent. Nor may we surmise that this message was merely communal, targeting Israel as a nation but not individuals. It is the wicked and unrighteous *individual*, whether Jewish or gentile, whom the prophet specifically addresses, and at any point in redemptive history.[42]

The demands for repentance enclosed in the Gospel do not abate in the NT era. The message of John, Jesus' precursor, resonates with the words, "Repent, for the kingdom of heaven is at hand!" (Mt. 3:1; cf. v. 8; Mk. 1:4). John's ministration of baptism is seen as requiring a public reflection of a repentant heart (Mt. 3:6). Jesus Himself continues John's message: "Repent, and believe the gospel" (Mk. 1:15), not merely as a prelude to the Gospel, but as "the gospel of the kingdom of God" (vv. 14-15). The call to repentance for sinners who wished salvation was a hallmark of Jesus' teaching (Mt. 9:9-13; 11:20-24; Lk. 13:1-5; 14:25-33). Against the self-righteous Jews He offered the parable of the Pharisee and the tax collector (Lk. 18:9-14). The Pharisee boasted before God of his own righteousness in the face the sinful tax collector, but the repentant tax collector humbly cried out for God's mercy, and he alone went down to his house justified. Sinners are justified only by a repentant faith.

Before his ascension, Jesus charged His disciples with the Gospel they were to propagate. Linked inextricably to the joyous fact of His own death and resurrection was the call to repentance (Lk. 24:44-49). The apostles recognized this sacred trust of the Gospel and preached a Christ-drenched message of repentance

---

42. Edward J. Young, *The Book of Isaiah* (Grand Rapids: Eerdmans, 1972), 3:380.

(Ac. 2:38; 3:19; 11:18; 17:30; 20:21; 2 Pet. 3:9) — it is not enough to believe *with a bare assent*; one must, as an aspect of believing in Jesus, turn from his sins.

Paul, in particular, preached a repentance-charged Gospel: while repentance is surely a necessity for sinning *believers* (Ac. 17:30, 31; 26:20; 2 Cor. 7:8-10; 12:20-21), it is also a requisite disclosed within the Gospel itself. For instance, Paul instructed Timothy in the manner of dealing with those ensnared by the Devil but to whom God may grant repentance (2 Tim. 2:24-26). In Romans 2:1-8, he warned the Jews not to boast in their exalted place in God's covenant, for God alone grants repentance and consequent eternal life. Toward the end of his ministry, he solemnly reminded the Ephesian elders that he had preached both to Jew and Greek "repentance toward God, and faith toward our Lord Jesus Christ" (Ac. 20:21). Paul saw the Gospel as a message demanding repentance.

While repentance is a gift of God that humans cannot conjure under their own power ("[T]urn thou me, and I shall be turned, Jer. 31:18, KJV; cf. Ps. 80:3, 7, 19; Ac. 11:18; 2 Tim. 2:24-26; Heb. 12:17), it is a fully human act, and God requires it; God does not repent on behalf of sinners. In Ezekiel 18:31, Jehovah even curtly demands that an apostate Israel "get yourselves a new heart and a new spirit."

Repentance no less than faith is a requirement imposed by the gracious Gospel message.

The Biblical picture is unmistakable: No repentance, no Gospel.[43]

And what is true of faith and repentance is equally true of *submission to Jesus' Lordship*,[44] of which, to be precise, faith and repentance are aspects. Interestingly, in the ancient world, the evangel, or Gospel, began in the cult of the emperor, and the emperor

---

43. On repentance as an essential correlate of faith by which individuals alone appropriate justification, see Norman Shepherd, "Justification By Faith Alone," *Reformation and Revival Journal*, Vol. 11, No. 2 [Spring 2002], 84-85.

44. John M. Frame, *Salvation Belongs to the Lord* (Phillipsburg, New Jersey: P & R Publishing, 2006), 191.

and his citizens used this very word.[45] The important days in the emperor's life, his birthday, how he came to power, and what his edicts demanded were announced throughout the realm as gospels, or pieces of good news, and festivals were held in honor of him.[46] These gospel messages were grand, resplendent public statements of joy and hope and reverence for the emperor. They constituted the Roman Empire's gospel.

The early Christians had their own, competing Gospel — the only true Gospel. It was not a secret, heavenly, esoteric message for a select few, for it would not have created such controversy and resistance had it been such a secret *gnosis*.[47] Rather, it was a grand, resplendent public message of joy and hope and reverence for Jesus Christ, Savior and Lord. It declared that He alone is the world's King, He alone is the world's hope, and in Him alone could the world find salvation.

This message had its roots in Jesus' ministry and the apostolic interpretation of it. The angel's annunciation to Mary highlighted the Kingship of Jesus in perpetuating the Davidic throne (Lk. 1:28-33). When the angel alerted Joseph of the impending incarnation and Mary's pregnancy with Jesus, he accented the meaning of "Jesus," Savior (Mt. 1:20-21). These angelic announcements should not be interpreted as two messages delineating two distinct ministries of the Messiah, but as two aspects of a single message and single ministry — Jesus as the Savior-King, redeeming His people by means of His overarching claims of royalty. When Jesus came proclaiming the message of the kingdom, we must infer that it was just this regal soteriology that He preached (Mk. 1:15).

The apostles after the resurrection understood this message. Peter's Pentecostal sermon (Ac. 2) indicting the Jews marshals OT evidence that Jesus is the Messiah, the risen Lord Who now rules from heaven (vv. 22-36). When the Jews, under searing conviction of their sin implored Peter for a course of action, he demanded

---

45. See also P. Andrew Sandlin, *The Full Gospel* (Vallecito, California: Chalcedon Foundation, 2001).
46. Ethelbert Stauffer, *New Testament Theology* (New York: MacMillan, 1955), 157.
47. Philip J. Lee, *Against the Protestant Gnostics* (New York: Oxford University Press, 1987).

that they repent and believe in Jesus and submit to baptism. It is evident that the objective message that convinced the hearers was not merely that they were sinners but that they had collaborated in crucifying the One Whom God had made both Lord and Christ ("Master" and "Anointed," v. 36). The incentive to repent is the exalted position of Jesus. They (and their Roman masters) had murdered the world's true King! Peter's Gospel is just this: that the One Who had been cruelly killed had risen from the dead, was now exalted in the heavens by the Father (v. 24), was showering His church with great gifts of power (vv. 14-21), and was summoning sinners over the known world (v. 39) to submit to His Kingship by exercising faith in Him and being baptized (v. 38) with the sure hope that all things will be subordinated to His authority (v. 35).

This is the message that the other apostles declared. For instance, we are not surprised that Paul begins his masterly statement in Romans of the eternal plan of God for humanity (vv. 1-7) with a declaration of the Davidic Kingship of Jesus that buttresses Paul's own Gospel ministry (v. 1). Here he employs the phrase "the obedience of faith" that constitutes his Gospel preaching. Like Peter at Pentecost, Paul accents the resurrection of Jesus as the visible, public demonstration of the power of God and that identifies Jesus as God's Son — and as the King. The implicit picture is not hard to discern. God has raised from the dead His Son, Who is the rightful heir of David's throne from which He now reigns and enlists His followers to declare to all nations the Gospel, the message that sinful men must submit to the King by exercising faith in and following Him.[48]

The chief features of this Pauline definition of the Gospel appear in Ephesians 1:15-23, in which Paul assures his readers of his prayer for them that they would understand their high calling as the inheritors of God's regal blessings in Jesus (vv. 18-19) to be fulfilled when God exalted Him to His Kingship and universal reign by means of the church (vv. 20-23). One infers that the message of

---

48. N. T. Wright, "Herald of the King," *What Saint Paul Really Said* (Grand Rapids: Eerdmans, 1997), ch. 3.

the Gospel by which Paul's readers first believed is the effect of Jesus' Kingship in putting down all human authority (v. 22).

Likewise, while Paul's summary of the Gospel in 1 Corinthians 15 is no stand-alone proposition but is rather part of his rationale against erroneous views of the resurrection, it is striking that he identifies the reign of Jesus as a part of the redemptive complex that includes the resurrection (vv. 22-28). This redemptive complex is just what the Gospel attests and interprets. The message of salvation is the message of what God has done in Christ in human history.[49] Central to that message is the present Kingship of Christ by which He accomplishes God's redemptive plan for humanity.

Therefore, while we agree with the motivation of theologians like Clark who espouse the antithetical Gospel-Law paradigm and who wish to avoid identifying the reception of the Gospel with human achievement, we cannot agree that the imposition of certain moral demands and reproof of certain transgressions as aspects of the Gospel open the door to human achievement. Nor do we agree that the imposition of these demands threatens a gracious, monergistic soteriology. Conversely, we are convinced that to wrench these requirements from the Gospel is to come dangerously close to succumbing to an antinomian message that Paul excoriates (Rom. 6:15).

Paul declares of his Gospel preaching, "For we are unto God a sweet savor [aroma] of Christ, in them that are saved, and in them that perish: To the one we are the savor of death unto death; and to the other the savor of life unto life" (2 Cor. 2:15-16, KJV; cf. 4:3-4; 1 Cor. 1:18ff).[50] Professor Clark suggests that we should first preach a rigorous Law to convict the sinner and then, only afterward, preach a gracious Gospel as a relief to the burden that the preaching of Law imposes (*CJPM*, 358-361). But Paul did not enlist the Law as a separate category in prelude to the Gospel —

---

49. George E. Ladd, "The Knowledge of God: The Saving Acts of God," in ed., Carl F. H. Henry, *Basic Christian Doctrines* (New York: Holt, Rinehart and Winston, 1962), 7-13.
50. Robert S. Rayburn, "The Contrast Between the Old and New Covenants in the New Testament," doctoral thesis, University of Aberdeen, 1978.

the Gospel *itself* sufficed to condemn the impenitent. The Gospel carries in its very bosom the broad ethical stipulation ("Law") that, since humanity stands condemned by its rebellion against God, coming to God in Christ for salvation entails a surrender of that rebellion and commitment to follow Jesus (Mt. 16:24-27).

Unfortunately, it is not often considered that man's chief dilemma is rebellion and that the Gospel was introduce to begin eliminating it. Part of the problem in Lutheran theology, for example, is that its soteriology is shaped more by Luther's own agonizing experience of wrestling with a burdened conscience before a holy God, and less by the picture of man's rebellion against God. The Gospel is then readily depicted in a rather imbalanced fashion — as a panacea to man's emotional plight. Luther drew parallels of his own dilemma with Paul's, but, as NT scholars are increasingly recognizing,[51] Paul did not seem to have suffered from a troubled conscience before his conversion. He did, however, describe himself (Phil. 3:3-9) and his Jewish countrymen (Rom. 2), as well as the Gentiles (Rom. 5:10-21; Eph. 2:1-3), as Christ-less rebels against God and in dire need of submission to Him. To picture Paul's chief problem as one of a troubled conscience under the weight of sin is to confuse effects with causes. Paul — and man's — great problem to which the Gospel is the solution is sin: in essence, man's rebellion against God.

This is why David P. Gushee is warranted when he writes in *Christianity Today* that the frequent evangelical way of answering the question of how we are to be saved by saying, "The only thing required of us is to believe that Jesus' blood saves us" is not the way Jesus talked. Jesus' pointed responses in Luke 10:25 and 18:18 included the necessity of a faith-filled *obedience*.[52] Salvation rests entirely on the finished work of Jesus on the Cross and from the empty tomb, and justification is appropriated by faith alone (elaborated below), but the faith by which we are justified is an obedient

---

51. Launched by the small classic, Krister Stendahl's "The Apostle Paul and the Introspective Conscience of the West," *Paul Among Jews and Gentiles* (Philadelphia: Fortress Press, 1976), 78-96.

52. David P. Gushee, "Jesus and the Sinner's Prayer," *Christianity Today*, March 2007, 72.

faith and, in Gushee's words, "If Jesus is to be believed, inheriting eternal life involves a comprehensive divine assessment at every step along our [spiritual] journey, not just at its inception."

In short, the Gospel is the message of the King, not merely the Savior — or, more positively, it is the message of the Savior-King. He atoned for the sins of humanity, rose from the dead for their justification (Rom. 4:25) and commands individuals to repent of their sins and follow Him. The goal of the Gospel is the worldwide submission of humanity to Christ the King (Phil. 2:5-11), and as His obedient servants we are charged to press His claims in all areas of life and thought, working toward the eventual and inevitable triumph of the Kingdom of Jesus Christ in earth, a kingdom engendered by the Gospel.[53] The Gospel is not only a message to be believed; it is a command to be obeyed.[54]

The obedience of faith, the demand for repentance, and the regal character of the Gospel all verify that the Gospel is not a message that one simply passively receives; one must actively affirm it and submit to its demands, contrary to Clark.

An active, obedient faith. Clark, citing the Westminster Confession, identifies faith exclusively as "resting and receiving" (*CJPM*, 357), and we dare not neglect this vital aspect of saving faith. If it is meant to denote that the object of man's confidence must be nothing or no one other than the crucified and risen Lord Jesus, it is an essential description of one aspect of the Biblical notion of saving faith. Sinners are not saved by trusting in themselves, their own good works or merit or achievement. They are saved by faith in Jesus Christ alone. In this sense, faith is rightly identified as resting and receiving. However, Clark equates this resting and receiving with *passivity* (*CJPM*, 362-363).[55] This passivity apparently prohibits the inclusion of repentance and submission to Jesus as constituent elements of faith: these acts may (even must) follow saving faith, but they are not of the essence of faith. For Clark, faith

---

53. H. Henry Meeter, *The Basic Ideas of Calvinism* (Grand Rapids: Kregel's, 1960 edition), ch. 7.
54. Barth, "Gospel and Law," 80.
55. See also Clark, "When the Good News Becomes Bad," 7.

cannot be living, active and obedient, but must be passive, merely resting on and receiving what Jesus has done in His "active" (lifelong obedience to the law) and "passive" (death and resurrection) obedience. Yet, as the argument above has attempted to demonstrate, faith is anything but passive; and an active, obedient faith is not incompatible with resting and receiving. This faith is the only means by which sinners appropriate justification.

The extent to which the antithetical Gospel-Law paradigm is forced nearly to the breaking point in its tension with Biblical exegesis appears in comments by Professor Clark's colleague, Michael Horton. Although Clark defines saving faith as "passive trust in the finished work of Christ,"[56] and Horton contends, "While our confessions affirm that the faith that justifies is a living, active, and obedient faith [!], they universally insist that faith is justifying faith only in its act of resting in Christ's merits" (*CJPM*, 205). That is, legitimate faith is living, active, and obedient, although one aspect of that faith (which Horton terms "justifying faith") is *not* "living, active, and obedient," but rather, passive, i.e., "resting in Christ's merits." The faith that justifies is "living, active, and obedient," but when it *actually does justify* (instrumentally), it is not "living, active, and obedient" but "passive trust in the finished work of Christ." This tangled terminology is an effect of a tangled soteriology. It is inconceivable that the Biblical authors — take as just one example the writer of Hebrews 11 — could have posited contrasting definitions of faith — "justifying faith" versus "the faith that justifies" or have isolated that aspect of faith that comprises "passive trust in the finished work of Christ" from that aspect of faith which is "living, active, and obedient." "[T]rust in the finished work of Christ" is not passive, and a "living, active, and obedient faith" casts itself wholly on the finished work of Christ. This is why Hebrews 11:6 identifies (saving!) faith not only as belief that God exists but also as belief that God rewards those who seek him out (actively!). The writer is encouraging believers whose assurance and conviction were flagging amid persecution (10:32-39) and whose loss of faith risked forfeiture of their standing

---

56. Clark, "When the Good News Becomes Bad," 7.

(v. 39). In chapter 10, faith and obedience (and unbelief and disobedience) are so intertwined as to render any isolation of one from the other impossible. Faith itself is an act of obedience, and in obeying, one exercises authentic faith. The faith by which one is saved (or justified) is this authentic "living, active, and obedient" faith that "trust(s) in the finished work of Christ."

The "works of the law." But what about those statements, notably by Paul, that contrast the faith of the Gospel and the "works of the law" (Gal. 2:16; 3:2, 11-12)? It comports remarkably with Paul's argument to interpret this expression as referring not to the revelatory law, but to the Pharisaic and Judaistic misinterpretations of the law by Paul's opponents.[57] Paul's negative comments about the law are almost always set in a polemical context, and there was no word group in Greek to designate "legalism," "legalist," or "legalistic."[58] If Paul can confirm the authority of the law and advocate the life-giving character of the Gospel within that revelatory law in the very contexts in which he distinguishes Law from grace (Gal. 6:1, 14; 6:2; Rom. 7:6-14), the most natural way to understand him is to recognize a contrast between a false and a genuine view of the law, and between a submissive relation to the law and a sinful relation to it.[59]

In Galatians the expression translated "works of the law" appears four times. It never appears in a positive light. It is set in sharp contrast with "the hearing of faith" (2:16, 3:2; 3:5), which is obviously positive. So, does "works of the law" denote the *genuine* commands of the OT law? Does it refer to commands that, while legitimate as stand-alone ethical standards, have nothing to do with eternal life, and are in fact commands that if read and obeyed will draw one *away* from Christ?[60] In other words, are they God-given

---

57. Fuller, *Gospel and Law*, ch. 4. See also Robert L. Dabney, *Lectures in Systematic Theology* (Grand Rapids: Zondervan, 1972), 458-462.
58. Fuller, "Paul and 'The Works of the Law,'" 28.
59. This position is at odds with Douglas J. Moo, "The Law of Moses or the Law of Christ," in ed., John S. Feinberg, *Continuity and Discontinuity* (Westchester, Illinois: Crossway, 1988), 203-218.
60. This is the sentiment of Rudolf Bultmann, *Theology of the New Testament* (New York: Scribner's, 1951), 1:259-269.

commands that sinners should at all costs avoid for fear that they will be seduced from Christ? This interpretation seems inconceivable.

In Romans 9:30-33 Paul states that unbelieving Israel did not seek righteousness by faith in Christ but by the "works of the law." Significantly, however, he clearly implies that they could have discovered the truth of *faith*-righteousness in the revelatory law. This means that "works of the law" *denotes not the revelatory law, but a perversion of the law by the self-righteous, a Law without Christ.*

The "works of the law" are not what the OT required. Read properly, the OT teaches (in anticipatory form) salvation solely in the redemptive work of Jesus (Rom. 10:4). OT law, therefore, is not a legalistic code. It is a covenant revelation of holy conduct that includes at its very heart the disclosure of salvation by grace through faith in Jesus apart from human merit or "good works" or any other human activity in which man can boast.

The contrast in Paul is never between Law, properly understood, and salvation by grace through faith in Christ. Rather, the contrast is between a perversion of the revelatory law that transforms it into a legalistic code apart from Jesus, and a proper understanding of the law at the heart of which is the Gospel message of faith in and obedience to the Redeemer.

This is why we read that remarkable statement in Romans 3:21, "But now the righteousness of God apart from the law is revealed, being witnessed by the Law and the Prophets." The revelatory law itself attested that righteousness is not by Law-keeping, which is a moralistic, exclusivist code such as the one that many Jews observed. By contrast, Paul calls the actual revelatory law a "law of faith" in verse 27. The problem is not the revelatory law, which, if properly kept, does not lead away from Christ — it leads to and reveals Christ. And those who understand and keep that law will trust in Christ alone for salvation; and as His disciples, they will obey Him.[61]

Paul contrasts faith with works (Rom. 4:1-8) and identifies faith as a human act compatible with God's grace — that is,

---

61 Daniel P. Fuller, "Only Disciples Are Saved," Berean Corner On-line, http://www.fuller.edu/ministry/berean/disciple.htm.

though a human act, it is not a human "work" in the sense of meritorious performance (4:2-4; cf. Gal. 3:22; Eph. 2:8-9).[62] This faith is an energetic, active, persevering belief (Rom. 4:18-24; Gal. 2:20; Heb. 11:6, 13-16). It engenders repentance for unbelief and disobedience, grasps with reckless abandon the promises of God, and submits to Jesus as Savior and Lord. It is the antithesis of moralism, legalistic works-righteousness, and merit-centered human performance. This faith receives and acts on the Gospel. "The term conditions," Sinclair Ferguson argues, "has a certain infelicity about it. But there is a difference between what we might call 'conditionality' (which compromises grace by saying, 'God will be gracious only if you do X or Y') and the fact that there are conditions for salvation which arise directly out of the gospel message and do not compromise its graciousness."[63] Ferguson goes on to mention, in addition to faith itself, confession (1 Jn. 1:9), repentance (Lk. 13:3), and suffering with Christ (Rom. 8:17) as such conditions that "[do] not compromise grace, but arise from it." These conditions, Ferguson correctly implies, do not violate justification by faith alone.

Gospel is the Good News of what God has accomplished in Jesus, and the reception of that message imposes obligation ("Law") on man, notably, faith alone as the instrument of justification, a living, active obedient faith. Gospel is gracious, just as it is obligatory, and its obligation does not undercut its gracious character. In the manner in which Clark uses these terms, Gospel includes Law.

The Law as Obligation Is Anchored in Salvation by Faith (Alone) in Jesus Christ ("Gospel")

But does Law include Gospel? According to Professor Clark, Law, in sharp contrast to Gospel, is a "relentless demand ... for perfect obedience (*CJPM*, 338); it "can do nothing but condemn[;]

---

62. John Murray, *The Epistle to the Romans* (Grand Rapids: Eerdmans, 1959, 1965), 1:127-133.
63 Sinclair B. Ferguson, "A Reformed Response [to the Lutheran View of Sanctification]," in ed., Donald L. Alexander, *Christian Spirituality: Five Views of Sanctification* (Downers Grove, Illinois: InterVarsity, 1988), 35, emphasis in original.

that [condemnation] is its office (*CJPM*, 341). While for believers "the law serves to structure Christian sanctity [i.e., contains God's standard of flawless sanctification they can never hope to meet] (*CJPM*, 350), for unbelievers it can only condemn, since Law requires unflinching obedience as a condition of eternal life. One must obey the Law unfailingly, or he is condemned to eternal death. There is no middle ground.

In defining Law as "God's unbending moral will,"[64] Clark cannot be referring to the revelatory law of the OT as such, that is, what is generally considered the entire segment of law(s) such as the Decalogue, the Ten Commandments, and the Jews' ceremonial stipulations. The sacrificial system is a crucial component of this law and thus was not "God's unbending moral will" but rather God's means of forgiving and restoring those who violate that will.[65] If the revelatory law had been "unbending," it would never have provided redemptive recourse for the Jews who bent it. We cannot hold that the law accepted nothing but infallible obedience if in its very structure God made ample provision for rectifying the Jews' disobedience. Therefore, Clark must be referring by "Law" to a subset of the revelatory law, a category of "active" commands (apart from the sacrificial system). When we are called actively to obey, we encounter the category of Law; when we are called passively to trust (in Jesus), we confront the category of Gospel.[66] That is, in Clark's view, we cannot mix active obedience with passive trust, and standing just behind this prohibition of mixture is the rationale for the Covenant of Works, the theory, explained previously, that eternal life can be achieved only by active obedience to God's commands, a reward that one merits. Since man has fallen into sin, he has forfeited his ability to win salvation by this meritorious obedience, so he must trust the meritorious obedience of another, Jesus. If man posits "active" commands as conditions of the Gospel, he is falling into the Law-keeping by which Jesus alone

---

64. Clark, "When the Good News Becomes Bad," 3.
65. Walter Kaiser, *Toward an Old Testament Theology* (Grand Rapids: Zondervan, 1978), 115-116.
66. Clark, "When the Good News Becomes Bad," 7.

wins God's favor and earns salvation for sinners. So, salvation (for man) is not about doing (Law) but about resting (Gospel). The Covenant of Grace is the Covenant of Works fulfilled by Jesus.[67]

No Covenant of Works. Yet this entire soteric scheme is wrong.[68] First, we must inquire whether obedience to the Law as a system of divine commands ever merited eternal life. The antithetical Gospel-Law paradigm asserts that it did — according to the Reformed version, in the Covenant of Works. Yet the Biblical arguments marshaled to justify this doctrine are tenuous, and the Biblical arguments against it are obvious.

In the Garden of Eden, before sin entered the world and before salvation from sin was necessary (the "prelapsarian" era), God did not offer eternal life contingent on man's merit or achievement or good works. In fact, the narrative of Genesis 1-2 asserts nothing whatever, explicitly or implicitly, about man's meriting or achieving eternal life, and neither does any other Biblical text.[69] Moreover, there is no covenant in the Garden, and certainly not a Covenant of Works, which is, according to John Murray "a grave misconception."[70] The text mentions only demerit — God threatens punishment for Adam and Eve if they eat of the forbidden tree (Gen. 2:17). Advocates of the antithetical Gospel-Law paradigm must import into Genesis 1-2 the idea that God promised to

---

67. Clark, "When the Good News Becomes Bad," 3.
68. For penetrating criticisms of the covenant of works notion, see Herman Hoeksema, *Reformed Dogmatics* (Grand Rapids: Reformed Free Publishing, 1966), 214-226. For a more recent repudiation, see Ralph Smith, *Eternal Covenant* (Moscow, Idaho: Canon Press), 61-83. While, contrary to Smith, I believe the launching point for treatment of the covenant is the historic Christ and not the orthodox Trinity, his criticism of the covenant of works is on target.
69. It is notable that in his otherwise excellent survey of the topic of covenant, O. Palmer Robertson does not offer proof that God's prelapsarian relation to man was covenantal, though he assumes this idea. See his *The Christ of the Covenants* (Phillipsburg, New Jersey: Presbyterian and Reformed, 1980), 67-107. See also C. F. Keil and F. Delitzsch, *The Pentateuch* (Grand Rapids: Eerdmans, 1988), 1:85-86.
70. John Murray, "The Adamic Administration," *Collected Writings of John Murray* (Edinburgh: Banner of Truth, 1977), 2:47-59. While Murray does not entirely abolish the rationale for the Covenant of Works (in avoiding mention of active, obedient faith as the condition of blessing in the Garden), his denial of merit delivers a welcome, critical blow to the theory.

reward eternal life to the first parents if they kept His commandments perfectly. This is an example of a "theological interpretation" (discussed above), by which they force the text into their own deductive theological grid: "Salvation at root is meritorious law-keeping; therefore, God must have promised to reward Adam and Eve with eternal life if they kept God's law." But this is not what Genesis 1-2 says, and it is not what it implies.[71] The threat of demerit does not necessitate the reward of merit, which cannot be found in Genesis 1-2.

Further, the idea that the Mosaic law is a republication of the Covenant of Works cannot sustain rigorous examination, not least because there was no Covenant of Works to republish.[72] The preamble of the Mosaic economy (Ex. 19:4; cf. Dt. 26:18-19) situates this covenant squarely as gracious (as all Biblical covenants between God and man are gracious), with no requirement that men must adhere to its commands in order to merit eternal life as some sort of reward. The gracious covenant relationship preceded the call to obedience (Jer. 31:32). The call to obedience is preceded by and established on the basis of God's gracious choice of Israel (Ex. 19:5f.). God initiated with Israel His gracious covenant relationship before He laid down the requirements to which His people were bound, requirements that were simply an aspect of that gracious covenant relationship and the keeping of which was never depicted as entitling one to eternal life.[73]

Not only does exegesis fail to support a Covenant of Works; it is a theologically impoverished doctrine. While the Bible describes Jesus Christ as the Lamb slain from the foundation of the world

---

71. John Bolt acknowledges that the Bible does not explicitly teach the Covenant of Works but argues that it teaches the doctrine implicitly, like the Trinity. He then relies on exegetical tradition to argue for the doctrine, which must be grounded (he says) in natural law. Bolt's chapter contains only theological observations and deductions, no exegesis: "Why the Covenant of Works Is a Necessary Doctrine," in eds., Johnson and Waters, *By Faith Alone*, 171-189.

72. Norman Shepherd, "Law and Gospel in Covenantal Perspective," *Reformation and Revival Journal*, Vol. 14, No. 1 [2005], 78.

73. Walter C. Kaiser, Jr., "Leviticus 18:5 and Paul: Do This and You Shall Live (Eternally?)," *Journal of the Evangelical Theological Society*, Vol. 14, No. 1 [Winter 1971], 22.

(Rev. 13:8), the Covenant of Works turns Him into a means within a deeper and different soteric scheme (*CJPM*, 243-244). Jesus in this soteric scheme is not the goal of man's salvation; He is the instrument for obtaining that goal, which is meritorious righteousness by which alone man is entitled to the reward of eternal life.[74] It is not Jesus (or, for that matter, the Father and Spirit) Whom we seek with all our heart as the treasure of eternal life (Col. 1:9-23), but rather a legal righteousness that earns for us a merited standing before God. Jesus is a means to a legalistic, moralistic end.

Conversely, if we recognize that in the Garden of Eden, just as in the postlapsarian economy after sin spoiled the earlier state, the promise of man's eternal life rests on the grace of God apart from human merit, good works, legal obedience or achievement, then we preserve the God- (and Christ-) centeredness of salvation. In the prelapsarian arrangement man would have been granted eternal life had he continued in a devout, uncomplicated faith in the Triune God, a faith that rested totally on God for all of man's needs and submitted to God as the loving heavenly Father. In the postlapsarian arrangement, man is granted eternal life as he exercises a devout, uncomplicated faith in Jesus Christ (God's express image [Heb. 1:1-3]), whose death and resurrection alone purge man's sin and restore his broken relationship with God (Rom. 5:6-11; Eph. 2:11-22; cf. Rom. 4:25). In both the pre- and postlapsarian arrangements, God is not the means to an end, the instrument for obtaining legal righteousness, but rather is the end toward which man looks by faith alone for eternal life. Salvation rests in Jesus alone (1 Cor. 1:30-31; Col. 2:9-10), not in righteousness that Jesus assists us in obtaining. Eternal life, therefore, is not merited by Law-keeping, and it has never been merited by Law-keeping.

Texts alleged to support this paradigm. Notwithstanding, Professor Clark offers several texts[75] in support of his view that eternal life is merited by Law-keeping (*CJPM*, 244-248). But do these texts

---

74. John Murray, "Covenant Theology," *Collected Writings of John Murray* (Edinburgh: Banner of Truth, 1984), 4:229-220.

75. The Westminster Confession lists Genesis 1:26-27; 2:17; Job 28:20; Ecclesiastes 7:29; Romans 2:14-15; 10:5; 5:12; and Galatians 3:10-12 as "proofs" of the Covenant of Works — that eternal life is merited by keeping the Law.

actually support the doctrine he advocates? (Recall that we denote the revelatory law as "law," but the category of Scriptural commands and requirements, a theological category as used by Clark, as "Law.")

He enlists Romans 1:18-2:16 to prove that "[e]ven in paradise the demands [of God] were unequivocal and the standard unforgiving." Clark cites Romans 2:6, that in the Final Day, God will give each man "according to his works [or deeds]." This statement, however, has nothing whatever to do with paradise (despite Clark's claim that v. 20 "frames the discussion in terms of Adam and the fall" *[CJPM*, 244]), and it does not otherwise support what Clark alleges. The context of Romans 2 is God's impartiality in judging the Jews, who have sinfully prided themselves as God's covenant people (vv. 11-12). In 1:18-32 God levels His indictment against law-breaking Gentiles, and He turns to an indictment of the Jews in chapter 2. God's rendering of judgment according to works (v. 6, citing Ps. 62:12) includes both the obedient and disobedient after the Fall (vv. 7-8). Those who possess the revelatory law (the Jews) will be judged by it, and those who do not possess it (the Gentiles) will perish without it (v. 12). Paul's point is not that the revelatory law has no claim on the Gentiles (this is the opposite of his intent [vv. 14-15; cf. 3:19]), but that lack of contact with the revelatory law is no excuse for the Gentiles' depravity, since God's revelation in creation, not just in Scripture, also discloses His law. None of this has anything to do with the Covenant of Works or "active obedience." The obedience implied in 2:7 is the "obedience of faith," an obedience the essence of which is the abandonment of all self-righteousness and constitutes confidence in Jesus Christ as Savior and Lord.[76] It does not refer to a meritorious "good works" in which one may boast but an obedient faith of the redeemed after the Fall. The depraved Jews and Gentiles are judged not because they violate a Covenant of Works (for the passage lauds good works done after the Fall, not in the Garden of Eden) but because they have turned their back on God (Rom.

---

76. Cranfield, *Romans 1-8*, 150-153..

1:19-21; 2:4). This abandonment of God and His grace leads naturally to the depravity of both Gentiles and Jews that Paul catalogs. There can be no doubt that Paul is reprimanding all humanity for its law-breaking (Rom. 3:19), and that "the divine command for obedience has existed since before the fall" (*CJPM*, 244), but God's reprimand nowhere implies that man is granted eternal life by Law-keeping. In Romans 2:13 he reminds the Jews that not the hearers of the law, but its doers, will be justified. It is tempting to see in that verse proof of a meritorious works-righteousness in the law by which one theoretically could be justified,[77] but since Paul has just applauded (v. 7) believers who live in terms of the law and in so doing trust in Christ for salvation, he must have in mind a righteousness of faith (Rom. 9:3) that excludes meritorious works-righteousness. The sense then would be that the Jews merely hear the law's teaching of justification by faith in Jesus but only those who do the law (actually exercise faith in Him apart from works-righteousness) will be justified.[78] Eternal life is not a reward for Law-keeping, a Covenant of Works. As in Genesis 1-2, so in Romans 1-2, God punishes disobedience with eternal death, but He does not reward obedience with eternal life. Eternal life is a gift conferred on those who place faith in Jesus.

Clark then cites Jesus' statement in Matthew 5:18-19 about the inviolability of the law (we are called to adhere to "the least of these commandments") and to our Lord's requirement of the self-righteous lawyer, "Do this and live" (Lk. 10:25-28). Yet Matthew 5:18-19 says nothing whatever about eternal life as a reward for Law-keeping, and Luke 10 (which will be addressed below) does not teach a meritorious self-righteousness.

Clark goes on to enlist Romans 10:5, Paul's citation from Leviticus 18:5, that the righteousness of the law is fulfilled by the man who lives by that law, to support the imputation of "active obedience," salvation by man's meritorious righteousness. Clark

---

77. John Calvin, *Commentaries on the Epistle of Paul the Apostle to the Romans* (Grand Rapids: Baker, 1993), 19:95.
78. Cranfield, *Romans 1-8*, 154-155. On a popular level, see N. T. Wright, *Romans: Part One* (Louisville, Kentucky: John Knox Press, 2004), 33.

ties this verse to 2:13, noted above. But what is true of 2:13 is true of 10:5 — "doers of the law" refers to those who act according to the revelatory law's plan of salvation in the promised Messiah. The contrast implied in 10:5 is not between those who keep the commands of God perfectly and those who do not, but between those who recognize that the revelatory law presents a righteousness of faith in Jesus and those who (sinfully) see this revelatory law as a means of their own merit and self-righteousness (9:30-32). The "but" (de) of 10:6 is not always adversative; it can also be transitional.[79] Verses 5 and 6, then, do not present a contrast between two legitimate ways to obtain eternal life, one by faith and one works; rather, these verses offer two examples of a single legitimate righteousness revealed in the OT, the righteousness of faith that persists in the NT and even today. If this is the case, Paul cited Deuteronomy 27:26 in Galatians 3:10 ("For as many as are of the works of the law are under the curse; for it is written, 'Cursed is everyone who does not continue in all things which are written in the book of the law, to do them'") to assert that the curse falls not on those who try to obey the law at all points and fail at any (this would be the very sin of ignorance for which Paul chides the Jews in Romans 9:32), but on those who do not continue in the only authentic righteousness of the law, the righteousness obtained by grace through faith in Messiah alone.

Clark is mistaken, therefore, to write that "[t]he demand [for eternal life] is not only for the absence of sin or even just punishment for sin but also for positive performance of all requirements [of the Bible]" (*CJPM*, 245). The revelatory law — and the entire Bible — teaches that "the demand for eternal life" necessitates the righteousness of faith, not "positive performance of all requirements."

Clark also cites Matthew 3:15, Christ's comment to John the Baptist that He must be baptized to "fulfill all righteousness," and Clark enrolls Galatians 4:4, that Christ was made under the law, to support his view. Yet neither of these texts verifies Clark's thesis. Matthew 3:15 has nothing to say about "active obedience" or a

---

79. Fuller, *Gospel and Law*, 67.

meritorious reward for obeying the Father. As the spotless Lamb of God, Jesus was obliged to walk in humble obedience (Heb. 9:14; 1 Pet. 1:19), but this obedience did not earn rewards or merit eternal life. In Christ's death and resurrection He substituted for sinners, and by union with that death and resurrection alone, a union typified in water baptism, we are saved (Rom. 6:1-4). Similarly, Galatians 4:4 (Jesus was "made under the law") does not denote "active obedience," but the death of Jesus, which is described as the bearing the Law's curse in 3:13. Man broke God's law, and Jesus paid the penalty for that law-breaking on the Cross.[80]

Clark's additional example (*CJPM*, 245, 359-360) of preaching the Law ("active obedience") as a "[t]he demand [for eternal life] ... not only for the absence of sin or even just punishment for sin but also for positive performance of all requirements [of the Bible]" is found in Jesus' conversation with a certain lawyer that provokes our Lord's parable of the Good Samaritan (Lk. 10:25-37). The controversial aspect of this conversation is Jesus' answer to the lawyer's simple question: "Teacher, what shall I do to inherit [or having done what, shall I inherit] eternal life?" Jesus' answer (in summary) is: "Love God with your entire being" (Dt. 6:5): "Do this,"Jesus stated, "and you will live." Clark interprets (1) the lawyer as assuming that his Law-keeping can merit eternal life and (2) Jesus as going along with this mistaken premise to show the lawyer that no mere mortal can meet that high standard. For Clark, the very idea that one would think he must "do" something to gain eternal life is wrongheaded. But the lawyer's question, while improperly motivated (v. 25) is not materially different from the question of Peter's audience in Acts 2:37 ("Men and brethren, what shall we do?") or the jailer's question to Paul and Silas in Acts 16:29, "Sirs, what must I do to be saved?" Neither question necessarily implies a lust for a program of works-righteousness, and both questions presuppose that salvation invites some human response and obligation. In the case of the lawyer, Jesus cited part

---

80. Herman N. Ridderbos, *The Epistle of Paul to the Churches of Galatia* (Grand Rapids: Eerdmans, 1953), 127-128.

of the Jewish Shema: "Love God with your entire being." How this answer could be construed as playing along with a mistaken premise grounded in attempts at self-righteousness is not clear. To love God with one's heart, soul, strength and might is to cast one's affectionate confidence on the Lord; to turn from one's self-centered, sinful life; and to submit to His Lordship. Jesus' answer, tailored to a Jew who likely had studied the revelatory law, was that salvation rests in a right relationship to God — loving Him with one's entire being. This is not somehow a message contradictory to the "righteousness of faith" that Paul mentions in Romans 9:30, a righteousness disclosed in the OT law that the majority of the Jews spurned to their own peril. Any Jew in the OT era who loved God with the entirety of his being was living authentically within the sphere of the law, trusting in the Messiah to whom the sacrificial system pointed, and not relying on his own good works or righteousness. Jesus' program for eternal life in Luke 10:25-37 has nothing to do with a Covenant of Works or attempts to merit eternal life by Law-keeping, when it is interpreted as flawless obedience to divine commands apart from trusting in Jesus.

The most popular text of traditional covenant theology is likely Romans 5:12-21, and it is not surprising that Clark enlists it for his purposes (*CJPM*, 246-248). This passage establishes a parallel between the First Adam (in the Garden of Eden) and the Second Adam (Jesus), or, more precisely, an antithetical parallel. Jesus is depicted as acting in such a way as to remedy and reverse the sinful act of Adam. Clark attempts to show that the one act of obedience by Jesus (vv. 18-19) includes the "active" (meritorious Law-keeping) obedience of Christ's life. Yet the passage says nothing about this form of obedience, and Clark is obliged to rely on an argument from silence ("Paul does not describe Christ's obedience as if it began only at Golgotha or on the cross" [*CJPM*, 248]). True enough, but Paul did not say precisely of what Christ's act consisted. He could have been referring to the obedience of Christ's death and resurrection. This passage cannot establish that Christ lived a meritorious life of good works that win the Father's favor, works that are imputed to sinners so that they can be deemed worthy of eternal life, as the Covenant of Works teaches. Romans 5:12-21 merely establishes (on this issue) that Jesus' obedience remedied what Adam's disobedience wrecked.[81]

The logic of the Covenant of Works appears also in Philippians 2:8, according to Professor Clark: Christ humbled Himself in His incarnation and became obedient to the point of death. Clark insists that Christ's obedience began with His incarnation and culminated in His death, implying that His "active" obedience preceded His "passive" obedience (*CJPM*, 248). There is no doubt that our Lord's entire life was characterized by flawless obedience (Heb. 5:8). Yet Paul does not identify the obedience to which he refers in Philippians 2:8 as a meritorious obedience of Christ's life imputed to believing sinners ("active obedience"). Nor is it clear that the obedience is other than the obedience of Christ's suffering for sinners ("passive").

The texts that Clark marshals to buttress his belief in the "active" obedience of Christ and in the Covenant of Works that is its framework do not teach what he asserts they teach.

Law is not designed to confer eternal life. All to the contrary, in Galatians 3:21 Paul writes, "Is the law then against the promises of God? Certainly not! For if there had been a law given which could have given life, truly righteousness would have been by the law." Paul has been contrasting salvation by faith in Christ with salvation by Law-keeping (vv. 1-18), especially by circumcision as the covenant mark (2:1-17). The promise of salvation to Abraham preceded chronologically the giving of the revelatory law at Sinai, and it is this gracious salvation apart from abstract Law-keeping that Paul is preaching and defending. The idea that the law as adherence to codes and standards and ethics could ever confer eternal life is abhorrent. The Galatians were convinced that the distinctive markers of the revelatory law — the external regulations that distinguished ancient Israel — could be imposed on the Gentiles. Paul's point is that conferring life is not the function of law — law is not against

---

81. Ben Witherington, *The Problem with Evangelical Theology* (Waco, Texas: Baylor, 2005), 10-20.

the promises of God because, unlike the promises, the law does not confer eternal life; only Jesus Christ does. Moisés Silva observes that in 3:12 Paul implies that the revelatory law may and should lead to eternal life but that it cannot generate that life — only Christ via the Gospel (which is found in the revelatory law) can do that.[82] Paul understood that the revelatory law carried within it the message of salvation by faith in the coming Messiah (Rom. 9:30-10:13). But the Galatians were teaching that the Mosaic law (and the economy of which it was a part [4:21-24]) as well as the Abrahamic covenant taught that the inheritance of eternal life was by Law-keeping, and not by promise-affirming (v. 18). The Abrahamic covenant (Gal. 3:15-20), which we understand as the pledge of salvation by grace through faith (vv. 7-9), they linked to circumcision and the human performance it implied as the inheritance by which sinners are saved. Unfortunately, the Galatians did not understand the revelatory law, which condemns those who lack faith (3:23-27) just as the NT gospel does. The Abrahamic and Mosaic covenants are indeed united — but as covenants of grace and not of "Law." To unbelievers, however, the Mosaic law becomes a tool of enslavement (4:1-11). This is not a description of the revelatory law, properly understood, but of the perversion of that law by those who wish to transform it into an instrument of self-righteousness.[83] As in Paul's teaching of Romans 7:13, "sin has co-opted law and pressed it into service for which it was not intended."[84] Though law was never intended to be employed as a system of works-righteousness, it was intended to reveal Israel's sinfulness. In Galatians 3:19 we read that law "was added because of transgressions."[85] God knew of Israel's wayward-

---

82. Moisés Silva, "Is the Law Against the Promises? The Significance of Galatians 3:21 for Covenant Continuity," in eds., William S. Barker and W. Robert Godfrey, *Theonomy: A Reformed Critique* (Grand Rapids: Zondervan, 1990), 165.
83. Rayburn, "The Contrast Between the Old and New Covenants in the New Testament," 93-128.
84. Klyne Snodgrass, "Spheres of Influence: A Possible Solution to the Problem of Paul and the Law," in ed., J. I. Packer, *The Best in Theology, Vol. 3* (Carol Stream, Illinois: Christianity Today, 1989), 86.
85. Note the penetrating insights of G. C. Berkouwer, *Sin* (Grand Rapids: Eerdmans, 1971), 173-186.

ness and gave them a law whose explicit covenant commands would reveal to them the extent of their rebellion (Dt. 1-4). Like the prohibition in the Garden of Eden, it laid down God's righteous standard, but this standard did not constitute a way to eternal life. Because the Gospel at the heart of the revelatory law includes requirements of those who will believe it, it is vulnerable to those who care for nothing but their own merit or self-righteousness. Just as the grace of the revelatory gospel can be turned into lasciviousness by antinomians (Jude 4), so the requirements of the revelatory law can be turned into self-righteousness by moralists. "The law saved," in the words of Donald Bloesch, "by directing us to the gospel, by relaying the message of the gospel to us. The law by itself abstracted from Jesus Christ does not save but only condemns. It is when Christ speaks to us through the law, it is when we perceive the law through the lens of the gospel, that we are convicted of sin and assured by the promise of the gospel."[86] The law (like the gospel) is lawful only if it is used lawfully (1 Tim. 1:8)! The law, however, is not against the promises of God, because, unlike the promises, it could never confer eternal life. Only Jesus Christ can confer eternal life. Paul's construction of Galatians 3:21 explicates not merely that the Mosaic law cannot generate life but, more generically, implies that it is not the function of Law of any kind to generate life.[87] A Covenant of Works of any kind is an impossibility.

It is true that Paul writes in Galatians 3 that the law is a schoolmaster to bring us to Christ. To those who do not believe, it condemns. Before faith comes, rebellious sinners see in the law only a condemnation. But this is no less true of the gospel, as we observed earlier. Paul tells us in 2 Thessalonians 1 that Jesus will one day return in flaming vengeance to wreak judgment on all those who do not obey the Gospel. The gospel is not only a message to be believed; it is a command to be obeyed. Both Biblical gospel and law convict the impenitent.

---

86. Donald G. Bloesch, *Jesus Christ, Savior and Lord* (Downers Grove, Illinois: InterVarsity, 1997), 202.
87. Walter C. Kaiser, Jr., "The Law as God's Gracious Guidance for the Promotion of Holiness," 190-192.

The antithetical Gospel-Law paradigm is wrong, therefore, to suggest that Law-keeping (as in fulfilling commandments) merits eternal life, because it is not the nature of law to occupy that function. Eternal life is the free gift of God to a faith-filled, submissive people, and it cannot — and could never have been — earned.

Professor Clark errs, consequently, to assert that the Gospel is the message not just that Christ has died and risen for our justification but, in addition that He "fulfilled the covenant of works" (*CJPM*, 352). There can be no doubt that our salvation has as its object only the crucified and risen Lord and that our justification and hope rest not in what we have done or ever could do, but in what Jesus has accomplished in His death and resurrection.

Clark acknowledges that the antithetical messages of Gospel and Law appear throughout the Bible (*CJPM*, 349), but the fact that they appear not just in close proximity but also interpenetrate one another renders his antithetical scheme arbitrary. There are not two, mutually antithetical messages — "Trust Jesus with all your heart and nothing else" and "Obey God with a trusting heart." These themes are inextricably bound in the Biblical Gospel.

Gospel at the heart of (Mosaic) law. We know that the message at the heart of the Mosaic law is a Gospel message. We learn from Paul (in Romans 10:4-10) that the law itself taught justification by faith.[88] In Luke 16, in the story of Lazarus and the rich man, we read that "Moses and the Prophets" (meaning large sections of OT revelation, and believing and acting on significant parts of the law) would have sufficed to protect the rich man's brothers from hell fire. We know that salvation is solely by the grace of God (Eph. 2:8-9), so it is clear that the aspects of the law mentioned in this paragraph are gracious, engulfed in the gospel. Men could be saved by hearing and believing the Christ-oriented teaching within the Mosaic law.

The most striking evidence of this wholly gracious soteriology in the Mosaic law was, as noted above, the sacrificial system, which was at the core of God's plan for His people, and not some

---

88. See Fuller, Gospel and Law, ch. 4. Consult, too, Norman Shepherd's *The Call of Grace* (Phillipsburg, New Jersey: P & R Publishing, 2000).

external code of legalistic salvation: "[T]he end [objective] of the Law lay beyond the obedience to such and such rules, that end being instruction in the knowledge of God and of individuals' relation to Him, and guidance in living as the children of such a God as he revealed Himself to be."[89] The law is integrally related to God's covenant with Israel and is sometimes even equated with that covenant (Ps. 78:10).[90] As a holistic revelation of God's standards for His covenant people, law and related terms like statutes, testimonies, and commandments, do not denote His demands devoid of His grace manifested in both communal and individual salvation but as "the teaching" reflect God's comprehensive revelation to Israel. Gracious salvation is, in fact, a chief aspect of that revelation in *tôrâ*, "the teaching" that God imposes on His covenant people for their salvation and well-being.

In Exodus 20:24, in the very giving of the Mosaic Law, Jehovah includes provision for the sacrificial system, at the center of which is (temporary, Heb. 10:1-4) forgiveness of sins pointing to Jesus, Who would one day cleanse His people from their sins. The sacrificial system as an integral component of the law refutes the notion that the Law as revelation was somehow an imposing, insuperable ethical standard, the smallest infraction of which elicits God's judgment.[91] In its every structure, the law contained the means for forgiveness of and rectification for sins committed.

While the OT contained only types and shadows, and while the reality to which (Whom!) they pointed comes to the fore only in the NT, the pattern of gracious salvation in which man can take no pride is a vital dimension of OT law.

---

89. Ulric Rule, "Law in the Old Testament," in ed., James Orr, *International Standard Bible Encyclopedia* (Grand Rapids: Eerdmans, 1939), 3:1852.
90. H[artley], J[ohn] E., "[L]aw, [T]eaching," in eds., R. Laird Harris, Gleason L. Archer, Jr., and Bruce K. Waltke, *Theological Wordbook of the OT* (Chicago: Moody, 1980), 1:403-405.
91. The Old Testament "denotes the covenant of works or the moral law given by Moses — the unbearable burden ... of legal ceremonies being added, absolutely and apart from the promise of grace," Francis Turretin, *Institutes of Elenctic Theology* (Phillipsburg, New Jersey: P & R Publishing, 1994), 2:234. It is hard to imagine a more mistaken view of the Old Testament law.

God did not reveal two *different* revelational components or classifications, one declaring the (non-obligatory) Gospel of a gracious salvation and the other laying out (non-gracious) legal stipulations by which His covenant people were to order their lives. All that "pertain[ed] to life and godliness" (2 Pet. 1:3) Jehovah had furnished in the Mosaic law that pointed to Jesus. This should not surprise us, since Jesus himself alerted the self-righteous Jews of His day (Jn. 5) that, while they trusted in an external conformity to Mosaic law (v. 16), they had missed the very center of that law — Jesus Himself:

> " ... Do not think that I shall accuse you to the Father; there is one who accuses you — Moses, in whom you trust. For if you believed Moses, you would believe Me; for he wrote about Me. But if you do not believe his writings, how will you believe My words?" (vv. 45-47)

The core of the Mosaic law is the revelation of the Messiah that was to come and salvation by faith in Him alone. When God exhorted Joshua to immerse himself in the law (Josh. 1:8), therefore, He was directing His servant not to a sort of code book of external law-keeping, but to the disclosure of Jesus and the justification by faith that belief in Him affords, apart from the righteousness of moralistic law-keeping (Rom. 10:6-13).

We confront also the psalmist's exaltation and exultation of the law in Psalm 119 in which he identifies his love for the law as a gracious, merciful, reviving, life-giving revelation (note especially vv. 17, 20, 25, 29, 32, 37, 40, 41, 50, 64, 77, 92, 105, 116, 144, 149, 154, 155, 166, 174). We discover from a careful reading of this psalm that David oriented his entire life — including his eternal life — to Jehovah by means of His revelation in the law. We detect not a single hint that David considered the law only a compendium of commands and threatenings terrifying all who swerve a single iota from it and containing nothing of God's grace; rather, the law is filled with Gospel, a gracious, vivifying force to all who submit to it in faith.

We should not be surprised, therefore, to read in Psalm 19 that the "law of the Lord is perfect, converting [or reviving] the soul" (v. 7). David sees the Gospel-enriched revelatory law as a tool of man's conversion in pointing us to Jesus, a fact that contradicts the idea that the revelatory law (as command) only and always threatens and lacks any instrumental salvific efficacy to sinners.

The Grace of Law in the New Testament. The NT presents a similar testimony about Law. Jesus, citing the Shema of Deuteronomy 6, identifies the first great commandment of the revelatory law as love for God with all of one's being and the second as love of one's neighbor (Mt. 22:34-40). The fact that the primary command of the law is passionate affection for God and, secondarily, for our fellow man militates against the idea that Law as requirements and commands (with which the revelatory law is filled) is a graceless, austere set of requirements, a meritorious Covenant of Works. It implies that Law is anchored in a covenant relation that entails reciprocity of affection and allegiance (Ex. 19:1-8; 24:1-8) — and neither without the other. God's covenant relationships with humanity as disclosed in the Bible are far from one-sided impositions of requirements and threatenings. They are bilateral relationships that include love and affection and forgiveness (Ps. 78:32-38; 86:5-7; 99:6-8) and agonizing longsuffering (Hos. 1-2) and means of rectifying grievances (Num. 4-5) and, in fact, instruments for obtaining eternal life in the Gospel (Dt. 30:11-20[92]).

This is why Jesus could on the one hand reprimand the Pharisees for their austere, external, legalistic approach to the law (Mt. 23), while He Himself advocated observance of the law in the smallest detail (Mt. 5:17-20).[93] He invites those souls burdened by sin and the cares of life to assume his easy yoke and light burden (Mt. 11:28-30). Yet His message clearly was not that the law is no longer in force. In other words, Jesus set forth a view of law that preserved its proper, Gospel-enriched character (Mt. 5:21f.) while

---

92. As indicated above, Paul introduces this passage in Romans 10 to buttress his argument for salvation by faith alone.
93. Greg L. Bahnsen, *Theonomy in Christian Ethics* (Nacogdoches, Texas: Covenant Media Press, 2002 edition).

rebuking those who perverted it by transforming it into a external, legalistic, burdensome code of works-righteousness (Mk. 7:1-13).

This portrait of Jesus' message does not fit within the constrictive antithetical Gospel-Law paradigm that sees the Law as only a series of commands backed up by dire threatenings, bracketed from the grace of God but filled with the promise of eternal life to all who keep them infallibly (an impossibility for all but Christ since the Fall).

Nor does Pauline theology conform to this restrictive, graceless view of the Law. While Paul repeatedly criticized those who turned the revelatory law into a Christ-less system of (often racial) pride and privilege (Gal. 3:1-9), he acknowledged the life-giving power disclosed in the law by which a man is justified by Jesus' redemption alone (Rom. 2:13; cf. 3:20-21!). The law is "spiritual" (Rom. 7:14), and is "ordained to life" (Rom. 7:10) — that is, the revelatory law contains at its very root the Gospel of salvation by grace through faith. Properly understood, it is not a death-dealing legal code but a glorious life-giving message of faith in Jesus alone and obedience to Him.

Nor is the law a rigorous code that one can never hope to meet. In Romans 10:4-9, Paul cites Deuteronomy 30:11-14 in assuring his readers that the law (in Christ, v. 7) is not far away from any of God's covenant people but is near them, in their mouth and heart (v. 8).[94] The "word" (v. 8) to which Paul refers is the word of the Gospel (v. 6), yet it is a Gospel nestled in and inextricably a part of the law. It is a Gospel message contained in the revelatory Law of Moses that is near God's covenant people and ready for them to appropriate by faith. It is not the imposition of codified demands apart from a gracious salvation. For this reason Karl Barth writes:

---

94. That Paul felt necessary to remind his readers that this Gospel message was preached to the Jews as a covenant people refutes the notion that membership in the church necessitates union with Jesus Christ, as the Roman Church holds: *Catechism of the Catholic Church* (Washington, D. C.: United States Catholic Conference [*Libreria Editrice Vaticana*], 1994, second edition), 204-205. For a Protestant example of this error, see Douglas Wilson, "Union with Christ: An Overview of the Federal Vision," in ed., E. Calvin Beisner, *The Auburn Avenue Theology: Pros and Cons* (Fort Lauderdale, Florida: Knox Theological Seminary), 5-6.

> With regard to the New Testament, must one not draw special attention to the fact that it, like the Old Testament, is law — i.e., ordinance, command and instruction for the new life of the people and children of God — but not therefore — not even in part — an authorization and invitation to self-justification and self-sanctification? It is therefore not a book of religion but rather the consistent proclamation of the justifying and sanctifying grace of God, thereby exposing the faithlessness of all religion.... One forgets ... what is so clear and self-evident, that the essence of the benefit of Jesus Christ and therefore of his gospel as experienced in the church of the New Testament is his *Lordship* over human beings. And there can be no purer, or more total *imperative* than the simple invitation directed to man in the New Testament — that he should believe in this Jesus Christ — and no stricter and fuller *obedience* than that which the New Testament describes precisely as faith.[95]

This simplified description of a unified message of Gospel and Law reflects the Biblical data more accurately than the antithetical Gospel-Law paradigm, which tends to surrender the Lordship of Christ in the Gospel on the one hand, and, on the other hand, transforms God's commands and requirements ("Law") into a system of works-righteousness. This paradigm breaks apart what God has joined together.

The exegetical impossibility of the antithetical Gospel-Law paradigm. When Clark isolates Gospel and Law into two messages, even two messages within a single Biblical passage, from a single speaker or writer, he strains credulity. For example, Clark suggests that Peter's Pentecostal message recorded in Acts 2 "moves freely between them [the messages of Law and Gospel]" thus indicating "no artificial separation" [!] between them (361, n. 95). As per Clark, Peter's words of condemnation are words of Law (vv. 22-23): "You have crucified Jesus." And in verse 36 ("Let every house of Israel know certainly, this Jesus whom you crucified, God made him Lord and Christ"), Peter includes both messages in a single statement — the

---

95. Karl Barth, *On Religion*, 69, emphasis in original.

message that one must obey God's commands flawlessly or be condemned (Law), as well as the message that one must passively trust in Christ for salvation in order to gain eternal life (Gospel).

Yet it is inconceivable that Peter would mix such inherently contradictory messages. How could he expect the unbelieving Jews to understand that they are bound to gain eternal life by keeping the law, which imparts that life only to those who conform to it infallibly, but that they cannot keep this law and therefore cannot gain eternal life, but that Jesus has actively kept this law for them and thus merited eternal life in his obedience, if only they trust Him to have obtained that obedience? Peter would in that case have been offering two contradictory roads to eternal life — one theoretical and one actual: the theoretical possibility of eternal life to any who could keep the law infallibly, and the actual fact of eternal life to all who trust in Jesus, Who did keep it infallibly.

This is the not Peter's conclusion. Rather, he insists that his hearers have sinned by crucifying Jesus, the Lord of glory, and that if they repent and cast faith on Him as Lord and Savior, the One they had murdered, they would be saved. Peter's sermon is not proof of the antithetical Gospel-Law paradigm but of the unity of Gospel and Law, of the wholehearted trust in Jesus (and in nothing else) characterized by submission to Him.[96]

Jesus Himself preached this unified message. To his disciples in Mark 8:34-38 (cf. Mt 16:21-23; Lk. 9:23-26; Jn. 12:20-26), Jesus suspends the gift of eternal life (gaining one's "soul," or life) on one's denying himself, taking up his cross and following Him. This message of repentance, self-denial, and obedience ("Law") is not a separate message, isolated from the initial call to trust in and follow Jesus ("Gospel"). It is not an "active" message ("Do this and live") contrasted with a "passive" message ("rest and receive"). There is simply no exegetical isolation of these two "moods" (Clark) in the message of Jesus. We are called to labor to enter into the rest of Jesus Christ (Heb. 4 — note that in this chapter the antithesis of

---

96. John R. W. Stott, *The Message of Acts* (Leicester, England: InterVarsity Press, 1990), 81.

godly rest in Jesus' redemptive ministry is disobedience, not merely unbelief). At the Final Judgment, God will judge all who have refused to rest in Jesus, following Him in repentant obedience.

When He healed the paralytic (Mk. 2:1-12), Jesus told the man, "Son, your sins are forgiven you," as well as "Arise, take up your bed and walk." Both statements proclaim the Good News (Gospel), yet the two are inseparable and imply a command and human obligation. Had the paralytic refused to believe Jesus by not rising from his bed, we have no reason to believe his sins would have been forgiven.[97]

A striking example of this unified message is the salvation of the wealthy tax collector Zacchaeus (Lk. 19:1-10). Jewish tax collectors in the ancient Roman world were reviled for their dishonest enrichment at the expense of their fellow Jews, and when Jesus agreed to visit Zacchaeus' home, the observing crowds complained of His decision. Immediately Zacchaeus promised Jesus that he would give half of his wealth to the poor and restore all ill-gotten wealth to its lawful owners. At this point, Jesus uttered, "Today, salvation has come to this house .... [F]or the Son of Man has come to seek and to save that which was lost" (vv. 9-10). Notably, Jesus affirmed the salvation of Zacchaeus on the evidence of his repentant obedience. The legitimate (obedient, submissive) faith of Zacchaeus assured him of salvation in Jesus, who did not insist on two messages, "Gospel" (the message of resting and receiving) of and "Law" (the message of doing).

This is an overarching Gospel message materially identical throughout redemptive history, though only foreshadowed in the OT: "You have sinned and thus elicited God's judgment, but Jesus has died and risen from the dead for your sins, and if you repent of those sins and trust in and commit your life to Him, you will be saved." This simple message avoids the tangled, convoluted attempts to ferret out two separate messages, two conflicting means of obtaining justification,[98] and situates man's hope entirely in

---

97. Donald G. Bloesch, "Law and Gospel in Reformed Perspective," *Grace Theological Journal*, Vol. 12, No. 2 [Fall 1991], 184.
98. As in Charles Hodge, *Systematic Theology* (Grand Rapids: Eerdmans, 1981), 3:129.

the death and resurrection of Jesus, a hope appropriated by a living, active obedient faith, a gift of God, in which one could never boast. In dividing the entire Bible message(s) into Gospel and Law as two, separate words or "moods," however, Professor Clark is compelled to stretch his antithetical Gospel-Law paradigm almost to the breaking point.

While we have presented here only sketchy evidence, one hopes it will give the reader pause in assuming that Law is always and only obligatory, a works-righteousness plan for eternal life quite in contradistinction to the redemptive work of Jesus. The antithetical Gospel-Law paradigm cannot do justice to those Scriptures that nestle commands and requirements ("active," not "passive") within the Gospel message, commands and requirements that in no way permit merit or good works or human achievement in which man may boast and that by no means compromise justification by faith alone. Likewise, the commands of the OT and the NT, properly understood, carry within them explicitly or implicitly the message that man's salvation rests exclusively in what Jesus has done on the Cross and from the empty tomb, and that only an active, obedient faith can appropriate the benefits of His redemptive work. In the manner in which Clark employs these terms, therefore, *Law includes Gospel*.

Summary and Conclusion

R. Scott Clark, following Martin Luther and a significant segment of the Reformed tradition, has argued that Gospel and Law are mutually exclusive divine messages from God to man: Law is the message of "Do this [actively] and live"; Gospel is the message of "Rest in Jesus [passively] and His work alone." Law is the demand for human performance before God. Gospel is the assurance of Jesus' performance on our behalf that invites our passive reliance ("resting and receiving"). Essential to this theological construct is the Covenant of Works, which holds that eternal life is the reward for man's entire, unblemished obedience to God's commands. Eternal life is merited by man's righteous works established by God. In the covenant administration before the Fall, Adam was capable of performing these works and therefore of winning eternal life for himself and the entire human race, but his sin disqualified both him and us from this path to gaining that life. Jesus Christ, as the New Adam, has fulfilled the standard demanded by the Covenant of Works in his active, Law-keeping life ("active obedience") as well as His Law-keeping death ("passive obedience"). In justification, this legal obedience is imputed (legally credited) to the believing sinner. Man is saved largely on the ground of Jesus' Law-keeping, which merits eternal life for man. At its foundation, eternal life is a reward for works-righteousness. Since man can no longer perform those works impeccably, Jesus performs them on his behalf. Foundationally, therefore, God deals with man on the basis of Law — "Do this and live; fail to do it and die." Gospel is the means of fulfilling this Law after the Fall: Jesus keeps the Law and merits God's favor as a substitute for man. This is the antithetical Gospel-Law paradigm.

Conversely, the unified Gospel-Law paradigm presented in this chapter asserts that God's relationship to man is not characterized by legality and merit. "Law" in the Bible often denotes teaching or instruction, not conditions or legality, and "gospel" denotes more than mere resting in Jesus and receiving God's grace. The traditional theological categories "Law" and "Gospel" employed by Clark do not correspond to their Biblical usage. More importantly, man by his very nature gains eternal life by faith alone, a wholehearted, obedient trust in God. After the Fall, man obtains the righteousness of eternal life on the ground of Jesus' atoning death and His bodily resurrection, which, respectively, paid the penalty for man's sin and which liberated him from the power of its grip. The only instrument by which to appropriate this righteousness is faith, a living, penitential, obedient faith. Sinners are justified by faith alone. They are saved entirely by the grace of God and not by means of works-righteousness or merit. The gospel message of the Bible is that one is saved only by Jesus' substitutionary death and bodily resurrection. This message is appropriated by an active faith, which rests on God's promises, repents of sin, and submits to the Lordship of Jesus. As Clark employs these terms, Gospel (resting and receiving) includes Law (obeying and performing), and Law includes at its source the message that man cannot be saved (and could never have been saved) by any good works, merit or achievement, but only by the redemptive work of Jesus Christ. Obedience grounded in a simple faith that looks only to Jesus is not antithetical to the grace of God.

Consequently, we can understand why C. van der Waal writes in his penetrating work *The Covenantal Gospel*: "The law was not outside of Christ, for the law and the gospel are not contradictory concepts, but, rather, interchangeable."[99] Not two laws, not two ways, not two means of justification — one holy gospel and law that tell man in Whom he must trust, and Whom he must obey.

This unified Biblical message can be and has been perverted by sinful man. To use the terms as Professor Clark uses them, if Law is reduced to nothing more than obligation, it becomes moralism; if Gospel is reduced to nothing more than offer, it becomes antinomianism. But we may not desist preaching the message of a penitent, obedient faith on the grounds that some people turn that message into a Christ-less works-righteousness, any more than we may cease declaring the message of salvation by grace through faith alone in Jesus Christ because other people transform that message into an excuse for lawlessness.

Professor Clark is correct, in fact, to draw attention to the momentous practical consequences of one's view of the Gospel-Law relationship (*CJPM*, 363), though this chapter disputes his theory of that relationship.

The Protestant Reformation originated principally as a reaction against a deadening moralism in the Latin Church, the abstraction of the Faith from the decisive work of God in Jesus Christ's death and resurrection and its transformation into a system of religious ethics — salvation ultimately in Jesus but instrumentally by human achievement centered in the sacraments within the context of the church. The Reformers correctly countered this moralistic soteriology with the gospel of the free grace of God in the redemptive work of Jesus Christ.[100]

---

99. C. van der Waal, *The Covenantal Gospel*, 62.
100. Alister McGrath, *Luther's Theology of the Cross* (Oxford, England: Blackwell, 1985, 1990).

Moralistic religion is not limited to the medieval West but is ever a hazard to authentic evangelical faith, which situates salvation in the apostolic *kerygma* — Christ's death and resurrection for our sins, appropriated only by a robust faith. Moralism, for example, survives in Protestant liberalism, notably in its substitution of man's efforts at goodness for the scandal of Jesus' atoning, agonizing death and of His "unscientific" bodily resurrection.[101] This moralism finds a foothold as well in those forms of high-church Christianity (whether Latin, Eastern or Protestant) that enclose salvation within the sacramental system and subordinate the *kerygma* to church priesthood or eldership, at the hands of which salvation is dispensed or withheld. Biblical, evangelical soteriology recognizes God's sovereign operation in applying the benefits of Christ's redemptive work directly to the human heart. High-church soteriology tends to domesticate God's freedom in man's salvation, reducing it to a naturalistic morality buttressed by the church and its hierarchy. Man is saved instrumentally by partaking of the sacraments and staying in the church's good graces.[102] This moralism is a bane to many conscientious souls, who despair that they can ever sufficiently adhere to the moral standard that wins God's favor; they have not been properly taught that salvation is accomplished for us by Jesus Christ; we do not accomplish it by laboring to achieve God's austere, righteous standard.[103] And a moralism that substitutes man's works for the finality of Jesus' atoning death and resurrection stands under apostolic curse (Gal. 1:6-9).[104]

But a soteriology of moralism is not the only enemy Christianity has to fear. In addition, a contemporary rampant antinomianism blights the Faith. In many churches, the gospel of free grace in Jesus has become a disgrace: it is held that since

---

101. Donald E. Miller, *The Case for Liberal Christianity* (San Francisco: Harper and Row, 1981).
102. Ludwig Ott, *Fundamentals of Catholic Dogma* (Rockford, Illinois: Tan Books, 1960), 251.
103. Peter Andrew Sandlin, "The Soteriology of Samuel Johnson," M. A. dissertation, University of South Africa, 1993.
104. Leon Morris, *Galatians* (Downers Grove, Illinois: InterVarsity, 1996), 38-47.

man is saved by grace, God makes few or no demands of him, demands whose persistent violation could threaten his standing as a believer. "Grace" becomes the antithesis of obedience, and any call for greater fidelity to the commands of the Bible is met with the derisive appellation "legalist." The seeds of this antinomianism are sown at the inception of the Christian life in an imbalanced, truncated evangelism. Sinners are told that they need do nothing but "trust in Jesus" — they need not repent of their sins or commit their lives to Jesus as Savior and Lord to be assured of eternal life.[105] They sometimes then join the church under the impression that the free grace of God in Christ is a cheap commodity designed to populate Heaven as quickly as possible. Obedience in the Christian life is desirable but optional — its lack could never threaten one's eternal life. This impoverished view of God's grace, refusing to recognize the agonizing cost it exacted from Jesus Christ on the Cross, has led too many to assume today, as they did in Paul's time (Rom. 6:1), that their sin only highlights the grace of God. To those who teach this antinomian gospel Paul issues an anathema (Rom. 3:5-8), just as he did toward those who undercut the free grace of God by polluting it with religious ceremonies and human merit (Gal. 1:6-9). In the contemporary world the greater danger likely springs from antinomianism: "The word of cheap grace," wrote the 20th century Christian theologian and martyr Dietrich Bonhoeffer, "has been the ruin of more Christians than any commandment of works."[106] But both moralism and antinomianism are fatal enemies of the Christian Faith.

The unified Gospel-Law paradigm of the Bible depicts salvation as the work of God entirely. God reconciles the world in the Person of Jesus, Who died for man's sins on the Cross and rose again for his justification. If man casts himself by faith on Jesus Christ alone, in a penitent faith that turns from his sins and submits to Jesus as Lord, trusting only in Him and not in himself or his deeds, he will be saved. This is a salvation wholly by God's

---

105. John MacArthur, *Faith Works* (Waco, Texas: Word, 1993).
106. Dietrich Bonhoeffer, *The Cost of Discipleship* (New York: MacMillan, 1937, 1959), 59.

grace, not of works, merit, or human achievement. It is the work of God, not of man.

This lawful gospel is the only authentic message of salvation to a dying world.

CHAPTER 7

The Imputation of Active Obedience

Norman Shepherd

In chapter 8 of *Covenant, Justification, and Pastoral Ministry*, R. Scott Clark offers an exposition and defense of the doctrine of the imputation of the active obedience of Christ for the justification of sinners. Clark makes use of the theological distinction between the active and passive obedience of Christ. Although "both adjectives are meant to describe, from different aspects, the entirety of Christ's work from the moment of his conception until his resurrection," he distinguishes between the two in a commonly accepted way. "*Active* denotes Christ's intentional and positive fulfillment of God's law for his people at every moment of his life, and *passive* (from the Latin adjective derived from the verb *patior*, to suffer) speaks to the concept that, in the course of his obedience, 'all the time he lived on earth, but especially at the end of his life, he bore, in body and soul, the wrath of God against the sin of the whole human race' (HC 37 [Schaff 3.319])" (*CJPM*, 230). In what follows we will use "active" and "passive obedience" in the sense that Clark has defined them here.

In Clark's view both the active and the passive obedience of Christ are imputed to sinners for their justification in the same, once-for-all justifying act of God. The first part of chapter 8 presents historical evidence beginning with Calvin to show that this view is the received Reformed view, although there were and are critics of this view both in the classic period of Reformed theology as well as in the modern discussion (15 pages). The second part presents the Biblical teaching on the imputation of active obedience (5 pages), and the third part offers "the theological context of the imputation of active obedience" (3 pages). A fourth and final section considers a series of objections to the doctrine of the imputation of active obedience (14 pages).

My response to Clark will follow the pattern of his presentation and will deal successively with the history of the doctrine, the Biblical warrant for it, its theological context, and some objections I have raised against it.

Because my response follows Clark's presentation, some key ideas are only developed later in the article. As a preview, note that the doctrine of the imputation of active obedience developed in the latter part of the sixteenth century as an correlate of the doctrine of the covenant of works. Prior to that development, in Reformed churches, justification was seen as forgiveness of sins based on Christ's passive obedience. In the covenant of works scheme, justification is both the imputation of Christ's passive obedience which forgives our sins thus keeping us out of hell *and* the imputation of Christ's active obedience which is necessary for us to get into heaven. This warped the Reformed church's understanding of both justification and sanctification.

History of the Doctrine

Clark holds that the imputation of Christ's active obedience for justification was the prevailing Reformed view from Calvin onward. He devotes a single paragraph to Calvin, referencing his 1539 commentary on Romans at 5:19 and the 1559 *Institutes* at 3:11:23, and concludes that for Calvin "God accepts sinners only because the *obedientia Christi* is imputed to us" (*CJPM*, 231). By "*obedientia*" Clark means the active obedience of Christ, his law keeping throughout the whole course of his life, in distinction from passive obedience, his suffering and death as sin bearer.[1]

---

[1] On occasion Clark may be using "active obedience" to include both the active and passive obedience and that may be the case here. However, in the preceding sentence he calls it "Christ's obedience to the law."

It is undoubtedly true that for Calvin the justification of sinners is grounded in the imputation of the obedience of Christ, but it is not at all clear that Calvin means by this the imputation of the *active* obedience of Christ.

Calvin begins his discussion of justification in the *Institutes* in Book 3, Chapter 11. At the end of section 2 Calvin writes, "Therefore, we explain justification simply as the acceptance with which God receives us into his favor as righteous men. And we say that it consists in the remission of sins and the imputation of Christ's righteousness."[2]

The key to understanding Calvin is his point that justification consists in the remission of sins. Because our sins are forgiven, we are accepted as righteous men and received into God's favor. This forgiveness is obtained by the imputation of Christ's righteousness, and (as will be discussed below) for Calvin the righteousness of Christ that obtains forgiveness of sin is the *passive* obedience of Christ, specifically his death on the cross for us and in our place. As Calvin goes on to explain his teaching in section 3, there is no mention of or reference to the imputation of active obedience because justification is the remission of sins, and this forgiveness is not grounded in the imputation of active obedience.

In section 3 Calvin rejects the Romanist view that justification means that sinners "acquire righteousness by well-doing." He says, "Therefore, 'to justify' means nothing else than to acquit of guilt him who was accused, as if his innocence were confirmed." And further on he says, "After pardon of sins has been obtained, the sinner is considered as a just man in God's sight. Therefore, he was righteous not by approval of works but by God's free absolution."[3] We are not justified by the approval of our works, as in the Romanist view, but by free absolution, the forgiveness of sins. We are reckoned righteous in Christ because his righteousness is imputed to us and the righteousness required for the forgiveness of sins is his passive obedience.

---

2. *Calvin: Institutes of the Christian Religion*, trans. F. L. Battles (Philadelphia: Westminster Press, 1960), 1:727.
3. *Institutes*, 1:727-8.

The passages of Scripture from which Calvin derives his teaching confirm this understanding. He refers to Romans 4:6, 7, where Paul cites Psalm 32:1, 2. "Blessed are they whose transgressions have been forgiven." Calvin says, "There [Paul] is obviously discussing not a part of justification but the whole of it."[4] The whole of justification consists in the forgiveness of sin. Calvin says that the best passage of all is 2 Corinthians 5:18-20. "Doubtless, he means by the word 'reconciled' nothing but 'justified.' Christ who was without sin was made sin for us, and we are justified when our sins are not counted against us."[5] Justification consists in the remission of sin. In this same context Calvin mentions Romans 5:19 that tells us we are made righteous by Christ's obedience. The obedience imputed to us in our justification is the righteousness of Christ that absolves us from our sin, and the righteousness that absolves us from our sin is his passive obedience, not his active obedience.

Toward the end of chapter 11, in section 21, Calvin writes, "It is obvious, therefore, that those whom God embraces are made righteous solely by the fact that they are purified when their spots are washed away by forgiveness of sins. Consequently, such righteousness can be called, in a word, 'remission of sins.'"[6] And referring once again to 2 Corinthians 5:21 in section 22 he writes, "Moreover, he teaches the way in which this righteousness is to be obtained: namely, when our sins are not counted against us."[7] Further on in section 22 Calvin comments on Acts 13:38, 39, where Luke writes, "Through this man forgiveness of sins is proclaimed to you, and everyone that believes in him is justified from all things from which you could not be justified by the law of Moses." He says, "The apostle so connects forgiveness of sins with righteousness that he shows them to be exactly the same."[8] He quotes Bernard approvingly to this effect, "Christ is our righteous-

---

4. *Institutes*, 1:729.
5. *Institutes*, 1:729.
6. *Institutes*, 1:751.
7. *Institutes*, 1:752.
8. *Institutes*, 1:752.

ness in absolution, and therefore those alone are righteous who obtain pardon from his mercy."[9]

Over against the Romanist view that justification consists in doing good, the consistent emphasis of Calvin in chapter 11 on justification is that justification consists in the forgiveness of sins grounded in the imputation of the righteousness of Christ. The righteousness of Christ that obtains the forgiveness of sins is not his law keeping throughout the whole course of his life, that is, his active obedience, but his suffering and death for us, his passive obedience.

We may examine Calvin's explanation of *how* Christ has fulfilled the function of Redeemer for us. Calvin begins the first paragraph in *Institutes* 2:16:5 this way: "Now someone asks, How has Christ abolished sin, banished the separation between us and God, and acquired righteousness to render God favorable and kindly toward us? To this we can in general reply that he has achieved this for us by the whole course of his obedience."[10] In support of this he cites Romans 5:19, Galatians 4:4, 5, and Matthew 3:15.

On the basis of a superficial reading of these words we might be tempted to conclude that here Calvin affirms the imputation of active obedience for justification, but it is a temptation we would do well to resist for the following reasons.

In this same paragraph in commenting on Galatians 4:4, 5, Calvin writes, "In another passage, to be sure, Paul extends the oasis of the pardon that frees us from the curse of the law to the whole life of Christ." He ends the paragraph with these words: "In short, from the time when he took on the form of a servant, he began to pay the price of liberation in order to redeem us."[11] Calvin is saying that the obedience of Christ throughout his life is to be seen as the source of the forgiveness of our sins. *In other words, the obedience in view is passive obedience because in fulfillment of the Father's will for him to die for the sins of his people he began to suffer as the sin bearer from the time of his incarnation.* In the words of the Heidelberg Catechism, Q&A 37, "During his whole life on earth, but especially at the end,

---

9. *Institutes*, 1:752.
10. *Institutes* 1: 507.
11. *Institutes* 1:507.

Christ sustained in body and soul the anger of God against the sin of the whole human race."[12]

Having made the point in the first paragraph that the way of salvation that secured freedom from the curse of the law (forgiveness, justification) included "the whole course of his obedience," Calvin begins the next paragraph by saying, "Yet to define the way of salvation more exactly, Scripture ascribes this as peculiar and proper to Christ's death."[13] He now cites a series of passages, all of which speak of justification and reconciliation with God through the death of Christ. This focuses Christ's lifelong passive obedience on his death. Calvin concludes, "For this reason the so-called 'Apostles' Creed' passes at once in the best order from the birth of Christ to his death and resurrection."[14]

There is nothing in the Apostles' Creed about the active obedience of Christ, and indeed, there is nothing in this whole section of Calvin's *Institutes* about the imputation of active obedience. His point is that Christ suffered because of our sins throughout his life in fulfillment of his Father's will for him. This is his righteousness, his obedience — his passive obedience — that is the ground of our justification, the forgiveness of our sins. Calvin writes, "And we must hold fast to this: that no proper sacrifice to God could have been offered unless Christ, disregarding his own feelings, subjected and yielded himself wholly to his Father's will."[15]

He ends section 5 by saying, "But because trembling consciences find repose only in sacrifice and cleansing by which sins are expiated, we are duly directed thither; and for us the substance of life is set in the death of Christ."[16] These words stand in marked contrast to the sub-title Clark gives to his chapter 8: "Christ's Active Obedience as the Ground of Justification." Calvin does not say that the substance of life is set in the imputation of the active obedience of Christ, but in the death of Christ.

---

12. *Ecumenical Creeds and Reformed Confessions* (Grand Rapids: CRC Publications, 1988), 28.
13. *Institutes*, 1:507.
14. *Institutes*, 1:508.
15. *Institutes*, 1:508
16. *Institutes*, 1:508

Clark briefly refers to Calvin's commentary on Romans 5:19 where Paul teaches that we are made righteous through the obedience of Christ, and of course, Calvin endorses this teaching. But again, it would be wrong to assume, as Clark apparently does, that Calvin is endorsing what later Reformed theologians had to say about the imputation of active obedience. The context of Calvin's comments on verse 19 makes this clear.

Commenting on verse 9 ("being now justified through his blood") Calvin says, "The import of the whole is, — since Christ has attained righteousness for sinners by his death, much more shall he protect them, being now justified, from destruction."[17] Christ does not attain righteousness for sinners by the imputation of his active obedience but by his death that secures the forgiveness of sins.

At the end of his comments on verse 18, just before his comments on verse 19, Calvin writes, "*Justification of Life* is to be taken, in my judgment, for remission, which restores life to us, as though he called it life-giving. For whence comes the hope of salvation, except that God is propitious to us; and we must be just, in order to be accepted. Then life proceeds from justification."[18]

Calvin could not be clearer than he is at this point. Justification is the forgiveness of sin. A sinner must be just in order to be accepted by God. How is he made just? Certainly not by the Roman Catholic method of inwrought (infused) and outwrought (his own active obedience) righteousness. On the other hand, is he made just by the *imputation* of Christ's *active* obedience? Calvin does not say so. The sinner is made just by the forgiveness of his sin. That is his justification. Remission of sin restores life to us, and Calvin concludes, "Then life proceeds from justification."

When Calvin goes on immediately to comment on Romans 5:19, he notes that the obedience imputed for our justification cannot be other than Christ's passive obedience, the obedience of his suffering and death in our place that secures the forgiveness of sin.

---

17. John Calvin, *Commentaries on the Epistle of Paul the Apostle to the Romans*, trans. John Owen (reprint, Grand Rapids: Baker Book House, 1979), 197.

18. Calvin, *Romans*, 212.

His commentary on Romans 5:19 concerning the imputation of obedience for justification corresponds to what we have found in the *Institutes*, 2:16:5.

The language of the decrees and canons of the Council of Trent on justification serves to confirm this understanding of Calvin and the early Reformers. The difference between Trent and the Reformation is often styled as the difference between justification on the ground of inwrought (infused) and outwrought (good works) righteousness as opposed to justification on the ground of imputed righteousness (Christ's active obedience). This is not how either Trent or Calvin describe the difference.

In the Decree on Justification (Sixth Session, Chapter 7) Trent declares that justification "is not the remission of sins merely, but also the sanctification and renewal of the inward man."[19] In Canon 11 Trent pronounces its curse on anyone who says that "men are justified, either by the sole imputation of the justice of Christ, or by the sole remission of sins, to the exclusion of the grace and the charity which is poured forth in their hearts by the Holy Ghost, and is inherent in them."[20]

Trent understood the Reformation (there was no distinction between Lutheran and Reformed at this point) to be teaching that justification consisted "merely" and "solely" in the remission of sins. This is clear not only from the words cited above but also from Canons 12, 13, and 14. The justice of Christ imputed to accomplish this is his passive obedience. There is nothing in the decrees and canons of Trent about the imputation of active obedience as the outstanding feature of the Reformation doctrine of justification to which Trent must now respond.

For Trent, justification cannot be merely the forgiveness of sin on the ground of Christ's death and received by faith alone as it was for the Reformers. For Trent, that was a legal fiction. Sin could only be forgiven by being expelled through the infusion of

---

19. Philip Schaff, *The Creeds of Christendom* (reprint, Grand Rapids: Baker Book House, 1977), 2:94. "justificatio ipsa ... quae non est sola peccatorum remissio." This is a Reformation "sola" that is most often overlooked: the remission of sins alone.
20. Schaff, *Creeds*, 2:112-3.

righteousness in the use of the sacramental system. Thus Trent defined justification as a process of sanctification, and for that reason confused justification with sanctification, as the Reformers charged.

Trent correctly understood the Reformation to be teaching that justification consisted in the remission of sins grounded in the passive obedience of Christ imputed to us; but Trent flatly rejected this Reformation doctrine. For his part, Calvin flatly rejects Trent when he takes up the very language of the anathema in Canon 11 to declare "that [justification] consists in the remission of sins and the imputation of Christ's righteousness."[21]

The evidence shows that Calvin did not teach the imputation of the active obedience of Christ for the justification of sinners. He defined justification as the forgiveness of sins, and the work of Christ that is the ground of this forgiveness is his passive obedience. This is the righteousness that is imputed for our justification.

Following his rather abrupt treatment of Calvin, Clark claims, "Among the early orthodox, the doctrine of the imputation of active obedience is found in Ursinus (e.g., *Summa theologiae* [1561])," but offers no argumentation to substantiate this claim (*CJPM*, 231). Is it a valid claim? In chapter 6 of *Backbone of the Bible* I offered a discussion of the view of Ursinus based on his *Commentary* on the Heidelberg Catechism, and presented further evidence from Ursinus in a related article showing that the claim Clark now makes is not valid.[22]

Like Calvin, Ursinus defines justification as the forgiveness of sins. He writes, "Justification and the forgiveness of sins are, therefore, the same: for to justify is that God should not impute sin

---

21. *Institutes* 3:11:2, 1:727.
22. P. Andrew Sandlin, ed., *Backbone of the Bible: Covenant in Contemporary Perspective* (Nacogdoches, TX: Covenant Media Press, 2004) 104-6. Norman Shepherd, "More on the Imputation of Active Obedience," *Christian Culture*, (Center for Cultural Leadership, P.O. Box 70, LaGrange, CA 95329), Feb. 2005, 2-4. In *CJPM* David VanDrunen takes note of the existence of *Backbone of the Bible* but says in n. 85 (51), "This work came into my hands too late to allow more specific interaction with the content of these essays." Dennis E. Johnson, however, does interact with my chapters in *Backbone of the Bible* in n. 17 (414). Clark nowhere refers to or deals with the material presented in either of these sources.

unto us, but accept of us and declare us righteous on the ground of the righteousness of Christ made over to us." He also tells us explicitly what this righteousness of Christ is. "*Evangelical justification* is the application of evangelical righteousness; or, it is the application of the righteousness of another, which is without us in Christ; or, it is the imputation and application of that righteousness which Christ wrought out for us by his death upon the cross, and by his resurrection from the dead."[23]

The view of Ursinus is the same as that of Calvin. We can summarize it in three points. First, justification consists in the remission of sins. Second, sins are remitted on the ground of the righteousness of Christ imputed to the believer. And third, the righteousness imputed is the suffering and death of our Lord to pay the penalty for sin. Contrary to Clark's assertion, the doctrine of the imputation of active obedience is not found in Ursinus any more than it is in Calvin.

The same must be said about the Heidelberg Catechism. The Heidelberg Catechism does not confess a belief in the imputation of Christ's active obedience for justification. This omission is not surprising, because Ursinus is generally recognized as the chief author of this Catechism dating from 1563.

Clark, however, holds that at least the "substance" of the imputation of active obedience is present in the Heidelberg Catechism and quotes Q&A 60 as follows: "God 'grants and imputes to me the perfect satisfaction, righteousness, and holiness of Christ, as if I had never committed nor had any sin, and had myself accomplished all the obedience which Christ has fulfilled for me' (HC 60 [Schaff 3.326-27])." He comments, "It hard [sic] to imagine what other expression the catechism might have used to teach the substance of the imputation of active obedience more clearly" (*CJPM*, 231-2).

Apparently Clark thinks that the use of the words "righteousness, and holiness of Christ" is a reference to the imputation of ac-

---

23. *The Commentary of Dr. Zacharias Ursinus on the Heidelberg Catechism*, trans. G. W. Williard (reprint, Grand Rapids: Eerdmans, 1954), 326-7.

tive obedience of Christ, but offers no evidence for this assumption apart from the rhetorical flourish. In *Backbone of the Bible* (106-11) I demonstrated that these three words — satisfaction, righteousness, and holiness — are used in the Catechism itself to refer to the suffering and death of Christ in obedience to the will of his Father in heaven as furnishing the ground for the justification of sinners.

First, the word "satisfaction" cannot refer to less than the death of our Lord on the cross to pay the penalty for sin. Second, Q&A 56 asks what we believe concerning the forgiveness of sins and says, "I believe that God, because of Christ's atonement, will never hold against me any of my sins nor my sinful nature which I need to struggle against all my life. Rather, in his grace God grants me the righteousness of Christ to free me forever from judgment." The righteousness of Christ is his atoning death that secures the forgiveness of sins (justification) and frees us from the judgment of God. And third, Q&A 36 tells us that Christ "is our mediator, and with his innocence and perfect holiness he removes from God's sight my sin — mine since I was conceived." What removes sin from God's sight is the death of Christ, "the precious blood of Christ, a lamb without blemish or defect" (1 Pet. 1:19). These three terms, satisfaction, righteousness, and holiness, used in Q&A 60 of the Heidelberg Catechism all refer to Christ's passive obedience, not the imputation of his active obedience.

The doctrine taught in the Heidelberg Catechism is representative of what was taught in the Reformed confessions of the early Reformation. In 1966 Arthur C. Cochrane published a collection of twelve of these confessions beginning with Zwingli's Sixty-seven Articles (1523) and concluding with The Second Helvetic Confession (1566).[24] None of them confess the doctrine of the imputation of active obedience.

It would be tedious to review all twelve of these confessions; but given the comment of Charles Hodge that "on some accounts" the Second Helvetic Confession is "the most authoritative

---

24. Arthur C. Cochrane, *Reformed Confessions of the 16th Century* (Philadelphia: Westminster Press, 1966).

symbol of the Reformed Church"[25] we can profitably take note of what this Confession says about justification and imputation.

In chapter 15 we have a definition of justification: "According to the apostle in his treatment of justification, to justify means to remit sins, to absolve from guilt and punishment, to receive into favor, and to pronounce a man just." And further, "solely by the grace of Christ and not from any merit of ours or consideration for us, we are justified, that is, absolved from sin and death by God the Judge."[26] This is to say, we are received into favor and pronounced just (forensic justification) by God when he forgives our sin, absolving us from guilt and punishment. There is nothing here about the imputation of active obedience.

The whole of the paragraph specifically describing imputed righteousness deserves to be quoted.

> *Imputed Righteousness.* For Christ took upon himself and bore the sins of the world, and satisfied divine justice. Therefore, solely on account of Christ's sufferings and resurrection God is propitious with respect to our sins and does not impute them to us, but imputes Christ's righteousness to us as our own (II Cor. 5:19ff.; Rom. 4:25), so that now we are not only cleansed and purged from sins or are holy, but also, granted the righteousness of Christ, and so absolved from sin, death and condemnation, are at last righteous and heirs of eternal life. Properly speaking, therefore, God alone justifies us, and justifies only on account of Christ, not imputing sins to us but imputing his righteousness to us.[27]

Here the view of Calvin is once again made abundantly clear both in the text of the Confession and especially in the Scripture passages cited. Justification consists in the remission of sin; remission is grounded in the imputation of the righteousness of Christ; and the righteousness imputed is Christ's death for us and in our place. We are holy both because we are cleansed and purged from sin (sancti-

---

25. Cochrane, 222.
26. Cochrane, 255.
27. Cochrane, 256.

fication) and because we are absolved from sin, condemnation, and death (justification). It is because our sins are forgiven that we are righteous and heirs of eternal life, not because the active obedience of Christ is imputed to us. There is nothing in this paragraph on imputation about the imputation of active obedience.

The Belgic Confession (1561) ought to be understood in the same way. Article 22 is sometimes cited as evidence for an early confession of the imputation of active obedience. In the form adopted by the Synod of Dordt more than fifty years later (not the original form) Article 22 says, "But Jesus Christ is our righteousness in making available to us all his merits and all the holy works he has done for us and in our place." However, these words are almost immediately followed by this often overlooked statement, "When those benefits are made ours they are more than enough to absolve us of our sins."[28] The antecedent of "those benefits" is "all his merits and all the holy works he has done for us and in our place." The merits and works that absolve us from sin are his passive obedience. There is no reference to active obedience, though many who subscribe to this confession choose to understand it that way.

Article 23 on "The Justification of Sinners" immediately follows Article 22 and begins by defining justification as the forgiveness of sins. "We believe that our blessedness lies in the forgiveness of our sins because of Jesus Christ, and that in it our righteousness before God is contained, as David and Paul teach us when they declare that man blessed to whom God grants righteousness apart from works."[29] The reference is to Psalm 32:1 and Romans 4:6. According to the Belgic Confession our righteousness before God is not contained in the imputation of active obedience but in the forgiveness of our sins.

The same article goes on to say that we must claim nothing for ourselves or our own merits. We must lean and rest "on the sole obedience of Christ crucified, which is ours when we believe in him. That is enough to cover all our sins." The obedience that is imputed

---

28. *Ecumenical Creeds and Reformed Confessions*, 99.
29. *Ecumenical Creeds and Reformed Confessions*, 100.

to us for our justification is the obedience of Christ *crucified*. That is the doctrine of Calvin and the early Reformed church.

The situation changes, however, in the latter part of the sixteenth century and on into the seventeenth century as we move from the "mature Reformation" into the period of "scholastic confessionalism."[30] The doctrine of the imputation of Christ's active obedience is embraced in tandem with the development of the doctrine of a covenant of works. The two go hand in hand and necessitate each other. Nevertheless, the rejection of the imputation of active obedience was represented by delegates to both the Synod of Dordt and the Westminster Assembly of Divines, and interestingly enough, by the chairmen of both these assemblies.[31] Therefore the Canons of Dordt and the Westminster Standards have to be understood historically as allowing for this position, though clearly it had become a minority view and has remained a minority view among the Reformed since that time.

As Clark points out, Johannes Piscator (1546-1625), an influential German theologian, defined justification as consisting only in the remission of sins and rejected the imputation of active obedience (*CJPM*, 232-3, 262-3). A series of French synods condemned his views, and the Synod of 1612 bound subscribers to the French Confession of 1559, to the authorized interpretation of this confession, that justification is not simply the remission of sins but also consists in the imputation of active obedience. This interpretation of the French Confession would certainly have to be enforced by a synodical decision, because the language of the Confession itself would never lead one to think that this interpretation is what the Confession meant to say.

Article 16 reads:

> We believe that God, in sending his Son, intended to show his love and inestimable goodness towards us, giving him up

---

30. The quoted expressions are Cochrane's in *Reformed Confessions*, 222.
31. See C. Vonk, *De Nederlandse Geloofsbelijdenis*, in *De Voorzeide Leer* (Barendrecht: Drukkerij "Barendrecht," 1956), 3b:41-2, and Alexander F. Mitchell, *The Westminster Assembly: Its History and Standards* (London: James Nisbet & Co., 1883), 149-56.

to die to accomplish all righteousness, and raising him from the dead to secure for us the heavenly life.[32]

Here the Confession says that in dying, Jesus accomplishes *all* righteousness and secures the forgiveness of sins. His death and resurrection secure eternal life for us. The Confession obviously alludes to Romans 4:25, "He was delivered over to death for our sins and was raised to life for our justification."

Article 17 reads:

> We believe that by the perfect sacrifice that the Lord Jesus offered on the cross, we are reconciled to God and justified before him; for we can not be acceptable to him, nor become partakers of the grace of adoption, except as he pardons [all] our sins, and blots them out. Thus we declare that through Jesus Christ we are cleansed and made perfect; by his death we are fully justified, and through him only can we be delivered from our iniquities and transgressions.[33]

Here the French Confession says, "by his death we are *fully* justified" (italics added). And Article 18 begins by saying, "We believe that all our justification rests upon the remission of our sins, in which also is our only blessedness, as saith the Psalmist (Ps. 32:2)." In all of this there is no place given to the imputation of active obedience.

The French Synod of 1612 furnishes us with a good example of what the Westminster Confession warns us about in chapter 31, section 3, when it says: "All synods or councils, since the apostles' times, whether general or particular, may err; and many have erred. Therefore they are not to be made the rule of faith, or practice; but to be used as a help in both."[34] We do not believe in the infallibility of our theological traditions or in the infallibility of the teaching magisterium of the church, as Rome does. There is nothing in our Reformed tradition or in our confessional documents

---

32. Cochrane, 150.
33. Cochrane, 150.
34. *The Westminster Standards*, (Suwanee, GA: Great Commission Publications, 2001), 32.

that may not be subjected to the searching light of God's word. Our only infallible rule of faith and practice is Holy Scripture, and in this spirit we turn now to Clark's treatment of the Biblical warrant for the imputation of active obedience.

Biblical Warrant for the Doctrine

This second main section of Clark's presentation is disappointing because it does not deliver what it promises. The title of this section is "Biblical Teaching of the Imputation of Active Obedience," but Clark offers no texts of Scripture where this doctrine is actually taught, nor does he offer a compelling exegetical argument for the doctrine. Instead, he offers a theological argument to show why the doctrine is necessary.

He prefaces the section by positing a statement of the covenant of works doctrine. Christ became incarnate in order to fulfill the legal obligations entailed both in the covenant of works made with Adam and in the covenant of works (called a covenant of redemption) between the Father and the Son. Because Adam failed to earn eternal life by the merit of his own good works, Christ has come to perform the good works necessary to earn eternal life, not for himself but for those to whom his obedience is imputed (*CJPM*, 243-4).

The Scripture then cited is designed to show that God's law requires obedience from mankind as a whole and from Christ in particular. The theological argument is that the disobedience of the first man "creates an expectation concerning remedial obedience" to be performed by the final Adam (*CJPM*, 246). Clark relies almost exclusively on Romans 5:19. "We are declared righteous because Jesus' obedience was that *dikaiwma*[35] *and met the terms of divine justice*" (*CJPM*, 246-7). The assumption is that this reference to obedience in verse 19 is a reference to the active obedience of Christ required by the works principle embedded in the covenant of works doctrine, and that this obedience is then imputed to the believer.

---

35. This Greek word actually appears in verse 18 and means "righteous deed."

I dealt at length with Romans 5:18, 19 in its surrounding Biblical context in *Backbone of the Bible* (87-9). I showed that justification in this passage is the forgiveness of sins (Rom. 3:25; 4:7, 8) grounded in the righteousness of Christ as revealed in the gospel. This righteousness is his sacrifice of atonement, his death on the cross, such that we are justified in the blood of Christ (3:25; 4:25; 5:9, 10). His death on the cross is the one act of righteousness that brings justification and life according to verse 18. It corresponds to the one trespass of Adam that brought condemnation and death. Just as the one trespass of Adam is the disobedience of the one man that made many to be sinners in verse 19, so also Christ's death on the cross, his one act of righteousness, is the obedience that made many to be righteous according to this same verse.

Paul is saying that the one act of obedience that justifies is Christ's death on the cross and that it secures the forgiveness of sins. This is clear from Romans, chapters 3 through 5. Over against this view, Clark holds that the one act of obedience is a whole lifetime of perfect and perpetual obedience that is then imputed to the believer as the meritorious ground for earning the right to eternal life as required by the theological doctrine of a covenant of works. There is no basis for this in Romans 3 through 5 or anywhere else in Scripture.[36]

When Paul writes in Galatians 4:4 that Jesus was born under the law, the purpose was not so that he could earn the right to eternal life by the perfect merit of his good works. Paul tells us why he was made under the law in verse 5. It was to redeem those under the law, and he tells us what this redemption is. Those under the law are redeemed from the *curse* of the law, and they are redeemed from this curse by Christ's death on the cross (Gal. 3:13). There is nothing here about the imputation of active obedience as the meritorious ground for achieving eternal life.

When Paul says in Philippians 2:8 that our Lord "became

---

36. Clark does not offer a satisfactory explanation for why Paul would refer to a lifetime of perfect obedience as "one act of righteousness." Adam's "one trespass" was clearly his eating the forbidden fruit; but Clark makes the biblically unwarranted comment, that "Adam's entire life to that point is characterized by his disobedience" (*CJPM*, 248).

obedient to death — even death on a cross," he does not mention the imputation of active obedience nor does he have that in view. Hebrews 5:8 tells us that "he learned obedience from what he suffered." In Philippians, Paul has in view this suffering as the sin bearer that climaxes with his death on the cross. It is the passive obedience of Christ that Paul has in view in Philippians 2:8.

The texts that Clark introduces in support of the imputation of active obedience are texts that Calvin, Ursinus, and other representatives of the early Reformation commonly introduced to show that Jesus secures for us the complete forgiveness of all our sins (justification) on the ground of what we are calling his passive obedience.

Strikingly absent from Clark's discussion of the Biblical teaching on the active obedience of Christ is any reference to the Old Testament, and the reason for this desideratum is apparent. There is abundant evidence in the Old Testament that forgiveness is secured through the shedding of blood, and the sacrificial system of the Mosaic economy is designed to prepare us for the coming of Christ and his mediatorial accomplishment on the cross. But there is nothing in the liturgical regulations of the law that corresponds to the imputation of active obedience. We read that the sins of God's people were laid on the animals that were slain; but there was no imputation of the legal obedience of the animals to God's people.

The Old Testament prepares us for understanding the threefold office of Christ as prophet, priest, and king in the work of the prophets, the priests, and the kings of the old economy. Throughout his public ministry Jesus served as a prophet announcing the coming of the kingdom of God and calling sinners to repentance. At the end of his ministry he offered himself as priest on the cross as a sacrifice for the sins of his people. After his resurrection he ascended into heaven to rule as king over his people and to build his church. In performing a lifetime of perfect and personal obedience, Christ is not doing the kind of official work assigned to prophets, priests, or kings as described in the Old Testament. However, in giving his life as a sacrifice for sin (passive obedience),

Jesus is clearly doing the work of a priest as the Book of Hebrews makes abundantly obvious. The imputation of active obedience does not correlate with the way Scripture presents Christ to us as our prophet, priest, and king.

Just as the priestly ministry of Christ is set out in the liturgical piety of the Old Testament, so also it is set out for us in the liturgical piety of the New. The Lord has given us two sacraments, baptism and the Lord's supper, both of which point to Christ's one sacrifice finished on the cross as the source of eternal life. There are no sacraments that point to the imputation of active obedience, even though it is actually the imputation of active obedience that secures eternal life for us according to the covenant of works scheme.

On this scheme the cross of Christ can do no more for us than deflect condemnation. It is not the source of eternal life. This view flatly contradicts the Heidelberg Catechism, Q&A 66: "This is God's gospel promise: to forgive our sins and give us eternal life by grace alone because of Christ's one sacrifice finished on the cross." In the covenant of works scheme the death and resurrection of Christ lose the centrality they have in Scripture, and the imputation of active obedience takes their place as the source of eternal life.

This is not to say that the lifelong, perfect and perpetual obedience of Jesus Christ is unnecessary for the accomplishment of his mediatorial office. Just as the sacrificial animals of the old covenant had to be whole and without blemish, so Jesus, born under the law, had to be without sin in order to offer himself as a sacrifice for the sins of his people. Our high priest is the Lamb of God who takes away the sins of the world. This lamb must be "a lamb without blemish or defect" (1 Pet. 1:19). He must be "one who is holy, blameless, pure, set apart from sinners, exalted above the heavens" (Heb. 7:26).

When the Heidelberg Catechism raises the question why Jesus must be truly righteous, the answer is not so that his lifelong perfect obedience could be imputed to believers as the ground of their acceptance with God. The answer is that Christ must be truly righteous because a sinner could not pay for others (Q&A 16). He must be the righteous one who dies for the unrighteous in order to bring them to God (1 Pet. 3:18).

In this second section of his chapter, Clark proposes to deal with the Biblical warrant for the imputation of active obedience for the justification of sinners. He succeeds in demonstrating that the Biblical warrant for the imputation of the active obedience of Christ is at best very sparse, and indeed, non-existent. Certainly this is true in comparison with both the quantity and the quality of the Scriptural evidence showing that the righteousness of Christ imputed for the forgiveness of sins (justification) is the passive obedience of Christ, and specifically his death on the cross. Surely some explanation is required to account for this disproportion, but Clark offers none.

Theological Context of the Doctrine

In the third main section of his chapter Clark proposes to take up the theological context for the doctrine of the imputation of active obedience. It is the briefest of the four sections and understandably so, because the theological context has already been presented in the previous section. The theological context is the covenant of works made with Adam and the covenant of works made with Christ. These covenants require the imputation of active obedience for justification, whether there is any Biblical warrant for the doctrine or not. That is why the doctrine of the imputation of active obedience developed in conjunction with the development of the covenant of works doctrine toward the latter part of the sixteenth century.

On the foundation of this covenant of works doctrine Clark tells us:

> According to the proponents of the imputation of active obedience, divine justice requires both obedience and punishment for sin such that Christ had to provide obedience and suffer the penalty for his elect. Proponents of the imputation of active obedience held to a twofold nature of sin and consequently a twofold remedy: the imputation of active obedience and remission of sins. (*CJPM*, 249)

In expounding this thesis Clark points to Piscator and Pareus who held (wrongly, in his view) that divine justice required *either* obedience to the law *or* punishment for disobedience, but not both. Clark leaves the impression that this line of argument was new with Piscator and Pareus toward the end of the sixteenth century and came about because of their supposedly innovative view that the active obedience of Christ is not imputed for justification.

Actually, this is the line of argument that Ursinus pursues in his *Commentary* on the Heidelberg Catechism and is evidence that the view of Piscator in rejecting the imputation of active obedience is really the view of the early Reformation. Or, more accurately, there was no doctrine of the imputation of active obedience in the early Reformation, and Piscator was simply espousing the original Reformation view as others began to add to Reformed theology the doctrines of a covenant of works and the imputation of active obedience. The real novelty is the introduction of the covenant of works requiring the further novelty of the imputation of active obedience.

I dealt at length with the view of Ursinus on this point in *Backbone of the Bible* (104-6) and in "More on the Imputation of Active Obedience."[37] Ursinus writes in his Heidelberg Catechism *Commentary*, "Legal righteousness is performed, either by obedience to the law, or by punishment. The law requires one or the other."[38] Earlier, as he began his comments on the second main division of the Catechism, he asks whether there is a way of escape from sin and misery and responds:

> To this question the catechism answers, that deliverance may be granted, if satisfaction be made to the law and justice of God, by a punishment sufficient for the sin that has been committed. The law binds all, either to obedience, or if this is not rendered, to punishment; and the performance or payment of either is perfect righteousness, which God approves of in whomsoever it is found.[39]

---

37. See above, note 22.
38. Ursinus, *Commentary*, 325.
39. Ursinus, *Commentary*, 77.

It is, of course, Christ who suffers and dies in the place of the believer, and this is the "perfect righteousness" that is imputed to him for his justification. Ursinus does not teach the imputation of active obedience for justification in addition to punishment.

We can probe still further into the theological context for the doctrine of justification. According to Genesis 2, if Adam sinned by disobeying the command of God, he would forfeit whatever eschatological blessing was otherwise in store for him. We can call this blessing eternal life and all that pertained to it. God said in effect, "When you eat from the tree of the knowledge of good and evil you will surely die" (Gen. 2:16, 17). However, this word of warning about disobedience is not the same as saying that if you keep every one of my commands you will earn the right to eternal life in terms of a principle of simple justice. God does not say this in Genesis. It is a mistaken logical inference that led to the theological invention of a covenant of works.[40]

Adam forfeited eternal life for himself and the posterity he represented by sinning against God; but God would not have his plan for the world and for the human race frustrated by Satan. He provided a way for the sin of Adam to be forgiven so that sinners would not have to suffer the penalty of death (justification). And he provided for the re-creation of the human race in his own image in righteousness and holiness (sanctification). God would be glorified not simply in the eternal salvation of sinners from sin, condemnation, and death, but even more so in the reconstitution of the organism of the human race so that we could carry out the work in this world that the Lord assigned to us from the beginning. The Lord commanded our first parents to "be fruitful and increase in number," to "fill the earth and subdue it." He gave them dominion over all the other living creatures and assigned them the task of developing and using the resources God put into the world for his glory. We refer to this task as the *cultural mandate*.

---

40. C. Vonk comments, "We still find it quite daring to conclude from the simple prohibition of Gen. 2:17 to a complete *covenant*. That is really going some!" "*De Heilige Schrift: Inleiding, Genesis, Exodus*" in *De Voorzeide Leer* (Barendrecht: Drukkerij "Barendrecht," 1960) 1a: 134 (trans., N.S.).

The covenant of works doctrine leads to the idea that the account of the historical Adam in Genesis 2 and 3 is all about how Adam can attain to eternal life. That narrows the scope of the account so that it is all about soteriology, a way of salvation from sin and its consequences, even before sin has entered into human experience! But God did not create Adam in order to see whether he would be strong enough to achieve the prize of eternal life by the merit of his own good works. God created Adam in his own image to magnify and reflect his glory by exercising dominion over all that God had made. God commanded him to be fruitful and multiply and as God's vicegerent to carry out the cultural mandate.

After the fall into sin there is, indeed, need for soteriology. There is need for a way to deal with both the guilt and the corruption of sin. God provides that way in and through Jesus Christ who bears the penalty for sin so that we can be forgiven and be assured of eternal life. But even more than this, God re-creates us in his own image in righteousness and holiness so that we can carry out the cultural task originally assigned to Adam and his posterity. All of that comes about through the second Adam, Jesus Christ, and specifically through his death and resurrection.

Salvation has two parts, the forgiveness of sin and the renewal of sinners; but salvation is not an end in itself. Most certainly God is glorified in the salvation of his people; but he saves them so that they can serve him in this created world and bring glory to him by developing the resources that God has deposited in his creation. God is glorified by at last achieving the goal that he set out when he created Adam in the beginning. God will not be frustrated by the machinations of Satan nor will he allow himself to become a cosmic laughing stock by failing to accomplish his plan for mankind and the world.

The controlling covenant of works doctrine reduces soteriology to justification so that sanctification and the cultural involvement of his image bearers take a subordinate place. In some traditions, sanctification becomes a second blessing, and in others it almost falls out of view all together. Clark's chapter helps us to see how this happens.

As noted above about the covenant of works and as Clark describes it, divine justice, and therefore justification, requires both the remission of sins and the imputation of active obedience. The cross can keep us out of hell, but it cannot get us into heaven. In this Clark is in full agreement with Trent that justification is not merely or solely the remission of sins as Calvin and the early Reformation taught, but also requires obedience.

For Trent, that obedience was an inwrought (infused) and outwrought (good works) obedience. Together these constitute sanctification, and sanctification defines what justification is. For Clark and those who share his commitment to the covenant of works, the required obedience is an imputed, active obedience. In other words, it is an imputed sanctification. Thus, just as Trent confuses justification and sanctification by defining justification as sanctification, so also Clark confuses justification and sanctification by defining justification as sanctification.

In his subtitle to chapter 8 Clark calls Christ's active obedience the ground of justification. That is to say, God justifies sinners by imputing sanctification to them. Even if Clark intends in this subtitle to include passive obedience because Christ was active in obeying the will of his Father to give his life as a ransom for sin, the emphasis is not on death as an atonement for sin, but on Christ's death as just another act of obedience to law.

Contrary to this Romanizing theology, the early Reformation clearly distinguished between justification and sanctification. Justification is the remission of sins and sanctification is the regeneration, renewal, resurrection, or recreation of the sinner in the image of God. They are quite distinct and should not be confused as they are in Clark's justification by works paradigm. Justification and sanctification are distinct, but they both flow from the cross and resurrection of Christ. They are ours as twin benefits when we are united to Christ by the indwelling of the Holy Spirit and the exercise of faith.

Because our more recent Reformed tradition has focused on calling this justification-defined-as-sanctification (the imputation of active obedience) the article on which the church stands or falls (Luther), or the main hinge on which religion turns (Calvin), we tend to subordinate the importance of transformation and renewal in a way that does not reflect the balance of Scripture. The Bible accents both. We are saved when our sins are forgiven and we are saved when the Holy Spirit washes us clean (Titus 3:4-7). This combination of twin benefits can be illustrated by reference to a number of passages in Scripture.

One of the clearest is 1 John 1:9. "If we confess our sins, he is faithful and just and will forgive us our sins and purify us from all unrighteousness." Here the twin benefits of justification (forgiveness) and sanctification (purification) are set side by side in a simple and obvious way. There is nothing here about the imputation of active obedience.

Hebrews 8:10-12 and 10:16 declare the blessings of the new covenant. The Lord will put his laws into our hearts and write them on our minds instead of on tablets of stone. This is sanctification. And he will no more remember our sins and lawless acts. This is justification. Again, there is no mention of the imputation of active obedience as constitutive for our salvation. Nor is it anticipated in the words of the prophet Jeremiah that the author to the Hebrews quotes in this passage.

In Ephesians 1:3-10 Paul describes the salvation that is ours in Christ arising from the predestinating plan and purpose of God for which we ought to give praise and thanksgiving. In verse 4 he begins with sanctification rather than justification. God chose us in Christ before the creation of the world "to be holy and blameless in his sight." Then he mentions the adoption as sons given us in his beloved Son (vss. 5, 6). He concludes with justification in verses 7 and 8 when he says that in Christ we have "redemption through his blood, the forgiveness of sins." Again, there is no mention of the imputation of active obedience.

The pattern of Paul's letter to the Romans shows us the clear distinction between justification and sanctification and at the same time their utter inseparability in the experience of the believer. He begins the letter by showing the sinfulness of the whole human race, both Jew and Gentile. He especially condemns the sinfulness of the Jews who were blessed by the possession of God's law and the promises of the covenant, but who were deliberately rebellious and disobedient (1:18-3:20). God deals with this problem by providing justification, the forgiveness of sins in the blood of Jesus (3:21-5:21). And he provides sanctification through union with the resurrected Christ. Sinners are transformed into obedient servants of righteousness (6:1-8:39). There is nothing in all of this about the imputation of active obedience because sinners are not saved by the merit of good works, a scenario the covenant of works requires. That was, in fact, the error of Rome. Instead, sinners are saved by the forgiveness of their sins and their renewal in the image of God in righteousness and holiness.

Although we can clearly distinguish between the twin benefits of justification as forgiveness of sins and sanctification as recreation in righteousness and holiness and must not confuse these two, we must not think that the Bible uses the word "justification" only with reference to forgiveness. In Romans 6:7, it is used where theologically we would expect the vocabulary of sanctification. Paul says that the sinner who has been crucified with Christ has died to sin and is no longer the slave of sin. He "has been freed from sin." Literally Paul writes that he has been "justified from sin."

We may well have a similar use of "justify" in Titus 3:5-7. "He saved us through the washing of rebirth and renewal by the Holy Spirit, . . . so that having been justified by his grace, we might become heirs having the hope of eternal life." Here Paul may be using "justify" in the sense of forgiveness; but the language also suggests that "justification" is simply another way of referring to the renewal by the Holy Spirit. This shows the close connection between justification and sanctification in the Scripture. We have to allow for and account for the flexibility of Biblical language where our theological vocabulary tends to be rigid and fixed. We can trust the Holy Spirit to say things more accurately than we can with our theological formulas.

Objections to the Doctrine

In the fourth main section of chapter 8 Clark proposes to deal with a series of objections that have been raised against the doctrine of the imputation of active obedience. I have already touched on some of these matters in this response; but I leave it to the reader to evaluate the validity of these objections and the validity of Clark's responses to them. I would like to summarize my own objections to the doctrine in three points.

My basic objection to the doctrine is simply that it has no Biblical warrant. It arose out of a need created by the imposition of a covenant of works on the text of Scripture and is actually defended as a "good and necessary consequence" flowing from that doctrine.

When Paul summarizes the gospel in 1 Corinthians 15 he says that what is of first importance is that "Christ died for our sins according to the Scriptures, that he was buried, that he was raised on the third day according to the Scriptures." What Paul puts in first place the theological program represented by Clark puts in second place. To Clark, the death of Christ only gets us back to where Adam was before the fall with the necessity still before us of earning eternal life by the performance and merit of good works. What really saves us and gives us eternal life is the imputation of active obedience. That is not the teaching of the New Testament. Paul preached Christ *crucified* (1 Cor. 1:23; 2:2), and following his example we must preach Christ crucified today.

My second objection is that the imputation of active obedience presupposes an unbiblical works principle. As pointed out earlier, Adam was commanded not to eat of the tree of the knowledge of good and evil. He was warned that to do so would result in death. At the end of the sixteenth century this warning was understood to imply that if Adam obeyed this command and all the other commands given to him, he would enter into eternal life as the earned reward for doing meritorious good works. That understanding was a misunderstanding. God did not create Adam for the purpose of challenging him to earn the right to eternal life by the merit of his performance. The probation in the Garden of Eden is not all about soteriology. God was teaching his image bearer to live in covenant fellowship with his Maker. He was teaching Adam whom he created as a just man to live by faith. It was Adam's faith that was being tested in the Garden, whether he was willing to live by every word that proceeds from the mouth of God.

After Adam sinned, God provided a way of salvation that included the forgiveness of sin (justification), and new life in Christ (sanctification). He would then be a just man living by faith and fulfilling the calling in this world God originally gave him.

Clark registers vigorous objection to my criticism of "merit" as "unbiblical" and "illegitimate." By "merit" I understand the works principle, the idea that eternal life and eschatological blessing are grounded in the perfect performance of good works over the whole course of one's life. In the words of R.C. Sproul, "Man's relationship to God in creation was based on works.... Ultimately the only way one can be justified is by works."[41] Indeed, I would say that this works principle is unbiblical and illegitimate.

In arguing his point, Clark does not attempt to show us that the works principle is in fact Biblical and therefore legitimate. His argument is that without a works principle the whole covenant of works scheme would collapse; and he is right, it would. He is overstating his case in saying that without the works principle we would have to repudiate most of two millennia of Western theology (*CJPM*, 254-5), although we would have to repudiate the same errors in Western theology that we repudiated at the time of the Protestant Reformation. And yes, we would have to turn back from the wrong turn that Reformed theology took toward the end of the sixteenth century with the development of a covenant of works doctrine requiring a covenant of redemption doctrine requiring in turn an imputation of active obedience doctrine.

With this unwieldy and totally unnecessary threefold burden lifted from our theological shoulders we can let the gospel shine forth with all of its brilliance, clarity, simplicity, and glory. God saves sinners by forgiving their sins and recreating them in his own image. He teaches them to love, serve, glorify, and enjoy their Creator in covenant fellowship throughout their lives; and when their work on earth is done they enter into eternal life in the pres-

---

41. R. C. Sproul, *Getting the Gospel Right* (Grand Rapids: Baker Book House, 1999), 160.

ence of their Savior Jesus Christ forever.

The word "merit" is often used to describe Christ's saving work on our behalf, including both his active and passive obedience. I would not want my rejection of "merit" to be understood as though we were not totally dependent on Christ for our salvation. We cannot make atonement for sin ourselves or contribute to atonement in any way. We cannot merit the forgiveness of our sins, nor can we do anything to secure the forgiveness of our sins. We can only suffer the penalty for sin, and that penalty is eternal condemnation. We cannot in any way reconstitute ourselves as righteous and holy persons or contribute to our transformation. Sanctification is wholly the work of the Holy Spirit grounded in the work of Christ for us in his death and resurrection. We are totally and exclusively dependent on what Jesus Christ has done for us to rescue us from sin, condemnation, and death.

The Heidelberg Catechism and the Belgic Confession use the word "merit" to refer to what Christ has done for us in his death and resurrection (his passive obedience). I have no theological objection to its use that way. However, because of the baggage that the word "merit" inevitably carries with it, it would be better not to use the word at all. I resonate with Calvin who writes about this term, "I wish that Christian writers had always exercised such restraint as not to take it into their heads to use terms foreign to Scripture that would produce great offense and very little fruit."[42]

My third objection to the imputation of active obedience is that it is not the view of the original Reformation. In a formal sense this is not a valid objection because we ought to be making progress in our understanding of the word of God, and progress will mean moving beyond and perhaps even moving away from the original Reformers in some ways. In the words of John Murray,

> However epochal have been the advances made at certain periods and however great the contributions of particular men we may not suppose that theological construction ever reaches definitive finality. There is the danger of a stagnant

---

42. *Institutes*, 3:15:2, 1:789.

traditionalism and we must be alert to this danger, on the one hand, as to that of discarding our historical moorings, on the other.[43]

The problem is that Reformed theology took a wrong turn toward the end of the sixteenth century with the introduction of an unbiblical works principle into soteriology. We need the humility now to go back to the point where we took the wrong turn in order to get our bearings from the word of God and to move on from there.

I recognize that at the present time the view Clark represents, the imputation of the active obedience of Christ for the justification of sinners, is the view that prevails in conservative Reformed denominations. It has been held and taught by a long line of able and distinguished Reformed theologians. It may seem presumptuous to challenge it.

However, I also believe that more recently enough evidence has been brought forward to make the validity of this doctrine a matter for discussion once again. Persons who question this doctrine and who are fully committed to the inerrancy, infallibility, and authority of Holy Scripture and have a high regard for the historic Reformed catechisms and confessions can participate in this discussion within the historic parameters of the Three Forms of Unity and the Westminster Standards.

We should not prematurely foreclose this discussion by the arbitrary, precipitous, and raw exercise of ecclesiastical power, as Rome did with the Protestant Reformation.

---

43. John Murray, "Systematic Theology," in *Collected Writings of John Murray* (Edinburgh: The Banner of Truth Trust, 1982), 4:8.

CHAPTER 8

The New Perspective, Mediation, and Justification

Don Garlington

Introduction

Professor S. M. Baugh, in his essay "The New Perspective, Mediation, and Justification" in *Covenant Justification and Pastoral Ministry*, summarizes and argues against the fundamental ideas and difficulties he sees in "The New Perspective on Paul" (hereafter NPP), and the scholars who advocate the NPP. It was J. D. G. Dunn who coined the phrase "The New Perspective on Paul" in the ground-breaking article of the same name.[1] We can summarize the elements of the NPP by letting Dunn himself describe his aims:

> This is what I meant and still mean when I speak of "the new perspective on Paul", as I attempted to work it out in fuller detail some years later in my *Theology of Paul*. In summary: (a) It builds on Sanders' new perspective on Second Temple Judaism, and Sanders' reassertion of the basic graciousness expressed in Judaism's understanding and practice of covenantal nomism. (b) It observes that a social function of the law was an integral aspect of Israel's covenantal nomism, where separateness to God (holiness) was understood to require separateness from the (other) nations as two sides of the one coin, and that the law was understood as the means

---

1. Dunn, "The New Perspective on Paul," *Bulletin of the John Rylands University Library of Manchester* 65 (1983): 95-122.

to maintaining both. (c) It notes that Paul's own teaching on justification focuses largely if not principally on the need to overcome the barrier which the law was seen to interpose between Jew and Gentile, so that the "all" of "to all who believe" (Rom. 1.17) signifies in the first place, Gentile as well as Jew. (d) It suggests that "works of law" became a key slogan in Paul's exposition of his justification gospel because so many of Paul's fellow Jewish believers were insisting on certain works as indispensable to their own (and others?) standing within the covenant, and therefore as indispensable to salvation. (e) It protests that failure to recognize this major dimension of Paul's doctrine of justification by faith may have ignored or excluded a vital factor in combating the nationalism and racialism which has so distorted and diminished Christianity past and present.[2]

This is a cogent and helpful summary of the issues involved in Dunn's understanding of Paul. (Please note that "nomism" denotes basing moral or religious conduct upon law, an idea we will encounter multiple times in this essay.) However, as I have written previously, there is no such thing as *the* NPP:

> There simply is no monolithic entity that can be designated as the "New Perspective" as such. It is surely telling that D. A. Carson, a noted critic of the NPP, acknowledges that it cannot be reduced to a single perspective. "Rather, it is a bundle of interpretive approaches to Paul, some of which are mere differences in emphasis, and others of which compete rather antagonistically." What goes by the moniker of the "New Perspective" is actually more like variations on a theme; and, in point of fact, this generic title is flexible enough to allow for individual thought and refinement of convictions….[3]

---

2. Dunn, *The New Perspective on Paul: Collected Essays*. Wissenschaftliche Untersuchungen zum Neuen Testament 185 (Tübingen: Mohr Siebeck, 2005), 15.
3. D. Garlington, "The New Perspective on Paul: An Appraisal Two Decades Later," *Criswell Theological Review* ns 2, no. 2 (2005), 18. The essay is reprinted in my *In Defense of the New Perspective on Paul: Essays and Reviews* (Eugene, OR: Wipf & Stock, 2007), 1-28. See Dunn's own admission in *New Perspective on Paul*, vii-viii. It is of more than passing inter-

Therefore, although I am much indebted to E. P. Sanders, J. D. G. Dunn, N. T. Wright and numerous others for invaluable insights, the following representation of the NPP does not correspond precisely to any of these scholars. The views expressed here are distinctly my own.

"The Fundamentals of the New Perspective"

Baugh asserts in his Introduction that the NPP consists of "a relatively small but vocal group," and that "the various positions of this group have been subject to considerable critique and rebuttal in scholarly literature, for its underlying analysis of both ancient Judaism and Paul's theology." He then outlines what he perceives to be the fundamentals of the NPP, including three "nonnegotiable ideas" (though Dunn numbers five).

First, according to Baugh, the NPP rejected the traditional Protestant vision of Judaism and Paul's Jewish-Christian opponents as "rank legalists" and instead understands ancient Judaism in terms of E. P. Sanders' "covenantal nomism:" one "gets in" the covenant by God's grace, but "stays in" by works of obedience to God's law.

As a basic summary of Sanders, this is fair enough, but oversimplified. To be sure, Baugh is right that NPP scholars have rejected the caricature of Second Temple Jews (the Jews in the period of Herod's temple, which was destroyed in AD 74) as "rank legalists," simply because it is a caricature, and for that reason *ought* to be rejected. The main issue Jewish writers in this time period faced was perseverance in the face of widespread apostasy, not the amassing of merits for the sake of some "self-salvation."[4] However, such a conclusion did not descend "straight down from above"

---

est that Dunn acknowledges that N. T. Wright was the first to recognize the significance of the work of E. P. Sanders ("The Paul of History and the Apostle of Faith," *Tyndale Bulletin* 29 [1978], 61-88). It was Wright who proposed that there should be "a new way of looking at Paul...(and) a *new perspective* on...Pauline problems" (cited by Dunn, *New Perspective on Paul*, 6, n. 24, italics added).

4. If I may refer to my discussion in *'The Obedience of Faith': A Pauline Phrase in Historical Context*. Wissenschaftliche Untersuchungen zum Neuen Testament 2/38 (Tübingen: Mohr Siebeck, 1991), 120, 265-67.

in 1977 with the publication of E. P. Sanders' *Paul and Palestinian Judaism*.. Baugh fails to present a sense of historical perspective, leaving the impression (from silence) that virtually no one before the advent of the "Sanders/Dunn trajectory" had taken issue with the Reformation understanding of the character of Second Temple Judaism.[5] Certainly this is not the case. Close to the turn of the twentieth-century, a group of Jewish scholars rightly protested against the Christian mishandling, not to say distortion, of the literature they knew so well. As a result, non-Jewish interpreters of Judaism and Paul, such as G. F. Moore, James Parkes and W. D. Davies, began to reassess.[6] Davies in particular concluded that at point after point in Paul's letters Paul and the rabbinic teachers agree, and the real difference is the question of whether Jesus of Nazareth is the Messiah.[7] Davies rightly, then, focused on Paul's christology.

R. N. Longenecker's *Paul: Apostle of Liberty*,[8] whose work predated the NPP, strangely has been overlooked (especially by evangelicals). Longenecker's treatment of the piety of Hebraic Judaism is a model of balanced scholarship.[9] He demonstrates, in the words of Israel Abrahams, that there are both "weeds" and "flowers" in the garden of Judaism and that the elements of nomism and spirituality must be kept in proper proportion to one another. Certainly ahead of his time, Longenecker had already distinguished between "acting legalism" and "reacting nomism," with the latter characterizing "the religion of a *nomist*."[10] It is true that Longenecker

---

5. The "Sanders/Dunn trajectory" is the phrase of Moisés Silva, "The Law and Christianity: Dunn's New Synthesis," *Westminster Theological Journal* 53 (1991), 341.

6. See the historical overview of E. P. Sanders, *Paul and Palestinian Judaism: A Comparison of Patterns of Religion* (Philadelphia: Fortress, 1977), 1-12.

7. W. D. Davies, *Paul and Rabbinic Judaism: Some Rabbinic Elements in Pauline Theology*. 4th ed. (Mifflintown, PA: Sigler Press, 1998), 323-24.

8. Longenecker, *Paul: Apostle of Liberty* (New York: Harper & Row, 1964).

9. Longenecker, Paul, 65-85.

10. Longenecker, Paul, 78, 79-83. Longenecker was later to (re)define "works of the law" as "a catch phrase to signal the whole legalistic complex of ideas having to do with winning God's favor by a merit-amassing observance of the Torah" (*Galatians*. Word Biblical Commentary 41 [Dallas: Word, 1990], 86). This is in apparent conflict with his endorsement of Sanders and the acknowledgement that "First-Century Judaism was *not*

takes the "weeds" of Judaism to be its tendency toward "externalism." Yet even here he does not absolutize external obedience to the law, because the "essential tension" of Judaism prior to the destruction of the Temple was not external versus inward obedience, but "fundamentally that of promise and fulfillment."[11]

In light of the actual development of Jewish and Pauline studies, Sanders' work is but the outcome of a process of rethinking. To be sure, his *Paul and Palestinian Judaism* managed to grab the attention of the scholarly world in a way none had done before. Nevertheless, his was not a unique epiphany straight out of the blue. As was so of Einstein's revolutionary accomplishments, Sanders also has stood on the shoulders of others ("giants") who came before him.[12]

Second, according to Baugh, what began as a "new perspective" on Second Temple Judaism turned into a complete recasting of Paul's theology. In particular, he chides Wright for indicting the Christian church for its supposed misunderstanding of justification for nearly two thousand years.

Baugh is right that Sanders in *Paul and Palestinian Judaism*, published in 1977, did little exegesis of Paul and that his sketch of Paul's theology has gained few followers.[13] Nevertheless, Baugh's main allegation is inaccurate. One of the most accessible windows into the NPP is a segment in Dunn's Introduction to his commentary on Romans.[14] In his own reflections on the movement, Dunn maintains that Protestant exegesis for too long allowed a typically

---

fundamentally legalistic" (ibid.). In any event, my point is that in his earlier work Longenecker formed an integral part of a developmental process culminating in Sanders.

11. Longenecker, *Paul*, 84.

12. This is especially evident from S. Westerholm's survey of scholarship in Perspectives Old and New on Paul: The "Lutheran" Paul and His Critics (Grand Rapids: Eerdmans, 2004), 3-258. It is also well to remember that before Dunn's Romans commentary there was U. Wilckens, Der Brief an die Römer. Evangelisch-Katholischer Kommentar zum Neuen Testament 6. 3 vols. (Zürich/Neukirchen: Benziger/Neukirchener, 1978-82). Wilcken's work may fairly be termed the first "NPP" commentary on Romans.

13. In fact, I have heard it whimsically said, and I agree, that Sanders' book should have been entitled Palestinian Judaism and Paul!

14. Dunn, *Romans*. 2 vols. Word Biblical Commentary 38 a, b (Dallas: Word, 1988), 1.lxiii-lxxii.

Lutheran emphasis on justification by faith to impose an interpretive grid on the text of Romans. The problem, according to Dunn, was not "justification by faith," but how its antithesis—"justification by works"—was defined. Lutherans understood "justification by works" in terms of a Roman Catholic system where believers *earned* salvation through the *merit* of *good works*.. This was based partly on the comparison suggested in Romans 4:4-5 and partly on the Reformation rejection of the Roman Catholic system that supposedly allowed one to accumulate merits and buy indulgences. But Dunn's qualification, that the Reformation's repudiation of merits and indulgences *is* an important emphasis, is often neglected. God is the one who justifies the ungodly (Romans 4:5), and, Dunn says, understandably this insight has become a powerful, integrating focus in Lutheran theology..

A careful reading of Dunn clearly reveals that his agenda is stated in hermeneutical terms. The protest against merits and indulgences was necessary, justified, and of lasting importance. But the hermeneutical mistake was to read *this* antithesis back into the New Testament period and to assume that Paul was protesting in Pharisaic Judaism precisely what Luther protested in the pre-Reformation church.[15] It is true that Dunn programmatically pursues this "new perspective" throughout his commentary, but Paul's theology is hardly given a complete overhaul. In many places, Dunn's comments on the text of Romans are as traditional as any other commentator.[16] It would be much more fair and accurate to say that Dunn and others have sought to make appropriate adjustments to our understanding of Paul in the light of his place in history and the issues actually under debate during his lifetime.[17] It is telling that the only aspect of Paul's theology that Baugh singled out is justification. Even if one believes that justification is the "article of standing

---

15. Dunn, *Romans*, 1.lxv. See the similar discussion in Dunn's *The Theology of Paul the Apostle* (Grand Rapids: Eerdmans, 1998), 335-40, and at length *New Perspective on Paul*, 1-88.
16. The same is true of his appreciation of justification by faith alone. See his *Theology of Paul*, 371-79; *New Perspective on Paul*, 21-22.
17. In a personal communication, Professor Dunn has confirmed the correctness of this characterization of his work.

and falling of the church" (*articulus stantis et cadentis ecclesiae*), it is a *non sequitur* that an adjusted definition of the term is tantamount to a wholesale revision of Paul's preaching, and Baugh has not demonstrated that such a sweeping alteration has occurred.

As for justification, it is necessary to distinguish between Dunn and Wright. Dunn is *not* of the opinion that the church has been "wrong" (as Baugh puts it) for the past two thousand years regarding justification by faith. According to his own statement, he has no particular problem in affirming that the doctrine of justification, in its fully orbed expression, is "the article of standing or falling of the church."[18] Some may question the phrase "fully orbed expression." But even allowing that this choice of words may not sit comfortably with some traditional views of justification, Dunn is basically consistent with the Reformation's recognition of how God justifies (vindicates) sinners.[19]

> This I say once again is what the "new perspective" is all about for me. It does *not* set this understanding of justification by faith in antithesis to the justification of the individual by faith. It is *not* opposed to the classic Reformed doctrine of justification. It simply observes that a social and ethnic dimension was part of the doctrine from its first formulation, was indeed integral to the first recorded exposition and defense of the doctrine—"Jew first but also Greek".... This is the lost theological dimension of the doctrine which needs to be brought afresh into the light, *not* to diminish the traditional doctrine, but to enrich the doctrine from its biblical roots and to recover the wholeness of Paul's teaching on the subject.[20]

---

18. Dunn, *New Perspective on Paul*, 21.
19. Dunn maintains that Luther's translation of Romans 3:28, "by faith alone," may be regarded as faithful to the thrust of Paul's argument so long as the scope of Paul's contrast of faith and works of the law is borne in mind (*Romans*, 1.187). In commenting on Galatians 2:16, Dunn doubts that the traditional reading of the verse has quite caught Paul's meaning. Nevertheless, he is entirely sympathetic with the proposition that humans cannot earn their salvation by their own efforts. In theological terms, this is an insight of "tremendous importance" (*The Epistle to the Galatians*. Black's New Testament Commentaries 9 [Peabody: Hendrickson, 1993], 135).
20. Dunn, *New Perspective on Paul*, 33(italics original).

Wright, by contrast, maintains that justification does not tell us how one can be saved; it is, rather, a way of saying how one can know that one belongs to the covenant community, or, in other words, how are the people of God to be defined?[21] Paul does indeed address the question, "Who is a member of the people of God?" Likewise, it is true that "justification...is the doctrine which insists that all who share faith in Christ belong at the same table, no matter what their racial differences, as together they wait for the final new creation."[22] This much said, it is to be acknowledged that Wright has distinguished too sharply between the identity of the people of God and salvation. In my view, it is closer to the mark to say that (among other things) Romans and Galatians do address the issue of entrance into the body of the saved, meaning that to belong to the new covenant *is* to belong to the saved community. Therefore, justification does indeed tell us how "to be saved," in that it depicts a method of redeeming sinners—*by faith* in Christ—and placing them in covenant standing with the God of Israel. If justification is *by faith*, then a mode of salvation is prescribed.[23]

---

21. Wright, *What Saint Paul Really Said: Was Paul of Tarsus the Real Founder of Christianity?* (Grand Rapids: Eerdmans, 1997), 119, 120-22, 131; id., *Paul: In Fresh Perspective* (Minneapolis: Fortress, 2005), 122. Wright is undoubtedly correct that such issues are to be judged in light of the covenant context of "the righteousness of God" and similar ideas.
22. Wright, *Saint Paul*, 122.
23. As regards Galatians particularly, better are E. P. Sanders, *Paul, The Law, and the Jewish People* (Philadelphia: Fortress, 1983), 18-19, and C. Cousar, *Galatians*. Interpretation (Louisville: John Knox, 1982), 61, both of whom acknowledge that soteriology lies at the heart of Paul's concerns in the letter. Moreover, I should have thought that with all of Wright's admirable and "justifiable" stress on the return from exile motif he would have been more inclined to play up justification as *salvation from bondage*. As he himself has labored to demonstrate, the very term "gospel" originates in Isaiah 40:9; 41:27; 52:7; 61:1-2; Joel 3:5 (Septuagint), where the announcement is made that Israel's captivity is at an end and that the people will embark on an exodus from Babylon, just as the wilderness generation had originally come out from Egypt, the "house of bondage." In the broader context of Isaiah 40-66, the "gospel" expands to entail Yahweh's return to Zion, his enthronement there and the commencement of the new creation. But if it is the "righteousness of God" that underlies and impels Israel's release from a new house of bondage, as Wright has argued, then why is justification not tantamount to a salvation, which, in biblical-theological terms, is played out with Jesus as the binder of the

Despite all this, Baugh still does not represent Wright entirely accurately. According to Baugh, Wright "indicts the church—principally because it has misunderstood ancient Judaism and has 'ransacked' Paul for mere proof-texts; therefore the Christian church has misunderstood Paul on justification 'for nearly two thousand years' and 'has systematically done violence to that text [Romans] for hundreds of years'." But let's examine Wright a bit more closely. In the pages referenced by Baugh,[24] Wright maintains that "the discussions of justification in much of the history of the church, certainly *since Augustine*, got off on the wrong foot—at least in terms of understanding Paul—and they have stayed there ever since."[25] Thereafter, he cites Alister McGrath to the effect that the doctrine of justification has come to develop a meaning quite independent of its biblical (Pauline) origins, that justification in Paul originated from his polemics against the Judaism of his day. He continues: "Whatever Paul means by a word, if the church has used that word or its equivalents in other languages to mean something else for nearly two thousand years, *that is neither here nor there*." Still, he writes, there remains a problem. In all the church's discussion of "justification," Paul's letters "are ransacked for statements, dare we even say proof-texts, on a subject which he may or may not himself have conceived of in those terms."[26] This leads to the proposal that if Paul meant by "justification" something which is "significantly different from what the subsequent debate has meant," then the appeal to him is "consistently flawed, maybe invalidated altogether."[27] And indeed, Wright does claim that the traditional way of reading Romans has "systemically done violence to that text for hundreds of years, and that it is time for the text itself to be heard again."[28]

---

strong man who plunders the latter's goods and releases those bound by him (Matthew 12:22-30; Luke 11:14-23; 10-17)?
24. Wright, *Saint Paul*, 115-17.
25. Wright, *Saint Paul*, 115.
26. Wright, *Saint Paul*, 115-16.
27. Wright, *Saint Paul*, 116.
28. Wright, *Saint Paul*, 117.

In presenting his peculiar approach to justification, Wright leaves no doubt that he is not satisfied with the terms in which the issue has been posed and with the Reformation's reading of Romans in particular, yet he does not describe the situation as dire. However, Baugh's truncated version of Wright's complaint that Paul's letters "are ransacked for statements, dare we even say proof-texts, on a subject which he may or may not himself have conceived of *in those terms*" leaves a different impression. Wright's own syntax, it would seem, has been subjected to a proof-texting method, leaving an overly negative impression of his actual claims. Wright does not say categorically that the church has misunderstood justification from the get-go. His discussion, unlike Baugh's, is more nuanced than that. Augustine, he writes, is the effective instigator of discussions of justification that have "got off on the wrong foot and have stayed there ever since." This is a statement of procedure, not a blanket denunciation of the entire pre-NPP understanding of Paul, especially if it is *"neither here nor there"* if the church has used the term "justification" or its equivalents to mean something else for nearly two thousand years.

Baugh has failed to notice Wright's acknowledgment that Paul does discuss the subject-matter that the church has referred to as "justification," though he does not use "justification language" for it. When it comes to a personal knowledge of God in Christ, Paul does not employ the language of justification, but rather he speaks of the proclamation of the gospel of Jesus, the work of the Spirit and the entry into the common life of the people of God.[29] Again, I should think if justification speaks to the issue of the deliverance of the believer from the bondage of sin, it is a false alternative to place this facet of soteriology over against the personal knowledge of God in Christ, as assured by the work of the Spirit and accompanied by our reckoning among the covenant people. Even so, Wright is considerably more balanced than as represented by Baugh, particularly relating to Wright's "threefold grid" for understanding "God's righteousness" that is provided by covenant lan-

---

29. Wright, *Saint Paul*, 117.

guage, law-court language and eschatology.[30] Whether one agrees or disagrees, it is evident that Wright is seeking to shift the terms in which justification has been discussed, from the dogmatic/confessional to the exegetical/historical, in keeping, I would say, with Paul's own world of thought.

Third, because Baugh perceives that the NPP has completely recast Paul, consequently any reading of Paul that "looks suspiciously like the Protestant view is ipso facto mistaken and excluded from consideration in the new perspective." Related to this, for Baugh, is the "curious fact that the new perspective Paul looks remarkably like his 'covenantal nomist' opponents described in Sanders's portrait of ancient Judaism."

The first allegation is an overstatement and attributes to proponents of the NPP an attitude they characteristically display. I simply defer again to Dunn's introductory essay to *The New Perspective on Paul*, "The New Perspective on Paul: Whence, What, Wither?" I might add my own piece, "The New Perspective on Paul" (especially pp. 26-29).[31]

As for the "curious fact that the new perspective on Paul looks remarkably like his 'covenantal nomist' opponents described in Sanders's portrait of ancient Judaism," I concede that there is a similarity. According to Baugh's reading of Sanders, one gets into covenant fellowship and salvation through a gracious, corporate election and retains title to these blessings only through "a sort of nonmeritorious obedience through works of law keeping." Yet this is not precisely Sanders' own articulation of his position. To be sure, Sanders does indeed speak of "good deeds" as the condition

---

30. Wright, *Saint Paul*, 117-18.
31. Other attempts to bridge the gap between the NPP and "the Protestant view" (admirably, in an irenic spirit) are   d, "When the Dust Finally Settles: Coming to a Post-New Perspective Perspective," *Criswell Theological Review* ns 2, no. 2 (2005), 57-69; id., "Justification as Forensic Declaration and Covenant Membership: A *Via Media* Between Reformed and Revisionist Readings of Paul," *Tyndale Bulletin* 57 (2006): 109-30; id., *The Saving Righteousness of God: Studies on Paul, Justification, and the New Perspective* (Carlisle: Paternoster), 2007; M. B. Thompson, *The New Perspective on Paul*. Grove Biblical Series (Cambridge: Grove Books, 2002). Baugh's quotation of Francis Watson (p. 140, n. 11) seems uncommonly like a suspicion that the NPP is ipso facto mistaken and consequently excluded from consideration.

of remaining in covenant relationship.[32] Likewise, he can state that the "proper response of man" is his "obedience to the commandments." But obedience is doing the will of the covenant Lord, who has provided atonement for transgressions.[33] In short, the faithful Israelite stayed in the covenant by perseverance, in keeping with Leviticus 18:5.[34] As Sanders is careful to state, the question is whether one is or is not an Israelite in good standing. Simple heredity did not ensure salvation: "That came to all those individual Israelites who were faithful."[35]

This being the case, both Paul and his Jewish counterparts were convinced that one must "get in" and then "stay in." While it is true that he and they differed as to requirements for getting in and staying in, and while it is also true that it is unhelpful to speak of Paul's theology in terms of a "nomism" (because Christ takes the place of the law), the basic pattern is the same. The difference is *christology*: for Paul, *Christ* is the "article of standing and falling of the church."[36] One gets in Christ by electing grace and stays in Christ by perseverance or "the obedience of faith" (Romans 1:5; 16:26), which itself is God's gift by virtue of the eschatological Spirit.[37]

"Methodological Difficulties in the New Perspective"

The first "methodological difficulty" that Baugh describes is "a pervasive tendency" on the part of NPP scholars to use a word, word group or phrase in Paul "as levers to shift our understanding of Paul's doctrines from what has been painstakingly established

---

32. Sanders, *Paul*, 517, as quoted by Baugh.
33. Sanders, *Paul*, 236, 420.
34. See further my *Obedience of Faith*, 263-65, and "Role Reversal and Paul's Use of Scripture in Galatians 3.10-13," *Journal for the Study of the New Testament* 65 (1997), 101-4.
35. Sanders, *Paul*, 237-38.
36. See further my "A 'New Perspective' Reading of Central Texts in Romans 1-4," http://www.thepaulpage.com, 47-48 (a paper presented at the Evangelical Theological Society annual meeting, Washington, DC, November, 2006).
37. As affirmed explicitly by Dunn, *New Perspective on Paul*, 77-80. If no one can call Jesus Lord but by the Spirit (1 Corinthians 12:3), and if faith itself is the gift of God (Ephesians 2:8), then everything is of grace, from beginning to end.

to their own eccentric interpretations." While this is obviously an *ad hominem* shot, as though advocates of the NPP are merely "eccentric" and have shirked from painstaking analysis of the data,[38] I can reply in brief to the words and phrases Baugh highlights.

The first is the hotly debated phrase "faith of Jesus Christ" (*pistis Iēsou Christou*). Space does not permit a full treatment of the phrase and the debate here, but the problem is that Baugh only cites scholars such as Douglas Campbell and Richard Hays, who interpret the phrase as subjective genitive (that is, Christ's own covenant fidelity). This creates in the reader the impression that this "eccentric interpretation" is characteristic of the NPP overall. Yet there is one glaringly obvious omission—J. D. G. Dunn. The scholar who actually coined the title "The New Perspective on Paul" has consistently resisted this reading of "faith of Jesus Christ!"[39] Baugh's argument for this first "methodological difficulty" suffers a methodological difficulty of its own.

Second, according to Baugh, the methodological problems of the NPP are further compounded by the phrase "the righteousness of God." Supposedly, this combination of words, along with the "righteousness" (*dik-*) word-group generally, warrants "the recasting of Paul's whole theology and especially the doctrine of

---

38. Such a bewildering contention can hardly be sustained in the face of the massive efforts of various NPP scholars. A fair reading of these materials is sufficient to establish that their labors are neither eccentric nor lacking in painstaking analysis. Besides Dunn and Wright, there are such "NPP sympathizers" as Udo Schnelle, Scott Hafemann, Scot McKnight, James Scott, David deSilva, Marcus Bockmuehl and Gordon Fee, to mention only a few, besides Jewish scholars on the order of Jacob Neusner, Pamela Eisenbaum and Mark Nanos. Various non-NPP scholars champion the analysis of the rabbinic materials by F. Avemarie, *Tora und Leben: Untersuchungen zur Heilsbedeutung der Tora in der frühen rabbinischen Literatur*. Texte und Studien zum Antiken Judentum 55 (Tübingen: Mohr-Siebeck, 1996). Yet it is to be noted that Avemarie acknowledges the grace-element in these sources, although he believes that there is a tension between grace/election, on the one hand, and works, on the other. Most strikingly, Avemarie grants that throughout this literature it is possible to speak of a "covenantal nomism." The Torah of the rabbis cannot be divorced from this context in which the law was given. In this sense, Sanders' coinage of the phrase, says Avemarie, is certainly justified (ibid., 584, n. 40).

39. As illustrated easily enough from Dunn's *Romans*, 1.166-67, and *Galatians*, 138-39. In more detail, see Dunn's "Once More, *PISTIS CHRISTOU*," *Pauline Theology. Volume IV: Looking Back, Pressing On*. eds. E. E. Johnson and D. M. Hay. Society of Biblical Literature Symposium Series 4 (Atlanta: Scholars Press, 1997), 61-81.

justification in the way in which new perspective adherents desire." His charge is that the NPP has focused too narrowly on a few words and phrases and has not appreciated that justification in Paul is a complex construction which must be established by *statements* and larger units of discourse.

Here once more is a baffling allegation, as though we on "the other side of the fence" have forgotten our basic James Barr: one cannot understand Scripture by working only from the meaning of words and phrases isolated from longer statements and from cultural understanding.[40] That the NPP has fixated atomisticly or myopically on mere words and phrases apart from an entire field of discourse simply does not comport with the facts. Quite the contrary, justification (as it takes its place within the broader parameters of "the righteousness of God") is rooted in the panorama of prophetic teaching about Israel's return from exile. Paul virtually brackets Romans with the declaration that his gospel is rooted in the prophetic Scriptures of Israel (Romans 1:2; 16:26); and, as we saw above, the very notion of gospel is rooted in the latter chapters of Isaiah.[41] Therefore, since the sum and substance of Isaiah and the other prophets is exile and return, some of us certainly cannot be fairly accused of disregarding Paul's entire universe of discourse in favor of simple words and phrases. Consequently, far from recasting Paul's whole theology, especially the doctrine of justification, I would maintain that we in the NPP camp have understood Paul in the manner in which he wished to be understood, i.e., as a theologian of salvation history who took the story of Israel and redrew it around Christ and the church.[42]

Singling out N. T. Wright in particular, Baugh cites an "extreme example" of ignoring context, claiming that Wright attempted to fix the content of Paul's gospel in two verses in Isaiah.[43]

---

40. Barr, *The Semantics of Biblical Language* (Oxford: Oxford University Press, 1961).
41. According to Mark 1:1-3, "the beginning of the gospel of Jesus Christ" *is* Isaiah 40:3 (and Malachi 3:1).
42. *A la* Wright, especially in *Jesus and the Victory of God*. Christian Origins and the Question of God 2 (Minneapolis: Fortress, 1996).
43. Citing Wright, *Saint Paul*, 42-43.

Actually, Wright does not limit his reference to Isaiah 40:9 and 52:7. He writes that the Jewish usage of the root "gospel," in its noun (*euangelion*) and verb (*euangelizesthai*) forms, *includes* these verses. Yet Baugh bypasses the fact that Wright proceeds to point out that these passages take their place in the company of others like Isaiah 60:6; 61:1, as they form the climactic statements of the great double theme of *the entire section of Isaiah 40-66*. Moreover, the return from exile was predicted by Isaiah, Jeremiah, Ezekiel and others, as reflected by several of the Qumran texts.[44] It would appear that Baugh is the one who has seized on certain words and has disregarded Wright's *statements* and larger units of discourse.[45]

To add to the problem, Baugh reasons that if Wright's identification of "gospel" with return from exile is correct, then we could just as likely trace Paul's gospel to Jeremiah 20:15, where the prophet curses the man who brought the "gospel" of his birth to his father; "hence, the gospel would be viewed as a curse." The obvious reply is that this "good news" (*ho euangelisamenos*) is not of the same variety as the end of the exile and the subsequent enthronement of Yahweh on Mount Zion.[46] Again, Baugh has neglected the actual *statement* of Jeremiah within his larger unit of discourse. It is he who is guilty of what Barr called "illegitimate totality transfer," and not Wright who, if anyone, is sensitive to the breadth of the prophetic setting of Paul's employment of "gospel."[47]

The second problem, for Baugh, pertains to the character of justification. Rather than a declaration by God that the sinner is accounted righteous in Christ by faith alone, the NPP, so says Baugh, envisages justification as "some sort of ongoing rela-

---

44. Wright, *Saint Paul*, 42-43.
45. Likewise, the citation of Sanders (*Paul*, 544) fails to appreciate Sanders' actual point, which is that the difference between Paul and Judaism resides in a different usage respectively of the "righteous" word-group.
46. J. A. Thompson points out that the underlying Hebrew is neutral and means merely "bring news," whether good or bad (*The Book of Jeremiah*. New International Commentary on the Old Testament [Grand Rapids: Eerdmans, 1980], 464, n. 4).
47. See further Wright, "Gospel and Theology in Galatians," *Gospel in Paul: Studies on Corinthians, Galatians and Romans for Richard N. Longenecker*. eds. L. A. Jervis and P. Richardson. Journal for the Study of the New Testament Supplement Series 108 (Sheffield: Sheffield Academic Press, 1994), 222-39.

tionship in covenant involving both God's obligation to save his covenant people and the individual's own obedience to maintain covenant with God." He then cites Dunn that such a conception is rooted in Hebrew thought, in which righteousness entails "a concept of relation." "Justification," consequently, means "to be acquitted, recognized as righteous…to be counted as one of God's own people *who had proven faithful* to the covenant."[48]

So, as Baugh would have it, Paul turns out for the NPP to be a "covenantal nomist" like his opponents. Baugh complains that the NPP sees Jewish and Greek conceptions of justice and justification as polar opposites, as though the former allowed no place for a norm (the law), and the latter recognized no element of relationship. It is true that Dunn contrasts the Hebrew relational (covenantal) ideal of righteousness with the Greco-Roman, which measured righteousness in terms of absolute ethical norms against which particular claims and duties could be measured. Failure to measure up to the Greco-Roman standard meant ethical or criminal liability. By comparison, in Hebrew thought, individuals are righteous when they meet the claims which others have on them by virtue of their relationship.[49] Baugh writes that a more accurate evaluation of Paul's historical backdrop would be "inconvenient for the rhetorical appeal of the new perspective," as though the rationale and argumentation were rhetorical and rhetorical alone.

It is difficult to conceive that anyone familiar with contemporary biblical studies would dismiss the relational nature of the Hebrew covenant, even if other factors enter in.[50] Even Mark Seifrid, who wants to downplay the definition of righteousness as covenant fidelity, has to concede that there are seven Old Testament texts that make the connection explicit.[51] Given that

---

48. Dunn, *Galatians*, 134-35.
49. Dunn, "The Justice of God: A Renewed Perspective on Justification by Faith," *Journal of Theological Studies* ns 43 (1992), 1-22; id. (with Alan Suggate), *The Justice of God: A Fresh Look at the Old Doctrine of Justification by Faith* (Grand Rapids: Eerdmans, 1993).
50. The literature is massive, but as good a starting point as any is Dunn, *Theology of Paul*, 334-89; id., *New Perspective on Paul*, 1-15 (both with other literature).
51. Seifrid, "Righteousness Language in the Hebrew Scriptures and Early Judaism," *Justification and Variegated Nomism. Volume 1: The Complexities of Second Temple Judaism.* eds. D.

righteousness is *at least* covenant fidelity, Dunn's appraisal of justification is apropos: Paul's doctrine entails being counted "as one of God's own people who had proven faithful to the covenant."[52] The issue, at the end of the day, is not achievement, merit or anything remotely resembling a method of self-salvation. It is, rather, the eschatological vindication of the servants of Christ who have remained loyal to him.

This approach is not antagonistic to the traditional understanding of Paul. Paul was not a "covenantal nomist" like his opponents, because the "nomists" were devotees of the law, whereas Paul was a devotee of Christ. In addition, many of us in the NPP are convinced that the declaration on the last day is a forensic acquittal. By definition, judgment *is* forensic, though we should remind ourselves that all of the judgment texts (Old and New Testaments) base final forensic acquittal on "works"—not the works of "saving ourselves" or "contributing to salvation," but the believer's "fruit" (John 15:2, 8, 16; Galatians 5:22-23) which is the inevitable product of faith. At the end of the day, what counts is faith(fulness), or, in Hebrew, *'emunah*.

As for the supposed antithesis of Jewish and Greek conceptions of justice and justification, Baugh typically paints with a very broad brush, and, apart from an allusion to Dunn, no "new perspective advocates" are named. However, Baugh makes a valid point that we should not oversimplify and thus exaggerate the differences between the Hebrew and Greco-Roman notions of righteousness, as though there were no overlap at all. Udo Schnelle, a decided "NPP sympathizer," in his recent volume on Paul notes that there was a degree of interpenetration between the Hebrew

---

A. Carson, P. T. O'Brien and M. A. Seifrid (Grand Rapids: Baker, 2001), 415-42. I have replied in detail to Seifrid in my *In Defense of the New Perspective on Paul: Essays and Reviews* (Eugene, OR: Wipf & Stock, 2005), 66-95.

52. See Dunn, *New Perspective on Paul*, 63-86; K. Yinger, *Paul, Judaism, and Judgment According to Deeds*. Society for New Testament Studies Monograph Series 105 (Cambridge: Cambridge University Press, 1999), esp. 146-82; Garlington, "New Perspective Reading," 18-24; id., *Faith, Obedience, and Perseverance: Aspects of Paul's Letter to the Romans*. Wissenschaftliche Untersuchungen zum Neuen Testament 79 (Tübingen: Mohr Siebeck, 1994), 44-71.

and Greco-Roman worlds.[53] But even with this qualification, the fact remains that Paul moved within the biblical/Jewish world of the covenant of Yahweh with Israel. Pagan notions of behavioral norms are of secondary importance in understanding Paul. The Old Testament understanding of righteousness allows us to understand justification within the society of the people of God. The judges of Israel were responsible for recognizing what these various obligations were as imposed on the people and for judging them accordingly, clearing the innocent and not deferring to the great (Exodus 23:7-8; Leviticus 19:15; Deuteronomy 25:1; Isaiah 5:23). This basic datum is a sufficient comeback to any claims that the NPP is concerned solely with relationships and not with the divine demand as expressed in the law. Dunn further comments that the more fully we recognize that Paul's teaching on divine righteousness is the Old Testament doctrine through and through, the more we must also recognize the social dimension of that righteousness (as demanded by none other than the law). By way of application, he writes, "this discovery of the horizontal and social dimension of justification by faith indicates that such social concerns lie at the heart of this so characteristic and fundamental Christian and *Protestant* doctrine."[54]

Third, Baugh argues that the NPP has "the consistent tendency to limit the meaning of Paul's own teaching to what his supposed Jewish contemporaries either taught or what they would have understood." Baugh illustrates with Galatians 5:3, which, in association with Galatians 3:10, has been taken to indicate that Paul interpreted the law to require perfect and entire obedience. Baugh contrasts this with Sanders' view (Sanders immediately preceded the NPP, and his perspective was formative), which he describes as "both Paul and contemporary Judaism taught a more relaxed view of the law in the form of covenant nomism." If Paul viewed the law as imposing an exacting and exhaustive requirement for personal obedience, then, according to Baugh, Sanders'

---

53. Schnelle, *Paul: His Life and Theology* (Grand Rapids: Baker, 2005), 460-63 (note Schnelle's comparison of Paul and Dio Chrysostom in particular, p. 463).
54. Dunn, "Justice of God," 20-21 (italics added).

analysis of Paul's opponents would in fail.

There are problems with this misrepresentation. At the very least, it is an oversimplification, and really a caricature, that NPP scholars reduce Paul's understanding to that of his contemporaries. True, Paul shared common values and outlooks with his Jewish kinsmen, particularly such theological terms as covenant, righteousness, faith and judgment. But at the same time, his perception of the role of the law and the Jewish people was radically altered by his encounter with the risen Christ on the Damascus Road.[55] Paul cannot be domesticated to Jewish standards because, for him, the crucified Messiah is all in all; he is the goal and termination (*telos*) of Israel's law (Romans 10:4); he is the reason the Torah was imposed as a disciplinarian on the covenant people (Galatians 3:23-25); he is the "body" to whom the shadows pointed (Colossians 2:17). Consequently, faith for Paul is Christ-centered: from now on, trust is to be placed specifically in Jesus of Nazareth, the crucified Messiah.[56]

The argument from Galatians 5:3 and Galatians 3:10 involves a good deal of assumption. As for the former, Paul's reasoning is obvious enough from the standpoint of the Torah: "For Paul the Law is a package deal, and one cannot separate out one portion of its commandments from another. All must be obeyed if one is under the law."[57] One was not, in other words, free to pick and choose in cafeteria style from among the commandments. What is in view is the typical Jewish mindset which understood "doing the [whole] law" (Leviticus 18:5; Deuteronomy 4:1, 10, 40; 5:29-33; 6:1-2, 18, 24; 7:12-13) as the obligation and privilege of those within the covenant.[58]

---

55. See my *Obedience of Faith*, 255-58.
56. C. H. Cosgrove confirms that the believer's faith is not in God per se, but in him as the vindicator of the crucified Messiah ("Justification in Paul: A Linguistic and Theological Reflection," *Journal of Biblical Literature* 106 [1987], 666). Wilckens speaks to the same effect: it is not faith as such that concerns Paul, but faith as directed to the crucified *Christ* as the basis of all righteousness before God (*Römer*, 1.89).
57. B. Witherington, *Grace in Galatia: A Commentary on Paul's Letter to the Galatians* (Grand Rapids: Eerdmans, 1998), 353. Cf. Longenecker, *Galatians*, 227; Dunn, *Galatians*, 267.
58. *If* there is any emphasis on "all" in Deuteronomy 27:26, which appears only in the

The Torah does not demand what is often claimed. In commenting on Deuteronomy 27:26, Peter Craigie, for example, maintains that "the reach of the law is so all-pervasive that man cannot claim justification before God on the basis of 'works of the law'."[59] But the "reach of the law," I would respond, is not perfect compliance with its demands, or anything approaching it, but fidelity to the God who graciously gave it to Israel. Craigie's other mistake is a failure to realize that the law is in fact performable. The Hebrew Scriptures never portray obedience to the Torah as an unobtainable goal. Rather, according to Deuteronomy 30:11-20, it is a thing within Israel's grasp ("this commandment...is not too hard for you, neither is it far off," v. 11). "Keeping the law," "obedience" and such expressions speak of perseverance, not sinless perfection.

For Protestants, Galatians 3:10 has also been understood as Baugh does, i.e., that the law demanded perfect, perpetual obedience. If this reading is correct, then Baugh has a case that Sanders' analysis of Paul's opponents would end in failure. Of course, perfect obedience is impossible for fallen human beings. However, the problem is that it assumes that as Paul penned Galatians 3:10, he had in his mind the "suppressed premise" that no one can actually keep the law perfectly.[60] This approach, to my mind, has been successfully rebuffed by several scholars.[61] I would suggest, as I have before, that Paul is using the context of the preceding por-

---

Septuagint, it is qualitative, not quantitative. Again, Israel was not free to pick and choose from the variety of the commandments: each one had its peculiar importance. It is in this vein that Paul writes in Galatians 5:3 that everyone who receives circumcision is bound to keep *the whole law*. Ironically enough, the Judaizers do not keep "the whole law" because of the absence of love on their part (5:14). Note how in Deuteronomy 30:16 loving God is correlated with walking in his ways and keeping his commandments.

59. Craigie, *The Book of Deuteronomy*. New International Commentary on the Old Testament (Grand Rapids: Eerdmans, 1976), 334.
60. As championed by B. Estelle in *CJPM*, 124-33.
61. Dunn, *Galatians*, 171; id., *Jesus, Paul*, 226; Wright, *The Climax of the Covenant: Christ and the Law in Pauline Theology* (Minneapolis: Fortress, 1991), 144-45; S. McKnight, *Galatians*. NIV Application Commentary (Grand Rapids: Eerdmans, 1995), 154-55; G. Howard, *Paul: Crisis in Galatia*. Society for New Testament Studies Monograph Series 35. 2nd ed. (Cambridge: Cambridge University Press, 1990), 51-54.

tion of Galatians, according to which the Judaizers have become "ministers of sin" and "transgressors" (2:17-18) because of their preaching of "another gospel." Therefore, the apostasy/perseverance texts of Deuteronomy 27:26; Habakkuk 2:4; Leviticus 18:5; Deuteronomy 21:23 are directly applicable to them by virtue of the phenomenon of role reversal.[62] The issue in Galatians 3:10, as in the Torah, is covenant fidelity or perseverance, not exhaustive perfect obedience to a "covenant of works" that demanded perfection for the Israelite to remain in covenant standing. Baugh and others have forgotten about the sacrificial system.[63]

Since, therefore, these two texts from Galatians can be explained in other terms than Baugh advocates, we are not compelled to concede that Sanders' analysis of Paul's opponents has failed. In fact, my proposed interpretation is entirely consistent with "the new perspective on Judaism" as advanced by Sanders.

While discussing his third methodological problem, Baugh keeps Sanders in his crosshairs. He maintains that Sanders changed his mind about Paul's conception of the law in relation to obedience. However, that is irrelevant, because Sanders is *not* an advocate of the NPP. As Dunn puts it, Sanders gave New Testament scholarship a "new perspective" on *Second Temple Judaism*.[64] The very reason why, in his Manson Memorial Lecture of 1982, Dunn coined the phrase "The New Perspective on Paul" was because Sanders, while providing legitimate insight into Judaism, still worked with an "old perspective" outlook on Paul himself. Consequently, to say, as Baugh does, that "the new perspective Paul can never break out of the box of his supposed pre-Christian convictions about the

---

62. Garlington, "Role Reversal." My take on Galatians 3:10 is supported by J. R. Wisdom, *Blessing for the Nations and the Curse of the Law: Paul's Citation of Genesis and Deuteronomy in Galatians 3.8-10*. Wissenschaftliche Untersuchungen zum Neuen Testament 2/133 (Tübingen: Mohr Siebeck, 2001), 43-62, 154-82, and N. Calvert-Koyzis, *Paul, Monotheism and the People of God: The Significance of Abraham Traditions for Early Judaism and Christianity*. Journal for the Study of the New Testament Supplement Series 273 (London: T & T Clark International, 2005), 96-97.
63. See further my reply to D. A. Carson and Mark Seifrid, *Defense of the New Perspective*, 183-85.
64. Dunn, *New Perspective on Paul*, 5.

nature of the law and its righteousness" is wrong in two regards. First, it dismisses Sanders' accurate portrait of the *pre-Christian* Paul, who understood that what the law required was fidelity, not sinless perfection, and who believed in the efficacy of the sacrificial system. And second, it fails to understand the eschatological situation: for the *Christian* Paul, the law and *its* righteousness has now given way to Christ and *his* righteousness (e.g., Romans 3:21; 10:3-4). To say it one more time, the question pertained to christology in relation to the Torah, and to the degree that Sanders has illuminated the Jewish position, we are in his debt.[65]

The fourth "methodological problem" takes up again the issue of justification, which forms a bridge into a lengthier section on Romans 5. In principle, I have already replied to Baugh's objections. Suffice it to say here that justification as a "definitive, judicial act" is falsely set in opposition to "continuance in the covenant relationship." It is not either/or but both/and. The believer's present justification as God's "definitive, judicial act" sets him upon the path of covenant fidelity—"continuance in the covenant relationship"—that ends in acquittal on the last day. Rather than cite Sanders to claim that one "gets in" by grace but "stays in" by works of obedience, it would have been more relevant to cite Dunn's affirmation that Paul expected his converts to "lead a life worthy of God" (1 Thessalonians 1:2), which is but their "harvest or fruit of righteousness in their lives" (2 Corinthians 9:9-10; Galatians 5:22-24; Philippians 1:11).[66]

In a mere footnote (n. 33), Baugh gives exceedingly short shrift to Paul's pivotal phrase "the obedience of faith" (Romans 1:5; 16:26). We are told that this combination of words is "often misunderstood." We are not told the "correct" understanding, but Baugh is quite sure that faith's obedience cannot be "faithfulness"

---

65. In another *ad hominem* barb, Baugh complains: "Anything he [Paul] says that does not conform to the views of this censorship board must be scrubbed of all offending material." Such a snide remark is not worthy of a reply.

66. Dunn, *New Perspective on Paul*, 63-72, esp. 67-68. Along these lines, an essay that really should have received more play is C. Loewe, "'There is No Condemnation' (Romans 8:1): But Why Not?" *Journal of the Evangelical Theological Society* 42 (1999), 231-50.

or "works of obedience" (I would add "perseverance"). Paul's Greek phrase *hypakoē pisteōs* ("the obedience of faith") has undergone a great deal of study in contemporary research, and some very competent scholars disagree with Baugh.[67] Baugh contends that certain NPP scholars committed the "etymological fallacy" or "root fallacy"[68] by relating the Greek noun *hypakoē* ("obedience") with the Hebrew verb *shamaʿ* ("hear"). According to Baugh, this is an "extreme example" of this particular exegetical failing. Carson explains that the etymological approach to word study entails word history and the drawing out "hidden meanings" based on a "meaning" inherent in the root of a word or a particular combination of letters. There are many examples, but Carson illustrates the fallaciousness of the method with the English word "nice," as derived from the Latin *nescius*, "ignorant." In terms of etymologizing, the "nice" person would be "ignorant" by definition![69] NPP (and other) scholars appeal to *hypakoē* not because of etymology but because of its usage in context. The Septuagint translators actually chose three variants of the Greek verb "hear" to render the Hebrew *shamaʿ*: *akouō*, *eisakouō* and *hypakouō*. All three are more or less synonymous. But still the questions arise, why are there variations, and do the variants convey at least different shades of meaning? As far as the verb *hypakouō* and the noun *hypakoē* are concerned, the prefix *hyp* ("under") cannot be dismissed as cavalierly as Baugh has done. While noting Carson's documentation of

---

67. In addition to Dunn's and Wright's numerous and various publications, Yinger's monograph and my own efforts to come to terms with "the obedience of faith," similar conclusions have been reached by G. N. Davies, *Faith and Obedience in Romans: A Study in Romans 1-4*. Journal for the Study of the New Testament Supplement Series (Sheffield: Sheffield Academic Press, 1990); J. Miller, *The Obedience of Faith, the Eschatological People of God, and the Purpose of Romans*. Society of Biblical Literature Dissertation Series 177 (Atlanta: Scholars Press, 2000); T. Berkeley, *From a Broken Covenant to Circumcision of the Heart: Pauline Intertextual Exegesis in Romans 2:17-29*. Society of Biblical Literature Dissertation Series 175 (Atlanta: Society of Biblical Literature, 2000). Outside of Paul, there is the excellent study of A. P. Stanley, *Did Jesus Teach Salvation by Works? The Role of Works in the Synoptic Gospels*. The Evangelical Theological Society Monograph Series 4 (Eugene, OR: Wipf & Stock), 2006.
68. Referring to D. A. Carson's *Exegetical Fallacies*. 2nd ed. (Grand Rapids: Baker, 1996).
69. Carson, *Exegetical Fallacies*, 27 (from my first edition of the book).

scholars who have pressed this prefix too far,[70] I would call to mind that as able a linguist as J. A. Fitzmyer—certainly no apologist for the NPP—discerns that: "Though that faith begins for Paul as a 'hearing'…it does not stop there. It involves the entire personal commitment of a man/woman to Christ Jesus as 'Lord'…. The word *hypakoē* implies the '*sub*mission' or total personal response of the believer to the risen Lord."[71] Granted, Paul and the Septuagint translators could have articulated the notions of submission and total personal response with the other forms of the Greek "hear." But, in their minds, there was apparently something about *hypakoē* that was especially suitable to their purposes.

"Hearing" in relation to obedience is significant enough that it is well to recall that in the Hebrew Scriptures the activity entails much more than audio-sensory processes. In point of fact, in Hebrew there are no distinctive words for "obey" and "obedience." Rather, the idea of obedience is consistently expressed by the vocabulary of hearing: to hear rightly is to obey.[72] As Wilckens affirms, the *Shema* of Deuteronomy 6:4—"Hear, O Israel"—has doing in view.[73] Dunn, then, can add that the respective appellations "hearers of the law" and "righteous" are complementary and overlap in large measure: hearing/believing and works are two ways of saying the same thing.[74] D. J. Moo is thus quite right that "obedience" (*hypakoē*) and "faith" are mutually interpreting: "Obedience always involves faith, and faith always involves obedience."[75]

---

70. Carson, *Exegetical Fallacies*, 27-28.
71. Fitzmyer, "The Semitic Background of the New Testament *Kyrios*-Title," *A Wandering Aramean: Collected Aramaic Essays*. Society of Biblical Literature Monograph Series 25 (Chico: Scholars Press, 1979), 132.
72. See further Garlington, *Obedience of Faith*, 11-13.
73. Wilckens, *Römer*, 1.132.
74. Dunn, *Romans*, 1.97, citing Deuteronomy 4:1, 5-6, 13-14; 30:11-14; 1 Maccabees 2:67; 13:48; *Sibylline Oracles* 3:70; Philo, *On the Preliminary Studies* 70; *On Rewards and Punishments* 79; Josephus, *Antiquities* 5.107, 132; 20.44.
75. Moo, *The Epistle to the Romans*. New International Commentary on the New Testament (Grand Rapids: Eerdmans, 1996), 52-53. Kindred statements can be found in T. N. Schreiner, *Romans*. Baker Exegetical Commentary on the New Testament (Grand Rapids: Baker, 1998), 35; C. E. B. Cranfield, *A Critical and Exegetical Commentary on the Epistle to*

As straightforward (and Pauline) as this is, there remains, as Wright observes, generations of theologians got anxious that any stress on obedience might create the impression that "good moral works" take priority over "pure faith." Wright, however, illustrates why this misses the point:

> When Paul thinks of Jesus as Lord, he thinks of himself as a slave and of the world as being called to obedience to Jesus' lordship. His apostolic commission is not to offer people a new religious option, but to summon them to allegiance to Jesus, which will mean abandoning their other loyalties. The gospel issues a command, an imperial summons; the appropriate response is obedience.[76]

"Covenant Mediation in Romans"

Baugh subsumes discussions of "Having Been Justified," "Justification and Mediation" and "The Development of Paul's Thought" under "Covenant Mediation in Romans." As for "Having been Justified," many of Professor Baugh's observations are well taken and are welcomed contributions to the study of Romans 5. I would simply affirm Dunn's contention that Romans 5:1 marks the beginning of the salvation process: justification is not a once-for-all act; it is the initial acceptance by God into restored fellowship (as indicated by the aorist tense "having been justified" (*dikaiōthentes*) of Romans 5:1).[77] But because "process" can be and has often been construed in a synergistic or Pelagian sense, I would just call to mind that the "process" corresponds to the basic archi-

---

the Romans. International Critical Commentary. 2 vols. (Edinburgh: T & T Clark, 1979), 1.66-67; J. Murray, *The Epistle to the Romans*. New International Commentary on the New Testament. 2 vols. (Grand Rapids: Eerdmans, 1959, 1965), 1.13-14; E. Lohse, *Der Brief an die Römer*. Kritisch-exegetischer Kommentar über das Neue Testament. 15th ed. (Göttingen: Vandenhoeck & Ruprecht, 2003), 68.

76. Wright, "Romans," *The New Interpreter's Bible*. 12 vols. (Nashville: Abingdon, 2002), 10.420.

77. Dunn, *Theology of Paul*, 386. It should be added that on the same page Dunn clearly acknowledges the reality of continuing sin in the life of the believer, even quoting Luther's famous *simul justus et peccator*. Writes Dunn: "Throughout this life the human partner will ever be dependent on God justifying the ungodly."

tecture of New Testament eschatology: the familiar "Already" and "Not Yet," or perhaps better, the "inauguration" and "consummation" of salvation. Since the present concern is with Romans 5, I would invoke the same verses as Dunn, Romans 5:9-10:

> If we have been justified by Christ's blood, then
> (how much more) shall we be saved from (eschatological) wrath.

> If we have been reconciled by Christ's death, then
> (how much more) shall we be saved by his (resurrection) life.

I have treated the passage elsewhere.[78] Suffice it to say here that Christ's resurrection gives the believer hope, a hope that looks forward to the future eschatological consummation of the new creation. Or, as Neil Elliott puts it, vv. 9-10 "relocate the soteriological fulcrum in the apocalyptic future: the gracious justification and reconciliation of the impious is made the basis for sure hope in the salvation to come."[79] Paul polarizes past and future in our salvation experience. Because of what Christ has already done, we have the assurance that although the consummation of redemption has not been completed, the believer can take comfort that God's purposes cannot fail. In this light, the aorist "having been justified" of Romans 5:1 is to be given its due within the spectrum of the "three tenses" of salvation history: "I have been saved, I am being saved, and I will be saved." It is the future tense of salvation that features prominently in Galatians 5:5 as well: "For through the Spirit, by faith, we await the hope of righteousness." When Paul uses the verb "await" (*apekdechomai*), he always describes future eschatological expectation (Romans 8:19, 23, 25; 1 Corinthians 1:7; Philippians 3:20). He anticipates a time when the believer's righteousness will be brought to its crowning conclusion at the end of

---

78. Garlington, *Faith, Obedience, and Perseverance*, 74-79.
79. Elliott, *The Rhetoric of Romans: Argumentative Constraint and Strategy and Paul's Dialogue with Judaism*. Journal for the Study of the New Testament Supplement Series 45 (Sheffield: Sheffield Academic Press, 1990), 229.

this age, when the character transformation that has already begun is completed.[80] We should not forget that the very first instance of the verb "justify" (*diakaioō*) in Romans is 2:13 occurs in the future tense: it is the doers of the law who will be justified (*dikaiōthēsontai*) in eschatological judgment. As I have argued elsewhere, the "doers of the law" are not "legalists," but those who have maintained faith with Christ.[81] Consequently, for Paul *sola fide* includes the obedience of faith.[82]

Baugh's work under the subheading of "Justification and Mediation" is again commendable. Those of us who espouse one variety or other of the NPP have no hesitation in concurring with Baugh: "We have no claim on God derived from anything in ourselves as worthy of redemption."[83] We heartily affirm that our redemption hinges from beginning to end on the mediatorial work of Christ. Likewise, I agree that the Already is the guarantee of the Not Yet. In Baugh's own words, the last-day verdict has already been rendered at the resurrection of Jesus for our justification (Romans 4:25).

Yet the other side of the coin is that Romans 5:9-10 sets up a movement (process) from present to future salvation. It is normally observed that Paul's assertion is akin to the rabbinic *qal wahomer* ("light and heavy") pattern: "from the lesser to the greater." On the surface, it might appear strange that Paul could place the past work of Christ in the "lesser" category. But without minimizing the significance of his death, Christ's sacrifice must accomplish the final salvation of his people. The process of salvation begins with present justification, but it will not be consummated until we are finally "saved" in the fullness of his glory. Judith Gundry Volf appropriately comments: "The process of consummating the work of salvation is more like an obstacle course than a downhill ride to the finish-line. For the destiny of Christians does not go

---

80. See my *An Exposition Of Galatians: A Reading From the New Perspective*. 3rd ed. (Eugene, OR: Wipf & Stock, 2007), 301-3.
81. Garlington, *Faith, Obedience, and Perseverance*, 56-71.
82. See further my "New Perspective Reading," 59-63.
83. See Wright's emphatic affirmation of this in *Saint Paul*, 116.

unchallenged in a world opposed to God's purposes. The powers of evil in the form of afflictions and trials threaten continuity in their salvation."[84] (Thus, Cranfield's remark that deliverance from eschatological wrath in relation to [past] justification is "very easy" fails to appreciate the formidable nature of the "obstacle course."[85]) Given the "tribulations" (Romans 5:3) that attend the life of faith this side of the resurrection, the great thing, from the perspective of the present passage, is yet to be accomplished. None of this calls into question the efficacy of the work of Jesus the mediator, but it is to affirm that his work is not complete until the day on which the good work he began in us will be completed and perfected (Philippians 1:6).[86] We should recall as well that Reformed theology has always been sensitive to the interplay of the *perseverance* of the saints and the *preservation* of the saints. It is not either/or, but both/and.

However, Baugh mistakenly subsumes "covenantal nomism" under the label of "synergism." It must be reiterated that the believer synergistically contributing to his salvation is not a characteristic of the NPP reading of Paul; covenant fidelity is characteristic. If anything, covenantal nomism is an expression of perseverance, not "synergism" or "contributing to salvation."

The final subsection, "The Development of Paul's Thought," contains relevant and useful exegetical observations on Romans 5:12-21. The main point is to reiterate that our justification in no way hinges on our personal performance of the law because our justification depends on Christ's obedience on the cross being imputed to us. Since I have already addressed this issue above, there is little to say but that Baugh refuses to recognize that justification, like most things in soteriology, occurs in stages, corresponding to

---

84. Gundry Volf, *Paul and Perseverance: Staying In and Falling Away* (Louisville: Westminster/John Knox Press, 1990), 81. G. C. Berkouwer also identifies "continuity in salvation" as the central problem of perseverance (*Faith and Perseverance*. Studies in Dogmatics [Grand Rapids: Eerdmans, 1958], 12).
85. Cranfield, *Romans*, 1.266.
86. We should recall that Hebrews focuses so much of its attention on the mediatorial aspect of Christ's priesthood as indispensable "in bringing many sons to glory" (5:10). The entire letter can be looked upon as an elaborate commentary on Romans 5:9-10.

unfolding of salvation history. No one I know in the NPP camp maintains that our present justification is contingent on any kind of "autosoteriosm" (i.e., saving ourselves). Dunn, for one, has expressed himself clearly enough (as quoted above).[87] And as to the justification of the last day, it has also been stated in the plainest terms possible that our ultimate vindication has nothing to do with "performance," "merit," "works-righteousness," "synergism" or any other pejorative terms that might be enlisted. To say it one last time, it is the "obedience of faith" or *the perseverance of the saints* that counts in the judgment. As for imputation, I have addressed the issue elsewhere.[88] It is true that a number of us who espouse the NPP see no particular exegetical evidence for the doctrine of imputation as espoused, say, in the Westminster Confession. But even so, a stance one way or the other toward imputation is not of the essence of the NPP. And even some who do embrace imputation are still in tune with an eschatological phrase of justification as the outgrowth of faith's obedience.[89]

Summary

Professor Baugh's essay has endeavored to expose what he perceives to be the methodological and exegetical weaknesses of the NPP. His attempt to come to terms with some of the Pauline texts that have been revisited many times since the "Sanders/Dunn trajectory" made its way onto the stage of New Testament Studies over a quarter of a century ago is commendable. A number of his exegetical observations on Roman 5 and his reaffirmation of the efficacy of the work of Christ are entirely apropos and

---

87. Wright is also clear: "There is simply no way that human beings can make themselves fit for the presence or salvation of God. What is more, I know of no serious theologian, Protestant, Catholic or Orthodox, who thinks otherwise" (*Saint Paul*, 116).
88. Garlington, *Defence of the New Perspective*, 107-97. See also the telling criticisms of R. H. Gundry, "The Nonimputation of Christ's Righteousness," *Justification: What's at Stake in the Current Debates?* eds. M. Husbands and D. J. Treier (Downers Grove Leicester: InterVarsity/Apollos, 2004), 17-45. I differ with Gundry in my conviction that it is *Christ's* righteousness that becomes ours by virtue of union with him.
89. For example, at least several of the (Reformed) contributors to the volume, *The Federal Vision*. eds. S. Wilkins and D. Garner (Monroe, LA: Athanasius Press, 2004).

are most welcomed. However, the downside of his paper largely outweighs its benefits. Throughout, there is the persistent misrepresentation that has plagued the Reformed response to the NPP since the outset of the debate. This includes painting with a very broad brush and, in several instances, imputing to proponents of the NPP positions that they do not advocate. Among other things, Baugh has not appreciated the variegated nature of the movement that generically bears the moniker of "The New Perspective on Paul." For instance, in the matter of justification he fails to take notice of the differences between Dunn and Wright (and others of us who have written on the subject). Especially egregious, moreover, is the allegation that the NPP has engaged in a recasting of Paul's entire theology. But as much as anything else, his essay is tarnished by its various *ad hominem* remarks. According to Baugh, the NPP has made the gains it has by the efforts of a small, eccentric, noisy but energetic band of rhetoricians who function as a censorship board to suppress any and all "offending" materials! I would hope that future discussions can be conducted in the spirit of "iron sharpening iron" on the part of those who, after the pattern of the Bereans, search the Scriptures daily to see if these things are so.

CHAPTER 9

Future Justification: Some Theological and Exegetical Proposals

Rich Lusk

Before offering my exegetical and theological proposals for a doctrine of "future justification," I need to offer a few preliminary principles that set the stage for this discussion.[1] First, "future justification," as will be shown, does not stand on its own. It presupposes and builds upon "initial justification," even as "initial justification" anticipates and foreshadows "final justification." In other words, everything in this essay needs to be read in conjunction with my other essay in this volume. The two essays together present something of a unified "Federal Vision" theology of justification (though, even then, there are numerous gaps that need to be filled in).

Second, I want to remind my reader of the word "proposals" in the title of this article. I am not attempting to offer a finished product, but another step along the way in doctrinal development. The doctrine of the final judgment/justification has remained fairly underdeveloped in Protestant thought and pastoral practice. In the Reformed tradition, we have not known exactly what to say

---

1. This chapter is not responding to any particular chapter in the *Covenant, Justification, and Pastoral Ministry* (*CJPM*) volume, but to its recurrent rejection of *any* doctrine of "future justification" (e.g., 205, 209, 294-296, 432, 442). My primary purpose is to set forth a positive case for this doctrine, but I also interact with various *CJPM* authors along the way.

about future judgment texts, and so we have not said much at all (as perusal of the standard systematic theologies shows). The result is that we have mitigated, and even muted, an important part of God's Word. This essay seeks to address that imbalance. As a result, it would be seriously premature to treat this essay as the "last word" on a massive topic. In particular, a number of "prooftexts" cited need more exegetical attention than I can give here. In terms of serious exegetical consideration, this paper limits itself to Romans 2:1-16 and James 2:14-26, and even then many, many important details have been omitted.

Third, while my focus in this essay is biblical-theological, not historical-theological, I will cite Reformational precedents at various points along the way. That historical material could be vastly expanded if time and space permitted. Also, while it is beyond my scope to interact with confessional materials, I feel the need to briefly sketch the confessional credentials of the doctrine on the front end so that my proposals can receive a fair hearing in the Reformed community. The Westminster Standards do not speak explicitly of a "future justification," but they do provide the conceptual framework within which I have developed the doctrine offered here. The Westminster Standards insist on obedience as a necessary condition of eschatological salvation in a variety of ways. Faith must bear "fruit," which has as its end "eternal life" (WCF 16.2). Forgiveness is only given to the repentant (WCF 15.3). Initial justification is inseparable from sanctification, perseverance, and good works (WCF 10-18). God requires repentance if we are to escape his wrath and curse (WSC 85). Holy obedience is not only evidence of salvation, but the *way* of salvation (WLC 32). Our good works are "accepted" by God in Christ, so that he, "looking upon them in His Son, is pleased to accept and reward" them (WCF 16.6). And so on. All of this, of course, reflects biblical teaching and reminds us that salvation, from beginning to end, in all its legal and transformative elements, is a gift of grace.

More directly related to the theme of this article, the WCF, following Scripture, teaches that all men will be judged at the last day, with the result that each will "receive according to what they have done in the body, whether good or evil." This eschatological, forensic judgment can only result in two possible outcomes: "For then shall the righteous go into everlasting life...but the wicked, who know not God, and obey not the Gospel of Jesus Christ, shall be cast into eternal torments." In view of this coming judicial examination, we should "shake off all carnal security, and be always watchful" (WCF 33.1-3). While the language of justification is missing here, the conceptual apparatus of justification is certainly present.

The same is true of WSC 38. The "benefits...believers receive from Christ at the resurrection" include being "openly acknowledged and acquitted in the day of judgment." "Judgment" language reminds us this is a forensic event, issuing forth in ether justification or condemnation. At that day, God will do more than "openly acknowledge" that believers have *already* received acquittal. He will actually acquit them *in* the day of judgment. While some might want to quibble over the precise term used here, no legitimate argument can be mounted against the notion that "acquittal" is a virtual synonym for "justification." To be acquitted is to be found "not guilty" in a court of law; the word describes a judicial deliverance in which the one on trial is freed from all charges. This acquittal/justification should be the eschatological expectation of all believers. The prooftexts do not carry authoritative weight, but they are of value in showing us how the Westminster divines read Scripture. In this case, the divines cited Matthew 25:23 ("His lord said to him, "Well done, good and faithful servant..."). As will be seen, this is a key prooftext in my doctrinal proposals as well.

Further, it should be remembered that final judgment according to works (with the expectation of acquittal for believers) is axiomatic in the ancient ecumenical creeds. The Apostles' Creed, Nicene Creed, and Athanasian Creed are all very forthright in asserting the coming reality of a final judgment by Christ.[2] The Athanasian Creed is the most comprehensive statement: "He will

---

2. The only reference to initial justification in the ecumenical creeds is baptismal. In the Nicene Creed, we confess to "acknowledge one baptism for the remission of sins."

come again to judge the living and the dead. At his coming all people shall rise bodily to give an account of their own deeds. Those who have done good will enter eternal life, those who have done evil will enter eternal fire." To deny this truth is to violate the most basic standards of Christian orthodoxy.

Third, my overarching rejection of "merit theology" should be kept in view. I utterly abhor and reject any notion that our works can have merit in God's sight, before or after conversion. Works do not "earn" anything from God. How could they? After all, the works themselves are the fruit of God's work in us. Who has given to God in such a way that he is obligated to repay (Rom. 11:35)? With merit out of the picture, we are in a much better position to assess the role of works in our salvation, including eschatological justification. As John Calvin says in his commentary on Romans 2:6 (God "will render to each one according to his deeds"),

> [A's he sanctifies those whom he has previously resolved to glorify, he will also crown their good works, but not on account of any merit: nor can this be proved from this verse; for though it declares what reward good works are to have, it does yet by no means show what they are worth, or what price is due to them. And it is an absurd inference, to deduce merit from reward.

In other words, though Calvin admits that good works *receive* eternal life, one cannot draw the conclusion that such works are the *meritorious cause* of eternal life. Final justification according to works, as articulated here, is *not* a way of sneaking works-righteousness in the back door. Rather, it is a way of acknowledging the comprehensive breadth and depth of God's gracious, redeeming work. Initial and final justifications are both in Christ. When God crowns our works at the last day with the reward of eternal life, he is not giving us a merited paycheck, but a promised inheritance, for the sake of his Son.

Fourth, I admit that my aim setting forth these exegetical and theological proposals is as pastoral as anything. It is often said that if we talk about the necessity of works – and especially if we talk about a final judgment/justification according to works – we will undercut the security of salvation and jeopardize the assurance of believers. But this is only because we have framed the doctrine in the wrong way. If we presuppose that God can never be pleased with human works, then a final judgment according to works will always appear as bad news. But if we look at the final judgment *from within* our union with Christ and initial justification, we can see how God can be pleased to declare us righteous according to our good-yet-imperfect works. All parties in the present controversy appear to agree that works will be the inevitable fruit of faith; further, all parties agree that there is some kind of final evaluation at the last day. Why not connect the doctrinal dots? Everything needed for a future justification to doers of the law (cf. Rom. 2:13) is in place.

I contend that it is actually *a great comfort* for believers to know that their works will be accepted in Christ at the last day. We are judged by Christ, who has already stood trial for us and taken condemnation for us on the cross. His blood covers our sins and washes the impurities out of our good-but-imperfect acts of obedience. Jesus judges us as the agent of our Heavenly Father, who looks upon our works in and through the work of his Son. He judges us with tenderness and compassion. He is hard to satisfy, to be sure, but easy to please. N. T. Wright gives a helpful pastoral application of this truth, commenting on 2 Corinthians 5:9:

> Many young people in the modern Western world find it, or at least believe it to be, very difficult to please their parents. Whatever we do just doesn't quite reach the high standard expected. Many continue through their whole adult life, even after their parents have died, still trying somehow to please them or at least appease them. Such people find the idea of pleasing God almost laughable. It seems quite impossible that God, being all-knowing and all-wise, could actually be pleased with them. You'd have to be an absolutely superb person on all fronts (they think) to please God. The chances are that God would look down on their best efforts and say, "Well, it's only nine out of ten, I'm afraid; that's not good enough."

Clearly Paul does not look at the matter like that at all. For Paul, God is pleased when he sees his image being reproduced in his human creatures by the Spirit. The slightest steps they take toward him, the slightest movements of faith and hope, and particularly of love, give God enormous delight. However difficult we may find this to believe, not least because of our own upbringing, it is a truth that Paul repeats quite often. Who we are in Christ, what we do in the Spirit, is pleasing to God; God delights in us, and, like a parent, he is thrilled when we, his children, take even the first small baby-steps towards the full Christian adulthood he has in store for us...

For Paul, if we are genuinely living in and by the Spirit of Jesus, then day by day, often without our even realizing it, we will have done many things that will give God pleasure — the smallest act of forgiveness, a great act of justice or mercy, a wonderful act of creativity enriching God's world. As a result of all these many things God will say, "Well done, good and faithful servant." When he says that, of course, we will rightly say, "Our competence, our sufficiency, comes from God." We never escape the wonderful circle of grace, gratitude and glory...

Although in these days of feeble relativism it is important to stress that God is indeed the judge who cares passionately about good and evil, and that he is a just God who will not allow sin for ever to flourish unchecked, we must remember that the warning of final judgment should not make Christians gloomy or anxious. We are not supposed to drag ourselves through our lives thinking, "Have I made it? Will I be all right?" We have assurance in the gospel that because Jesus died for us and rose again, we are completely forgiven and accepted in him. This assurance is matched by the delight we can and should take in the work of the Spirit. Through the Spirit we are enabled to do many things by God's grace so that, when we appear before the judgment seat of Christ, we will find we have pleased him in countless ways that for now we can only guess at.[3]

---

3. N. T. Wright, *Reflecting the Glory* (Minneapolis: Augsburg, 1998), 45-46.

So the ordinary believer should have nothing to fear regarding the final judgment according to works. Unless he is living as an orphan, he should hope to hear the Father's approval – not because his works are perfect, not because they earn the Father's approbation, not because his works have merit in and of themselves, but because his works are being evaluated according to a covenantal, familial relationship. If believers are not trained to eagerly anticipate the final judgment in this way, we who are pastors are robbing them of a comfort and security that rightly belongs to them.

The fifth and final preliminary principle is a hermeneutical one. Many of the problems regarding the final judgment according to works crop up because of a law/gospel pattern of reading to Scriptures. I cannot go into a full scale analysis here. But I will point out one key point germane to our discussion. In this law/gospel schema (which is obviously prominent in the *CJPM* book; cf. ch. 12), the law requires perfect obedience and condemns even the smallest infraction. The gospel requires no works, but only a bare faith. It is self-evident, then, that there is no place left for God's acceptance of our good-but-imperfect works performed as believers. They do not meet the criteria of the "law" and they are irrelevant as far as the "gospel" is concerned. The law/gospel hermeneutic requires that works either be perfect, in which case they merit blessing, or else they are worthless.[4]

A covenantal, eschatological hermeneutic is able to do better justice to Scripture at this point. In this hermeneutic, the "law" in Scripture is *usually* the Mosaic Torah, understood as an adminis-

---

4. This is precisely why Michael Horton is not able to grasp my argument (following John Calvin) for the *non-meritorious worth* of works done by believers. See *CJPM*, ch. 7 and compare to my essay "Blurring the Federal Vision," available at http://www.trinity-pres.net/pastor.php.

Scott Clark's utter confusion on this issue is evident on page 244. He writes, "The essence of *the law* (Rom. 2:6) is that God will 'give to each man according to his works'" (emphasis added). But when Paul concludes his discussion of how God will render to each one according to his works, he declares this to be an aspect of "*my gospel*" (Rom. 2:16). For Paul, contra Clark, the coming judgment is good news for believers. How this is so will become evident when we exegete the passage itself (including the background text of Psalm 62:12, which Paul is quoting in Romans 2:6).

tration of the covenant of grace.[5] And the "gospel," while certainly including a free promise of forgiveness and acceptance (initial justification), also promises Spirit-empowered transformation (leading to final justification). The pastoral "cash value" of this way of reading the Bible is seen in the Wright quotation above, and should emerge more fully as we move though the discussion.

Initial and Final Justification

I have already sketched out several main features of the biblical doctrine of justification in my preceding essay in this volume. Now it's time to project our picture of justification into the future. It is not unreformed to view the NT's already/not-yet dynamic as cutting across the entirety of salvation, including justification. In other words, while we are already justified (cf. Rom. 3:24, 26; 5:1, 9; 8:30; 1 Cor. 1:30; 6:11; Tit. 3:7; etc.), there is a dimension of justification that remains to be received by the people of God, when we will be found worthy and blameless in his sight (Mt. 12:37;

---

5. WCF 19.1 says the law, regarded as "a covenant of works" binds Adamic humanity to "personal, entire, exact, and perpetual obedience." But the moral content of this law never appears to us in the bare form of a covenant of works. Rather, it comes clothed in the administration of the covenant of grace, as in the Mosaic law (WCF 7.5). To be regarded as a covenant keeper, under the covenants of Abraham, Moses, and Christ, does not require perfect obedience, but rather the obedience of faith (Rom. 1:5), that is an evangelical obedience that presupposes forgiveness and the grace of the Spirit. Of course, this is not to flatten out the real redemptive-historical movement and maturation that takes places as one follows along the trajectory of the biblical narrative (cf. WCF 7.6).

To state this truth another way, the "law" is more than merely a set of absolute moral requirements (cf. Ex. 20:1-2). The "law" as given in the Mosaic covenant (that is, the Torah) not only reveals God's holiness (and thus, serves as a perfect standard of righteousness), it also reveals his grace (and thus, includes typological provision for forgiveness, pointing ahead to the cross of Christ). Of course, both aspects of the law's revelatory function are celebrated in Psalm 119 – but note that the psalmist is very much at odds with the law/gospel antithesis as a biblical hermeneutic.

Or to put the truth yet another way, believers will not be judged at the last day according to the law understood as a perfect rule of righteousness that condemns even the smallest infraction. They will be judged in Christ by the Father's gracious application of his moral standards. Thus, what is good in the works of believers will be accepted with praise, while their faults and shortcomings are forgiven. Just as parents can require "perfection" of their children but be pleased with less, so it will be with the Father on the last day. This does not excuse sin or sloth in present; indeed, just the opposite. Knowing that our Father *can* be pleased with us gives us great incentive to seek his pleasure.

Rom. 2:1-16; 2:26-29; 5:9-10; 8:33-34; 14:10-18; 1 Cor. 1:8; 4:2-4; 2 Cor. 5:9-10; Gal. 2:17; 5:4-5; Phil. 3:9; Col. 1:22; 1 Thess. 3:13; 2 Thess. 1:5; 2 Tim. 4:8, 16; Rev. 20:12-13; 22:12, 14; etc.).[6] There is a final judgment still to come, and judicial pronouncements of approbation and condemnation will be made by the divine Judge on that day. This final day of reckoning is axiomatic in the OT and NT. Inevitably, then, the biblical-theological architecture of justification includes a future verdict, a final imputation (or reckoning; cf. Rom. 2:26; Phil. 4:17; 2 Tim. 4:16) still to come, for God's people. This declaration will be pronounced over the entirety of our lives.[7]

Paul never says that a bare faith will be sufficient at the last day. Instead, he insists that only a faith that works through love will avail for the final, hoped for justification (Gal. 5:5-6). He never says faith substitutes for deeds at the last day. Instead, he says, deeds are

---

6. Soteriologically speaking, everything comes in two stages. For a thorough discussion of this already/not yet dynamic, as well as exegesis of several alleged "future justification" texts, see Paul Rainbow, *The Way of Salvation* (Waynesboro, GA: Paternoster, 2005), ch. 12-17, especially the summaries on pages 172, 186f, 203, and 212. Rainbow decisively demonstrates that the issue at stake in the final judgment is not one's degree of reward or punishment (though that is included), but ultimate realities (salvation and condemnation). Note that some texts (e.g., Rom. 5, 8) weave the "already" and "not yet" aspects of justification together, without any hint of tension. If we sense an incompatibility, it is because we are not sufficiently attuned to biblical theology.

7. Some have suggested that we should speak of a "final *vindication*" instead of a "final *justification*" in order to avoid confusion (e.g., Michael Horton in *CJPM*, 222). Perhaps that is so, but I am not yet convinced. The problems with this proposal are twofold. First, vindication and justification are heavily overlapping categories. To be *justified* in a court of law is to be *vindicated* against your accusers. The Bible uses the same family of terms to cover both justification and vindication; they are not sharply distinguishable (as many English Bible translations attest), and they apply in a wide range of contexts, some of which are not as purely "legal" as others (e.g., judgments made in the context of the family rather than a civil court). Second, there are clearly places where justification language and imagery are used to describe the favorable verdict God will pass over his faithful people at the last day (e.g., Rom. 2:13, 8:33; 1 Cor. 4:4-5; Gal. 5:4-5; cf. also the future law court scene of Mt. 25:31-46). Biblically, judgment is inseparable from justification; whenever a judgment is passed, the outcome is either justification or condemnation. Thus, (I would suggest) to deny the legitimacy of a "future justification" is to reject the plain teaching of Scripture. Scripture clearly speaks of two distinct moments of justification, at the time of conversion/baptism and at the last day. Whether we think of this as a single justification unfolding in two phases, or two discrete-but-related justifications, makes little difference as far as I can tell.

necessary as the fruit and evidence of faith, so that we can be established in blamelessness and holiness at the day of reckoning (1 Thess. 3:12-13). The apostle never says that our initial justification cancels out the need for a future, final judgment. Instead, he says the goal of final salvation remains contingent on conditions which are yet to be fulfilled (Phil. 2:12-13; Col. 1:22-25). He never says that the righteousness of Christ takes the place of our obedience, such that our own personal righteousness is superfluous. Instead, he says we will only be pronounced "worthy" at the last day if we have pleased him with a working faith (2 Thess. 1:3-12, especially verse 11). He never says that works play no role in the culmination of our salvation or our final acquittal. Instead, he explicitly insists that works are the criterion of the final judgment (2 Cor. 5:9-10).

All that to say: In the final installment of our justification, there is a very real sense in which works will be the *decisive* factor. If we take time to bother with the actual words of Scripture, this conclusion is unavoidable. It is so plain, one wonders how it could be missed or suppressed. God requires obedience just as surely as he requires faith. Obedience is not optional, but essential.

At the same time, it is crucial for us to relate initial and final justification to one another in the proper way. We will develop the biblical picture as we go, but note at this point that initial justification by faith alone must, in some sense, serve as *the foundation* for final justification by works. At the very least, we can say initial justification puts us in a state of justification with God, which makes a final justification according to works possible. Exactly what that means will be clarified as we explore Romans 2 and James 2.

Justification and Doing the Law: Romans 2:1-16

Romans 2:1-16 is obviously a key passage in this discussion. Paul says "the doers of the law will be justified" (2:13). Some have argued that Paul must be thinking hypothetically since he elsewhere argues that no one can do good (Rom. 3:10-20) and works of Torah cannot justify (Rom. 3:28). On that reading, this section is simply preparation for the gospel message to come later in the epistle. While that is certainly an aspect of the text, Paul is actually prophesying of a future, actual event, which will culminate and complete God's saving work. While Paul shows that covenant breaking leads to wrath, he also reveals a way of escape – a way that will be unpacked more fully in the rest of the letter. That way of escape is fidelity to the terms of the new covenant – in Christ and by the Spirit. Note the following points.

First, Paul's indictment against human sin in 1:18-2:11 includes both Jews and Gentiles. He most likely has in view a Jewish unbeliever (non-Christian) in 2:1ff. The "man" who is "inexcusable" is Jewish; Paul is reminding him that just because God will condemn Gentiles (Rom. 1:18ff) does not mean the Jew will be acquitted by the mere fact of his Jewishness. If he breaks the law, he will be judged as a lawbreaker. Whereas 1:18-32 deals with Jew and Gentile together, in 2:1, Paul singles out the Jew who would object to being lumped in with the Gentile under "the wrath of God revealed from heaven" (1:18). Jews are objects of wrath as well, if they are covenant breakers (2:9). They stand in judgment on Gentiles, but are in danger of being judged themselves (2:1, 3).

Second, Paul is speaking in the future tense in 2:13. In other words, this is a reference to final justification, not initial justification. Everywhere else the NT addresses the future judgment, it is shown to be a judgment of works (e.g., Matt. 25:31-46; 2 Cor. 5:10). Even within Romans, this is an important theme (14:10-13). Thus, reading Romans 2:13 as a description of forthcoming reality is not necessarily at odds with those passages that deny *present* justification by works. Present justification by faith alone is not in tension with a future justification to doers of the law (for reasons that will be clearer as we go). If the acquittal to (Gentile) lawkeepers in 2:13 is actually counter-factual, Paul's entire polemic against arrogant and hypocritical Jewish moralism unravels. The sting of the passage is in its actuality: righteousness Gentiles will rise up and condemn self-assured, presumptuous Jews at the last day. The covenant people must show covenant obedience if they are to inherit the covenant blessings.[8]

---

8. There is a lot of evidence that Paul is targeting Jewish covenant breaking in the text,

Third, keeping/doing the law (in the sense of covenant faithfulness, not sinless perfection) and practicing righteousness (as an ordinary pattern of life) are realities, not merely hypotheticals, as numerous texts attest (e.g., Gen. 6:9; Job 1:1; Luke 1:6; 1 John 3:7; cf. Deut. 30:11-20). Romans 2:1-16 does not require perfection, but rather the seeking of "glory, honor, and immortality," all of which can only be done by faith (2:7; cf. 14:23). The law in view throughout the discussion is the Torah, and the Torah clearly did not require sinless perfection from believers since it was given to sinners and included sacrifices.[9] Thus, why not plug law-keepers, as described elsewhere in Scripture, into this verse, instead of leaving it an empty set of sinlessly perfect people? Scripture interprets Scripture, after all – and the rest of Scripture most certainly attests that "doers of the law" is not a null set (e.g., Luke 1:6). Why not

---

though much of it occurs at the level of intertextuality and allusion. For example, in 2:5, Paul mentions "your hardness and your impenitent heart," leading to "wrath," echoing the Deuteronomic description of Israel (Deut. 9:6; 29:19 LXX). The blind self-righteousness of Paul's Jewish interlocutor might be rooted in Deuteronomy 9:4-8. The thrust of the argument is straightforward: in the day of wrath, the covenant will provide no protection to those who have broken it by impenitent unbelief.

Given the "Jew first" language in 2:9, it is possible Paul has in view a 70 A. D. judgment, bringing the end of the old covenant era. I am not yet convinced of a preterist reading of the passage, but even if I were, the theological dimensions of the text would still have application to the final judgment. Most likely, Paul is contemplating the *final* judgment from his pre-70 A. D. vantage point. See Peter Leithart's post "Day of Wrath (Romans 2)" for some thoughts on this interpretive issue: http://www.leithart.com/archives/000246.php.

9. In one way or another, the hypothetical reading requires treating the "law" in Romans 2 as a republication of the Adamic covenant of works. See, e.g., Michael Horton in *CJPM*, 200. But in context, "law" clearly refers to the Mosaic Torah, given uniquely to Israel (cf. Deut. 4:5-8), *after* God redeemed the nation from slavery in Egypt. Jews have this law, while Gentiles do not (Rom. 2:12). Following WCF 7, my reading of Romans 2 treats the law/Torah not as a "works principle" but as an administration of the covenant of grace. As an administration of the covenant of grace, the Torah did not require perfect obedience in order to be regarded as a "covenant keeper" or "doer of the law." The view that "doers of the law" must be sinless can be refuted with one question: Did doing the law (Torah) in the old covenant era include doing the sin offerings?

This view of the law in Romans 2 is strengthened if we keep in mind the Deuteronomic underpinnings of the passage as a whole, culminating with the Deuteronomic promise of a circumcised heart (Rom. 2:29 and Deut. 30:6). The law in Deuteronomy required obedience because God is an impartial judge (Deut. 10:17), but it did not require sinless perfection as a condition of covenant keeping (Deut. 30:11-20).

match the "doing good" of 2:7 with the "Well done!" of Matthew 25:21, 23 and the "good works" of Ephesians 2:8-10? Romans 2:10 says those who "work what is good" will receive "glory, honor, and peace." Why not link that with John 5:29, where Jesus says those who have "done good" will enter the "resurrection of life"? Or with Galatians 6:7-10, where Paul urges believers to "not grow weary while doing good" so that they may "reap everlasting life"? In other words, there is more than enough non-hypothetical material in the rest of the NT that speaks in the same terms as Romans 2.

Fourth, Paul's precise language in 2:6-7 is crucial to a proper understanding of 2:13 since they obviously have in view the same group of people. Paul says "eternal life" will be the reward of those who "by patient continuance in doing good seek for glory, honor, and immortality." "Patience" emerges as a virtual synonym for faith in the rest of the letter (5:3-4; 8:25; 12:12; 15:4-5), and indeed, in the rest of the NT (e.g., James 5:7). Though the exact term is not used, "patient continuance" would also be an apt way to describe Abraham's faith in 4:16-21. The pair "glory" and "honor" (2:7, 10) trace back to Psalm 8:5. To strive for glory and honor is to strive for the eschatological destiny God originally intended for humanity, and now offers in Christ, the true "Son of Man" (cf. Ps. 8:4). In short, Romans 2:13 is clearly *not* a description of people who are attempting to earn salvation in their own power. If Paul had wanted to describe proto-Pelagianism in this context, he could have done so in a much more straight-forward fashion, without dropping so many hints that the "doing" in question is a "doing" that arises from faith. As the text stands, every indication is that the faithful (who will be justified) are being contrasted with the unfaithful (who will perish). Beneath the "doing good" and the "doing of the law" (2:7, 13) lies a posture of faith. How could it be otherwise?

Fifth, the justification described in Romans 2 is set over against perishing (2:13). Thus, final justification at the last day includes a rescue from death and wrath (cf. 5:9). It must be an all inclusive deliverance. Final justification, then, takes the form of bodily resurrection and entrance into glory. When God justifies the doers of the law in that day, his deliverance vindicates them against the claims of death and ushers them into the new creation. In this sense, final justification should be regarded as the completion of what God began in our initial justification. To be found righteous at the last day is to be picked out for salvation and spared from judicial wrath. We were delivered from wrath and death definitively in our first justification, but the delivering verdict does not take fully embodied shape until the last day when we are raised from the grave. At that point, the creation is finally and fully put to rights. In other words, the judgment event in 2:1-16 includes an element of restorative righteousness for God's people; it is not merely punitive.

Sixth, there is no conditional or counterfactual clause in this section. There is no hint that Paul is claiming "*if* anyone could do the law....that person would be justified." Paul's point in Romans 2:1-16 is *not* that God will universally condemn the human race;[10] his point is that God's judgment will treat Jews and Gentiles with equity (2:6, 10-16).[11] Divine impartiality was not a point that all Jews were willing to grant in Paul's day (cf. 2:1-2); at least some Jews grounded their hope in some combination of non-moral factors such as election, covenant, and ethnicity; others boasted of moral performance. It is precisely these grounds for confidence that Paul makes his target in the chapter as a whole: in 2:1-11, he subverts the Jews' delusions of moral superiority by exposing their hypocrisy; in 2:12-16, he shows their possession of the Torah by nature does not bring immunity to judgment; in 2:17-24, their national privileges are shown to be worthless apart from obedience; and in 2:25-29, the covenant badge of circumcision is turned against them because of their covenant breaking. Paul's point is that none of these, considered in themselves, can secure eschato-

---

10. Paul's case against humanity in 1:18-3:20 obviously applies only to humanity outside of Christ. In the nature of the case, Christians are exempted from the wrath Paul describes.
11. Of course, Jews should have already known from their own Scriptures that God is an impartial judge (cf. Deut. 10:12-22), not "bribed" by religious heritage or ethnicity in themselves. This impartiality, in Deuteronomy and Romans, shows itself in an even-handed judgment according to works.

logical justification. The Torah is a Jewish privilege to be sure (cf. 3:1-8; 9:1-5), but that privilege will only serve to intensify their judgment if they persist in unbelief and disobedience.

Seventh, the condemnation is obviously real, not hypothetical. Romans 2:8, 9, 15 describe an actual state of affairs (condemnation of the wicked). Why not 2:10, 13 as well, especially since Scripture repeatedly stresses that works performed in this life play a decisive role in one's final destiny (e.g., Matt. 25:31-46; Jas. 2:14-26)? Romans 2:6 uses the same verb ("will render") to apply to *both* final condemnation and justification. It simply does not make sense to say that none will be justified in this context, given that the Psalmist himself (whose words are being quoted; cf. Ps. 62:12) expected his final "performance review" to issue forth in salvation (cf. Ps. 62:1-2). That is to say, he expected God to "render" to him justification, "according to his work." The hypothetical reading actually pits Paul against the Psalmist, instead of allowing Paul to apply the words of the Psalm according to their natural meaning.

Eighth, further confirmation that Paul is *not* speaking in hypothetical terms is found in the nature of the contrast he draws in 2:13. Paul does not pit *faith* against *doing*, as two potential ways of justification. Rather he pits mere *hearing of the law* (without doing) against *doing the law* (which implicitly includes faith). If justification by doing is supposed to be hypothetical here, this is a very odd, and even confusing, way to develop the argument. On that reading, Paul ends up describing two false ways of justification (hearing and doing) rather than the false way (hearing) compared to the true way (doing). Again, on this reading, the passage loses its ability to deconstruct Jewish presumption that arises from reliance on mere hearing (and having) the law. In truth, it is obvious that Paul's Jewish interlocutor is deluded about the heinousness of his own sin, which causes the Gentiles to blaspheme God (2:1-3, 17-25). The problem with Paul's Jewish dialogue partner in Romans 2 is *not* that he is trying to earn justification by doing; the problem is that he thinks his bare hearing/possession of the law and circumcision will save him, no matter how he lives. The real issue in 2:1-16 is not legalism but antinomianism (cf. Matt. 3:7-10). The issue is not that the Jews in view keep the law to a certain point, but just don't go far enough. The issue is that they do not keep the law *at all*. They are covenant-breaking apostates. Again, the problem Paul is addressing is not overly scrupulous obedience on the part of Jews, but Jews who live like pagan Gentiles and abuse God's grace, all the while thinking they will be justified anyway because they "hear" Torah regularly. Paul's antidote to such false assurance and carelessness is a reminder that at the last judgment, God will act as an impartial judge and will only justify those who have demonstrated the obedience of faith, *whether Jew or Gentile* (cf. 1:5). Thus, as Paul says in 2:3-4, the Jews in view need to consider God's longsuffering goodness to them (basically summing up the whole of Israel's history) and repent (and it is surely significant that *repentance* rather than *faith* comes to the fore in this context!).

Ninth, when Paul speaks of "doers of the law," he is hinting at things to come as the argument of Romans unfolds. In the rest of the letter, he will unpack and transform what it means to do the law. Ultimately, Paul resolves law-keeping into the obedience of faith. Keeping the law, transformed by the arrival of the new covenant, means fulfilling the law's true intentions and eschatological *telos*, by trusting in Christ and living in the Spirit (Rom. 2:26; 3:31; 8:1-4; 10:1-4; 13:8-10).[12] Romans 2:13 no more affirms that human nature can autonomously achieve righteousness in the law apart from God's grace, than Romans 3:28 rules out the good

---

12. In other words, if we were to interrupt Paul in Romans 2:13 and ask him what he means by "doing the law" he would jump right into his discussion at the beginning of Romans 8. To do the work of the law is to fulfill its righteous requirement by walking according to the Spirit. The fulfillment of the law obviously presupposes faith, a point Paul throws into the discussion in 3:31. Paul is obviously playing around with the meaning of "law"in 2:25-26, where the uncircumcised actually keep the law (2:25-26)! Obviously this cannot be law-keeping in a straightforward "doing what Moses said" fashion. There is an implicit Christianization of the law at work. Note also Paul's ironic phrases, such "the law of faith" (3:27) and "the law of the Spirit of life" (8:2). Moreover, there are texts in Romans 2 that echo later descriptions of Christians in the letter (2:26 and 8:3; 2:29 and 7:6). In an important sense, the interpretation of 2:13 comes down to one question: *Are Christians doers of the law?* Paul would bring in various qualifications, but would certainly answer in the affirmative (cf. Rom. 8:4-9; 1 Cor. 7:19). For Paul, the categories of "believers" and "doers of the law" are identical because true faith is a "doing faith."

works that must follow from our initial acceptance. Each passage must be read in its own context and according to its own purpose.

Tenth, to further the point just made: The language of Romans 2:15 ("who show the work of the law written on the heart") is linked to Jeremiah 31:33 ("I will put my law in their minds and write it on their hearts").[13] Paul is speaking of Christians – specifically new covenant Gentile Christians[14] – who fulfill the true meaning of Torah through trusting in Christ and walking in the Spirit. This interpretation is further confirmed by Paul's redefinition of Jewishness in 2:25-29. These "doers of the law" are new covenant believers;[15] they will hear God's praise at the last day (Rom. 2:29). They are not circumcised bodily, but they have experienced a circumcision of the heart (cf. Deut. 30:6 and Phil. 3:3). In other words, they have become the true Israel. The ironic fact that Gentiles are fulfilling the law (cf. Rom. 2:27) and entering the kingdom ahead of Jews is, of course, a major NT theme (cf. Rom. 11; cf. Matt. 12:38-42; Luke 13:22-30). Gentiles do not have

---

13. Likewise, 2:24-29 alludes to another new covenant prophecy, Ezekiel 36. It is instructive to remember that Ezekiel condemns Jews for sinning in the eyes of the Gentiles (36:22; cf. Rom. 2:24), but he also promises a time when Israel will be reconstituted and renewed, with members drawn from every nation (36:24). Moreover, Ezekiel 36:24 promises that this reconstructed Israel will have the Spirit (cf. Rom. 2:29) and will keep the law (cf. Rom. 2:13). Those who are justified in Romans 2 are the fulfillment of Ezekiel's prophecy, the promised new Israel.

14. That Paul would include Gentiles in the fulfillment of the new covenant promise is not problematic. Jeremiah's promise was delivered to the nation when she was in exile, surrounded by pagan neighbors. It is precisely these "neighbors" who come to know the Lord on a massive scale in Jeremiah 31:34. While Jews might not have detected it, the prophetic promise of a new covenant implicitly included a marginalizing of the Jew/Gentile distinction, which Paul now builds into his argument. These Gentile believers participate in the blessings promised to Israel, and thus have the Torah (in a transformed, new covenant way) inscribed on their hearts.

15. Some have suggested they could be God-fearing Gentiles living in the old covenant era (e.g., Ps. 115:13), especially given that in some sense Jeremiah's (and Ezekiel's) "new covenant" went into effect in a preliminary way after the return from exile. The same issue comes up in Romans 4:9-12, where the Gentile believers could be old covenant God-fearers as well. But in both cases, I think it is more likely that new covenant Gentile Christians are in view. There are two decisive factors: first, the reference to the Spirit in 2:29 seems to point to the new covenant in its fully inaugurated sense; and second the fact that the whole Jew/Gentile divide seems to be dissolving in 2:25-29 into one category of "true Jews" (whether Jew or Gentile by nature) who have heart circumcision.

the Torah "by nature" (that is, by birth and culture; Rom. 2:14, 27);[16] as outsiders to the historic covenants, they are wild branches that must be grafted into the covenant tree. Meanwhile, the natural branches (Jews) are being broken out of the covenant through unbelief and disobedience (Rom. 11:17-25). This is the dynamic Paul is describing in Romans 2 as well, albeit in somewhat different terms than Romans 11. Jews should be teaching Gentiles, but instead are being bested by them (Rom. 2:17-29). Paul's overall argument is (at least in some measure) aiming to arouse Jewish jealousy and fidelity by demonstrating that God's intentions for Israel are being realized among Gentiles who have embraced Jesus Christ and entered the promised new covenant. Unbelieving Israel, meanwhile, remains in exile and under wrath, until and unless she embraces Jesus' new way of being Israel. The sharp contrast between Gentile Christians who keep the law (in an eschatologized sense) and Jews who break the law (and thus will perish) is the thrust of the text. There is nothing hypothetical about that.[17]

---

16. For a defense of this reading of "by nature" in 2:14, see N. T Wright "The Law in Romans 2" in *Paul and the Mosaic Law*, edited by James D. G. Dunn (Grand Rapids, MI: Eerdmans, 2001), 131-150.

17. This larger section of Romans, 1:18-3:20, of course, is aimed at demonstrating that both Jew and Gentile (apart from Christ) are under sin. But that does not suggest that justification by doing the law is a hypothetical perfect standard that Paul invokes only in order to show that no one measures up. Paul has already demonstrated God's response to human sin in 1:18-32. In 2:1-29, he is especially showing Jews are under the power of sin, and thus share in the predicament of the nations, even though they seem to think they are exempt. They thought of themselves as the solution to the curse, but in reality have become part of the problem. They are sick physicians. One way Paul shows them their true condition is by exposing their hypocrisy – they rely on a law they refuse to keep. The sharp edge of his argument contrasts unbelieving Jews to a group of Gentiles who have become their moral (and covenantal) superiors. Their boast of Torah has actually backfired; instead of freeing them from sin, Torah binds them to the rest of Adamic humanity and focuses the curse on them (Rom. 5:20).

Neither does 3:19-20 force a hypothetical reading back onto 2:13. The "law" in view in the two passages is different as the immediate contexts prove. In 2:12-13, the law is the Jewish Torah, the Mosaic covenant which Gentiles by nature do not posses. The law in play in 3:19-20 is actually the whole of Scripture. Note that the immediately preceding catena of quotations in 3:9-18 does not cite Moses at all, but relies on Psalms, Wisdom literature, and the prophets. "Under the law" in 3:19-20 does not have to do with the distinctively Jewish Mosaic covenant (the meaning of "law" in 2:12-13, as well as 5:13, 20); rather, it refers to the word and authority of God in the broadest sense, thus

Eleventh, the clinching argument is Paul's OT intertextual echo. Psalm 62 (and probably also Proverbs 24:12) stands in the background of the entire passage. In Romans 2:6, the apostle is alluding to Psalm 62:12, which provides the background for a *gracious* judgment of the believer's works. The psalmist says "Also to You, O Lord, belongs mercy [or steadfast love]; For You render to each one according to his work." Those who take the hypothetical view of 2:13 are sawing off the very branch the apostle is sitting on in 2:6. The hypothetical reading severs Paul from his roots in the Hebrew Scriptures. Those Scriptures foretold of a gracious final judgment in which God would vindicate his faithful, obedient people according to their works; Paul has picked up on that theme and brought it into a new covenant context. In the OT background texts (Ps. 62; Prov. 24), those who seek to walk with God (by faith; note Ps. 62:8) have every reason to expect a favorable verdict at the last day; Paul takes hold of that expectation and affirms it. Paul, like the Psalmist, can regard a judgment according to deeds as good news precisely because that judgment is shot through with God's covenant love (Romans 2:16) and God has promised to provide the needed transformation (that is, heart circumcision; Rom. 2:29 and Deut. 30:6). But because the Jews Paul is addressing do not share in the righteousness of the Psalmist, they are deluded to think they will share his glorious destiny. They have rejected God's "mercy" (or "steadfast love") in Christ and so will be judged without mercy. Contrary to their expectations, the coming day will bring them wrath and tribulation, not vindication.

---

encompassing Gentiles (cf. "Scripture" in Gal. 3:22). The point in 3:19-20 is to summarize the witness of Scripture as a whole to the sinful condition of humanity as a whole. The question, then, is how Israel's unique national privileges fit into the global problem of humanity's sin, in which Israel is just as implicated as every other people group. Further confirmation of this interpretation is found in 2:12, where Paul speaks of those who perish "without the law." See also 5:20-21, where Paul acknowledges the problem of sin (and death) is of wider scope than the reach of the law; in other words, sin is bigger than the law and condemns even those who are not under the law (the Mosaic Torah) if they remain in union with Adam. For more on the meaning of 3:19-20, see the discussion in Richard Hays, *The Conversion of the Imagination: Paul as Interpreter of Israel's Scripture* (Grand Rapids, MI: Eerdmans, 2005), 85ff. All of this stands as a refutation of Michael's Horton's remarkably odd claim in *CJPM* that Gentiles were actually under the Torah (204).

So what do we see here? Paul, with the Judaism of his day, believed in a final judgment according to works. But we also get the sense that this common presupposition is functioning very differently now that Paul has been taught the truth in Christ. For Paul, the judgment will not result in the automatic justification of the Jews that so many of his countrymen were presuming.

For Paul, the expectation of a future judgment has been overhauled and transformed in Christ. If the Jews of Paul's day had drifted into some combination of presumptuous antinomianism and prideful legalism (cf. Rom. 2:1-6), Paul calls them back to the OT expectation of a coming judgment according to deeds, but now with a new twist: Those who will be regarded as law keepers at the last day will not be mere possessors of the law, but those who have faithfully upheld the law in Christ. If the Judaism of Paul's day was some variety of covenant nomism (with different parties in Judaism putting varying degrees of emphasis on the "covenant" part, or the "nomos" part), Paul *radically re-centers* biblical theology on Christ and the Spirit, within the framework of inaugurated, new covenant eschatology.

Thus, whatever similarities there might have been in formal structure, Paul has filled the covenantal framework with fundamentally different content than his contemporary countrymen.[18] For Paul, faith in Christ, rather than works of Torah, is the way of deliverance. But those who trust Christ are, ironically, fulfilling Torah, because the Torah bears witness to Christ (cf. Rom. 3:21, 31) and faith in Christ inevitably bears Torah-fulfilling fruits (cf. Rom. 8:1-4; 13:8-10). National Israel was supposed to be the solution to the sin of the nations; instead she has become part of the

---

18. A recurring flaw in the *CJPM* book is the conflation of the "Federal Vision" with covenant nomism (e.g., 19, 22; see also chaps. 3, 7). This is often subtle. For example, Scott Clark says that in covenant nomism, "justification is a matter of obtaining and retaining status as God's covenant people." This implies that in nomism, maintaining covenant status is something earned by works. No one associated with the "Federal Vision" has taught such a monstrosity. We would certainly affirm that there are conditions to be met in order to maintain one's place within the covenant (e.g., Paul's "if" statements in texts like Col. 1:22-25), but these conditions are always met by grace through faith. They are not a matter of "nomism" but of relying on Christ in the power of the Spirit.

problem. Her only hope is to join Gentile Christians in pledging allegiance to Jesus Christ as her Redeemer and King.

Paul's radical departure from Judaism, then, is found in his Christology, pneumatology, and soteriology. Christologically, Paul and Judaism differ in that Paul believes Jesus to be Israel's promised Messiah. Jesus has single-handedly redeemed Israel from the burden of the Torah's curse (and Adam's curse) through his cross. Pneumatologically, Paul grounds human ability in the work of the Spirit. Apart from the Spirit, humans are enslaved to sin; in the Spirit, humans are set free to please God (Rom. 8:1-17). Life in the Spirit bridges the apparent chasm between *sola fide* at the beginning of the Christian life, and judgment according to works at the end. As Michael Bird points out, Paul's pessimism about human depravity is only matched by his optimism about the ability of a Spirit-empowered people.[19] Finally, Paul eschatologizes soteriology, including justification. The verdict of the final day is already declared ahead of time in the present in Christ. God justifies believers *right now* in anticipation of the final verdict that is to come. But that does not negate the reality of the final verdict as a distinct event, any more than our being raised with Christ in the present (Eph. 2:5) negates the reality of a still-to-come resurrection (1 Cor. 15). Only a counterfeit gospel of cheap grace would deny the need for Christians to be preparing themselves to meet their Maker and Judge at the last day by striving for obedience and maturation in the present.

How Future Justification Works

We have started to get a picture of future justification, but we still need to fill in this sketch in various ways. The classic Reformed emphasis on initial justification is fully understandable. Historically, initial justification by faith through grace was the main aspect of the gospel needed in the 16th century, and its recovery was the

---

19. Bird, *The Saving Righteousness of God*, (Waynesboro, GA: Paternoster, 2007), 173. Some Reformed folk need a reminder the label "totally depraved" is a description of unbelievers, not Christians!

sparkplug that ignited a long overdue reformation of the church. Theologically, Paul admits that initial justification is a "bigger deal" than final justification. This is the logic of Romans 5:6-11, especially verse 9. If God has already done the much harder thing – giving his Son to die for sinners who are at enmity with him – *how much more* will he save us from the wrath to be poured out at the last day? If God was willing to give his Son for the sake of sinners to reconcile them to himself, surely he will rescue us at the last day now that we are his friends! The hard thing has been done; the easy thing is sure to follow. Initial justification by faith is *the really decisive thing* because it reverses our status from condemned to acquitted; the justification of the last day serves to confirm, concretize, and embody that status. While final justification is undoubtedly the ultimate *goal* of redemption, the major *obstacle* to redemption is tackled at the beginning when God reconciles us to himself. Since that obstacle has been overcome, we have no reason to fear failing to reach the goal.

If initial justification is already settled by faith alone, why is there a final justification according to works?[20] *Because there is more to salvation than bare acceptance.* That acceptance is glorious, but it is only the beginning, not the end. Ultimately salvation is about glorification (or *theopoiesis*, as the church fathers put it).[21] Salvation

---

20. Obviously, many answers could be given to this question. See, e.g., the discussion in Anthony Hoekema, *The Bible and the Future* (Grand Rapids, MI: Eerdmans, 1979), 254. The final judgment is not simply concerned with parceling out rewards, but with eternal salvation and destruction. It is not my aim to be comprehensive here, but to focus on what is most relevant to the present controversy. My point is very similar to Richard Gaffin's when he writes, "Our sanctification is strategically more ultimate than our justification" (in "Biblical Theology and the Westminster Standards," *WTJ* 65 [2003], 179). In other words, present justification is part of a larger soteriological scheme, which has actual, embodied conformity to Christ as it its ultimate *telos* (Rom. 8:29-30). Initial justification plays a foundational role in God's "master plan" of salvation, but his soteric intentions towards us are not fulfilled until we have become actually righteous before him. The final judgment stamps us with the character of Christ comprehensively (including bodily). In other words, salvation from wrath and the completion of our transformation is not finally consummated until the last day. This is why final justification is so important: without it, our redemption is not yet a finished product.

21. John Calvin was in agreement with the fathers. Commenting on 2 Peter 1:4, he wrote, "Let us then mark, that the end of the gospel is, to render us eventually conform-

is not just about getting sins forgiven; it's about growing, maturing, and reaching full godlikeness.[22] The final aim of our union with Christ is that his life might be wholly reproduced in us, that his death and resurrection would become the pattern of our lives (Rom. 6). The day of judgment is the finish line, the completion of what God started when he began a good work in us by calling us into union with Christ by faith (Phil. 1:6). Those who have run their race in persevering trust will be crowned with resurrection glory at the last day. This is the final "much more" of Romans 5:15, 17, and 20-21 that is added to our initial justification. Final justification ratifies that process of maturation into restored images of God, as he passes a favorable verdict over his faithful, obedient people. Final justification is the public, cosmic declaration at the end of all things, announcing that God is eternally pleased with his children.

To put it another way, final justification is God's approval of the Spirit's work *in* us, just as initial justification is his approval of Christ's work *for* us. If initial justification is rooted in Christ's work for us on the cross, final justification takes into account Christ's work in us by his Spirit, which is equally essential to our redemption. The divine Judge will not look at the Spirit's work in us at the last day and say, "I'm sorry; that's not good enough." The Spirit's work will not be condemned, but accepted and glorified. The Spirit's work in us has real value before the judgment of the

---

able to God, and, if we may so speak, to deify us."

22. This is why it is also inadequate to reduce the role of obedience to mere evidence that we are indeed justified. It's not as if God needs proof of our election and faith; these things are matters of his own decree and work. Rather, obedience has value as the very goal, end, and essence of God's work of salvation. Salvation aims at the rectification and restoration of human life in its entirely. But restored human life is obedient life.

One might wonder if we are conflating final justification with final salvation. After all, Reformed theology rightly sees justification as a smaller piece within the overall program of salvation. Justification is the judicial aspect of salvation, but does not exhaust the meaning of salvation, which also has experiential aspects. But at the last day, final justification and final salvation,while still distinguishable in certain respects, nearly merge together. Final justification is God's favorable verdict over us, which ultimately takes the shape of a glorified, bodily resurrection, even as it did for Jesus (1 Tim. 3:16). Of course, this bodily resurrection is the complete restoration and fulfillment of our humanity, and therefore caps off the process of salvation as a whole.

Father and the Son. In Galatians, Paul lists the fruit of the Spirit and then concludes, "Against such there is no law" (Gal. 5:22-23). *But where there is no law, there cannot be condemnation.* Hence, even the imperfect fruit the Spirit has borne in our lives will meet with divine pleasure and acceptance.

Every Christian needs to continually be reminded of his first justification *and* pointed ahead to his future justification. In other words, every Christian needs to continually hear, "Your sins are forgiven!" as well as "Well done good and faithful servant!" (Matt. 25:21, 23). That "well done," of course, is really God's evaluation of the Spirit's work in us, since the Spirit enables and empowers our obedience. At the last day, when our works are approved and accepted, *God will only be crowning his own gifts* (as Augustine put it). To deny that our works have value before God, so far from magnifying grace, actually belittles the work of the Spirit.[23]

We insist that works do not *earn* final justification. Rather, final justification is God's gracious, fatherly, judicial approval and praise of the Spirit-wrought works his people have performed. Our works are pleasing only through God's merciful pardon. Even as God says to us "Well done good and faithful servant," we will say about ourselves, "We are unprofitable servants" (Luke 17:10). We do not boast in what we have accomplished because it isn't really our doing anyway. We do not rely on ourselves or our works. Moreover, faith still has a role to play even in a judgment of works. The works themselves, after all, are only the fruit and evidence of faith. But more than that, it is only as we trust God to show us mercy in Christ that our works can find acceptance and favor. At the last day, we still have to trust God to forgive our sinful works in this life, as well as cover over and fill in the imperfections of our good works. In no sense do our works make satisfaction for sin or procure pardon – but, then, there is no need to do those things because they have already been accomplished by the cross.

Thus, final justification is God's gift every bit as much as ini-

---

23. Do not confuse "value" with "merit." See the complete discussion in my "Blurring the Federal Vision" and John Calvin's *Institutes of the Christian Religion* (Philadelphia: The Westminster Press, 1960), 3.17.3.

tial justification. Final justification is in Christ every bit as much as initial justification. There is even a sense in which future justification is by faith alone, like initial justification, because faith remains the sole instrument of union with Christ, in whom our persons *and works* are accepted. When God recompenses our comparatively paltry works with the gift of eternal life, we will be full of gratitude for all eternity. But note that God only justifies works in the end because he has *already* justified us apart from works at the beginning. The first justification is of sinners in Christ; the second justification is of the righteous in Christ. The first justification secures forgiveness of our sins; the second justification announces approval of our Spirit-empowered obedience. In the first justification, God accepts our persons; in the second justification, God accepts our works. In the first justification, we appear before God empty-handed; in the final justification, we come bearing gifts (Deut. 16:16). In the first justification, the Father judges the Son in our place according to strict justice; in the final justification, Christ judges us as the Father's agent, according to familial compassion.

Double Justification in Old Testament Typology: Numbers 19

This double justification pattern got some traction at the time of the Reformation, though anti-Roman polemics probably kept it from becoming the standard form of expression.[24] But, of course,

---

24. Contrary to the claims of Michael Horton in *CJPM*, 210, 221 a double justification doctrine, quite distinct from anything found in "covenant nomism" or medieval Catholicism, has precedent within our Reformational heritage. See Anthony N. S. Lane, *Justification By Faith in Catholic-Protestant Dialogue: An Evangelical Assessment* (New York: T and T Clark, 2002), 33ff. See also Rainbow, *The Way of Salvation*, ch. 20, for Reformed antecedents. As Rainbow shows, Philip Melanchthon and George Major openly advocated a view of double justification very similar to what I have offered here. Martin Bucer was forthright in teaching a double justification, first of the ungodly by faith, then of the godly by works. He was very concerned to show that the Reformers were teaching the same doctrine as the church fathers. Bucer also played a vital role in the Regensburg Colloquy (along with John Calvin), which developed a double justification model, as part of an ecumenical effort with some Roman Catholic theologians. Calvin occasionally spoke in terms of a double justification model. In John T. McNeil's edition of Calvin's *Institutes*, page 816, footnote 14, the editor makes reference to Calvin's *Sermons on Various*

the more critical point is that it is widely attested in Scripture. We cannot do a full overview here. We will limit ourselves to a cursory look at a crucial OT text and its role as a hermeneutical grid for other texts. Double justification is woven deeply into the typology of the OT. Numbers 19 is a particularly clear example. The laws of purification in Numbers 19 required those under Torah to be cleansed from defilement any time they came into contact with death (19:11-22). Ceremonially and symbolically, death "spreads to all men" (cf. Rom. 5:12) under the old covenant. Any time an Israelite touched death in any form, he drew that "death" and uncleanness onto himself. Thus, he needed a "resurrection" and purification to answer to his condition. In the Torah, that resurrection/purification unfolds in two phases over seven days. The unclean person would be cleansed by a sprinkling on the third and seventh days. In other words there are two resurrection (or justification) events, one in the middle of the week, and one at the end of the week.[25]

Passages of Genesis, in which Calvin "speaks of double justification—first a general pardon of those who are called, and thereafter 'justification even in our works by pure faith.'" In *Institutes* 3.14-18, Calvin beautifully and extensively develops a double acceptance doctrine, showing that God regards the works of his justified people as righteous in the final judgment, all due to his fatherly favor. In his commentary materials on Romans 4:6-8 and Psalm 106:31, Calvin argues that Phinehas received a double justification. His act of obedience was only imputed to him as righteousness because he was (implicitly) justified by faith alone at an earlier point. Calvin says, "In short, faith alone, and not human merit, procures both for persons and for works the character of righteousness." The Westminster Standards describe the final judgment in judicial terms (WCF 33) and speak of an "open acquittal" at the last day in WSC 38 and WLC 90. Recent and contemporary Reformed proponents of an already/not yet shape to justification include Geerhardus Vos, William Hendriksen, Herman Ridderbos, William Dumbrell, Scott Hafemann, Peter O'Brien, Don Garlington, Richard Gaffin, Sinclair Ferguson, Anthony Lane, Peter Lillback, John Frame, Robert Letham, Simon Gathercole, Mark Seifrid, Michael Bird, Thomas Schreiner, and Paul Rainbow. Of course not all these scholars agree (with me or with each other) on all the details. Nevertheless, Rainbow claims that a "future moment of justification" is now the "common view of most Pauline scholars" (158). My own research confirms that observation – though, admittedly, there is still a great deal of work to be done.

25. The rite described in Numbers 19 probably stands behind Paul's cryptic reference to "baptisms for the dead" in 1 Corinthians 15:29, and also his linkage of baptism with death and resurrection in Romans 6. It also undergirds the NT's twofold resurrection schema, found in passages such as John 5 and Revelation 20.

Jews would have been quite accustomed to this double-resurrection/cleansing pattern, given how often they would have needed to bury friends or family members. It is easy to see that the third day resurrection/cleansing is apart from works. The unclean person is washed by a clean person. The cleansing is not his own work but that of another. On the seventh day, the unclean person is once again washed by a clean person. But this time, he *also* washes himself (Num. 19:19). In other words, his own "work" is now included. The first cleansing event is apart from work; the second, final cleansing event includes his work.

This is the already/not yet pattern of redemptive history: Jesus is raised in the "middle" of history (the third day). Then, there is a general resurrection at the end of history (the seventh day). But those who were not initially cleansed on the "third day" in Christ's resurrection will be "cut off" forever (Num. 19:20) at the last day. Thus, the cleansing by Another on the third day makes way for the person's own work to be acceptable on the seventh day. The third day cleansing makes it possible for a person to grow to maturity in a way that pleases God, so that his work is accepted at the last day and his renewal is complete. Having been purified by Christ, he can acceptably purify himself (cf. Jas. 4:8).

How does the pattern of Numbers 19 play out in this two-stage justification? How does the rest of Scripture fill in our understanding of this model of justification? In initial and final justification, *the ground* of acceptance before God remains the same, namely the death and resurrection of Christ. He is the Cleanser from death and defilement. In both initial and final justification, our union with Christ is *by faith alone* (Rom. 5:1-11; 8:1-11). Furthermore, Christ is our Advocate in both initial and final justification, interceding on our behalf. But whereas in initial justification, we appear before God's court empty-handed ("nothing in my hands I bring, simply to thy cross I cling"), at the last day, we present to God the works of our hands, to be established forever (Ps. 90:17; cf. Rev. 14:13; 21:24).[26]

---

26. In this sense, then, we can say that God not only justifies us according to works in the final judgment; he justifies our works themselves. Or, to put it another way: while we are not saved by our works, our works themselves are saved. God effects a comprehensive

Through the mediation of Christ, these good-but-imperfect works are made perfect, so that we can appear before the final judgment "blameless in holiness" (1 Thess. 3:13; cf. Col. 1:22; 1 Cor. 1:8) and may be "counted worthy of the kingdom of God" (2 Thess. 1:5). While we do not hope in our own obedience, but in Christ who makes our obedience acceptable, we also know that without obedience, we have no hope (cf. Matt. 5:17-20; 7:13-27; 25:31-46; Rom. 8:13; Gal. 5:5-6; Heb 12:14; etc.). God justifies us from sin (Rom. 6:7) so that we bear the fruit of holiness, with the end goal of "righteousness" and "eternal life" (Rom. 6:16, 22), all of which is his free gift (Rom. 6:23). Faith-filled works are related to eternal life as sowing is related to reaping (Gal. 6:7). Thus: Initial justification flows out into progressive growth in sanctification, which flows back into final justification, forming a holistic salvation that rescues us from sin it all its dimensions, legal and experiential.

This twofold resurrection/justification also explains the texts in the Psalms where the psalmist pleads *his own* righteousness before God's law court (e.g., Ps. 7:8).[27] At the last day, the upright in heart will be saved – and none other (Ps. 7:10). These psalms are referring to covenant members who have already trusted in the Lord. In other words, they are already initially justified apart from any works on their part (cf. Ps. 7:1). Now, they expect an eschato-

---

deliverance, bringing us into the glory, honor, and eternal life we have been seeking. Justification according to works means that our works are not burned up; rather, they are accepted into God's eternal kingdom and woven into the final form of the new creation (1 Cor. 15:20-28). The justice of the last day is restorative justice for the people of God. The final justification will be, to use Peter Leithart's term, a "deliverdict" in the most comprehensive sense.

27. For a complete study, see the outstanding volume by Gert Kwakkel, *"According to My Righteousness": Upright Behavior as Grounds for Deliverance in Psalms 7, 17, 18, 26 and 44* (Leiden: Brill, 2002). Though these psalms may ultimately have a christological referent, Kwakkel shows that at the historical-literary level, the claims of righteousness in the psalter do not have to be understood as sinless perfection (which would render the sacrificial system meaningless). Instead, the psalmist is claiming covenant fidelity as an overarching pattern of life. This loyalty to the Lord provides a basis for expecting him to (keep his covenant and) judge in the psalmist's favor in the eschatological assize. The presupposition of these passages is that the psalmist is already a covenant member, and therefore already in a state of initial justification by faith when he pleads for some fuller (final?) vindication against enemies or accusers.

logical confirmation of that already received verdict, when God will manifest their right status and cast down their enemies. The evidence in the court at that last day will be their works of loyalty to the Lord. Because they have already been accepted into a covenant relationship with God, they do not fear the coming judgment; indeed (like Paul; cf. 2 Tim. 4:8), they fully expect to be vindicated. Ultimately, we can say that present justification is a matter of trusting God to forgive our ongoing sin so that we can remain in a right relationship with him; final justification is a matter of trusting God to vindicate and glorify us in the future. We need both.

This also explains the twofold clothing metaphor Scripture uses. In initial justification, God clothes us with Christ (Gal. 3:27). Afterwards, we see the saints clothed with the white robes of their own righteous acts (Rev. 3:4; 19:8). This is not an either/or but a both/and. The robing imagery points to both our new status in Christ and the transformation that flows from it. The fact that the same symbolism can be used both ways show how indivisible these different aspects of our salvation are.

Finally, this same pattern is seen in various historical types of the final judgment. We find that, again and again, the ethically righteous are picked out to be saved from coming wrath. The cases of Noah, Lot, and the demolition of the Jerusalem temple in 70 A. D. are especially instructive. These events (the flood, the destruction of Sodom and Gomorrah, and the end of the old covenant) are rightly taken as pictures anticipating the last day. In each case those who were delivered had God's favor already, but their survival at the coming judgment was not apart from obedience. We are told Noah "found favor" before we are told he "was a just man, perfect in his generations" (Gen. 6:8-9). He had obviously been justified before God for a long time before his obedience culminated in the salvation of his family in the ark (Heb. 11:7; 1 Pet. 3:20; 2 Pet. 2:5). While Lot had his share of struggles, he was certainly among the "righteous" as far as Abraham and Peter were concerned (Gen. 18:16-33; 2 Pet. 2:6-9). His "final" salvation in Genesis 19:1-29 clearly presupposed an earlier standing in God's favor. When Jesus spoke of the judgment to fall on Jerusalem, he made it clear that deliverance presupposed trusting him *and* living obediently (Matt. 16:24-29). In other words, justification according to works at the "final" judgment of 70 A. D. built upon an earlier justification by faith when the disciples first responded to the call of Jesus, received forgiveness, and began following him.

In sum, Paul Rainbow is exactly right when he says,

> For persons to be justified in the full sense, God's present imputation of righteousness to those who are incorporate in Christ by faith must be legitimized in the end by his approbation of an actual righteousness which he brings about in them during the meantime. While faith is the ultimate condition for both events, deeds are proximately conditional in their own right for the culminating event...*Sola fide* is true when it describes how we first enter into a new standing with God, but it oversimplifies the nature of the Christian journey into the coming age, with potentially disastrous effects.[28]

Of course, Rainbow is just following Calvin, who said that *sola fide* is "false," unless a "prudent and sound interpretation is given to it,"[29] and also spoke of a "double acceptance of man before God":

> For we dream neither of a faith devoid of good works nor of a justification that stands without them...

> [God] takes works into account...[T]hose good works which he has bestowed upon us the Lord calls "ours," and testifies they not only are acceptable to him but also will have their reward...

---

28. Rainbow, *The Way of Salvation*, xvi. Despite my reliance on Rainbow at points, there are several problems in his book, including the fact that he vastly underestimates how much Calvin agrees with his thesis. My major complaint is his failure to expound on the role of Christ and faith at the last judgment.

29. See Peter Lillback, *The Binding of God: Calvin's Role in the Development of Covenant Theology* (Grand Rapids: Baker Academic, 2001), 192. Lillback's work is a masterful and balanced study of the Reformer's thought, showing that he wrestled with the same biblical issues that this paper studies, arriving at a very complex and nuanced understanding of justification, faith, and union with Christ.

> The promises of the gospel...not only make us acceptable to God but also render our works pleasing to him...
>
> After forgiveness of sins is set forth, the good works that now follow are appraised otherwise than on their own merit...[T]he good works done by believers are accounted righteous, or, what is the same thing, are reckoned as righteousness...
>
> Therefore, we ourselves, when we have been engrafted in Christ, are righteous in God's sight because our iniquities are covered by Christ's sinlessness, so our works are righteous and are thus regarded because whatever fault is otherwise in them is buried in Christ's purity, and is not charged to our account. Accordingly, we can deservedly say that by faith alone not only we ourselves but our works as well are justified.[30]

The twofold justification scheme is one with many analogies in our own experience. When parents welcome a newborn into the home, they do so apart from any works or contribution the child might make. There are no demands. The child's status is "righteous" in the eyes of his parents. But when the child grows up, mature works are expected, and it is even possible that the child could live in such a way that parents would disinherit/disown him altogether. In a healthy situation, when a child reaches a certain age, the parents will look at their work "in" the child and give their judgment of approval. They will tell their mature son, "Well done! We're pleased with you! You are worthy of our inheritance!" This is the capstone of the initial welcome they gave to the child before he could do anything that would commend their praise. The inheritance he receives will still be a gracious gift, but he has shown himself to be a fitting recipient of such additional blessing. Obviously this analogy has limitations, but it helps to connect these biblical truths to everyday life.

Twofold Justification and the Necessity of Obedience

Contrary to some of the "Federal Vision" critics, Scripture never says that our deeds will be irrelevant to our standing in the

---

30. Calvin, *Institutes*, 3.16.1, 3.15.4, 3.15.3, 3.17.3, 3.17.8, 3.17.10.

final judgment. The language of the Bible could not be plainer in tying together obedience and final blessedness (Matt. 7:21-23; Heb. 12:14). The end goal of our obedience is "righteousness" (right-standing in God's law-court) and "everlasting life" (Rom. 6:16, 21-22; cf. WCF 16.2, which confesses the "end," or goal, of our good works to be "eternal life"). Works are related to final vindication as a means to an end, or a way to a destination (Gal. 6:7-8; cf. WLC 32). Turning the point around, Scripture teaches that inheriting the eschatological kingdom of God is contingent upon avoiding (or repenting of) certain patterns of behavior which constitute apostasy (cf. 1 Cor. 6:9-10; Gal. 5:19-21).

The necessity of grace-wrought works is the presupposition of the final judgment. But how should we classify and categorize the role of these works? Are works *instrumental* in final justification? No, at least not in the same sense that faith is instrumental. Works cannot unite us to Christ; that is the special function of faith. But many biblical passages could be easily construed in a way that works are instrumental in a variety of other ways that complement the unique instrumentality of faith. As Gathercole says, reflecting on Matthew 12:37, "It is dangerous to attempt to be more orthodox than Jesus by insisting that 'fruit' [of faith] cannot be described as an instrumental cause of eschatological justification."[31]

Should we then say that works are (merely) *evidence* in the final court scene? Perhaps. Then we could say God's vindicating verdict is rendered on the basis of the public evidence. But if we formulate the place of works in terms of evidence, we need to be careful to avoid certain pitfalls. The evidential view can make it seem as though works are tacked onto the real essence of salvation, which is forgiveness/imputed righteousness. The evidential view can make works appear to be extrinsic to the whole process of

---

31. Gathercole, "The Doctrine of Justification in Paul and Beyond: Some Proposals," in *Justification in Perspective*, edited by Bruce L. McCormack (Grand Rapids, MI: Baker Academic, 2006), 233. But note that Gathercole immediately points out that when Jesus is describing *initial* justification (in Luke 18:13-14), he leaves works out of the picture. It is a justification of the ungodly, received solely by the cry of faith. That is to say, Jesus and Paul are fully compatible in their teaching on present and final justification.

salvation. Salvation is one thing; evidence of salvation something else. The evidential view can make it look like trusting and obeying are two separate responses to God's word, even two different ways of relating to God, rather than distinct-but-integrated aspects of a single response. The evidential view can make obedience look like a second stage in the Christian living, rather than inextricably tied into faith from the outset.[32]

In reality, obedience is the "essential expression of what it means to trust Christ in and of itself."[33] This is why Paul speaks of the "obedience of faith" (Rom. 1:5). Faith itself is obedience to the gospel announcement, but it also carries within itself the seeds of obedience that are bound to bear fruit. Obedience is not a second step added to faith. Obedience is not a supplement to faith. Obedience is not merely proof of faith. Rather obedience is the reflex of faith to God's imperatives, the same way taking medicine is the reflex of a patient's trust in his doctor. Obedience is just what faith does; it is faith in action. Obedience is what saved, renewed, restored human life looks like.[34]

---

32. Rainbow, *The Way of Salvation*, 206ff makes a case for going beyond "works as evidence" at the last day. He ends up advocating an "instrumental" view, much like Gathercole, in which works are a "means" unto final salvation. Calvin also describes works as "inferior causes" and "means" of final salvation (*Institutes*, 3.14.21).
33. Scott Hafemann, *The God of Promise and the Life of Faith* (Wheaton, IL: Crossway, 2001), 188. Hafemann goes on to say, "There is only one thing, not two, that we must do to be saved: trust God with the needs of our lives. This one thing, trust in God's provision (now supremely manifested in Christ) will show itself, from beginning to end, in our *many* acts of repentance and obedience..." (192).
34. We can go one step further and describe obedience as a perichoretic reality. "Perichoresis" is a theological term used to describe the inner "choreography" (or "dance") of God's triune life, as the three persons of the Godhead mutually fill and indwell one another in love, giving, receiving, and returning to one another. As Jesus describes obedience in John 14:20-21, 23-24, we find that (faith-filled) obedience is a means to ever-deepening communion with God. The Father and Son indwell one another; the Son indwells us, and therefore the Father dwells in us as well (14:20). As we give ourselves to the Son in loving obedience, we are loved in turn by the Father, and the Son gives himself to us even more deeply (14:21). As we obey, we prepare our hearts into homes for the Father and Son to take up residence (14:23). Jesus seems to be saying that obedience leads us deeper into the heart of God's triune life, even as it opens the way for the persons of the Godhead to dwell more fully in our hearts. As Father and Son give themselves to us, we give ourselves to them in return, and the bond between us grows and strengthens. In this way, obedience may be thought of as "dancing" with(in) the Trinity; it is the way

All that being the case, it might be better to call works a *condition* of final justification. Works do more than demonstrate that we are already saved; growth into mature obedience is the whole point of salvation, after all. As we are rounded out into renewed, Christ-like image bearers, we are being made mature sons, ready to claim our inheritance in God's renewed creation. Thus, obedience is not merely verification of salvation; it is the point of salvation. God's desire has always been to have a mature, obedient humanity at the helm of his creation. At the last day, God will look at his finished work of re-creation in Christ and judge it as "good." Final justification is the declaration that God is pleased with his work in us by his Spirit; he finally has what he was aiming at when he created man in the first place. Good works in the present are signs of God's benevolence to us, showing that we are on the road to eschatological glory, to be received in full in the future.

The Bible repeatedly describes two ways of life, two paths one can travel: the path of faithful obedience and the path of unfaithful disobedience.[35] The first path ends with the Father declaring his pleasure and granting the crown of life. The other path ends with condemnation and the lake of fire. There is no third way.

Given that the critics of the "Federal Vision" will generally admit that obedience is necessary, it is hard to see why they would so strenuously object to the Bible's plain teaching regarding a final justification. If there is no final judgment/justification, in which works play a decisive role, *why* are works necessary?

The Grace of Judgment Day

Like Paul, the "Federal Vision" sees a final judgment according to works as good news for believers (cf. Rom. 2:16), whereas

---

we come to enjoy and fulfill the communion with the Triune God that we were created to experience. Again, this brings us back to our point above: obedience (flowing out of faith, manifesting love) is not simply tacked on to salvation; rather, is the very shape and goal of our salvation.

35. See Deuteronomy 27-30; Psalm 1; the book of Proverbs; the Sermon on the Mount in Matthew's gospel; the "way" theme in Mark's gospel; Romans 8:1-17; Galatians 6:7-10; etc.

(implicitly, at least) the critics see it as bad news.[36] While many aspects of the present controversy may be written off due to misunderstanding, here we seem to have a real, substantive disagreement, one that can only be solved in the old fashioned way – by an appeal to the Law and the Testimony!

How can it be good news to hear that our justification has been inaugurated, but not yet consummated? That our final approbation is contingent on certain conditions which must still be fulfilled in this life? That the criteria for final acquittal includes our performance of good works? What does it mean for already justified believers to *hope* for justification by faith (Gal. 5:5)?

As already noted, the Bible uses very blunt, plain language to express the reality that our deeds in this life bear upon our final destiny (cf. Matt. 5:17-20; 7:21-23; John 5:29; Gal. 6:7-10; etc.). *But this does not have to be taken as bad news.* Indeed, Paul considers it part of the gospel (Rom. 2:16). The gospel not only delivers us from the penalty of sin, but from the power and presence of sin as well. Jesus died not only to win the acquittal of convicted criminals, but also to secure their rehabilitation through the work of his Spirit. The cross and resurrection not only serve as the ground of our acceptance by God (Rom. 4:25), but also as the dynamic of our renewal and transformation (Rom. 6:1-23). The faith that justifies also works (Jas. 2:14-26) through love (Gal. 5:6). At the last day, those, and only those, who have persevered in faithfulness by grace will hear the Father's praise (1 Cor. 4:5).

We have to distinguish working hard to make ourselves right with God from working hard because we have already been made right with God (1 Cor. 15:10). The works that justify at the last day are the works that flow out of a faith that has already received initial acceptance and the promise of forgiveness. When Paul sets faith over against works, the works he has in view are either [a] works done in an outdated, old covenant mode of life, according to the Torah, apart from Christ and the Spirit, and these works are now obsolete in light of the great redemptive-historical shift that has taken place;

---

36. See the remarks of Hywel Jones in *CJPM*, 295-296.

or [b] works done pre-conversion, in a vain attempt to merit God's favor in the flesh.[37] But Paul *never* says works are optional for believers; he always insists that works (flowing out of faith) are necessary to receive God's final approbation on the last day.[38]

The problem is that we have shrunk down the gospel. It is all too typical for the gospel to be reduced to the forgiveness of sin and imputation of righteousness. But the gospel not only promises free pardon and acceptance through Christ; it also ensures that God transforms us and matures us into Christ's image. This much neglected aspect of the gospel needs to be recovered so that we can eagerly anticipate God's praise on the final day of reckoning the same way Paul did (cf. Rom. 2:10; 1 Cor. 4:2-5; 2 Tim. 4:8).

This does not have anything to do with shifting the *ground* of justification (in the present or in the future) away from Christ. Rather, it is to suggest that Christ does even more for us than perhaps we have thought. God is not going to destroy my life's work because it was stained with sins and flaws. Rather, at the last day, he will establish the work of my hands forever, perfecting, glorifying, and beautifying it (Ps. 90:17).[39] That is part of the gospel hope as well. Christ is not only the ground on which God accepts me; he is the ground on which God accepts my deeds as well.

If the ordinary Christian doubts whether or not his works are "good enough," such that he fears a final judgment according to works, *the problem is that he is not sufficiently believing the gospel.* In Christ, even the most meager, baby steps of obedience delight

---

37. Too many "Federal Vision" critics have failed to make a distinction between these worthless works, done outside of union with Christ, and the good works of Spirit-indwelt believers. The critics are suspicious that *any* human effort is a sign that one is motivated by merit rather than grace. But there is no generic category of "works" that covers every type of human effort. We have to make distinctions between works that arise out of different modes of living. The works of the flesh are radically different from the works done in the realm of the Spirit, as Romans 8 shows.

38. See Rainbow's survey of every passage in the Pauline corpus which contrasts faith with works, *The Way of Salvation*, 84ff.

39. For a beautiful literary picture of the way the final judgment purifies, perfects, completes, and glorifies our life's work, read J. R. R. Tolkien's story "Leaf By Niggle" in *Tree and Leaf* (London: Harper Collins, 2001). For a more theological account, see Darrell Cosden, *The Heavenly Good of Earthly Work* (Peabody, MA: Hendriksen, 2006).

the Father. Indeed, even our struggles to obey bring him pleasure, though we often falter. Once we know the Father is pleased with our efforts, we can go out into the world and live for him, full of joy and confidence. We can leave behind the old, and strain ahead to the new, knowing that our Father's glorious and gracious approbation awaits us. We are motivated out of gratitude for an already received justification, but love also compels us and presses us ahead towards the goal of pleasing our Father in all that we do so that we can hear his fatherly praise at the last day.

But the critics of the "Federal Vision" balk at these notions. They do not believe even regenerate humans can do anything that pleases the heavenly Father. For example, in *CJPM*, Michael Horton writes, "A final justification based on our works, even works done in faith, would reverse the verdict pronounced in our present justification" (226). This is so, as Horton explains, because the law demands perfect obedience. God simply cannot pass a favorable judgment over the works of his people, even when those works are regarded as gifts of grace and fruit of the Spirit. Of course, the fundamental problem here is that Horton regards believers as still under the law, contra Romans 6:14 and Galatians 5:23.

Likewise, in *CJPM* (411), Dennis Johnson writes,

> Some federal vision advocates draw a distinction between God's "strict" justice, which only Christ's perfection can satisfy, and God's "fatherly" assessment, which accepts our less-than-perfect obedience, calling it 'pleasing' and "good." Rich Lusk, for example, asserts...
>
> In another essay Lusk attempts to soften the daunting prospect of final judgment based on works....

Johnson goes on to say that my view of the final judgment undermines both grace and justice and eliminates love as a motivation for obedience.

But just the opposite is the case. On Johnson's view, no matter how hard the believer tries, his works are always going to be worthless before God. In Johnson's view, living in a state of justification makes absolutely no difference in how God regards our deeds. According to Johnson, a believer should not desire to hear his Father say "Well done!" – and he never will anyway. (Perhaps he would say Matthew 25:21, 23 are hypothetical in the manner that the other *CJPM* authors read Romans 2:13.) We serve a Master who simply cannot be pleased with us. Nothing we ever do is praiseworthy. And to seek the Father's approbation is to fall into works-righteousness. The result of this approach, of course, can easily be apathy, listlessness, and even despair, as God's people are robbed of comfort and encouragement that is due to them. Indeed, the doctrine taught in *CJPM* seems demeaning and dehumanizing in its insistence that nothing humans ever do (even in faith) can have value before God.

Compare Horton's and Johnson's view with that of Paul. Yes, Paul knew that his only hope was the free grace of God in Christ. He was motivated not by an attempt to obligate God. But nevertheless, he wrote, "Therefore we make it our aim...to be well pleasing to him. For we must all appear before the judgment seat of Christ, that each one may receive the things done in the body, whether good or bad" (2 Cor. 5:9-10). By Johnson's standards, Paul was poorly motivated since he took account of God's approbation at the last day.[40] By Horton's standards, all Paul could hope to "receive" before the "judgment seat" is condemnation since he brings works into view. The claim of the "Federal Vision" is that Paul, not Horton or Johnson, got it right.

James 2 and Eschatological Justification

The picture of justification drawn in James 2 may be brought into the discussion at this point. We will find that James 2 and

---

40. On *CJPM*, 411, Johnson seems oblivious to any distinction between seeking to please God by faith and seeking to earn his favor. Virtually everything Johnson says about Luke 7:36ff is fine as far as it goes, and I would agree with it. But the problem is what he leaves out. The parable in Luke 7:41-47 is a beautiful story of how initial justification compels us to love God, but it does not bear upon my point, which is established by appeal to a different set of texts.

In addition, it is not just the "Federal Vision" theologians who argue for a distinction between God's "strict" and "fatherly" justice. The same distinction is found in Calvin. See my essay, "Blurring the 'Federal Vision'" for a complete discussion of Calvin's view.

Romans 2 align perfectly. I will not comprehensively exegete this much contested passage, but I do want to point out that most discussions of the text go astray because they start at the wrong point. Unfortunately, many of our English Bible put a section break between James 2:13 and 2:14. But 2:12-13 provide one of the key premises in the argument that follows (and it turns out to be a premise that Johnson, in the above mentioned discussion, flatly rejects). James says, "So speak and do as those who will be judged by the law of liberty. For judgment is without mercy to the one who has shown no mercy. Mercy triumphs over judgment." Then, the apostle launches into a discussion of God's future judgment. But he has already contextualized the meaning of God's judgment. God judges the merciful with mercy. That is to say, believers (who inevitably show faith by their deeds of mercy; cf. Jas. 1:26-27; 2:1-6, 15-16 and Matt. 25:31-46) will be judged mercifully at the last day.[41] Mercy receives mercy. The law of judgment for believers is the "law of liberty." Of course, we have seen Paul make the same point by incorporating Psalm 62 into his teaching on final justification in Romans 2.[42]

What do we find in the rest of James 2? And how does it mesh with Jesus' and Paul's teachings?

First, James clearly has in view works which do not follow from justification, but which precede and lead to the pronounce-

---

41. Degrees of judgment are also hinted at in James 3:1.
42. What if we press back further into the early part of James 2? How does James' statement about the perfectionism of the law in 2:10 comport with the merciful judgment of 2:13? The key is in James' turn of phrase in 2:12, where he speaks of "the law of liberty," already referred to back in 1:25. There is no doubt the law in view in 2:10 is absolute in its demands. James speaks of "stumbling at one point" in 2:10; in 3:2, he confirms that we do all in fact "stumble in many things." So we would all be judged as law-breakers according to the standard of 2:10. But the law of 2:10 is *not* the standard by which believers will be judged. They have come under the "law of liberty." This law still brings a judgment of deeds (1:25, 2:12), and it appears that is has similar moral content to the law of 2:10, since both laws condemn partiality (2:9). But the law of liberty is distinct in that it brings a judgment of mercy to the merciful. This merciful law is actually an incentive to obedience rather than an excuse for lowering our standards (cf. 2:8, 12). Obviously, this meshes well with what we saw in Romans 2:1-16, as it rests upon Psalm 62:12. The "law of liberty" may also be connected with Paul's discussion of liberty in Galatians 5 and the law of Christ in 1 Corinthians 9:21 and Galatians 6:2.

ment of the verdict. This is a justification that is *posterior* to works. In other words, this passage has *nothing* (directly) to do with initial justification, which clearly precedes works. James deals here with eschatological salvation (2:12-14). In the illustrations given (Abraham and Rahab), it is clear that they are already believers well before the justification in view is declared.[43] (This is clearer in the case of Abraham, obviously.) These illustrations foreshadow, model, and typify eschatological justification. James is discussing our final acquittal before the judgment seat of God; he is providing historical paradigms for understanding future justification.[44]

Second, salvific realities pervade the text. James is concerned with the same kinds of questions that drive Paul – questions about salvation (2:14), being reckoned righteous (2:23), friendship/reconciliation with God (2:23), the relationship of faith to works, and the connection between works and justification. Like Paul, James is concerned with those who are mere hearers of the law rather than doers (1:22-27). Like Paul, James relies on the example of Abraham, and even uses the same prooftext (Gen. 15:6). James uses a typical Pauline grammatical construction (the preposition "by" followed by a genitive case) to express justification's instrumentality (2:24; cf. Gal. 2:16; Rom. 3:26; etc.). In other words,

---

43. In other words, the tension between James and Paul is a mirage. The statements of the apostles that appear to conflict are talking about different justification events. The justification and works that Paul opposes to one another in Romans 3:28 are different from the justification and works that James coordinates in James 2:24. Romans 3:28 teaches pre-Christian works cannot attain initial acceptance with God. James 2:24 is about future justification by faith-filled good works. When we recognize this, we see that James easily harmonizes with Paul's teaching on *future* justification (e.g., Rom. 2:13; Gal. 5:5-6). If we could get away from the unhealthy tendency to force James through the grid of a few select Pauline passages, and let him speak for himself as an inspired apostle, we would be able to deal much more faithfully with the text. We do need to harmonize various texts, but we cannot let that short circuit the work of exegeting each text on its own. We cannot let a handful of Pauline passages muzzle what James has to say.

44. It is possible that James that laying down the requirements his readers must meet if they are to be justified not at the last day, but at an historical judgment that is much nearer at hand (cf. Jas. 5:1-12; Mt. 16:27-28), perhaps 70 A. D. But even if this is so, such that James 2:14ff is describing historically intermediate judgments, this still serves as a picture and type of the final, eschatological judgment, and that would be the primary application for today's readers.

James 2 breathes the same air as Paul's theology. There is every reason to suppose that James is using "justification" terminology in a roughly Pauline way (forensic acquittal).

Third, James is dealing with the way to secure ultimate salvation.[45] James has already alluded to the future completion of salvation in 1:12, using language that could easily be construed in a judicial way ("approved"). James says a faith that does not demonstrate itself in works will not profit for salvation in the day of judgment (2:14, 16; cf. 1:26). Indeed, James frames the situation in the harshest of terms: a non-working faith is not only dead (2:17), but demonic (2:18). In other words, faith is not a matter of mere assent (for even demons can assent to propositional truths and shudder). Faith is a whole-souled commitment, an entrusting of one's life and ways to God. This is why James can insist that saving, justifying faith will show itself in deeds. The way to God's final approval is the way of faith, as that faith is completed in works (2:22). Faith is as faith does. And only a "doing" faith can yield justification. The whole of the epistle points in this direction.

Fourth, James states his conclusion three times: final justification is "by works" (2:21, 24, 25). To be sure, the verdict is not given to works apart from faith, as though these works could stand on their own as an independent human contribution to salvation. Rather, James says works and faith combine together to attain final justification (2:24). In this way, James maintains the unique role of faith, even though it is not a prominent theme. While he does

---

45. Contra Jones, *CJPM,* 295, who says (without any substantial proof) that James' main question is "How can faith be demonstrated?" That is a subsidiary point, to be sure, but Jones' approach begs the key issues. Jones says that the recurring theme is that "works 'justify' faith." But that is precisely what James *never* says. Yes, works "show" faith, but in the passage, it is *persons* (Abraham, Rahab), not *faith,* that are *justified.* Paying close attention to grammar is critical to sound exegesis, and Jones has failed in that respect. Further, Jones' view that "to justify" means "to demonstrate righteousness" makes non-sense of James' formula in 2:22, 24: How could faith "demonstrate" faith? After all, James does not deny faith's role in justification when he insists that works have a role as well. But in a demonstrative justification, faith would be *entirely* excluded.

However, to Jones' credit he admits the exegesis of Douglas Moo (which is very similar to what I am offering here) is "open to question." In other words, Jones has not totally closed the door on giving the passage a more faithful reading.

not use the language of union with Christ, his overall point is one that is found in Paul as well. As radical as James 2:24 sounds, it is actually rather easy to find Pauline equivalents (e.g., Rom. 2:13; Gal. 5:5-6). When Paul denies that works justify, he has in view pre-Christian works (e.g., Rom 3:28). When James says faith alone cannot justify, he has in view an inadequate, workless faith that amounts to mere assent (2:19, 24). When Paul and James speak of works that will justify eschatologically (Rom. 2:13; Jas. 2:24), they have in view the Spirit-driven works of an already accepted believer.

Fifth, it is impossible that James is using the verb "to justify" in the sense of "to demonstrate as just." Besides the well documented linguistic problems with this view,[46] it simply does not fit the sense of the passage, [47] especially the use of Genesis 15:6 in 2:23.[48] In James' discussion, works are evidential, but they evidence *faith*, not *justification*. James does not say "show me your justification," but "show me your faith" (cf. 2:18). In James 2, justification *follows from* faith and works. Or to put it differently, only a demonstrated faith will lead to justification (eschatological right-standing). Verse 24 is the clincher: When James says that faith and works justify, he cannot mean that faith and works demonstrate one's status (or character) as just. Faith, in itself, does not demonstrate anything. Rather,

---

46. See e.g., Norman Shepherd, "The Grace of Justification," available at http://www.hornes.org/theologia/content/norman_shepherd/the_grace_of_justification.htm. See also Rainbow, *The Way of Salvation*, 223n. This stands against Jones, *CJPM*, 295. Jones questions whether or not God is the subject of the verb "to justify" throughout James' discussion. But Genesis 15:6 definitively answers that question. God is the one who does the justifying. Who else could it be? Who else would justify Abraham by faith, even in combination with works? Besides, James identifies God as the Judge elsewhere in the epistle, e.g., 4:11-12.

47. To be sure, works can be regarded as proof that *initial* justification has taken place. Only the initially justified will do good works; these works flow out of initial justification and verify its reality. So the *theological* point of those who interpret James in this way is entirely valid, even if it is *exegetically* false. My desire here, obviously, is to deal with James' actual point.

48. Those who want to argue that James uses justification language in a demonstrative sense, rather than in the Pauline, forensic sense are still left with a contradiction, since then James and Paul are using the same example (Abraham), and even the same prooftext (Gen. 15:6), in radically different ways.

it is the very thing that needs demonstrating, so that one can be (eschatologically) justified.

Sixth, some have argued that James is talking about a justification before men, not God. In other words, our good works are not needed as far as God is concerned, but in order to prove our righteous status to other humans, we need to have works. While it is true that works demonstrate our identity in Christ to others (cf. 1 Pet. 2:12), it is not at all clear that that function of works is in view in James 2. The whole context seems to be salvation and acquittal before God. Not only that, but in the two illustrations offered (Abraham, Rahab), a human audience is not in view. Abraham went *alone* with Isaac up the mountain. Obviously Rahab's covert action had to be kept a secret from the other citizens of Jericho. James is apparently answering those who think that a non-working faith (mere assent) can profit towards final *salvation*. The issue at stake is not our witness before men (as important as that is), but our standing before God.

Seventh, James' way of relating faith and works seems counter-intuitive at first. In his analogy in verse 26, faith = the body and works = spirit/breath. But upon further reflection, it makes perfect sense. James is saying that a living faith is a *breathing* faith. Faith inhales God's promises (implicit in the examples of Abraham and Rahab), and exhales good works. A faith that does not breathe out good works is suffocated. It is a corpse. It is worthless. A body separated from its breath is dead. Thus, only a vital faith can justify. But because justifying faith is a working faith, good works must always be considered as the works *of faith*, not something added to or tacked on to faith. Thus, in a very important sense, a justification by works is still *really* a justification by faith at the deepest level.

Eighth, why does James think that Abraham's obedience in Genesis 22 (cited in James 2:21) "fulfilled" the declaration of Abraham's righteousness in Genesis 15 (cited in James 2:23)? Why does James think of God's imputation of righteousness to Abraham's faith in Genesis 15:6 as somehow prophetic of Abraham's later obedience, when he offered Isaac? Some have suggested that God imputes believers as righteous in the present in view of who he will make them to be in the future. In other words, justification by faith in the present is really future justification by works announced ahead of time, much like a doctor declaring a sick patient cured as soon as he begins to take medicine, because the medicine is so sure to take effect in due time. This may be what James is saying, but it seems to me more consistent with the overall witness of Scripture to say that the point is a bit different. James is pointing out that the same faith that clung to God's promises in Genesis 15 concerning the seed grew into mature obedience in Genesis 22, so that it could offer the seed back to God. In other words, the kind of faith that justifies in the present is the kind of faith that will produce good works in the future. The good works that flow out of faith actually mature and perfect faith (2:22; cf. 1:4). Faith reaches its *telos*, its goal, in obedient human action, as the life of Abraham demonstrates. God then mercifully declares his approval of that faith-filled obedience (cf. 1:12). The maturity theme runs straight through the epistle and it is not out of place to see it lurking in 2:14-26. The final judgment is God crowning his mature sons with approbation.

Ninth, the example of Rahab is especially instructive in terms of discerning James' overall intentions. In Jewish eyes, she is everything Abraham wasn't: a woman, a Gentile, a flagrant sinner. Obviously, God's judgment is not partial to Israel (cf. Romans 2:1-16). Her inclusion in a passage that focuses on justification by works shows unmistakably that James is not thinking in terms of legalistic demands, but of God's gracious acceptance. He is not thinking in terms of the works of the self-help moralist, who tries to make himself presentable to God. Rather, he is thinking of the believer who has cast himself upon the sheer mercy of God – but in the act of doing so, is also transformed by the Spirit of God. Rahab's justification – even when it is according to works – must be a gift. Rahab reminds us that the question "How much obedience is enough to justify?" is seriously misguided. The point is that *any measure* of true faith will demonstrate itself in embodied action. And that is sufficient.

Tenth, if we ask, "How can a perfect, holy God accept our imperfect works? How can flawed obedience justify?" James is ready with an answer. We have already noted that James views the final judgment as a merciful evaluation of believers (2:13) according to the law of liberty (1:25, 2:12). God shows mercy to those who show mercy. Further insight is offered in 2:23, which reflects back on Genesis 15:6. Because Abraham believed God, God called him his friend. So when God judged his actions later on (Gen. 22), God judged him in a friendly way. It was not a judgment of strict justice (since that has been meted out at the cross), but a covenantal judgment. God looked at Abraham's work through the lens of covenant friendship.[49] Forensic justification issues forth into a state of friendship, which provides the context for a future forensic event. Of course, outside of that covenant relationship, there is no mercy mixed into the judgment (Jas. 2:10).

Eleventh, James should not be read in such a way that he denies the truth of *sola fide*. Grammatically, James identifies two instruments of justification (faith and works), but that is not necessarily the case theologically. While James' (inspired!) formulation rejects *sola fide* on the surface (2:24), there is another sense in which his teaching can be squared with the intentions of *sola fide*. James does not teach that faith and works play identical, or interchangeable,

---

49. If we fill this out with the rest of Scripture, we can say that God not only exercises a *friendly* judgment towards believers, but also a *fatherly* judgment. We are judged as a father judges his children, which is a comforting thought (cf. Ps. 103:13-14). Calvin put a great deal of emphasis on the fatherhood of God in relation to his judgment of believer's works at the last day. Of course, ultimately, God's judgment is merciful, friendly, and fatherly only because we are *in Christ*. Christ has already satisfied God's wrath against our sin, even as Christians. Christ continually intercedes for us, making our flawed works acceptable and ensuring that our sins will be forgiven. The cross, resurrection, and mediation of Christ puts believers on new footing with God, so that our works really can meet with God's good pleasure. Our works are not tacked onto faith in an extrinsic way; rather, as the product of our faith, they are now evaluated by God from within our union with Christ. This was all prefigured in the sacrificial system, where the tribute/grain offerings (representing human labor) were also offered on the heels of sin offerings and ascension/ whole burnt offerings (representing Christ's sacrifice). Our works become acceptable to God only after our persons have been accepted. And all of this is enveloped by Christ's work on our behalf. See WCF 16 for a Reformed statement of this truth regarding God's acceptance of our good works through Christ. See also my "Blurring the Federal Vision" for a larger theological discussion, drawing heavily on Calvin.

or equal, roles in justification. In fact, his quotation of Genesis 15:6 is a powerful affirmation of the priority of faith. Works and faith cooperate (2:22), but only as works flow out of faith. Works follow faith as a secondary and subordinate condition. So while James says that faith and works justify conjointly (2:24), this does not necessitate blurring their respective functions. In the hands of Reformed theologians, James' dual instrument formula (justification by faith plus works) has resolved into a singular instrument (justification by a working faith). *This is an entirely legitimate move, and one I would endorse.* It is not an improvement on James, but a summary of James. The faith that alone justifies is never alone. Believing and doing are distinct, but they can never be divorced. Faith and works are integral to one another, but not identical.

Now we are prepared to state the biblical doctrine of justification more fully. Initial justification is by faith alone. But it is by a faith that will prove itself in works. Final justification is by faith and works together. Or, to put it differently, it is by a faith that has proven itself in obedience and borne the fruit of the Spirit. This is the teaching found across the board in the NT. Jesus (Luke 18:14/Matt. 12:37), James (2:23/2:22), and Paul (Rom. 3:28/Rom. 2:13) all provide a synthesis of present justification by faith and future justification to doers. So far from there being tension, there is complete compatibility. This is because salvation is a complete package, which includes initial forgiveness, final vindication, and growth in the obedience of faith in between. God's purpose, beginning in the eternal election of a people, reaching achievement in the death and resurrection of Christ, coming to fruition in the applicatory work of the Spirit, and finally culminating with resurrection and new creation, is all of one piece. In other words, there is no tension between the two poles of justification because, eschatologically and decretally, "believers" and "doers" become the same group. Those who are declared righteous at the start are practically righteous at the end.[50]

---

[50] Horton wrongly accuses this twofold pattern of justification as being indistinguishable from the Roman Catholic Tridentine view of justification (*CJPM*, 210). But Horton can only make such a claim by radically twisting my arguments out of shape (which

he quite adept at doing) and/or misunderstanding the Tridentine view of justification. Which canon from the Council of Trent teaches a doctrine of initial justification anything like I have proposed, in this book? Which canon of Trent proposes a future justification in which the mediation of Christ is foundational to the acceptance of our works (rather than merit), as I have argued? Where does Trent articulate the role of faith as I have done?

CHAPTER 10

Covenantal Nomism and the Exile

Don Garlington

Introduction

Professor I. M. Duguid's essay commences with a rudimentary analysis of E. P. Sanders' now famous phrase "covenantal nomism."[1] His concern, however, is not to address Sanders as such but rather "the rise of similar formulations within the modern church." The discussion is intended to focus on "the accuracy of covenantal nomism as a description of the Old Testament relations between God and his people and in particular on the pastoral crisis that faced God's people during and after the exile." The question is: "Can covenantal nomism account for the persistence of God's relationship with his people after the exile." Or, stated otherwise: "After Israel's unfaithfulness had led to the ultimate sanction of exile, did the prophets promise covenant blessing dependent on human faithfulness, or did they look for something new in which God himself would fulfill the covenant conditions?" As in my reply to S. M. Baugh in this volume, this response to Professor Duguid will follow his organization, first summarizing the arguments and then responding to them.

"Maintenance of Marriage"

Duguid acknowledges that "at first sight" covenantal nomism may seem to be supported by the analogy of the marriage

---

1. Throughout Sanders' *Paul and Palestinian Judaism: A Comparison of Patterns of Religion* (Philadelphia: Fortress, 1977).

relationship in the Old Testament. Thus, he remarks, it could be well argued that a wife's faithfulness is necessarily a key element in the marital relationship. By analogy, then, our faithfulness would be a key element in maintaining our relationship with God. But the question is, How is this analogy worked out in Scripture? In answering the question, Duguid appeals to several passages in the prophets. The first is Ezekiel 16. After a vivid depiction of Israel's adoption, nurturing by the Lord and yet adulterous response to his grace, the bottom line is that after Yahweh's wrath is poured out on Jerusalem he will have mercy on her. Judgment is thus not the end of Israel's relationship with her God. According to Duguid, "The Israelites will experience the curses that the covenant threatened, but the covenant relationship itself will not be annulled by their unfaithfulness."

Next, Hosea 2, Isaiah 50 and Jeremiah 3 are considered in tandem. As for Hosea 2, the prophet's unfaithful wife was chosen for no merit in her. When she runs after other lovers, she is punished, but divorce could not be the end of the story, because ultimately the Lord would restore her to himself. Isaiah 50 is stated in similar terms: Yahweh's divorce of Israel was because of her transgressions. Nevertheless, even such iniquities cannot ultimately destroy the marriage. The Lord has remained faithful to his bride and for that reason speaks comfort to Zion. The Lord will raise up a faithful servant who will bring deliverance to his unfaithful bride. Jeremiah 3 pictures the breach between the Lord and his people in the strongest possible terms. But even so, the relationship, writes Duguid, cannot ultimately be severed by their unfaithfulness: "The marriage relationship between God and his people cannot ultimately be destroyed by the unfaithfulness of the bride."

The response to these data can be brief. On the one hand, Duguid is quite right that it is the mercy of God toward Israel that will ultimately restore her to the marriage covenant. This is beyond dispute and is simply not a bone of contention between a "covenantal nomism" reading of God's relation to Israel and any other. On the other side, a rather obvious fact has been downplayed: it is for no other reason than *infidelity* that a divorce has occurred and the nation is sent packing into exile. Hosea 2, Isaiah 50 and Jeremiah 3 all draw on the divorce metaphor and cite as the cause of the dissolution of the marriage Israel's adultery. One may say, as Duguid does, that the marriage relationship between God and his people cannot ultimately be destroyed by the unfaithfulness of the bride. But the fact remains that God's restorative action (return from exile) is intended to repair a relationship that was broken by none other than an unfaithful bride. The old marriage is dissolved and the Lord "marries" a new "wife" who enters into a "new covenant" with him.

"Renovation of the Covenant"

The thesis of this rubric is stated as follows:

> ....the future prospect after the exile is not merely a return to the status ante quo. It would be no comfort to tell a generation who had experienced the full weight of the covenant curses for their disobedience and that of their forefathers that future blessing depended on their future faithfulness. Rather, the prophets repeatedly pointed their hearers to a new intervention of God that would radically alter the constitution of the people.

In pursuing this proposition, appeal is made to the well known passages of Jeremiah 31, Ezekiel 34 and Ezekiel 36. As for Jeremiah 31, the "new covenant" (31:31-34) is radically unlike the Sinai covenant in some significant regards, most notably in terms of internal transformation, the writing of the law on the heart, the universal knowledge of God and the definitive forgiveness of sins. At the same time, Duguid notes, the new covenant represents the fulfillment of the Mosaic covenant, when the blessings of that conditional covenant will be received unconditionally, through a sovereign act of God's mercy and grace. The same, he writes, pertains to the Davidic covenant. Even though the persistent unfaithfulness of David's heirs had now led to comprehensive judgment,

Jeremiah promised a renewal of the Davidic covenant in the days to come. To wit: "Neither God's covenant with David nor his covenant with the descendants of Jacob could ultimately be broken, in spite of all of the unfaithfulness of the human parties, for these covenants were as unbreakable as God's covenant with night and day (33:19-26)."

Identical themes emerge from Ezekiel 34. The "covenant of peace" will bring about a new future for Israel. No longer will the exiles undergo the curses of the Sinai covenant, but rather they will now enjoy the blessings of that covenant. Duguid specifies that the "covenant of peace" is "a new covenant in the sense that they will in the future experience the blessings promised in the original (Mosaic) covenant rather than the curses merited by their breaches in the covenant." The same is true of the blessings of the Davidic covenant. In place of the monarchy divided by sin, the returned exiles will be united under one shepherd. They will now know blessing instead of curse. Adam's original act of unfaithfulness will be undone through an act of salvation on the Lord's part.

Such ideas are further developed in Ezekiel 36:16-38. God's wrath is called forth by Israel's unfaithfulness, as evidenced by her many and various misdeeds. But, says Duguid, this action creates a new problem for God: it now appears that he is unable to bring about what he had promised, i.e., to maintain his people in the land within the special relationship of the Mosaic covenant, as symbolized by the tabernacle, the visible dwelling of God in their midst. The Lord might have blotted out Israel from the pages of history, except for his concern for his own name, which he had inextricably linked to Israel by entering covenant with them. "Because of that sovereign, irrevocable act at Sinai," comments Duguid, "mercy not only may be but must be shown to Israel." Consequently, not only is there a mere physical return to the land, but the people must be redeemed inwardly and effectively. The old heart of stone will be replaced by one of flesh, and as a result: "Israel will experience the blessings of the Mosaic covenant, the fruitfulness of the land, rather than experiencing the covenant curse of famine that had made them such a reproach among the nations." Duguid then rightly maintains that the Lord's favor toward his people does not flow from this inner transformation but is the cause of it. All this corresponds, in Ezekiel, to the new creation that will restore the land to a "better-than-original" condition. The various data from these selected passages are summarized by Duguid:

> The central point being made by the prophet is clear: the blessings promised in all of God's covenants—conditional and unconditional—will ultimately be experienced by God's people. This will take place not through their faithfulness but through a sovereign act of God's grace in providing for them a new and faithful shepherd.

By way of positive reaction, Professor Duguid has presented us with an exceedingly lucid and useful overview of these prophetic texts. His treatment makes for a very handy biblical theology of exile and return. A great many of his points are clearly rooted in the Scriptures, and I know of no one who would take issue with the bulk of his analysis, certainly not respecting the sovereign power and grace of God exercised to restore Israel to the land and to establish a new covenant, wherein the exiles are purged of their old sins, sanctified and renewed in their service of the Lord.

In terms of critical response, several observations are in order. For one, Duguid drives a wedge between the "new intervention of God that would radically alter the constitution of the people" and the necessity of a renewed fidelity on their part. Students of biblical theology are well aware that every covenant is established sovereignly and unilaterally, but always with a view to bilateral relations.[2] Even the Mosaic covenant (modeled on the Hittite Suzerain treaties), with all its declarations of naked sovereignty, has in view the faithful obedience of Israel, the people of a marriage-like bond with Yahweh. The operational principle of this covenant is stated in Leviticus 18:4-5: "You shall do my ordinances and keep my statutes and walk in them. I am the Lord your

---

2. For example, O. P. Robertson, *The Christ of the Covenants* (Grand Rapids: Baker, 1980), 3-15.

God. You shall therefore keep my statutes and my ordinances, by doing which a man shall live: I am the Lord." This is, as it were, covenantal nomism. In context, this demand for obedience stands over against idolatry, in particular: "You shall not do as they do in the land of Egypt, where you dwelt, and you shall not do as they do in the land of Canaan, to which I am bringing you. You shall not walk in their statutes" (Leviticus 18:3). In short, the faithful Israelite stayed in the covenant by doing the will of the covenant Lord, or perseverance.[3] The same perspective is evident in the recurring refrain of Deuteronomy: "This do and live" (Deuteronomy 4:1, 10, 40; 5:29-33; 6:1-2, 18, 24; 7:12-13; cf. 29:9, 29; 30:2, 6, 8, 10, 11, 16, 20; 31:12-13; 33:46). Given that the context of this doing of the law is the covenant graciously established at the time of the Exodus, the point of Leviticus 18:5 is hardly that of Israel having to earn God's favor or obtain life by performance. Rather, the people would continue to live in the land and enjoy the abundant blessing of the Lord if they remained within the parameters of the law and turned away from idolatry—this is to "do the law."

Second, for Duguid, "It would be no comfort to tell a generation who had experienced the full weight of the covenant curses for their disobedience and that of their forefathers that future blessing depended on their future faithfulness." Moreover, return from exile and the establishment of the new covenant "will take place not through their faithfulness but through a sovereign act of God's grace in providing for them a new and faithful shepherd." Of course, this is undeniably true, but there seems to be some confusion regarding the establishment of the covenant and its continuance—"getting in" and "staying in" (as per immediately above). Israel could never have been the prime mover in the redemptive actions that took place in connection with her deliverance from the bondage of exile. But let's not forget that faithfulness is the intended product of this "sovereign act of God's grace."

---

3. See further my 'The Obedience of Faith': A Pauline Phrase in Historical Context. Wissenschaftliche Untersuchungen zum Neuen Testament 2/38 (Tübingen: Mohr Siebeck, 1991), 263-65, and "Role Reversal and Paul's Use of Scripture in Galatians 3.10-13," *Journal for the Study of the New Testament* 65 (1997), 101-4.

Everything is of grace, from beginning to end, but it is grace that empowers and enables human fidelity. This is what Gordon Fee calls "God's empowering presence" by the Spirit.[4] Consequently, it is a false dichotomy to set God's power and grace over against the necessity of human fidelity. It is both/and not either/or: the one is the means to the other.

It is true that Duguid singles out the Spirit and his work in the prophetic passages selected. But we need to take matters to another level and consider the relation of Spirit to "fruit" in the prophets. The imagery of fruit is first encountered in the Genesis creation account and later in the flood narrative (itself a new beginning) (Genesis 1:11, 12, 22, 28, 29; 3:2, 3, 6, 12; 8:17; 9:1, 7). Later, the fruitfulness of the land features prominently in the prophecies respecting Israel's return from exile (Isaiah 4:2; 11:1-5; 27:5b-6; 29:17; 32:15-18; 44:2-4; 51:3; 57:18; 60:21; 61:1; 65:21; Jeremiah 23:3; 31:5; Ezekiel 17:23; 34:27; 36:8, 11, 30; 47:12; Amos 9:14; Joel 2:22; Zechariah 8:12). In the prophetic vision, Palestine was to be made like the Garden of Eden before Adam's fall, a veritable new creation.[5]

G. K. Beale's study of the prophetic backdrop of these verses has demonstrated that Isaiah 32 and 57, particularly in the Septuagint, are distinguished in their depiction of the restoration of Israel as a time of fruitfulness.[6] But the prosperity goes beyond material abundance to embrace ethical and spiritual qualities. According Isaiah 32:16-18:

> Then justice will dwell in the wilderness,
> and righteousness abide in the fruitful field.
> And the effect of righteousness will be peace,
> and the result of righteousness, quietness and trust
> for ever.

---

4. Fee, *God's Empowering Presence: The Holy Spirit in the Letters of Paul* (Peabody: Hendrickson, 1994).
5. One of the central promises of the Abrahamic covenant is fruitfulness in terms of the patriarch's descendants (Genesis 17:6; 28:3; 35:11; 47:27; 48:4; Exodus 1:7). This carries over into Galatians: Paul's Gentile converts are the actualization of Abraham's seed.
6. Beale, "The Old Testament Background of Paul's Reference to 'the Fruit of the Spirit' in Galatians 5:22," *Bulletin for Biblical Research* 15 (2005), 1-38.

> My people will abide in a peaceful habitation,
> in secure dwellings, and in quiet resting places.

Such is the result of the outpouring of the Spirit from on high (v. 15). Likewise, Isaiah 57:18 contains the assurance:

> I have seen his ways, but I will heal him;
> I will lead him and requite him with comfort,
> creating for his mourners the fruit of the lips.

All this carries over into Paul's letter to the Galatians. In commending to his readers "the fruit of the Spirit" (Galatians 5:22-23), Paul confirms that the new creation has arrived in Galatia. His converts have entered that new creation not by virtue of Torah observance, but because of the descent of the Spirit upon them in Pentecostal blessing. It is they, uncircumcised as they are, who fulfill the imagery of the productive land; they are the new Israel which has returned from exile; they are the fruitful vine the old Israel failed to be (John 15:2-8, in contrast to Isaiah 5:1-7; Jeremiah 8:13; Hosea 9:10; 14:6-7; Habakkuk 3:17); they are the nation producing the fruit of the kingdom (Matthew 21:43).[7]

Beale further roots the Christian life of 5:22-25 in the resurrection of the end-time Israel. Phrases such as "the fruit of the Spirit," "living by the Spirit" and "walking by the Spirit" are best understood as "resurrection living." It is Ezekiel 37:3-14 that links resurrection directly with Spirit, and the Septuagint of Isaiah 57:15-19 assigns to the Spirit the giving of resurrection life. Therefore, Galatians 5:22-25 is like Isaiah 57:15-19 in not only combining "Spirit" and "fruit," along with the mention of "joy," "peace" and "patience," but also in making the Spirit the source of resurrection life. Such resurrection existence finds a precedent in Galatians 2:19-20, which sets the pattern of crucifixion-resurrection, whereby the believer's experience is identified with Christ's own death and resurrection.[8] It should be added that these

---

7. Beale shows that in certain strains of Jewish literature eschatological Israel was expected to be spiritually fruitful ("Background," 16-20).
8. Beale, "Background," 20-22.

pictures of resurrection and fruitful living stand in the sharpest contrast to the chaos so disturbingly exhibited by "the works of the flesh" in Galatians 5:19-21. If the bulk of those works is hatred and its attendant phenomena, mainly discord and strife, then the fruit of the Spirit, commencing with love, finds its unifying factor in a community at rest and enjoying the benefits of mutual understanding, support and encouragement.

All of the above suggests very plainly that the outpouring of the Spirit at the time of restoration from exile and the establishment of the new covenant is to the end that Israel be a fruitful vine (in contrast to what she was in Isaiah's day [e.g., Isaiah 5:1-7 = Matthew 21:33-43]). The writing of the law on the heart (Jeremiah 31:33) has no other purpose than bringing Israel full-circle back to the very terms of the Sinai covenant (Leviticus 18:5; Deuteronomy 4:1, 10, 40; 5:29-33; 6:1-2, 18, 24; 7:12-13; cf. 29:9, 29; 30:2, 6, 8, 10, 11, 16, 20; 31:12-13; 33:46), of being God's people and he being their God.[9] The new covenant thus realizes the purpose for which the old covenant was instituted.[10] If faith, perseverance and

---

9. See the excellent treatment of Jeremiah 31:33-34 by C. F. Keil, *The Prophecies of Jeremiah.*. Commentary on the Old Testament. 10 vols. (Peabody: Hendrickson, rep. 2006), 8.282-85. Among other insights, Keil relates that the writing of the law on the heart is tantamount to an animating life-principle (2 Corinthians 3:3).

10. Duguid thinks that Isaiah's "covenant of peace" (Isaiah 54:10) is a *new* covenant in the sense that the returned exiles will experience the blessings promised in the original (Mosaic) covenant rather than the curses merited by their breaches of that covenant. Without denying the validity of this insight, I would stress that the new covenant is *eschatologically* new. It is rooted in the old covenant and brings its essential ideals to realization. Yet, in terms of Jesus' own teaching, the new covenant brings a new wine that cannot be contained by the old wine skins (Mark 2:21-22, as accompanied by 2 Corinthians 3 and Hebrews 8). By definition, newness is an eschatological concept. See C. B. Hoch, *All Things New: The Significance of Newness for Biblical Theology* (Grand Rapids: Baker, 1995). The new covenant is not simply the old covenant *redidivus*. Despite the continuity observable between old and new, the discontinuity of the two is underscored by the datum that, according to Ezekiel 37 and numerous other passages, the exile is reckoned as Israel's death, to be followed by her resurrection. See D. E. Gowan, *Theology of the Prophetic Books: The Death and Resurrection of Israel* (Louisville: Westminster/John Knox, 1998); J. D. Levenson, *Resurrection and the Restoration of Israel: The Ultimate Victory of the God of Life* (New Haven: Yale University Press, 2006). The difference between the two Israels is thus like the disparity of life and death. By contrast, the new covenant for Second Temple Judaism was, as S. Lehne writes, "a return to the *old* relationship with God and a *renewal* of the old covenantal promises by God in response." As she further notes, the Qumran

fruitfulness were non-negotiables under Moses, the same is true of the eschatological covenant. Not to bear the fruit of the Spirit is by definition to engage in the "works of the flesh" (Galatians 5:19-21), the effect of which is that one will not inherit the kingdom of God, but rather reap a harvest of "corruption" (Galatians 6:8). Bear in mind that Paul writes Galatians for the purpose of averting the apostasy from Christ that was already under way.[11]

We can now return to Duguid's original proposition: "It would be no comfort to tell a generation who had experienced the full weight of the covenant curses for their disobedience and that of their forefathers that future blessing depended on their future faithfulness." The straightforward reply is that the returned exiles would take comfort from the promise that, at the time of the restoration, the Spirit would be outpoured in copious measure to ensure the inscription of the law on their hearts, i.e., to grant them a heart compliant with the will of the covenant Lord, and to transform them from a fruitless vine into a field that bears abundant fruit. Their renewed and continued fidelity to the new covenant *is* required, but the wherewithal to comply is the gift of the sovereign Spirit. In that they could take supreme comfort and derive ultimate encouragement.

In the third place, there is the issue of conditionality in the covenants. I would submit that each biblical covenant is conditional, in the sense that the human partner is obliged to maintain faith with the God of the covenant.[12] Since it is always best to begin at

---

sectarians' ideal of the new covenant "consists in a return to the original intentions of the Mosaic Torah as they have come to understand its true import under the guidance of the Teacher of Righteousness" (*The New Covenant in Hebrews*. Journal for the Study of the New Testament Supplement Series 44 [Sheffield: Sheffield Academic Press, 1990], 58).
11. On the apostasy factor, see T. A. Wilson, "Wilderness Apostasy and Paul's Portrayal of the Crisis in Galatia," *New Testament Studies* 50 (2004), 550-71.
12. Duguid cites a comment from my review of D. A. Carson, P. T. O'Brien and M. A. Seifrid, eds., *Justification and Variegated Nomism. Volume 1: The Complexities of Second Temple Judaism* (Grand Rapids: Baker, 2001), posted on thepaulpage.com and replicated in my *In Defense of the New Perspective on Paul: Essays and Reviews* (Eugene, OR: Wipf & Stock, 2005), 59-105. The comment is: "The very existence of the marriage-covenant is contingent on the righteous/faithful behavior of its partners." This was written in response to Mark Seifrid's downplay of righteousness as covenant fidelity. And the point still stands: our righteousness and God's are required to maintain the marital bond known as a covenant. On the identification of marriage and covenant, see G. P. Hugenberger, *Marriage as a Cov-*

the beginning, I would first call attention to the *creation covenant* of Genesis 1-3. While there are no "ifs" on the surface of the text, it is obvious enough that Adam was obliged to fulfill the mandates set before him (procreation and subduing the earth), while obeying the command not to eat of the tree of the knowledge of good and evil.[13] If he failed to comply, then on the day he sinned he would die (Genesis 2:15-17); and, of course, that is what happened. That Adam died on the very day he sinned makes sense in light of Israel's exile.[14] That is to say, death by definition is banishment from the presence of God, which is precisely what transpired when Adam and Eve were expelled from the garden (Genesis 3:22-24). In brief, Adam was the first to suffer the pain of exile = death. The creation does carry on, with two of Adam's sons (Able and afterward Seth) to take the lead of the godly line. But as for Adam himself, Paul can view him as the head of the old creation tainted by sin and death, whose place has been taken by Christ, the life-giving Spirit (Romans 5:12-19; 1 Corinthians 15:21-22; 45-50). G. C. Berkouwer, then, justifiably writes that although the word "fall"

---

enant: Biblical Law and Ethics as Developed from Malachi. Biblical Studies Library (Grand Rapids: Baker, 1994). It is in terms of the marriage-covenant that "grace" and related words make sense as God's "covenant love" and "and covenant fidelity." See N. Glueck, *Hesed in the Bible* (New York: KTAV, 1975); G. R. Clark, *The Word Hesed in the Hebrew Bible*. Journal for the Study of the Old Testament Supplement Series 157 (Sheffield: Sheffield Academic Press, 1993); N. H. Snaith, *The Distinctive Ideas of the Old Testament* (London: Epworth, 1944), 94-130; T. F. Torrance, *The Doctrine of Grace in the Apostolic Fathers* (Grand Rapids: Eerdmans, 1959), 10-20. As Torrance in particular puts it, "grace" is God's self-giving to Israel (*Grace*, 15). If God gives himself to Israel in a marriage-like relationship, then he commits himself to the maintenance of his bond with her. The classic passage is Exodus 33:19-34:9, especially against the backdrop of the golden calf incident (Exodus 32).

13. Bryan Estelle's excellent account of the creation covenant (*CJPM*, 99-116) is rich and rewarding and, if anything, serves to confirm the conditional character of that covenant. I would just submit that rather than a "covenant of works," the relationship depicted in the opening chapters of Genesis is simply a conditional covenant, like any other. As for Estelle's treatment of Romans 5:12-21 and Galatians 3:10, which, for him, support the traditional doctrine of the covenant of works, I have proposed alternative understandings respectively in *Faith, Obedience, and Perseverance: Aspects of Paul's Letter to the Romans*. Wissenschaftliche Untersuchungen zum Neuen Testament 79 (Tübingen: Mohr Siebeck, 1994), 79-108; "Role Reversal and Paul's Use of Scripture in Galatians 3.10-13," *Journal for the Study of the New Testament* 65 (1997), 85-121.

14. Again, Gowan, *Theology of The Prophetic Books*; Levenson, *Resurrection and the Restoration of Israel*..

does not occur in Genesis 3, "sin is pictured as *apostasy from God*."[15] Adam, in short, was the first to break faith and fall away.

As for the *Noahic covenant*, again there are no "ifs" observable. Yet in the narrative of Genesis, the events of the flood and its aftermath are represented as a new creation: the earth is initially covered with water (Genesis 1:2) and then the dry land emerges (Genesis 1:6-8). In fact, there are numerous parallels, but the essential point is that once the chaos of the flood waters subside, Noah and his family emerge from the ark as the new humanity, a people of a new beginning. Such being the case, one would expect that the Noahic covenant would follow suit with the state of affairs in the garden. One very telling indication that conditionality is involved in this renewed creation covenant is the presence of curse. Ham looked upon the nakedness of his father (euphemistic for a sexual act), and when Noah woke up, he placed the curse on Ham's son Canaan (Genesis 9:24). The curse was fulfilled when Israel invaded and conquered the land of Canaan. The very factor of curse argues rather compellingly that one could (and in Ham's case did) forsake the ideals and practices of the creation covenant and thus incur the judgment of the Creator.

As regards the *covenant with Abraham*, the text of Genesis is replete with assurances that the Lord will fulfill his promise of a seed that would become the source of blessing for the nations (Genesis 12:1-3, etc.). However, by the time of Genesis 15, his faith begins to wane as he complains that he is still childless (v. 3). In response, the Lord does two things. First, he reassures Abraham that his progeny will be as numerous as the stars of heaven (vv. 4-6), to which Abraham responds in faith. Second, there is Yahweh's self-maledictory oath (vv. 7-16). As is well known by now, the symbolism inherent in the cutting of the animals is that the one who undertakes an oath swears that he will suffer the same fate as the animals if he does not fulfill his covenant commitment. Or, as M.

---

15. Berkouwer, *Sin*. Studies in Dogmatics (Grand Rapids: Eerdmans, 1971), 268 (italics added). Likewise, Calvin, *Institutes*, 2.1.4. See at more length my *Faith, Obedience, and Perseverance: Aspects of Paul's Letter to the Romans*. Wissenschaftliche Untersuchungen zum Neuen Testament 79 (Tübingen: Mohr Siebeck, 1994), 79-109.

G. Kline explains, "Passing between the slain and divided beasts beneath the threatening birds of prey...God invoked the curse of the oath upon himself should he prove false to it."[16] Later, when the Lord's oath seems to be very much in doubt, Abraham is called upon to sacrifice the son miraculously born in his old age (Genesis 22). But, as we know so well, the Angel of the Lord called from heaven: "By myself I have sworn, says the Lord, because you have done this, and have not withheld your son, your only son, I will indeed bless you, and I will multiply your descendants as the stars of heaven and as the sand which is on the seashore" (vv. 16-17). Here the voice refers back to Genesis 15 and reiterates the familiar promise that Abraham's children would one day be innumerable. We recall that Hebrews 6:13-18 picks up on both the oath and the word of promise in order to encourage the readers that the same oath and promise are for their benefit as well.

We will revisit the Abrahamic covenant below, but for the moment we note simply that the story of Abraham contains another dimension. According to Genesis 17:1-2, a requirement was placed on the patriarch: "When Abram was ninety-nine years old the Lord appeared to Abram, and said to him, 'I am God Almighty; walk before me, and be blameless. And I will make my covenant between me and you, and will multiply you exceedingly'." Gordon Wenham very helpfully observes that the Lord bids Abraham to walk "in his presence," recalling the way in which Enoch and Noah walked with God (Genesis 5:22, 24; 6:9). Wenham then defers to Claus Westermann for the meaning of this command: "God directs Abraham (who here represents Israel) to live life before him, a life in which every step is taken looking to God and every day of which is accompanied by him." However, Wenham rightly takes issue with Westermann's denial that this was a high demand, for certainly it was.[17]

Of particular interest is the syntax of 17:2. The requirement that Abraham live a certain kind of life is followed here by the conjunction *waw* as expressing result: "*so that* I may make (literally

---

16. Kline, *By Oath Consigned: A Reinterpretation of the Covenant Signs of Circumcision and Baptism* (Grand Rapids: Eerdmans, 1968), 16-17.
17. Wenham, *Genesis 16-50*. Word Biblical Commentary 2 (Dallas: Word, 1994), 20.

"give") my covenant with you. As Wenham further explains, this verse goes straight to the heart of the topic: "Whereas inaugurating the covenant was entirely the result of divine initiative, confirming it involves a human response, summed up in v 1 by 'walk in my presence and be blameless' and spelled out in the demand to circumcise every male."[18] It should be added that "blameless" is not sinless perfection but a wholehearted compliance with every aspect of God's revealed will. Noah was the first to be called "blameless" and "righteous" (Genesis 6:9; 7:1). Much later, these very terms are applied by Luke to Elizabeth and Zechariah: "they were both righteous before God, walking in all the commandments and ordinances of the Lord blameless" (Luke 1:6; cf. Philippians 3:6).[19] Notice the correlation of "righteous," "walking" and "blameless." In both Genesis and Luke, the three are tantamount to one another: all denote perseverance as a godly way of life. A significant confirmation is provided by Hebrews 6:15. After invoking the oath and the word of God as assuring Abraham, the writer adds: "And thus Abraham, *having patiently endured*, obtained the promise." For this author, there are two side to the same coin: God's assurance and Abraham's perseverance (walking blameless before God).

Conditionality is obvious in the case of the *Sinai covenant*. Deuteronomy 28-30, for example, is all about the blessings of the covenant for obedience and the curses of the same covenant for disobedience. On the one hand, "All these blessings shall come upon you and overtake you, *if* you obey the voice of the Lord your God (28:2);" and "The Lord will establish you as a people holy to himself, as he has sworn to you, *if* you keep the commandments of the Lord your God, and walk in his ways" (28:9). On the other, "But *if* you will not obey the voice of the Lord your God or be careful to do all

---

18. Wenham, *Genesis 16-50*, 20. Confirmation is provided by V. P. Hamilton, *The Book of Genesis*. New International Commentary on the Old Testament. 2 vols. (Grand Rapids: Eerdmans, 1990, 1995), 1. 461-63.
19. See further J. Nolland, *Luke 1-9:20*. Word Biblical Commentary 35a (Dallas: Word, 1989), 26-27; J. Green, *The Gospel of Luke*. New International Commentary on the New Testament (Grand Rapids: Eerdmans, 1997), 65. Green notes that the image of living lives that conform to God's will as a journey is an important one for Luke, as developed the central "journey" section of the Gospel.

his commandments and his statutes which I command you this day, then all these curses shall come upon you and overtake you" (28:15). Such is a constant refrain throughout this section of the book, having to do with exile and return. The whole is distilled in 30:15-20. Even a glance at the text is sufficient to establish that the issue placed before the nation is not the mere loss of rewards but life itself, if she chooses to disregard the Lord's commandments, statutes and ordinances in favor of idols.[20] For this reason, Moses pleads with the people to choose life instead of death.[21]

The promise to *David* constitutes a covenant within the covenant, with a specific view to a future Israelite ruler who would take charge of the kingdom. It is true that, according to 2 Samuel 7:15, God's steadfast love would never be removed from David's progeny. But in virtually the same breath, the Lord requires obedience on his part, and when such obedience is not rendered, then he will be chastised "with the stripes of the sons of men" (2 Samuel 7:14). Additionally, Psalm 89:29-33, as it echoes 2 Samuel 7:14-15, speaks precisely in the same terms:

> I will establish his line for ever
> and his throne as the days of the heavens.
> *If* his children forsake my law
> and do not walk according to my ordinances,
> *if* they violate my statutes
> and do not keep my commandments,
> *then* I will punish their transgression with the rod
> and their iniquity with scourges;
> but I will not remove from him my steadfast love,
> or be false to my faithfulness.

---

20. Robertson stresses this very factor: "A covenant is a bond-in-blood. It involves commitments with life-and-death consequences. At the point of covenantal inauguration, the parties of the covenant are committed to one another by a formalizing process of bloodshedding. This blood-shedding represents the intensity of the commitment of the covenant. By the covenant they are bound for life and death" (*Christ of the Covenants*, 14-15).

21. The "covenant lawsuit" of Isaiah 1 echoes Deuteronomy: "If you are willing and obedient, you shall eat the good of the land; But if you refuse and rebel, you shall be devoured by the sword; for the mouth of the Lord has spoken" (vv. 19-20).

Here too, the Lord promises continued fidelity to David, but to the end that his descendents will fulfill the terms of the covenant. And *if* they do not do what is required, certain consequences will result, which is precisely what happened when Israel was banished into Babylonian exile (as preceded by the dispersion of the two northern tribes into Assyrian captivity).

As for the *new covenant*, foreseen by Israel's prophets, the one who established it in his blood (Luke 22:20) speaks in this manner (John 15:1-11):

> I am the true vine, and my Father is the vinedresser. Every branch of mine that bears no fruit, he takes away, and every branch that does bear fruit he prunes, that it may bear more fruit. You are already made clean by the word which I have spoken to you. *Abide* in me, and I in you. As the branch cannot bear fruit by itself, unless it *abides* in the vine, neither can you, unless you *abide* in me. I am the vine, you are the branches. He who *abides* in me, and I in him, he it is that bears much fruit, for apart from me you can do nothing. *If* a man does *not abide* in me, he is cast forth as a branch and withers; and the branches are gathered, thrown into the fire and burned. *If* you *abide* in me, and my words *abide* in you, ask whatever you will, and it shall be done for you. By this my Father is glorified, that you bear much fruit, and so prove to be my disciples. As the Father has loved me, so have I loved you; *abide* in my love. *If* you keep my commandments, you will *abide* in my love, just as I have kept my Father's commandments and *abide* in his love. These things I have spoken to you, that my joy may be in you, and that your joy may be full.

The imagery of the passage is derived from Psalm 80:8-19; Isaiah 5:1-7; 27:2-11; Jeremiah 2:21-28; Ezekiel 15:1-8; 19:10-14, where Israel is depicted as an unfruitful vine. In each instance, the consequence is exile. As Andreas Köstenberger observes, in contrast to

Israel's failure, Jesus claims to be the "true vine," who brings forth the fruit that the nation failed to produce. "Thus Jesus, the Messiah and Son of God, fulfills Israel's destiny as the true vine of God" (Psalm 80:14-17).[22] And as an advance on the vine imagery of the Old Testament, Jesus is not only the vine, the disciples are the "branches" that adhere to him: they derive their life and identity by virtue of union with him; without him, they can do nothing.

Of the many factors that stand out in the passage, Jesus' relationship to the disciples is characterized by conditionality, by "ifs." If one does not abide in Christ the vine, judgment is the sure outcome. But if one abides in him and keep his commandments, the result is fruit-bearing and continuance in his love. Note especially the latter: Christ's love for individuals is contingent on keeping his commandments. No doubt, there are systems of theology that would gladly explain away the *prima facie* meaning of the text, but it will always resist every effort.[23] Below we will take up the question of the divine and the human in the process of perseverance and fruitfulness. Suffice it to say here that both dimensions of the evidence must be marshaled in support of an overall understanding of the perseverance of the saints as balanced by the preservation of the saints.

Apart from "if," of particular interest is the phrase "abide in" or "remain in," which occurs no less than ten times in John 15:1-11. The English renders the Greek *menō en*. In fact, Jesus' language is rooted in the Septuagint of Deuteronomy 27:26: "Cursed be he who does not confirm the words of this law by doing them." The Septuagint translates the verse as "cursed is every man who does not *remain in* all the words of this law to do them." The underlying Hebrew of the Greek "remain" (*emmenō*) is a verb which literally means "to uphold" (*yakim*) the words of the Torah. The

---

22. Köstenberger, *John*.. Baker Exegetical Commentary on the New Testament 4 (Grand Rapids: Baker, 2004), 450. The Septuagint of Jeremiah 2:21 names Israel a "true vine," but the succeeding context makes it plain that this "true vine" was deeply flawed.

23. The same pertains to the conditionality inherent in Matthew 6:14-15: "For *if you forgive* men their trespasses, your heavenly Father also will forgive you; but *if you do not forgive* men their trespasses, neither will your Father forgive your trespasses." Plainly, the precondition of eschatological forgiveness is our forgiveness of others here and now.

force of *yakim* is not to be overlooked: the Israelite was to "uphold" or "support" "the words of this law," which were given to regulate the relationship between Yahweh and Israel. In so doing, one would honor one's prior faith-commitment to the Lord.[24] At heart, then, the point of Deuteronomy 27:26 is: "Cursed be anyone who is fundamentally disloyal to the law—anyone who does not, by his actions, show that he is on the side of the law and anxious to 'make the law stand'.."[25]

That the Septuagint chose *emmenō* for *yakim* is understandable, given that the verb has the meaning of "remaining within a specified territory."[26] Its selection may reflect the climate in which portions of the translation took place, i.e., the necessity of persevering in "the holy covenant" (1 Maccabees 1:15) in the face of the Hellenistic onslaught. Elsewhere, *emmenō* likewise means "persevere in" (Sirach 2:10; 6:20; 11:21 [in parallel to "believe" = *pisteuō*]; 1 Maccabees 10:26, 27; Philo, *On the Preliminary Studies* 125; Josephus, *Against Apion* 2.257; cf. Numbers 23:19). Furthermore, in other crucial passages in Deuteronomy, the kindred *menō en* (as it reproduces *dabaq b^e*) denotes dedication to Yahweh and continuance in his ways (e.g., 11:22; 13:4; 30:20; cf. Joshua 22:5; 23:8-11). In these verses, the phrase stands in parallel with the synonymous expressions "keeping the commandments" and "loving Yahweh." It is just this usage that carries over into John 15:1-11, according to which the disciples must "abide in" (*menō en*) him, the vine.[27] That such "abiding" is tantamount to continuing faith is evident from

---

24. The same note of allegiance to (or renewal of) the covenant is sounded by the hiphil stem of the verb *qum* in, e.g., 2 Kings 23:3, 24. By way of further illustration, 1 Samuel 15:11, 13; Jeremiah 35:15, 16 present us with a study in contrast: as over against those who have broken faith with the Lord, there are individuals who have "upheld" the Torah.
25. J. Bligh, *Galatians: A Discussion of St. Paul's Epistle*. Householder Commentaries 1 (London: St. Paul, 1970), 257.
26. H. Schlier, *Der Brief an die Galater*. Kritisch-exegetischer Kommentar über das Neue Testament. 5th ed. (Göttingen: Vandenhoeck & Ruprecht, 1971), 132.
27. Not surprisingly, the idea of "remaining"/"abiding"/"cleaving" is taken up by later Jewish literature. Ben Sira, for example, more than once correlates cleaving to God with obedience (e.g., Sirach 11:22; 13:4; 30:20). To cleave to God entails dispositions such as love, fear and faith, virtues commended by the scribe throughout his book.

John 14:1: "Keep on believing in God, and keep on believing in me."[28]

By way of qualification, there are differences between John and Deuteronomy. (1) Christ takes the place of the Torah: the believer remains in him, not the law. (2) Consequently, Jesus provides the model for us: it is he who has kept the Father's commandments and has remained in his love. (3) There is the factor of mutual indwelling, a characteristic of the Fourth Gospel. Not only do the disciples abide in Christ, his words abide in them, as he himself does (17:23). And not only so, there is the advent of "the Spirit of truth" who dwells with them and is in them (14:17). Here is the factor of divine enablement: by virtue of Christ and the Spirit (as sent by the Father, 14:26), the disciples will go forth and fulfill the mandate of the service of their Lord (cf. 16:1-4). Perhaps the best summary of the farewell discourses of John 14-17 is 14:23-24. In answer to a question by Judas, Jesus replies: "*If* a man loves me, he will keep my word, *then* [*kai*] my Father will love him,[29] and we will come to him and make our home with him. He who does not love me does not keep my words; and the word which you hear is not mine but the Father's who sent me." It is surely striking that divine sovereignty and enablement are not set over against the conditionality of loving Christ and keeping his word. Rather, entirely in keeping with the character of a biblical covenant, it is both at the same time.

In light of such considerations, one may say with Duguid that the blessings of the covenant are *received* unconditionally when the exile comes to an end. But as the return from exile motif carries over into the New Testament, we find the same outlook as in the Torah and the prophets, namely, that blessings unconditionally received *must result* in the bearing of much fruit and the keeping of Christ's commandments. Conditionality characterizes life not

---

28. Because in the present tense the Greek indicative and imperative assume the same form, John 14:1 can actually be translated in four different ways. But the rendering that makes the most consistent sense is to take *pisteuō* as imperative in both instances.

29. That *kai* can function to introduce an apodosis ("then") is well documented. See, for example, *BDAG*, 494-95. *Kai* here is much like the *waw* of Genesis 17:2.

only under Moses but under Christ as well: "*If* you love me, you will keep my commandments. *Then* [*kai*] I will pray the Father, and he will give you another Counselor, to be with you forever" (John 14:15-16, as elaborated by 14:21-24). Certainly without meaning to do so, I should think, Duguid leaves the impression that faithful obedience (perseverance) is unnecessary for members of the new covenant community. But if that were so, documents such as Hebrews and 1 John (and several others) were written for no purpose.

"Transformation of the People"

Under this heading are subsumed several passages, Ezekiel 37, Haggai 2 and Zechariah 3, all making the same essential point: resurrection and cleansing from defilement are the products of a divine transformation, with the result that the people experience blessing. These observations are well-taken, apropos and could hardly be called into question. But once more, such data do not preclude a "covenantal nomism" understanding God's relations with Israel. Indeed, Duguid's assessment falls directly into line with my own: "The order of these two acts of God [resurrection and change of status before God] is irreversible: first the people must be made clean and acceptable in God's sight; only after that could the process of being transformed into a new obedience be begun." I would only underscore what I have written above: such divine deeds are to the end that Israel be a faithful and fruitful people, not merely as desirable commodities, but as constituting the *sine qua non* of covenant responsibilities and privileges.

Duguid makes a particular issue of the enjoinder of the Angel of the Lord to the high priest Joshua: "Thus says the Lord of hosts: If you will walk in my ways and keep my charge, then you shall rule my house and have charge of my courts, and I will give you the right of access among those who are standing here" (Zechariah 3:7). This follows upon the injunction for Joshua to exchange his filthy garments for clean ones. Duguid concedes that the "right of *access*" is not certain, but the important point (for him) is that what is dependent on Joshua's faithfulness is "not his standing in the covenant community but the experience of extraordinary blessing." Duguid perceives Joshua's "standing in the Lord's presence" as more akin to prophetic privilege than that of a "normal Israelite," "a blessing beyond mere salvation." In any event, the passage is sufficiently singular that little, if anything, of it can be placed in service of Duguid's desire to play down the factor of conditionality in the covenant, especially as Duguid himself is not certain of the meaning of "right of access."

"Rewards for Faithfulness"

In this segment, Duguid takes up his thesis derived from Zechariah 3, as now buttressed by Haggai 2 and Ezekiel 40-48. That is to say, the theme of faithfulness *is* important, not as the means of staying within the covenant but rather as the source of receiving rewards. In taking up Haggai 2, Duguid maintains that because of Zerubbabel's faithfulness in obeying the Lord during the day of small things (Zechariah 4:10), he is promised "special status" on the day of cosmic shaking (Haggai 2:6-7). The presence of Zerubbabel, the chosen "signet ring," is evidence that the stump is not dead; he is a green shoot emerging from the stump of the old line. The question is: "What has Zerubbabel done to deserve this mark of approval?" The answer is: "He has simply done what the kings of Judah ought to have done, but often failed to do, namely listen to God's word through the prophet and obey it." Consequently, Zerubbabel would effectively hear: "Well done, good and faithful servant! You have been faithful over a little; I will set you over much. Enter into the joy of your master" (Mathew 25:21).

Up to a point, these observations are fair enough. Duguid is certainly right that the issue is that of Zerubbabel's faithfulness over against the failure of the kings of Judah to obey. But there is a flaw in his line of argumentation. Rather than disproving that continued covenant blessings are contingent on faithfulness, the case is *proven* just by the obedience of Zerubbabel. Had he fared like his predecessors, Jerusalem and the temple would not have been rebuilt. When the eschatological shaking of the heavens and the earth would occur, there would be no place to serve as a repository of the wealth of the nations that was to flow into the new temple (Haggai 2:6-9). The city and the temple must be rebuilt, and the rebuilding is contingent on the fidelity of the workers, and especially that of Zerubbabel, the governor. To be sure, "desert" is not even an issue, because the Lord was with Zerubbabel (Haggai 1:13; 2:4). But if anything, it is nothing other than the fidelity factor that is placed in "boldface print" by the books of Ezra and Nehemiah. According to those accounts, the workers were required to be loyal and true to the task, with defectors and opponents singled out for particular scorn. In order to take his meaning, the prophecy of Haggai has to be read in the historical context of his ministry to the returned exiles.

One may grant that Zerubbabel enjoyed a "special status" in salvation history. Yet the issue was not merely reward for himself as an individual; rather, his privilege was that of being a vital link in the chain that would eventuate in the coming of the new creation, as symbolized apocalyptically by the shaking of the heavens and the earth. It is surely impressive that Hebrews 12:25-29 takes up this passage in Haggai and applies it to the necessity of perseverance in view of the coming last day. The writer's bottom line is: "Therefore let us be grateful for receiving a kingdom that cannot be shaken, and thus let us offer to God acceptable worship, with reverence and awe; for our God is a consuming fire" (v. 29). For this author, the events that transpired in Zerubbabel's day find their definitive fulfillment in the *parousia* of Christ and the necessity of our faithfulness against that day. Notice in this text the presence of the two elements that form a constant in the biblical outlook for the future: (1) the kingdom cannot be shaken because of God's sovereignty and determined purpose; (2) it is possible to refuse him who is speaking (v. 25) and thus be devoured by the "consuming fire" that is the eschatological wrath of God.

It is well to add that Duguid's reference to Matthew 25:21 is appropriate enough, but with one important proviso. According to the parables of Mathew 25 and parallels, there are *unfaithful servants*. In the very parable of the "Talents," there is the condemnation of the "wicked and slothful servant" who is consigned to "outer darkness," where there will be weeping and grinding of teeth—the unmistakable language of judgment as reflective of ancient Oriental funerals (cf. Luke 7:32; 8:52). See further Matthew 24:48-51; Luke 12:45-46; 19:19-27. According to Jesus, the good and faithful servants will indeed enter into the joy of their Lord, but the others will be put with the unfaithful (Luke 12:46). The issue, then, is much larger than individual rewards: *nothing less than life and death are at stake.*

Duguid's argument is thereafter extended into Ezekiel 40-48, which, he believes, supports the principle of reward for faithful service. In particular, it is the faithful Zadokite priests who are rewarded with the central role in the new temple. They are not perfect, but because they have been the most faithful, they may expect a reward in the heavenly realm. By contrast, the Levites had been unfaithful in their spiritual adultery. Yet even they are not excluded from the visionary promised land because of their unfaithfulness; they are restored to their God-given place as ministers of the sanctuary. The covenant between the Lord and the tribe of Levi cannot be broken by their faithlessness. For Duguid, "All of God's chosen people enter and remain in the covenant relationship through the Lord's faithfulness, yet there are greater rewards for those who have been more faithful in that service. Faithfulness in the Lord's service finds its reward in enhanced access to the presence of the Lord."

To judge by the comments of another commentator on Ezekiel, Daniel Block, Duguid's observations on the text of Ezekiel 44 are entirely accurate. Block shows how vv. 10-11 and 12-14 respectively of chapter 44 stand in parallel.[30] The upshot is that the Levites are held accountable for their idolatry, but even so, they are reinstated and reassigned to different duties. They may not function as priests, but theirs is still a privileged role.[31] The covenant with Levi, therefore, remains unbroken (Jeremiah 33:20-22).

---

30. Block, *The Book of Ezekiel: Chapters 25-44*. New International Commentary on the Old Testament (Grand Rapids: Eerdmans, 1998), 627.
31. Block, *Ezekiel*, 632. Block denies that the Levites are demoted in privilege. It would appear to me that they are, but Duguid's essential point remains intact.

The problem, however, is one of methodology in the application of these observations. Without expressly invoking the category of "typology," the only way to make real sense of Duguid's proposal is to assume that he sees the Levites telegraphing ahead of time glimpses of the actual new temple, with a constituency of faithful and not so faithful priestly servants. Otherwise, an appeal to Ezekiel 44 is simply irrelevant, if there is no parallel to be encountered in the new covenant community. But as in the case of Joshua in Zechariah 3, there is a failure to appreciate that something as singular and context-specific (not to say obscure) as the service of the Levites in Ezekiel's temple can hardly be paradigmatic for the relationship that believers sustain to Christ in the new covenant. Reasoning in terms of a biblical typology, this projected temple serves to foreshadow in a grandiose manner the eschatological sanctuary, which ultimately will expand to encompass the new heavens and the new earth.[32] Nevertheless, typology does not normally, if ever, conform to a one-for-one correspondence between the respective elements of prediction and fulfillment; it is normally "looser" than some are willing to allow. What is important in typology is the conviction that there is an overall consistency of divine activity in salvation history: God's acts in the Old Testament set in motion a rhythmic pattern which is brought to a climax in the New Testament. R. T. France expresses it well: "New Testament typology is…essentially the tracing of the constant principles of God's working in history, revealing a 'recurring rhythm in past history which is taken up more fully and perfectly in the Gospel events'."[33] Scripture thus largely consists of parallel persons and events that culminate in the Christ-event.[34]

---

32. See G. K. Beale, *The Temple and the Church's Mission: A Biblical Theology of the Dwelling Place of God*. New Studies in Biblical Theology 17 (Downers Grove: InterVarsity, 2004), 335-64.
33. France, *Jesus and the Old Testament: His Application of Old Testament Passages to Himself and His Mission* (Downers Grove: InterVarsity, 1971), 39, quoting G. W. H. Lampe, *Essays on Typology*. Studies in Biblical Theology 1/22 (London: SCM, 1957), 27.
34. See, for example, D. C. Allison, *The New Moses: A Matthean Typology* (Minneapolis: Fortress, 1993), 11-95.

Such being the nature of typology, one must be very careful in bringing elements of the type over into the finished antitype. The points of correspondence between the two were never meant to be precisely exact. If the type were perfect, there would be no need for an antitype, and we must ever resist the temptation to confuse typology with allegory. In the present case, it will not do to import idolatrous Levites into the body of Christ, destined to inherit the universe.[35] Duguid's argument is that even though the Levites were faithless and idolatrous, they are still occupy a place in the new temple, though with a reassignment of responsibilities and diminished access into the presence of God. But the suggestion that "Levites" can be translated into "carnal Christians" who still get "in" the "heavenly realm" (if that is the point) simply does not wash with the New Testament (or the Old). Myriads of texts could be cited, but some rather obvious ones are Romans 1:18-32 (all about idolatry); 8:5-8; 13:11-14; 1 Corinthians 6:9-10 (including idolaters); Galatians 6:19-21; Hebrews 12:14; Revelation 21:8 (again idolaters). Perhaps Duguid understands the Levites to be "penitent sinners." But apart from the fact that the text of Ezekiel does not actually say so, the fundamental problem is still that of extrapolating from a very specific setting and making the application far too broadly.[36] It is the whole flow of salvation history that must inform not only our conception of typology but the constituency of the people of God; and in light of the "big picture" of the redemptive narrative, Duguid's proposal fails to measure up to the ideal and the reality of covenant relationships.

---

35. Especially in light of Revelation 21:1-22:5, according to which the coming universe is depicted as a city, a temple and a garden all-in-one. It is into this realm that no unclean thing can enter. See Beale, *Temple*, 23-25, 365-73.

36. Even granting that the Levites might be viewed as "penitent sinners," the fact remains that restoration always follows upon genuine *repentance*, i.e., turning from idols to serve the true and the living God (1 Thessalonians 1:9). In this case, renewed fidelity as embodied in repentance is hardly optional. And the picture of a temple served by the "more faithful" and the "less faithful" is incongruous in terms of obedience as the worship and service of the Creator rather than the creature. Some believers may be more fruitful and productive than others, but faithfulness by definition is commitment to the person of the Lord and the standards of his covenant. Idolatry is *ipso facto* precluded.

"Theological Reflections"

Professor Duguid's essay moves into its final phase with this series of theological reflections. In introducing this segment, Duguid recapitulates what has gone before: "All of the Old Testament covenants, both conditional and unconditional, would have ended in failure if left to the faithfulness of sinful human beings." To this is added the comment that although the covenants with Abraham, Israel (Sinai) and David were endangered on several occasions, human faithlessness could not annul God's covenant commitment.

At the risk of belaboring the point, the foundational problem with this formulation is that there are no unconditional covenants in Scripture. At the very least, the data presented in the previous part of this undertaking are sufficient to call into question Duguid's claim that such covenants are in evidence. At bottom, it is an oversimplification to push the divine determination to maintain the covenant at the expense of the bilateral character of the arrangement. As intimated more than once, Duguid is not wrong that the final deciding factor is God's covenant commitment. At the end of the day: "so shall my word be that goes forth from my mouth; it shall not return to me empty, but it shall accomplish that which I purpose, and prosper in the thing for which I sent it" (Isaiah 55:11). Yet it is Isaiah 55 as a whole which is so very instructive. On the one side, there is the proclamation of v. 11 that nothing can thwart the Lord's purposes in regathering Israel from her dispersion among the nations. But on the other, if anything characterizes this specimen of "gospel preaching," it is the repeated and impassioned pleas for the people to return to the Lord and thus enter into the blessings of the new creation; and unless they return, the covenant will not be established.

Texts can be multiplied many times over, but simply sticking with the instances cited by Duguid—the patriarchs, Israel and David (Levi)—we can briefly review the data. As for Abraham and his progeny, it was pointed out above that Abraham was required to walk before God and be blameless (Genesis 17:1); and there is no reason why the same operative principle should not apply to Isaac and Jacob. In fact, the entire narrative of Jacob can be viewed as the process of turning the "rascal" Jacob into the man he should have been, all culminating in his wrestling with the Angel of the Lord and his consequent transformation (Genesis 32:22-32).[37] Additionally, we should not forget about Esau, the one who despised his birthright by bartering it away (Genesis 25:29-34). Equally a member of the Abrahamic community, it is Esau who is set forth as a prototype of the Christian apostate by the Letter to the Hebrews (12:15). Of course, the covenant continued and found its fulfillment in the Mosaic and Davidic covenants and finally in the new covenant. Even an Esau could not frustrate the Lord's designs. Nevertheless, Esau and those like him function as warning posts to the reality of apostasy.

Regarding the Sinai covenant, comment has been offered previously. Duguid correctly points to Moses' impassioned appeal that the people choose life rather than death (Deuteronomy 30:19). It is likewise obvious that the repeated unfaithfulness of the people did not demolish the bond established on the mountain—nor could it. Yet something rather conspicuous has been omitted, namely, on those occasions when there was an egregious display of rebellion against the Lord, reprisal was taken against those who chose to denounce Yahweh as their God: they were cut off from the covenant. One is the worship of the golden calf (Exodus 32). Moses' intercession for Israel staves off the total destruction of the congregation, but even so, about three thousand of them are put to the sword by the Levites because of their breach of faith (vv. 25-29). It is just in this setting that the question rings out, Who is on the Lord's side (v. 26)? One had to decide and come to Moses, or not. Another occasion is that related in Numbers 21:4-9. When the Israelites began to "murmur" against God and Moses—the

---

37. Geerhardus Vos describes the Jacob narrative in these terms: "The main principle embodied in the history of Jacob-Israel is that of subjective transformation of life, with a renewed stress of the productive activity of the divine factor." Vos acknowledges, as everyone must, that Jacob is represented as the least ideal of the patriarchs. But, "This is done in order to show that divine grace is not the reward for, but the source of noble traits. Grace overcoming human sin and transforming human nature is the keynote of the revelation here" (*Biblical Theology: Old and New Testaments* [Edinburgh: Banner of Truth, rep. 1975], 93).

noise of rebellion and apostasy—the fiery serpents killed many of them.[38] Yet the community is not entirely obliterated because of the brazen serpent placed on a standard to be their salvation. Here again we see both sides of the coin. A third instance is refusal to trust God in view of the report of the spies, Joshua and Caleb (Numbers 13-14). Again, there is murmuring which provokes the anger of the Lord and calls forth his judgment. Only Joshua and Caleb are allowed to enter the promised land, while the entire generation of those who left Egypt were consigned to wander in the wilderness for forty years. We may say that the two men who remained faithful represent a "remnant" of the larger community. The Lord rewards their fidelity, and their entry into the land ensures that the covenant will continue. Yet a terrible price is paid by those who chose rebellion and unbelief.

The covenant with David is of the same species as the others. We may acknowledge with Duguid that the narrator of 2 Samuel demonstrates that human unfaithfulness cannot annul God's covenant commitment. But again, a vital datum has been overlooked. Even a year after David's twofold sin of adultery and murder, there was no repentance on his part. And because there was no admission of guilt, Nathan the prophet was sent to denounce David as one who had stolen the ewe lamb of another (2 Samuel 12:1-15). It is only when Nathan exclaims "you are the man" that David realizes the depth of his sin and repents of it (as echoed in Psalms 32 and 51). As in all the examples examined in this study, a bilateral arrangement is in place here. Yes, God is resolved that the covenant not be annulled, yet his determination is not played out in the abstract, because apart from David's repentance and renewal of the covenant, no son of his would sit on the throne of Israel. (I think it is quite on purpose that the birth of Solomon follows immediately upon David's confession and the death of the child conceived out of wedlock with Bathsheba.) God's determination

---

38. In Philippians 2:14-16, Paul is concerned that his readers not repeat the murmuring and questioning of Israel in the wilderness. Rather, they should be the blameless children of God who shine as lights in the midst of a perverse and crooked generation, so that his labors among them would not have been in vain.

to sustain the covenant is enacted in no other way than in bringing David to repentance and confession. We may say that the Lord's dealings with David were the means to the end of ensuring the perpetuity of the covenant with him.

Before descending to the particulars of this final portion of Duguid's essay, I should say that all the above observations are commonplace to any reader of the Old Testament, and I have sought only to remind us of what we know already. Yet these familiar stories are to be read in the scope and breadth intended by their authors in order to determine their overall aims and objectives. It is thus the full weight of the narratives that are to be brought to bear on "covenantal nomism" debate, simply because one of the worst enemies of biblical interpretation is imbalance and oversimplification in one direction or the other.

Marshaled under this concluding rubric of "Theological Reflections" are two subheadings. The first is "Jesus Christ, the Fulfiller of the Covenants." The question is, "If Israel is a nation of promise breakers, how then will these covenants be fulfilled and bring about the blessing that God has irrevocably committed himself to give his people?" The answer of the Old Testament is twofold: "there must be a substitute who suffers in the place of his people and a covenant keeper who takes Israel's place (and, even more profoundly, Adam's place) in fulfilling the righteousness that God demands as the condition of the blessing." The answer of the New Testament is that Jesus Christ is the suffering substitute and obedient servant. This premise is then unpacked with reference to various biblical texts.

The great bulk of what Duguid has written is indisputable. I know of no evangelical who endorses covenantal nomism as an accurate evaluation of Judaism or who embraces the new perspective on Paul who would call into question the substitutionary work of Christ, the one who endured the curse for us, with a view to the fulfillment of the blessings that all the covenants promised to covenant keepers.[39] It is in this regard that Christ's

---

39. Among other considerations, Duguid's appeal to Jesus' wilderness experience, suc-

death and resurrection are "the climax of the covenant." "He *is* Israel, going down to death under the curse of the law, and going through that curse to the new covenant life beyond."[40] Nor is it a matter of debate that Christ has clothed us with the garments of his own righteousness (Isaiah 61:10; Jeremiah 23:6; 33:16).[41] This section of Duguid's essay is excellent gospel preaching, but, I must say, it is preaching to the converted!

My only critical comeback concerns the stance that "covenantal nomists" take toward the Old Testament sacrificial system. According to Duguid, too much weight is placed by them on the efficacy of the sacrifices. But the answer is easy. First of all, a recognition of the place and function of the sacrifices is not peculiar to covenantal nomism. It is only a matter of coming to terms with the typological significance of this portion of the cultus. Certainly, the offering of animals, including the day of atonement, was provisional for old covenant Israel and had no inherent efficacy; its only purpose was to point forward to Christ and his sacrifice of himself. Such things are simply not in dispute. Second, those of us who embrace a covenantal nomism understanding of Judaism are *not* "covenantal nomists." Covenantal nomism is an assessment of Judaism, not Christianity. Christ has taken the place of the law. We are devotees not of the law but of Christ![42]

Finally, we come to "The Place of Human Faithfulness." Duguid's recapitulated thesis is that our faithfulness is to be rewarded, but it is not the condition by which we remain in the covenant. Then follows a brief discussion of reward, with the bottom line being: "There is only one way to enter this reward of eternal life in

---

ceeding where Israel failed, is certainly to the point. Both the Gospel temptation narratives and Hebrews set forth Jesus as the man of faith who persevered through the wilderness. Perhaps I could pass on my own study, "Jesus, the Unique Son of God, Tested and Faithful," *Exegetical Essays*. 3rd ed. (Eugene, OR: Wipf & Stock, 2003), 79-132. An abbreviated version appears in *Bibliotheca Sacra* 151 (1994), 284-308.

40. N. T. Wright, *The Climax of the Covenant: Christ and the Law in Pauline Theology* (Minneapolis: Fortress, 1991), 152 (italics original). See as well J. M. Scott, "Paul's Use of the Deuteronomic Tradition," *Journal of Biblical Literature* 112 (1993), 217-221.

41. I have affirmed this explicitly in my *Defense of the New Perspective*, 107, 121, 150.

42. I have addressed this in my reply to S. M. Baugh in this book.

the close presence of God: through faith in that looks to his righteousness imputed to us and depends on his faithfulness—not our own—to bring to completion our salvation."

In light of the entire above discussion and analyses of texts, there is little to say but that this is a decided oversimplification, even to the point of distortion. Of course, the finished work of Christ, including not least his faithfulness, is the reason for our salvation. But to say that our fidelity is not the condition for remaining in the covenant does violence to every Old and New Testament passage we have considered. Duguid would have us decide between the faithfulness of Christ and our own. Yet if there was ever a false alternative, this is it, just because Christ's work is not complete until the day on which he perfects the "good work" that he has begun in us (Philippians 1:6). According to Romans 5:9-10, there is a salvation yet to be. For Paul, the past redemptive event in Christ has given rise to hope in the believer, a hope which has as its primary focus the future eschatological consummation of the new creation.[43] It is not either Christ's faithfulness or ours: it is both at the same time. But since the fidelity of the believer is an obvious bone of contention for Duguid, let me affirm once more that Christ, the Servant of the Lord, has fulfilled the conditions of the covenant, but in so doing he has imparted the gift of his Spirit to ensure our own covenant fidelity and thus to bear his image.[44] If no one can call Jesus Lord but by the Spirit (1 Corinthians 12:3), and if faith itself is the gift of God (Ephesians 2:8), then everything is of grace, from beginning to end. A recognition of our faithfulness is hardly a denial of divine mercy and grace. Quite the contrary, it is none other than God's empowering presence that enables us to run the race set before us, looking to Jesus, the author and perfecter of *our faith* (Hebrews 12:2).

---

43. See my discussion of Romans 5:9-10 in the reply to S. M. Baugh.
44. See J. D. G. Dunn, *The New Perspective on Paul: Collected Essays*. Wissenschaftliche Untersuchungen zum Neuen Testament 185 (Tübingen: Mohr Siebeck, 2005), 77-80, along with the relevant portion of my reply to S. M. Baugh.

Summary and Reflections

In his essay, Professor Duguid has endeavored to challenge the ideology lying behind the coinage of E. P. Sanders' phrase "covenantal nomism." The gist of the argument is that this moniker cannot be an accurate portrayal of covenant relationships, because it is the faithfulness of the Lord, not human beings, that ensures the continuance of the covenant. According to Duguid, there are both conditional and unconditional covenants in Scripture. Among the most prominent of the conditional covenants is the Mosaic. But even the blessings of that covenant are to be received unconditionally, through a sovereign act of God's mercy and grace, at the time of Israel's return from exile, when the new covenant is established. In the final analysis, it is Christ the covenant servant who has fulfilled the conditions of the covenant. As I read him, however, these findings are placed in service of a rather startling conclusion: for all practical purposes, *perseverance is unnecessary and unrequired.*. I doubt that Duguid would want to express it in these terms, but such is the consistent outcome of his thesis.

In my response, I have concurred that God's grace is always primary, indispensable and the source of every blessing that flows from the covenant(s). Each biblical covenant is initiated sovereignly and graciously in fulfillment of the Lord's eternal design to have a people for himself, and we are kept by the power of God for a salvation to be revealed in the last day (1 Peter 1:5). And yes, the Lord Jesus Christ is the faithful and obedient servant (Philippians 2:5-11) who has fulfilled the conditions of the covenant. None of these data are in dispute, and it is inconceivable that any believer would call them into question. *Without him, we can do nothing.*

Where I differ is in my assertion that every covenant is conditional, in the sense that the human partner is obliged to maintain faith with the God of the covenant. Therefore, if Christ has fulfilled the conditions of the covenant, it is to the end that we do the same. In the very context where Paul declares Jesus to be the servant obedient unto death, he calls on the Philippians to imitate his example: the obedient one is to be obeyed, and the readers are to work out their own salvation with fear and trembling (Philippians

2:12-13; cf. Hebrews 5:9). As Gordon Fee so aptly comments, the connection of "work out your own salvation" with "obedience" is verified by both the grammar and the context. As he remarks, the outworking of the Philippians' common salvation consists in their continued obedience to Christ. In their concrete situation, the immediate demand is for them to stop their internal squabbling (4:2-3) and get on with being God's blameless children in pagan Philippi. As regards the qualification that God is at work in them, Fee adds that Paul writes this not to protect himself theologically, but to encourage the readers that God is really on the side of his people actively working on their behalf.[45] Fee's introductory remark to this passage is telling. He notes that the text has long been difficult for evangelical Protestants, who cannot imagine that Paul is suggesting that salvation is something that must be "worked out," even with God's help.[46] Yet Fee's exposition demonstrates clearly that Paul is making such a demand.[47] I would add that Philippians 2:12-13 furnishes an outstanding instance of how theology must adapt itself to the text of Paul and not force the text into its mold.

Therefore, given that Christ is the man of faith, who made his own trek through the wilderness of this world, and given that we can do nothing apart from him, it follows that our feet are to tread where his have trod. If we are being conformed to his

---

45. Fee, *Paul's Letter to the Philippians.*. New International Commentary on the New Testament (Grand Rapids: Eerdmans, 1995), 235-36, 237-38.
46. Fee, *Philippians*, 231.
47. Fee's recent volume on Paul's christology makes the same point. In responding to those commentators on Philippians 2:6-8 who have an aversion to the idea of imitating Christ, as though ethics were based finally on self-effort rather than on grace, Fee writes: "But these objections are based on a fundamental misunderstanding of *imitatio* in Paul's thought, which does not mean 'repeat after me' but rather (in the present context) 'have a frame of mind which lives on behalf of others the way Christ did in his becoming incarnate and dying by crucifixion.' One can appreciate the desire not to let this profound passage lose its power by making it simply an exemplary paradigm, but Paul himself seems to have done that very thing. He then follows up with his own story in 3:5-14 as one who lives out the Christ paradigm and urges the Philippians to follow his example of following the primary example (3:15-17) and thus to live in the present in a cruciform way" (*Pauline Christology: An Exegetical-Theological Study* [Peabody: Hendrickson, 2007], 372, n. 6).

image (Romans 8:29; Ephesians 4:24; Colossians 3:10), then we are to learn obedience in precisely the same manner as he, i.e., through testing, trial and temptation. According to the author of Hebrews: "Although he was a Son, he learned obedience through what he suffered; and being made perfect he became the source of eternal salvation *to all who obey him*" (Hebrews 5:8-9). Faithful obedience to Christ, or perseverance, is so much of the essence of new covenant life that Paul had to exercise self-control in all things, lest, having preached to others, he himself would be rejected (1 Corinthians 9:24-27). As Fee explains, the image in view is that of being "disqualified" (*adokimos*) to receive the eschatological prize of the Christian race. "This has been the point of the [athletic] metaphors from the beginning, that the Corinthians exercise self-control lest they fail to obtain the eschatological prize."[48]

In Philippians 3:12-14, Paul again invokes the figure of the race: because he has not yet attained to the resurrection of the dead, he presses on toward the goal of the upward calling of God in Christ. In the immediately preceding statements of 3:10-11, Paul wants to know Christ and the power of his resurrection, as well as participate in his sufferings and death (v. 10), "that, if somehow, I may attain the resurrection from the dead." The phrase "if somehow" (*ei pōs*) appears curious, if not troubling. Peter O'Brien points to recent interpretations of 3:11 that seize on the route by which Paul will experience the resurrection, either through martyrdom or some other kind of death, or he might be alive at Christ's coming.[49] In this case, Paul writes, "if by whatever means...." Such makes for a plausible reading and avoids a potential clash with Paul's stated confidence elsewhere that he will certainly be with the Lord (e.g., Philippians 1:23; 2 Corinthians 5:1-9). Be that as it may, we should not miss the obvious: Paul has not yet been raised

---

48. Fee, *The First Epistle to the Corinthians*.. New International Commentary on the New Testament (Grand Rapids: Eerdmans, 1987), 440. Fee adds: "...we have been called to a higher life of service that includes self-control and the willingness to endure hardship as concomitants. Perhaps too many contemporary Christians have lost sight of their eschatological goal and are running aimlessly, if they are in the 'contest' at all" (ibid., 441).
49. O'Brien, *The Epistle to the Philippians*. New International Greek Testament Commentary (Grand Rapids: Eerdmans, 1991), 412-13.

eschatologically with Christ, and for that reason he must forget what lies behind and press on to lay hold of the future prize. Even he must persevere to that end.

All this serves to underscore what I have attempted to say in the body of this response: because of sovereign grace, the covenant itself can never be broken, but there are individuals who may and do forsake it. The pronounced weakness of Duguid's approach to the materials is one of imbalance: only one part of the evidence is presented and the other is virtually ignored. But when both sides of the coin are kept in sight, it should be self-evident that it is not either/or but both/and. In Christ, God has reconciled the world to himself (2 Corinthians 5:19) by establishing an everlasting covenant with a new humanity, the "Israel of God" (Galatians 6:16). Yet the Lord of this new covenant not only requests but requires that his "branches" abide in himself, the "vine." If they do, they will bear abundant fruit; if they do not, they will be cut off and cast into the fire (John 15:1-11). And once more, the author of Hebrews understood very well that Christ has offered to the Father the sacrifice that ends all sacrifice (9:11-14). Yet the cross does not render endurance unnecessary, but rather mandates it: "let us run with perseverance the race that is set before us" (12:1), of course, "looking to Jesus the pioneer and perfecter of our faith," the very one who apprised his disciples that "he who endures to the end will be saved" (Matthew 10:22).

The perseverance debate is hardly new, as per the encounters of Calvinism and Arminianism over the centuries. But I fear that these interchanges may have actually muddied the waters. The problem is that the "five points" of both systems are schematized and tend to be artificial, as both are based on a systematic rather than a biblical theology. Without reproducing my observations on the Already and the Not Yet from the reply to Professor Baugh, God's grace *and* "the obedience of faith" on our part (Romans 1:5; 16:26) are simply what one would expect, given that the salvation inaugurated here and now must be consummated hereafter (Romans 5:9-10). Our trek through the wildness has commenced, but we have not yet entered into God's eschatological rest, and the possibility remains that some may fail to enter because of "the disobedience of unbelief" (Hebrews 3).[50] Note especially the parallel of Hebrews 3:18-19: "And to whom did he swear that they should never enter his rest, but to those who were *disobedient?* So we see that they were unable to enter because of *unbelief.*" The Already is the guarantee of the Not Yet, but not in such a manner as to preclude the necessity of perseverance.

For some, what I am proposing may seem like a contradiction of terms, or, at the very least, a theological tension. It is in the study of Paul in particular that recent debate has centered around whether there is such a "tension" in his thought respecting election and grace, on the one hand, and final vindication according to faith's obedience, on the other. Even someone as conservative as Simon Gathercole believes that such is the case, and the massive volume of Gathercole's Aberdeen colleague, Francis Watson, has this putative tension as its central thesis.[51] In my view, however, such an assessment of Paul's theology fails to "get into his head," as he assumes his place in the context of Second Temple Judaism, with the Old Testament as common to both. Altogether on target, I would say, is Kent Yinger's study of *Paul, Judaism, and Judgment According to Deeds.*.[52] According to Yinger's findings, there simply is no tension in Jewish thinking between God's grace and God's demand; the two simply coexist in complete harmony.[53] For a final

---

50. See the excellent studies respectively of S. McKnight, "The Warning Passages of Hebrews: A Formal Analysis and Theological Conclusions," *Trinity Journal* ns 13 (1992), 21-59; D. deSilva, "Entering God's Rest: Eschatology and the Socio-Rhetorical Strategy of Hebrews," *Trinity Journal* ns 21 (2000), 25-43.
51. Gathercole, *Where is Boasting? Early Jewish Soteriology and Paul's Response in Romans 1-5* (Grand Rapids: Eerdmans, 2002), 226, 265; Watson, *Paul and the Hermeneutics of Faith* (London: T & T Clark International, 2004).
52. Yinger, *Paul, Judaism, and Judgment According to Deeds*. Society for New Testament Studies Monograph Series 105 (Cambridge: Cambridge University Press, 1999).
53. Brad Young very helpfully confirms that Paul's thinking is Jewish in character, a telling point when it comes to comprehending and unpacking his universe of discourse. Those who scruple about hard-and-fast distinctions between "justification" and "sanctification" should consider that what appears to the Western mind to be a "blurring" of ideas is, in the Jewish mindset, what Young calls "a cycle of interactive concepts." According to Young, "The apostle understands God and his great love for all humanity as a vibrant whole. One concept belongs to a complex of interactive ideas. Each term he

time, we do not have to choose between either/or, because it is always both/and at the same time. As a notable instance, Psalm 62:12 (normally considered to be the source of Romans 2:6), actually says: "to you, O Lord, belongs *steadfast love*, for you requite a person *according to his work*."[54] It is for this reason that the great "assurance chapter" of Scripture, Romans 8, promises "no condemnation for those who are in Christ Jesus" (v. 1); and yet the recipients of this guarantee are those who walk according to the Spirit and put to death the deeds of the body (vv. 4-8). To set the mind on the Spirit is life, but the mindset of the flesh must result in death (v. 6).[55]

On a final note, I would ask why Professor Duguid did not engage more of the recent literature devoted to the return from exile motif. He does touch base briefly with a couple of Wright's books.[56] But Wright's pursuance of the matter hardly ends there, and others have taken up the cause as well. To be sure, the literature on the motif is voluminous, but in addressing the theme in relation to "covenantal nomism," some interaction with these scholars would have been appreciated.[57]

---

uses to communicate his thought is clustered with other interactive concepts concerning God's relationship to people.... When the contours of Pauline thought are considered in a cycle of interactive concepts rather than in a straight line where each new idea supersedes and eliminates the previous one, the apostle's conceptual approach to God is given fresh vigor. It is a Jewish way of thinking" (*Paul the Jewish Theologian: A Pharisee among Christians, Jews, and Gentiles* [Peabody: Hendrickson, 1997], 40-41, 42). The hermeneutical impact of this observation should be apparent enough: modern interpreters must be prepared to undergo a paradigm shift to this Jewish way of thinking in order to enter the thought processes of Paul and the other biblical writers.

54. On the theology of Romans 2, see further my *Faith, Obedience, and Perseverance*, chapter 3; K. R. Snodgrass, "Justification by Grace—to the Doers: an Analysis of the Place of Romans 2 in the Theology of Paul," *New Testament Studies* 32 (1986), 72-93.

55. See further C. Loewe, "'There is No Condemnation' (Romans 8:1): But Why Not?" *Journal of the Evangelical Theological Society* 42 (1999), 231-50. At the risk of throwing out an inflammatory term, we should remember that classic antinomianism was devoted to the proposition that grace does not entail obligation.

56. Wright, *Climax of the Covenant*, and *What Saint Paul Really Said: Was Paul of Tarsus the Real Founder of Christianity?* (Grand Rapids: Eerdmans, 1997).

57. I think particularly of Wright, *The New Testament and the People of God*. Christian Origins and the Question of God 1 (Minneapolis: Fortress, 1991); id., *Jesus and the Victory of God*. Christian Origins and the Question of God 2 (Minneapolis: Fortress, 1996); id., *The*

Challenge of Jesus: Rediscovering Who Jesus Was and Is (Downers Grove: InterVarsity, 1999); id., *Paul: In Fresh Perspective* (Minneapolis: Fortress, 2005); Levenson, *Resurrection and the Restoration of Israel*; J. M. Scott, ed., *Exile: Old Testament, Jewish, and Christian Conceptions*. Supplements to the Journal for the Study of Judaism 56 (Leiden: Brill, 1997); C. A. Evans, "Jesus and the Continuing Exile of Israel," *Jesus and the Restoration of Israel: A Critical Assessment of N. T. Wright's Jesus and the Victory of God*. ed. C. C. Newman (Downers Grove: InterVarsity, 1999), 77-100; B. Pitre, *Jesus, the Tribulation, and the End of the Exile: Restoration Eschatology and the Origin of the Atonement* (Grand Rapids: Baker, 2005); M. Fuller, *The Restoration of Israel: Israel's Re-gathering and the Fate of the Nations in Early Jewish Literature and Luke-Acts*. Beihefte zur Zeitschrift für die neutestamentliche Wissenschaft und die Kunde der älteren Kirche 138 (Berlin: de Gruyter, 2006). There are also the older contributions of M. Knibb, "The Exile in the Literature of the Intertestamental Period," *Heythrop Journal* 17 (1976), 253-72; id., "Exile in the Damascus Document," *Journal for the Study of the Old Testament* 25 (1983), 99-117.

Contributors

John H. Armstrong (B.A., M.A., Wheaton College; D. Min., Luther Rice Seminary) is president of ACT 3: Advancing the Christian Tradition in the Third Millennium, based in Carol Stream, Illinois. He is an adjunct professor of evangelism at Wheaton College Graduate School and a member of the board of Biblical Theological Seminary and the Institute on Religion & Democracy. He is a frequent guest on numerous radio programs, a contributing writer for several major periodicals and the author of hundreds of articles and essays. He is also the author/editor of eight books, the most recent being *Understanding Four Views of Baptism* (Zondervan, 2007). John has been married for thirty-seven years and is the father of two married children and the grandfather of two.

Don Garlington (B.A., Harding University; M.Div., Th.M., Westminster Theological Seminary in Philadelphia; Ph.D., University of Durham) has been a lecturer in Biblical studies at Trinity Ministerial Academy, Montville, New Jersey; professor of New Testament at Toronto Baptist Seminary; and adjunct professor of New Testament at Tyndale Seminary, Toronto. He continues to make his home in Toronto and is currently engaged in a variety of writing projects. His publications include: *'The Obedience of Faith': A Pauline Phrase in Historical Context* (Tübingen: Mohr Siebeck, 1991); *Faith, Obedience, and Perseverance: Aspects of Paul's Letter to the Romans* (Tübingen: Mohr Siebeck, 1994); *An Exposition Of Galatians: A Reading From the New Perspective* (3rd ed.; Eugene, OR: Wipf & Stock, 2007); *Exegetical Essays* (3rd ed.; Eugene, OR: Wipf & Stock, 2003); *In Defense of the New Perspective on Paul: Essays and Reviews* (Eugene, OR: Wipf & Stock, 2005), along with numerous essays in various periodicals.

Mark Horne (B.A. Houghton College, M.Div, Covenant Theological Seminary, St. Louis, Missouri) is an assistant pastor at Providence Reformed Presbyterian Church (PCA) in St. Louis, Missouri. He has written several books, including *The Victory According to Mark* (Canon, 2002) and *Why Baptize Babies* (Athanasius Press, forthcoming). He and his wife Jennifer have four children.

Peter J. Leithart (B.A., Hillsdale College; M.A.R., Th.M., Westminster Theological Seminary in Philadelphia; Ph.D., University of Cambridge) is senior fellow of theology and literature at New St. Andrews College, Moscow, Idaho, and pastor of Trinity Reformed Church (CREC), also in Moscow. He has written a number of books, including *Solomon Among the Postmoderns* (Brazos, forthcoming) and *1 & 2 Kings* (Brazos, 2006). He is a contributing editor to *Touchstone* magazine and to *Credenda/Agenda*. He and his wife Noel have ten children and one grandchild.

Rich Lusk (B.S., Auburn University; M.Phil., University of Texas) is pastor of Trinity Presbyterian Church (CREC) in Birmingham, Alabama. He has written numerous internet and journal articles. He is also the author of *Paedofaith: A Handbook for Covenant Parents*, as well as contributor to several volumes, including *The Federal Vision* and *The Case for Covenant Communion*. Rich and his beautiful wife Jenny have four young children who love the Lord and enjoy playing in the creek beside their house.

P. Andrew Sandlin (B.A., University of the State of New York; M.A., University of South Africa; S.T.D., Juan Calvino Theological Seminary) is president of the Center for Cultural Leadership; preacher at Church of the King-Santa Cruz, California; and theological consultant of ACT 3 Ministries. He has written many essays and articles and several books, the latest of which is *Un-Inventing the Church: Toward a Modest Ecclesiology*. He is married and has five adult children and two grandchildren.

Norman Shepherd (B.A., Westminster College; B.D., Th.M., Westminster Theological Seminary in Philadelphia) served as associate professor of systematic theology at Westminster Seminary in Philadelphia, and subsequently pastored two congregations in the Christian Reformed Church (CRC) before retirement. He is the author of *The Call of Grace* (2000), *Women in the Service of Christ* (a booklet, 1992), and several journal articles and reviews. He contributed two chapters to *Backbone of the Bible* (2004) on "Justification by Faith in Pauline Theology," and "Justification by Works in Reformed Theology." He is widowed with two married daughters, and grandfather to four children.

www.ingramcontent.com/pod-product-compliance
Lightning Source LLC
Chambersburg PA
CBHW022058150426
43195CB00008B/185